D0204685

ARTICLES ON ⎯⎯⎯⎯⎯⎯⎯⎯⎯

COLONIALISM AND NATIONALISM IN AFRICA

A Four-Volume Anthology of Scholarly Articles

Series Editors

GREGORY MADDOX
Texas Southern University

TIMOTHY K. WELLIVER
Bellarmine College

A GARLAND SERIES

Series Contents

VOLUME
3

AFRICAN NATIONALISM AND INDEPENDENCE

Edited with introduction by
TIMOTHY K. WELLIVER

GARLAND PUBLISHING, Inc.
New York & London
1993

Library of Congress Cataloging-in-Publication Data

African nationalism and independence / edited with an introduction
by Timothy K. Welliver.
    p.   cm. — (Colonialism and nationalism in Africa ; v. 3)
    ISBN 0–8153–1390–X
    1. Africa—Politics and government. 2. Africa—History—
Autonomy and independence movements. 3. Nationalism—
Africa—History—20th century. I. Welliver, Timothy K.
II. Series.
DT29.A33 1993
960—dc20   93–27885
                                         CIP

Printed on acid-free, 250-year-life paper
Manufactured in the United States of America

CONTENTS

SERIES INTRODUCTION

The study of African history as an academic discipline is a rather new field and one that still has its detractors both within and outside academics. The eminent British historian Hugh Trevor-Roper, now Lord Dacre, is once reputed to have said that African history consisted of nothing but "the murderous gyrations of barbarous tribes," while more recently the Czech novelist Milan Kundera has written to the effect that even if it could be proved that hundreds of thousands of Africans died horrendous deaths in the Middle Ages it would all count for nothing. At the very least, such views are a matter of perspective; for the 400 million or so people living in the nations of sub-Saharan Africa today history still shapes the rhythm of their destiny.

This collection of articles highlights for students and scholars the modern era in African history. It brings together published research on the colonial era in Africa, an era relatively brief but one that saw dramatic change in African societies. It highlights the ongoing research into the struggles for independence and social transformation that continue to the present. The authors of these articles eloquently rebut the Euro-centric bias of critics like Trevor-Roper and Kundera and claim for African societies and Africans their rightful place as agents of history.

The articles collected here cover the period between the "Scramble for Africa" in the late nineteenth century, when all but two nations in Africa became colonies of European powers, and the struggles to define the meaning of independence in Africa and throw off the last vestiges of white rule in the southern part of the continent. Such a concentration by no means implies that African societies before the late nineteenth century were tradition-bound or unchanging. They developed according to their own pace and played significant roles in world affairs from the days when West Africa provided a major proportion of the Old World's gold before 1500 through the era of the Atlantic slave trade. However, the colonial era created the modern map of Africa, and Africans transformed their societies politically, economically, and socially in the face of their forced integration into the world economy as producers of raw materials.

The articles in this collection chart the development of African historical studies. As the field emerged in the late 1950s and early 1960s, many historians sought to place the struggle by African peoples to liberate themselves from colonialism and racial domination within a historical tradition. Some scholars, inspired by T. O. Ranger's work, sought to link modern nationalist movements to resistance to colonial rule in the late nineteenth century. They also focused on the development of what they saw as a national consciousness that overlaid existing economic, ethnic, and religious communities.

The reaction to this approach was not long in coming within both African politics and historical scholarship. The ongoing struggles within African nations, often defined in ethnic terms, find their image reflected in early critical works such as those of Steinhart and Denoon and Kuper included here that question the development of national consciousness. More generally, as I. N. Kimambo of Tanzania has argued, there was a turn towards economic and social history that concentrated on the transformation and relative impoverishment of African societies under colonialism. Some scholars have gone so far in the search for the origins and meanings of community in Africa as to reject the modern nation state as of much use as a unit of analysis. Basil Davidson, one of the most influential pioneers in African historical research and a long time supporter of African liberation, has recently produced a volume that calls for a reconfiguration of African political life to fit the reality of African communities (*The Black Man's Burden: Africa and the Curse of the Nation State*). This collection demonstrates the competition between these views and the shifts that have occurred over the last three decades.

This collection intends to make available to students and scholars a sample of the historical scholarship on twentieth century Africa. The articles come mainly from Africanist scholarly journals, many of which had and have limited circulations. It includes some seminal works heretofore extremely difficult to locate and many works from journals published in Africa. It also includes some works collected elsewhere but shown here in the context of other scholarship.

The articles collected here represent a growing and distinguished tradition of scholarship. Some are foundation works upon which the field has built. Many pioneer methodological innovations as historians have sought ways of understanding the past. All go beyond the often abstract generalities common to basic texts. Taken together they reveal the diversity and the continuity of the African experience.

Several people have contributed greatly to this project. Leo Balk and Carole Puccino of Garland Publishing have guided it through all its stages. Cary Wintz was the catalyst for the project. I. N. Kimambo critiqued the project and made many suggestions. The library staffs of the Ralph J. Terry Library at Texas Southern University, the Fondren Library at Rice University, and the University Library of Northwestern University, and especially Dan Britz of the Africana Collection at Northwestern, provided critical help. Bernadette Pruitt did some of the leg work. Pamela Maack was always supportive, and Katie provided the diversions.

INTRODUCTION

Decolonization in Africa[1] occurred with a rapidity that surprised both the colonial rulers and those Africans who struggled for independence. At the end of the Second World War, British and French leaders continued to resist the prospect of giving up their colonies. Churchill refused to preside over the dissolution of the empire, and the 1944 Brazzaville Declaration by French governors stated that "even at a distant date, there will be no self-government in the colonies." But in 1956, Sudan, Morocco, and Tunisia became independent, and by 1966, when Botswana and Lesotho were freed, some thirty-five sovereign African states had appeared on the map.[2] The process peaked in 1960; during that year all of French West Africa and French Equatorial Africa gained independence, along with the most populous African nation, Nigeria, and the Belgian Congo (Zaire), Somalia, and Cameroon—seventeen countries in all.

Although the circumstances of decolonization varied, depending on imperial policies and local conditions, there were certain patterns that emerged. With some exceptions, North Africa gained independence first, followed by West Africa, then East and Central Africa, and finally southern Africa. This was largely a consequence of the fact that colonies with white settlers—for the most part located in eastern, central, and southern Africa—were slower to gain independence due to obstruction by the white minorities. Territories without settler populations gained independence peacefully, whereas violence typified the struggle for freedom in many settler colonies.

Britain was the first imperial power to consider granting independence to its African colonies and spent more time than others preparing the colonies for independence. France, facing armed resistance in Indochina and then Algeria, quickly reversed its policies and granted independence relatively rapidly. Belgium made so few preparations for the independence of the Congo (Zaire) that chaos ensued (see the article by Jitendra Mohan). Portugal sought to hold its colonies in the face of several effective armed liberation movements and held out until 1974, when the repressive regime in Lisbon collapsed under the strain.

Much of the scholarly debate over independence revolves around the question, "from where did the impetus come?" Was African independence "planned" by the metropolitan powers, or was it the product of intense struggle on the part of African nationalists? The terminology one chooses to describe the process is important. "Decolonization" implies European initiative and tends to deny that any real "freedom" resulted. On the other hand, "liberation" indicates initiative on the part of African nationalists. "Independence" is more neutral, although many scholars would object that the independence achieved in the 1950s and 1960s was incomplete (see below). The rather bland phrase "transfer of power" is therefore favored by many.

Those who stress the initiative of the Europeans tend to focus on the impact of the Second World War, which weakened the European powers economically and militarily. The rival superpowers—The U.S. and U.S.S.R.—were both publicly opposed to imperialism. The 1941 Atlantic Charter, signed by Churchill and Roosevelt, mentioned "the right of all peoples to choose their form of government." The ideology of the war itself, fought as it was against a racist regime, exposed the hypocrisy of the colonial powers. Some (such as John Flint, in this volume) have argued that the British were already planning reforms in the African colonies before the war broke out. This argument may apply to Britain and perhaps to France, but one could hardly claim that Belgium and Portugal "planned" for the independence of their African colonies.

Those who stress African initiative point out that, whether or not the colonial powers intended to grant independence at some point in the distant future, African nationalist agitation forced the Europeans to address the issue immediately and thus won their independence much earlier than anticipated. Here the emphasis is on the rise of nationalist leaders and their ability to mobilize the masses against colonial rule. There is no doubt that the post-war years witnessed an intensification of nationalist agitation in Africa. This generally has been attributed to factors such as the emergence of an educated African elite, the wartime sacrifices made—and hardships endured—by Africans, and the politicization of military veterans. Whatever the circumstances, the achievement of the nationalist leaders of the 1950s—Sekou Touré, Jomo Kenyatta, and Julius Nyerere, to name but a few—was the mobilization of people of diverse ethnic and class identities in support of an agenda of independence and national unity. Conferences, strikes, boycotts, demonstrations, and appeals for democracy and justice were the weapons in their arsenal.[3] At the forefront of African liberation was Kwame Nkrumah, whose Convention People's Party (CPP) led the Gold Coast (Ghana) to independence in 1957. Nkrumah was committed to the liberation not only of Ghana, but of the entire continent, and to the unification of all African peoples. Although his dreams of a united Africa were to be dashed (and he himself was ousted in a military coup in 1966), he inspired an entire generation of Africans with the ideals of freedom and unity.

That Nkrumah was able to oust the British with minimal violence is indicative of the changing atmosphere in the 1950s. The major colonial powers—Britain and France—generally did not wait for violent upheavals to drive them out of sub-Saharan colonies, in contrast to their behavior elsewhere. Independence for the French colonies was clearly accelerated by developments in Indochina (where the French withdrew after the Dien Bien Phu debacle in 1954) and in Algeria, where from 1954 they faced an armed insurgency. Britain in the 1940s was already pulling out of parts of the Middle East and Asia, areas that were of even greater economic and strategic importance than Africa. These events were on the minds of nationalist African leaders, colonial bureaucrats, and European politicians. Thus in many colonies, demands by African leaders for independence were met with what amounted to panic. Although the Europeans practiced delaying tactics and occasional rear-guard actions in Africa, the movement was less an imperial retreat than an imperial rout.

Or was it either? It has long been argued by many that the "independence" of the 1950s and 1960s was at best incomplete and at worst was not true independence at all. Scholars using the concepts of "development of underdevelopment," "neocolonialism" and "dependency" have maintained that the colonial powers (representing the capitalist world as a whole) merely handed nominal political power to African elites, who continued the economic exploitation of Africa for the benefit of the developed world.[4] According to this view, neocolonial exploitation represents a higher stage in the incorporation of African economies into the "world-economy" and the subordination of Africa's resources and labor to the needs of international capital. Thus the transfer of local political authority from Europeans to Africans produced no real change in the circumstances of the African masses. In many ways, this school of thought was the product of the disappointment that attended the failure of the newly-independent states to live up to expectations, as economic growth stalled, Cold War rivalries were played out, and assorted repressive regimes quickly replaced the parliamentary systems left by the Europeans. In order to

gain complete independence from the West, many African governments decided in the 1960s and 1970s to nationalize their industries
(see the article by Leslie Rood) and to turn to various socialist models
of development.

The decade of the 1980s was a disaster for Africa—output actually
fell in some countries while the population continued to grow rapidly.
Famines, wars, and AIDS dominated news coverage of Africa. In this
atmosphere, more radical reassessments of African independence were
produced. In the article by the late Michael Crowder reproduced
here, Crowder criticizes those who "judge the past twenty five years in
terms of a dream manufactured in Europe not Africa" and who hold
Africa to a model of liberal-democratic nation-states that correspond
little to Africa's circumstances and to the legacies of colonial rule. Basil
Davidson has recently published a scathing attack on the nation-state
model, which, having caused immeasurable suffering in Europe, has
now become a "shackle on progress" in Africa.[5] The fact is that few
African countries fit the ideal of a nation; most are beset with ethnic
and religious divisions that are easily exploited for political advantage.
As several of the articles included here attest,[6] the politics of ethnicity
(or "tribalism", as some have labeled it) was already playing a role in
the independence struggle. With hindsight, it is easy to conclude that
one of the great shortcomings of African and western observers alike
was their failure to recognize the fragility of the "nations" that had
been created.

It is possible to view these difficulties as symptomatic of an even
greater dilemma that has faced Africans (and many others) for generations: the rules of the game had all been written by the West. Colonial
rule shaped the boundaries, infrastructures, economies, institutions,
and even the official languages of the new African states. Furthermore,
independence could not be realized except by using the intellectual
structures and concepts of the West. Hence, the language of resistance
to Europe was itself a European language, replete with concepts such
as liberation and nationalism, revolution and freedom, socialism and
democracy. For decades there has been a search underway for suitable
African models for organizing the state, distributing wealth, and
nurturing national cultures.[7] Perhaps only when this search is successful will it be possible to say that the dream of independence has been
fulfilled.

NOTES

1. The most comprehensive survey of the topic of decolonization is contained in the two volumes edited by Prosser Gifford and W. Roger Louis: *The Transfer of Power in Africa: Decolonization 1940–1960* (New Haven, 1982), and *Decolonization and African Independence: The Transfers of Power, 1960–1980* (New Haven, 1988).

2. In addition, Rhodesia in 1965 unilaterally declared independence from Britain under a white-dominated government.

3. See articles by Susan Geiger, Jan Van Donge, R. W. Johnson, Jean Suret-Canale, 'Ladipo Adamolekun, and Finn Fugelstad for specific examples.

4. A good example of this scholarship, which has today fallen somewhat out of fashion, is Peter C.W. Gutkind and Immanuel Wallerstein, ed., *Political Economy of Contemporary Africa*, 2nd ed. (Beverly Hills, 1985). For a critique of this approach to the transfer of power, see the article by John Flint in this volume.

5. Basil Davidson, *The Black Man's Burden: Africa and the Curse of the Nation-State* (New York, 1992), p. 290.

6. See the articles by Victor Amaazee, Jean Allman, I.R. Hancock, and Tekena Tamuno.

7. See the articles by Derek Wright, Robert July, and Michael Crowder.

The Journal of Modern African Studies, 24, 4 (1986), pp. 679-689

Fanon and Africa: a Retrospect

by DEREK WRIGHT*

THE work of Frantz Fanon, who died 25 years ago, was the *locus* of many clashing contradictions. There were many Fanons, living uneasily together. The prophet of a cleansing revolutionary violence, which would re-unite what lethargic white self-interest had put asunder, found strange company in the psychiatrist whose case-histories recorded its traumatic effects: violence was both socially regenerative and personally degenerative, a renovating healer and a destructive sickness, a mystical release and a dehumanising barbarity. The devotee of French culture reviled French colonialism, and the humanitarian realist who acknowledged the revolutionary sacrifices of Algeria's Europeans was no doubt uncomfortable about the partisan propagandist whose necessary racism could not afford concessions to white altruism. Most relevant to the situation and prospects of independent Africa, however, was the deadlocked struggle fought between the committed nationalist in Fanon and the pan-Africanist who sought to make the nation the magical springboard into continental unity.

The latter ambivalence had to do with the fact that African political structures began with those which Europe left behind: in one way or another, the black man started with what the white man had finished with, and was then left to finish what the white man had started. The contradictions were, initially, those of Europe. Largely impervious to the presence of these in its own behaviour, colonialism was, in Fanon's phrase, 'used to putting all Negroes in the same bag',[1] and yet preserved and exploited the tribal barriers which showed them to be different, thus triggering irreconcilable tensions between tribalism, nationalism, and African continentalism. On the one hand Fanon, whose basic position was that culture was national but consciousness continental and racial, made his nationalistic best of the botched job of colonial boundaries inherited by Africa whilst, on the other hand, making a pan-African virtue of the colonial 'necessity' of race prejudice.

The continentalist turned white racialisation of black identity to serve the purposes of a spurious cross-cultural unity; the nationalist who

---

* Lecturer in English, University College of the Northern Territory, Darwin, Australia.
[1] Frantz Fanon, *The Wretched of the Earth*, translated by Constance Farrington (Harmondsworth, 1967), p. 173.

urged the breaking of bonds with Europe turned the same divisive structures created by Europe into the equally spurious focus of the liberation struggle and decolonisation programme. It was the fate of blacks to fight from within the prison house of white national boundaries, racial concepts, and political myths. Whichever turning was taken to divest the psychic geography of colonial patterns led deeper into whiteness:

We have taken everything from the other side; and the other side gives us nothing unless by a thousand detours we swing finally round in their direction, unless by ten thousand wiles and a hundred thousand tricks they manage to draw us towards them to seduce us and to imprison us. Taking means in nearly every case being taken...[1]

'Colonialism wants everything to come from it', Fanon wrote in *L'An cinq de la révolution algérienne* (Paris, 1959).[2]

In his first book, *Peau noire/Masques blancs* (Paris, 1952), Fanon spoke of the 'infernal cycle' through which a white-owned world led everything back into its own total reality, causing all energy and movement towards black liberation to run itself into a circle of frustration and enslaved dependence. This is his conclusion:

I am a man, and what I have to recapture is the whole past of the world... In no way should I dedicate myself to the revival of an unjustly unrecognized Negro civilisation... I am not a prisoner of history. I should constantly remind myself that the real leap consists in introducing invention into existence. In the world through which I travel, I am endlessly creating myself... Let us be clearly understood. I am convinced that it would be of the greatest interest to be able to have contact with a Negro literature or architecture of the third century before Christ. I should be very happy to know that a correspondence had flourished between some Negro philosopher and Plato. But I can absolutely not see how this fact would change anything in the lives of the eight-year-old children who labour in the cane fields of Martinique or Guadeloupe.[3]

And here is Fanon again, nine years later, in *Les Damnés de la terre* (Paris, 1961), published shortly before his death:

I admit that all the proofs of a wonderful Songhai civilisation will not change the fact that today the Songhais are underfed and illiterate... But this passionate search for a national culture which existed before the colonial era finds its legitimate reason in the anxiety shared by native intellectuals to shrink

---

[1] Ibid. p. 182.
[2] Frantz Fanon, *Studies in a Dying Colonialism*, translated by Haakon Chevalier (New York, 1967), p. 63.
[3] Frantz Fanon, *Black Skin, White Masks*, translated by Charles Lam Markmann (New York, 1967), pp. 226 and 229–30.

away from that Western culture in which they all risk being swamped...It was with the greatest delight that they discovered that there was nothing to be ashamed of in the past, but rather dignity, glory and solemnity...Colonialism is not satisfied merely with holding a people in its grip and emptying the native's brain of all form and content. By a kind of perverted logic, it turns to the past of the oppressed people, and distorts, disfigures and destroys it. This work of devaluing pre-colonial history takes on a dialectical significance today...The native intellectual who decides to give battle to colonial lies fights on the field of the whole continent. The past is given back its value.[1]

In the passage of time between these poles the black intellectual's pursuit of a new, integrated black identity in a white world had given way to an embittered and desperate decontamination of himself from that environment and all its goods. Personal liberation was now to be found only in the context of political revolution. There were, of course, underlying continuities. *Négritude* remained for Fanon a mystifying irrelevance, and his 1961 account of its narcissistic chauvinism and exhibitionistic cultural theatricals chimed perfectly with his 1956 remarks on the rushed revalorisation of fossilised cultures.[2] He was alert to the pernicious glorification of the African past, by leaders such as Léopold Sédar Senghor and Kwame Nkrumah, as an opiate to divert the masses from their suffering in the present. Cultural retrievals of usable alternative pasts, though necessary to extricate Africa from the corrupting swamp of colonial culture, had a small part to play in the alleviation of suffering. But in the later version the qualifier had become the qualified. Although their historical achievements changed nothing for the Songhai of the present day, the rehabilitation of a 'future national culture' was now seen to be politically worthwhile. The moral pragmatist had given way to the tactical propagandist: the preoccupations were the same, but the order of priorities had been reversed.

Fanon offered a few not very far-sighted pointers to the way out of the impasse of whitening westernisation. At the political level, he habitually opposed an inventive revolutionary consciousness to an imitative middle-class mentality. His solution to the deceptions of neo-colonial leadership in independent Africa was to teach the masses 'that everything depends on them', and 'that there is no such thing as a demiurge, that there is no famous man who will take the responsibility for everything'.[3] Fanon had already concluded, at the end of *Peau*

---

[1] Fanon, *The Wretched of the Earth*, pp. 168–70.

[2] See ibid. pp. 173–83, and Frantz Fanon's speech to the First Congress of Negro Writers and Artists, Paris, September 1956, published in *Pour la Révolution africaine* (Paris, 1964) and as 'Racism and Culture' in *Toward the African Revolution*, translated by Haakon Chevalier (Harmondsworth, 1970), pp. 51–3.   [3] Fanon, *The Wretched of the Earth*, p. 159.

noir/Masques blancs, that middle-class society strangled 'all evolution, all progress, all discovery' and was 'a closed society in which life has no taste, in which the air is tainted, in which ideas and men are corrupt'.[1] But he failed to foresee, in 1952, that this stagnant uncreative ethos would become the norm for the government of much of independent Africa and that 'introducing invention into existence' on the merely personal level could be only the most partial and provisional of remedies. The Algerian combatant of his last writings was forced 'to face problems of building, of organizing, or inventing the new society that must come into being'.[2]

By this stage Fanon was certain that 'the greatest danger that threatens Africa is the absence of ideology'.[3] The only way to break the grip of European influence and forestall the inevitable slipping back into intellectual dependency was to devise an original non-western ideology. What had happened in reality was that African impatience with both colonial capitalism and its Marxist counter-products, together with the obligation to be original and to refuse the loan of foreign conceptual tools, had driven the new political and intellectual leaders back upon doubtfully derived 'African Socialisms' which were in truth neither 'African' nor 'Socialist' but variants on western bourgeois hegemonies. These experiments, leading neither outward into a new stage of political history nor genuinely inward into African traditional thought, had taken newly independent Africa – Fanon had Ghana in mind – nowhere except into deeper political and economic dependency upon the West.

But the social and political analysis of post-colonial Africa on which Fanon based his own recommendations was severely flawed by inaccuracy and simplification. David Caute wrote in his book on Fanon: 'The wide canvas of the Third World is filled in with sweeping strokes of a brush almost exclusively dipped in African paint.[4] More specifically, the African paint had a strong Algerian pigment. Arguing always from the revolutionary model of Algeria, even when he was writing about the power-élites of West Africa, Fanon found no place on his monochromatic canvas for the crucial distinction between administrative and settler colonies. His emphasis fell upon 'authentic' and 'inauthentic' decolonisation, not on the corresponding modes of initial colonisation.

---

[1] Fanon, *Black Skin, White Masks*, p. 224.
[2] Fanon, *Toward the African Revolution*, p. 114.
[3] Ibid. p. 196.   [4] David Caute, *Fanon* (London, 1970), p. 68.

The uprooted Martinican and adopted Algerian failed to take into account the strength and length of the political dialogue between the colonial powers and a long-established, propertied, and prosperous West African bourgeoisie: a class which was not suddenly fabricated in the panic rush of decolonisation, as in Fanon's model, and for which violent revolution was neither possible nor desirable. He defined the imperial decoloniser's purpose as 'to capture the vanguard, to turn the movement of liberation towards the right and to disarm the people'.[1] But in Nigeria, Ghana, and Côte d'Ivoire these movements were already turned well towards the right, and national liberation had become a heavily class-coloured concept. In much of sub-Saharan Africa, where there were no white lands to seize and the admission of the native bourgeoisie to positions of influence and partial authority had pre-dated independence, what Fanon called 'inauthentic decolonization' proceeded from historical determinants which were entirely different from those operating in the more violently and thoroughly colonised – and decolonised – settler colonies.

Fanon rejected the two-phase model of revolution imported from European Marxism and insisted that social revolution, to be effective, had to be integrated immediately into the struggle for national independence, as in China, Indo-China, and less-developed European countries like Yugoslavia. It was essential that the 'neo-colonial phase' of bourgeois nationalism be kept 'necessarily brief' and be made to give way promptly to 'the second phase of total liberation...required by the popular masses.'[2] If this did not happen, the second stage might not occur at all. The partisan analyst's tendency to lapse into a mystique of determinism, subsuming what will be, or what ought to be, into what actually is, in statements that are half-prophecy, half-appeal – 'The peoples demand this; the historic process requires it'[3] – is only part of the problem here. Caute comments on the two-phase revolutionary model: 'One searches in vain for an example of the two-stage strategy operating effectively...Wherever the national bourgeoisie has established its power in Africa or Asia, it has retained that power.'[4]

The historical currents which brought the middle class to social dominance in the West African colonies, and the national independence movements which consolidated its political power are, of course, only loosely analogous to the two stages of the revolutionary strategy and should not be confused with them. But Fanon's analytical model prefers to overlook the fact that these were neither simultaneous operations nor

[1] Fanon, *The Wretched of the Earth*, p. 55.
[2] Fanon, *Toward the African Revolution*, pp. 131 and 135.
[3] Ibid. p. 136.   [4] Caute, op.cit. pp. 76–7.

continuous phases of a single campaign, but quite separate processes existing at different times. The effective transposition of western bourgeois traditions to Africa during the colonial period gave to this class a rooted tenacity and, subsequently, an enduring presence. Thus, in some African colonies, notably the merely administrative West African ones, unfavourable socio-historical conditions prevented the otherwise sound two-stage strategy from gaining any ground, rendering it less invalid than inoperative. Not all decolonisation started from the same point.

Secondly, there was a strong temptation in Fanon to regard both tribal and social divisions as the conjurings of colonialism, and an attendant reluctance to concede pre-colonial status to tribal violence. The overwhelming trend of Fanon's rhetoric is to see this violence as a construct or emanation of colonialism, which is violence pure and simple, 'violence in its natural state' – a colonialism from which everything comes and which makes everything like itself. Tribal antagonism is everywhere something which is preserved by colonialism, not something which survives in spite of it:

> By its very structure, colonialism, is separatist and regionalist. Colonialism does not simply state the existence of tribes; it also reinforces it and separates them...Violence is in action all-inclusive and national. It follows that it is closely involved in the liquidation of regionalism and of tribalism.[1]

Fanon went on to smuggle a doubtful 'biological' integrity into those fictions of political geography, the arbitrary national boundaries left behind by the colonists, and ignored the tribal structures which were the only properly organic bases of African society. What resulted was the contradictory view that the tribalism supposedly fomented by Europeans would disappear if the people rallied to the truly divisive European construct of the nation. In Fanon's mind, violence was naïvely opposed to tribalism, and was viewed not as an expression of tribal or social struggles, but as the cleansing, unifying power which would sweep these away. At the worst, violence arose when protesting tribal energies were deflected back upon themselves and turned inward in a 'collective auto-destruction' by the colonial authority which was their true target. The tribal feud was seen, puzzlingly, as an organic release from the 'muscular tension' induced by colonial oppression, a 'pattern of avoidance behaviour' which was both a carefully engineered response to colonial reality and an evasive deferment of effective opposition to it.[2]

[1] Fanon, *The Wretched of the Earth*, p. 74.   [2] Ibid. p. 42.

According to Fanon's post-independence conspiracy theory, the ex-colonial oppressor, who 'pulls every string shamelessly' and 'never loses a chance of setting the niggers against each other', continued to exercise a neo-colonial remote control through *agents provocateurs* and *agent-régimes* which retribalised the state after the colonial pattern and fomented internal antagonisms to divert opposition from themselves. The revival of tribalism was supposed to derive from the laziness and duplicity of ruling élites, not from any traditional inborn strength: 'Everywhere where that national bourgeoisie has shown itself incapable of extending its vision of the world sufficiently, we observe a falling back towards old tribal attitudes.'[1] At the outer limits of Fanon's fantasy, tribalism became not merely a tool but the very creation of colonialism, contemporaneous with it, and violent, 'authentic' decolonisation became the guarantor of a delirious detribalisation:

In a veritable collective ecstasy...traditional enemies decide to rub out old scores and to forgive and forget...There is a permanent outpouring in all the villages of spectacular generosity, of disarming kindness...Even tribes whose stubborn rivalry is well known now disarm with joyful tears and pledge help and succour to each other. Marching shoulder to shoulder in the armed struggle these men join with those who yesterday were their enemies...Solidarity between tribes and between villages, national solidarity, is in the first place expressed by the increasing blows struck at the enemy.[2]

This was not to happen, in Fanon's Algeria or anywhere else. Events in West Africa only a few years after his death demonstrated that the really catastrophic imperial legacy was not the preservation and hurried patching over, at the colonial exodus, of tribal divisions, but the imposition across these divisions of the artificial structure of the nation-state, the European importation which Fanon made the base for the liberation struggle.

The state of Nigeria was built out of what were really three nations, ethnically diverse and, when pressed into a spurious unity, equally incapable of living together or apart. The idealism generated by a united struggle against savage colonial repression blunted Fanon's awareness of many temporarily shelved internal antagonisms. Whatever the value of his precarious thesis that violent decolonisation burns away tribal antagonisms whilst peaceful succession leaves them dormant or even re-awakens them, Fanon's faith in the unifying and liberative potential of the largely makeshift nation-state did not allow him to foresee the advancing threat of a horrific neo-tribal civil war in a newly independent state five years after his death. What happened

---

[1] Ibid. pp. 127 and 129.   [2] Ibid. pp. 105–6.

in decolonised Nigeria was neither the premature arrival at 'the stage of social consciousness before the stage of nationalism' which Fanon feared might lead to a revival of 'primitive tribalism',[1] nor a series of colonially conjured micro-nationalisms. It was a fragile, full-scale nationalism in which few believed.

Fanon also attributed the formation of social classes in Africa to the divisive impositions of colonialism, in spite of strong evidence of stratified, hierarchical social structures and indigenous colonial practices within pre-colonial societies. His Algerian-biased attribution of almost all internal rivalries and divisions to colonial machinations ironically gave some credence to the converse myth of a classless or 'communalist' pre-colonial Africa, from which the eccentric and largely fabricated 'socialist' ideologies of Senghor, Nkrumah and Julius Nyerere were derived. By the mystifications of the communalist-socialist syndrome, the new nationalist leaders were able to plead traditional Africa's social and political homogeneity in order to justify the abolition of opposition parties and to entrench the bourgeois dictatorships that Fanon so deplored: 'The single party is the modern form of the dictatorship of the bourgeoisie, unmasked, unpainted, unscrupulous and cynical.'[2]

Fantasies of pre-tribal, pre-class unity were used to bolster the monolith of the modern totalitarian state. Corrupt hegemonies, which in reality caricatured the values of the former colonial bourgeoisie, were allowed to masquerade as revivals of 'pre-colonial' solidarities. Unwittingly, the demystifier helped to fashion a new mystification: only in Fanon's case this turned out to be the peasant-based, revolutionary one-party state in which everyone would 'have to be compromised in the fight for the common good' and 'associate himself with the whole of the nation'; in which all will follow a dangerously undefined and unlocated 'national interest' and 'every onlooker is either a coward or a traitor'.[3]

Thirdly, Fanon's prophetic exemption of Algeria's violently won independence from the fate of sub-Saharan decolonisation was questionable. The heady atmosphere of revolutionary struggle gave Fanon an idealistic faith in the Algerian people's potential for a solidarity which was not realised after 1962. The revolution stimulated political consciousness and gave a temporary equality to bourgeois and *fellah*, male and female, Muslim and infidel, but did not permanently dissolve social, sexual, and religious divisions. Fanon saw the post-war com-

[1] Ibid. p. 164.   [2] Ibid. p. 132.   [3] Ibid. pp. 161–2.

munity as 'renovated and free of any psychological, emotional or legal subjection, prepared...to assume modern and democratic responsibilities of exceptional moment', and claimed that French and Jewish sacrifice in the Algerian cause 'attested to the multi-racial reality of the Algerian Nation.'[1]

According to Simone de Beauvoir, the analyst knew better than the activist about the internal dissensions which were destined to break out into violent conflict later on.[2] After independence, faction-fighting resulted in a succession of dictatorships and a monolithic political and cultural structure: not quite the 'theocratic, feudal Moslem state that frowned on foreigners' feared by the French Algerian in the appendix to *L'An cinq de la révolution algérienne*, but one which contained many of its exclusive and reactionary elements. Algerian socialism, no less than its Kenyan and Tanzanian counterparts, was tailored to fit a single dominant interest: in this case, Islam. Fanon's revolutionary peasantry dispersed into small landholders and took no further part in the direction of the revolution, and Ben Bella's limited and short-lived programme for female emancipation did not justify Fanon's westernised liberal belief that the liberation struggle had 'developed new values governing sexual relations' and led to 'the birth of a new woman'.[3]

Most importantly, the anti-colonial struggle did not produce a decolonised Algeria with the instantaneous efficacy which Fanon expected: he had leapt from the realisation that peaceful succession does not authentically decolonise to the fallacy that violent revolution would. But the crippling effect of the war left Algeria dependent upon heavily conditional French economic and technical aid, and western modernisation programmes prevented the reshaping of the French legal, educational, and bureaucratic systems. French atomic tests in the Sahara went on and Algeria continued to supply raw materials within the structure of an essentially colonial economy. Samuel Rohdie argued, in 1966, that the tragedy of Algeria was that the personal and social transformations wrenched by the war from the traditional order 'had no context after the war to grow, solidify and alter creatively Algerian society'.[4]

[1] Fanon, *A Dying Colonialism*, pp. 157 and 179.

[2] Simone de Beauvoir, *Force of Circumstance*, translated by Richard Howard (Harmondsworth, 1968), p. 609.

[3] Fanon, *A Dying Colonialism*, pp. 107 and 109.

[4] Samuel Rohdie, 'Liberation and Violence in Algeria', in *Studies on the Left* (London), 6, 3, May–June 1966, p. 88.

9

Finally, there was Fanon's propagandising hope for national consciousness as 'the only thing that will give us an international dimension',[1] and his subsequent assumption that Algerian nationalism might, mysteriously, help to launch Africa towards continental unity:

More and more the effects of the Algerian Revolution in Black Africa become noticeable...and a community of interests develops beween the peoples living north and south of the Sahara.[2]
The Algerian people knows that the peoples of Africa south of the Sahara are watching its struggle against French colonialism with sympathy and enthusiasm.[3]

This magical solidarity between sub-Saharan Africa and the Mahgreb was, like the trans-Saharan invasion force which was to seal it, a dream. It has long been a commonplace that the Fanonian body of thought thrown up by the Algerian Revolution had more real influence in Europe and America than in Africa, and the western connection in Fanon should not be understated. Fanon advised the total abjuration of Europe, even to the extent of dismissing Marxism as the inverted handmaiden of colonialism and its myth of the revolutionary proletariat as an opiate imported with the European class-structure which gave it existence.

Let us decide not to imitate Europe...Let us not pay tribute to Europe by creating states, institutions and societies which draw their inspiration from her...Leave this Europe where they are never done talking of Man, yet murder men wherever they find them.[4]

But this was policy and prophecy, not practice, and Fanon made no claim to have done this himself. If he had turned his back on Europe, at least one eye looked over his shoulder and was still fixed unerringly on it, notably on the treacherous French Left, which seems to have been the main target of his shock therapy. The book in which Europe was written off was prefaced by a French philosopher whose insistence that the Third World 'speaks to itself' through Fanon's voice now sounds odd in the light of his minimal influence of African thought.[5] Fanon's Bakunin-like upholding of the revolutionary value of sub-proletariats, as an alternative to orthodox Marxism, made his books the staple reading

[1] Fanon, *The Wretched of the Earth*, p. 199.
[2] Quoted by Peter Geismar, 'Frantz Fanon: evolution of a revolutionary. A Biographical Sketch', in *Monthly Review* (New York), May 1969, p. 28.
[3] Fanon, *Toward the African Revolution*, p. 116.
[4] Fanon, *The Wretched of the Earth*, pp. 251–4.
[5] See preface by Jean-Paul Sartre to *Les Damnés de la terre*, p. 9.

of black radicals and racially-repressed urban slum-dwellers of the developed world, not the inhabitants of African shanty-towns or South American *favelas*. Fanonism, as western analysts have never tired of pointing out, became the gospel of urban riot and terrorism in Europe and the United States.

PLANNED DECOLONIZATION AND ITS FAILURE IN BRITISH AFRICA

JOHN FLINT

TWO BROAD interpretations of the movement for decolonization have been put forward. The first of these may be described as 'liberal-nationalist' (some might prefer 'bourgeois') and the second as 'dependentista' or 'neo-colonialist' (though here again some might opt for the epithet 'vulgar Marxist'). Both theses, unfortunately, tend to be heavy with theory but lightweight in their evidential base. Both have originated largely in the speculations of political scientists, though the theories tend to reappear with monotonous regularity in the general historical literature, especially in textbooks. In this article I propose to examine how the decolonization movement originated as a movement for colonial reform in British Africa; what the theoretical assumptions behind this movement were; and how the British proposed, from London, to plan African evolution to self-government. My sources will be, almost entirely, the Colonial Office files for the period after 1938. I make no apologies for this because the dynamic for change, before 1946 at the earliest, lay there, and not in Africa.

I shall devote more space to a critique of the *dependentista* thesis than the the liberal-nationalist theory, because the former is more complex and nearer to reality, while the latter can be somewhat quickly demolished. The liberal nationalist interpretation was itself an ideological by-product of the decolonization process (and essential to it); its evidential base lay in the largely propagandist published sources, both nationalist and imperial, of the time, and the interpretation is largely the stuff of drama and myth. Both need conflict between firmly-drawn characters, a struggle of wills, an unfolding plot and a final resolution of conflict, with hero taking on villain, and a happy ending in which even the villain is mellowed, Scrooge-like, in the contemplation of the final generosity forced on him by the dire warnings of his helpful and enlightened friends and the ghosts of dead empires.

Act I of this drama must surely have been the Second World War (though there was a spectral prologue of forebodings and prophecies from the European catastrophe of 1914–18). As the entire northern half of the world moved through what was to prove the bloodiest period of human history the moral and physical bases of pre-war imperialism collapsed—the Axis Powers rep-

The author is professor of history at Dalhousie Univeristy, Halifax, Nova Scotia, and already a distinguished authority on the earlier partition of Africa through his biography of Sir George Goldie (OUP, 1960). The article was originally presented as a paper at the Australian National University conference on decolonization in August 1982.

389

resented the ultimate racism, the ultimate irrational autocracy, the ultimate evil. The 'United Nations' (how quickly we forget historical origins!) stood for the ideological opposites—self-determination, the equality of mankind, democracy. The outcome in 1945 was the defeat of Axis imperialism and the triumph of the anti-imperialist Soviet and American super-powers. Western Europe, the historical fountainhead of imperialism, lay in ruins, with France and Britain, the 'greatest' imperial powers, exhausted and weak, dependent on the financial generosity of the USA. The era of European domination had ended; roused by the new *Zeitgeist* the nationalists of the third world (seen as an opposite polarity to colonial rulers) could rally the masses and challenge their masters. The 'struggle' for decolonization had begun. Its victory was inevitable.

Even at a common sense level this story will not hold together. If willingness to decolonize was the result of struggle by nationalists and weakness of the colonial powers then the chronology of declonization makes no sense. By any sensible estimate the British, in 1945, were the strongest of the colonial powers in Africa, with the French next, followed by Belgium and Portugal. These powers should therefore have decolonized in exactly the opposite chronological order. In reality, however, strength represents exactly an index of willingness to decolonize, while political weakness appears to have bred imperialist resistance.

Examination of the documentary evidence undermines the liberal-nationalist myth entirely. It reveals clearly that consideration of policies of decolonization were entirely British in inspiration (with no other colonial power in Africa contemplating such steps before 1958) and that these British ideas antedated the outbreak of the war. They were not the reaction of an 'exhausted' power realizing its own weakness, but contemplated as means of strengthening British economic and international influence. American influence, though exerted, was really of little significance in shaping actual policy, as distinct from public relations.[1] The element of nationalism played no part in these developments until they had reached a relatively advanced stage; we may indeed go further than this and suggest that the emergence of nationalist political parties seeking mass support was the *result* of decisions to decolonize and a creation of imperial policy. Far from nationalists and imperialists standing at opposite poles, they were indeed historically aspects one of the other. No fundamental ideological gulf separated 'nationalists' from imperial policy once colonial reform planning was under way after 1938; the 'struggle' was merely tactical and concerned almost entirely with timing. The 'nationalists' wished to inherit

---

1. Wm. Roger Louis, *Imperialism at Bay: the United States and the Decolonization of the British Empire,* Clarendon Press, Oxford, 1977, deals extensively with this theme. The Anglo-American conflict about colonial goals was very largely a battle of words, with semantic issues looming large. In my work I can find no evidence that the British were willing to trim their sails to an American wind, except in matters of propaganda and drafting. Louis's book seems to suggest that US influence rather stiffened the 'imperial' temper in Britain.

the colonial state, the colonial frontiers and the colonial apparatus of power in all its ramifications.   The British had equal need of 'nationalist' cadres who could carry through exactly such aspirations, and if the nationalists were not there they would have to be created and nurtured.   This argument will be supported through detailed examples later in the context of a critique of the *dependentista* thesis.

The theory which attempts to explain decolonization in terms of under-development theory and the concept of neocolonialism is too well known to require extensive elaboration here.   It has been succinctly summarized by Colin Leys as an outline of the final stages of colonial rule:

'new social strata and ultimately social classes were either brought in (through colonial settlement), or created from among the indigenous population, which had an interest in organizing and facilitating the new economic activities involved (trade, mining, crop production, and so on).   In the course of time these strata or classes became powerful enough to render direct rule by the metropolitan power unnecessary . . . the need for the continuous and overt use of force by the government to back up the process of accumulation declined.   This facilitated by replacement of direct colonial administration by 'independent' governments representing local strata and classes with an interest in sustaining the colonial economic relationships'.[2]

The cooption or even creation of a 'comprador' class, followed by the transfer of formal political and administrative power to it, is thus seen by the *dependentista* school as the essential, yet illusory, element of the decolonization process, which may be seen as a kind of mirror image of the earlier phase of partition.

The *dependentista* thesis is certainly more attractive than the liberal-nationalist mythology and it takes care of all the devastating objections which can be raised against the legend of nationalist-imperialist struggle.   Moreover, although it was originally a mechanistic series of theoretical postulates erected on the flimsiest base of historical evidence, when such evidence is examined in detail it lends itself much more to interpretation along *dependentista* than liberal-nationalist lines.

At the outset, however, it should be pointed out that much of this lies in the large element of truism and tautology that runs through the *dependentista* jargon.   It is, for example, impossible to conceive that the decolonizing power had any alternative but to use 'new social strata . . . which had an interest in organizing and facilitating the new economic activities' created in the period of formal imperialism; Britain was hardly likely to foster the growth of

2.   Colin Leys, *Underdevelopment in Kenya: the political economy of neo-colonialism, 1964–1971*, Heinemann, London, 1975, p. 9.   On the previous page, footnote 13, Leys runs through the major literature on neo-colonialism and underdevelopment published before 1975.

revolutionary communist parties to which it might transfer sovereignty! The only other alternative, the deliberate exclusion of such groups with the objective of returning sovereignty to African precolonial nations controlled by precolonial social elites, an idea favoured in some colonial service circles of Nigeria, was in fact totally impractical, and amounted in fact to a disguised resistance to the very concept of self-government and decolonization.[3]

The crucial element in the *dependentista* thesis, therefore, lies not in the transfer of power to a 'new strata', but in the description of that 'class' as 'comprador'[4] The comprador bourgeoisie is not, cannot be, and must not be, a national bourgeoisie, capable of supporting itself by accumulation from a national economy. It is therefore not fully a capitalist class, but dependent as a class (symbolizing the dependency of the neo-colonial economy) on 'international capitalism' which is seen as dominated by the multinational corporations, generally regarded as linked ultimately to those of the USA. All it can do is preserve, develop and intensify underdevelopment and dependency in the forms of monoculture and raw material production which are the economic legacy of the colonial period. The creation of such a system was the planned purpose of decolonization.[5]

3. See below p. 399. An elaboration of indirect rule institutions could, at most, have led to 'self-administration' of small units and the creation of a permanent need for a cadre of colonial service personnel to co-ordinate these units, maintain transport and technical services and organize relations, economic and political, with the outside world. The concept had a good deal in common with that of the 'Bantustans' in South Africa today.

4. The historiography of empire is, of course, beset with the problems arising from the use of words which carry emotional, instead of rational, overtones. The liberal-nationalist school introduced the emotive terminology of the second world war and the struggle against Nazism in studies of 'resistance' and 'collaboration'. 'Comprador' in its Latin American historical context, appears to carry a more perjorative connotation than 'collaborator', though the terms are often used interchangeably. 'Collaborator', as the memories of Nazism recede, seems to be losing its hateful overtones, with the verbal form coming back into diplomatic and journalistic use to indicate moderation, co-operation and a friendly attitude. This is perhaps why the term 'comprador' is more favoured.

5. The neocolonialist and *dependentista* literature is too vast to summarize here. The above paragraph tries to summarise a number of strains or themes about which most of these theorists are agreed. Paul Baran's *The Political Economy of Growth*, first published in New York in 1957, outlined the view that decolonization hardly affected the realities of formal colonial rule because all the territories were handed over to 'comprador governments'. These were not merely 'fortuitous coincidences' but the result of 'the totality of imperialism' (p. 218). André Gundar Frank emphasized the view that underdevelopment was a systematic purpose of neocolonialism by which the USA (or rather its multinational corporations) intensified 'structural underdevelopment' (*Capitalism and Underdevelopment in Latin America*, London, 1969, p. 336 and *passim*). The writings of Samir Amin (*Accumulation on a World Scale: A critique of the theory of underdevelopment*, 2 vols., New York, 1974 and *Imperialism and Unequal Development*, Sussex, 1977) emphasizes the view that peripheral economies are only partially involved in the world system, which prevents their 'autocentric' development, and fixes them into patterns of transport and monoculture useful to the metropolis. Pre-industrial forms of reproduction thus coexist with incomplete and limited forms of advanced technology; these are fixed and immutable (except to violent revolution) by the dominance of metropolitan multinational corporations who use the comprador regimes to maintain the local order in the system in the periphery. Tautology runs rife through all these arguments; the term 'imperialism' seems to mean nothing more or less than the international capitalist system itself.

It is interesting that Kwame Nkrumah, himself one of the most crucial historical actors in the process of British decolonisation of Africa, was one of the first to elaborate the neocolonial idea and to castigate comprador regimes (though he did not use the Latin American term). He avoids

Footnote 5 continued on next page

In all of these writings there is scarcely any reference to what historians would call primary sources, other than published reports and economic statistics: indeed, the school seems to feed, vampire-like, on the writings of its own members, citing and reciting them monotonously as if they were evidence in themselves. But the historian can now look at the documentary evidence of British political thinking which lay behind the profound changes in policy which developed steadily after 1938. In particular we can look at British ideas about the emergence of social classes in Africa, what should be their roles in political and economic life and what should be the relationship between political, and economic and social, change. Did the British plan the transfer of power to 'compradors', or even to create compradors, in a purpose of perpetuating underdevelopment, peripheral economies and the interests of multinational (or even British national) corporations?

The Colonial Office files certainly do reveal that an almost complete reversal of attitudes towards social change in the British African territories developed in London after 1938.[6] Before that time the indirect rule philosophy, which had been developed entirely outside the Colonial Office by colonial service personnel, held virtually unchallenged sway, as did the economic doctrine, sacrosanct in the Treasury, that colonies should live off their own resources.[7] Indeed, if the historian looks for the roots of the 'development of under-development', the fostering of monocultures and metropolitan-oriented transport networks and the creation of 'compradors', they are to be found in the policy of rule through 'native authorities' (truly a 'comprador group' in a state of total dependence upon the British) combined with the concept that infrastructural development to serve the interests of cash-cropping and mining had to be financed from local resources. Before 1938 reform of 'native administration' could be argued by advocates who wished to improve its effectiveness, but those who argued for its abolition and replacement by some other system

the rather obvious implied question about his own role in the events of 1948–57 in Ghana, then the Gold Coast colony, as well as the strong implication that a continuation of direct colonial rule would have been preferable. Nkrumah outlines neocolonialism as worse than colonial rule because it left no imperial redress against the corruption, mismanagement and autocracy of collaborationist regimes: '... it means power without responsibility, and for those who suffer from it, it means exploitation without redress. In the days of old-fashioned colonialism, the imperial power had at least to explain and justify at home the actions it was taking abroad. In the colony those who served the ruling imperial power could at least look to its protection against any violent move by their opponents. With neo-colonialism neither is the case.' (K. Nkrumah, *Neo-colonialism, the Last Stage of Capitalism*, London, 1965, Introduction, p. xi.)

6. The development of a dichotomy of attitudes and thinking between the colonial service in the field and 'London' is a major theme which cannot be dealt with extensively here. By London in this context I mean not only the officials in the Colonial Office but also other informed groups who helped to shape opinion and attitudes, including members of parliament, the Fabian Colonial Bureau, the British trade unions and interest groups like the Anti-Slavery and Aborigines Protection Society as well as academic and university opinion, especially that which was interested in the development of higher educational institutions in colonial territories.

7. The two doctrines were closely connected, although the colonial service never embraced the latter with enthusiasm. Treasury parsimony was at the root of the origins of the indirect rule system, which became codified and dogmatized because it was without doubt the cheapest form of African administration.

17

were regarded as a lunatic fringe.   The aim of colonial rule was seen as the preservation of precolonial social organization.   The emergence of 'classes', whether bourgeois or proletarian, betokened a failure of policy.   Urbanization was thus frowned upon, migrant labour preferred to settled working men with their families, and the emergence of clerical and professional groups was regarded as an unfortunate by-product, alien in spirit and even in nationality to Africa itself. 'Detribalization' was the ghost which haunted the system.

All these assumptions began to be rather suddenly undermined by quite new attitudes and sentiments which made their appearance in the Colonial Office in 1938–9.   The timing is of significance; although the outbreak of war against Nazi Germany solidified these changes and added a strong anti-racist element to them, it is clear that the process began well before the war started.   What these changes amounted to, we can now see with hindsight, was the beginning of a movement for colonial reform in which lay the origins of decolonization.[8]

It is interesting to speculate on why these changes should have emerged at that time; Britain was recovering from the long years of economic depression; the strident racism and imperialism of Nazi propaganda was producing reactions of repulsion even on the right-wing of the British political establishment and the German demand for colonial concessions, as well as the Italian conquest of Ethiopia, revived interest in the question of the moral justification for colonial rule and how this might be linked with the values of democratic ideas which were under attack from fascism.   But three specific events of the later 1930s were directly responsible for the shift in attitudes in London. These were the widespread riots in the British West Indies during 1937 and 1938, which shattered the complacency of the Colonial Office and in their aftermath destroyed the long held axiom that colonial territories must live off their own resources on *laissez faire* principles; the almost simultaneous publication of Lord Hailey's *African Survey* in 1938; and the appointment in the same year of Malcom Macdonald as Secretary of State for the Colonies.

The new sentiments, taken together, amounted to an almost total reversal of the attitudes of the 1929s and early 1930s.   The indirect rule philosophy now came under fundamental and often stridently hostile attack.   It was not so much a matter of reforming the system (unless reform could be of such a nature as to alter its very basis and transform it into a system of local government) but of getting rid of its 'traditional' basis and the very concept of 'natural' rulers.   Such ideas were linked with a new concern for the role of the educated elements.   In January 1939 in a long minute commenting on Hailey's *African Survey* as part of a review of judicial administration in Africa initiated by

8.   Much ink can be wasted in trying to determine when a policy of 'decolonization' was finally decided.   The question, however, is ahistorical.   Just as it is nonsense to ascribe to Durham's Report a plan for the creation of independent nations in Australia, New Zealand and Canada, so no one in Britain intended 'decolonisation' in Africa until it actually occurred.   Decolonization was envisaged at best as centuries ahead in Africa in the 1940s; in the 1950s it emerged as a 'solution' to problems created by the failure of colonial reform.

Macdonald, the Colonial Office legal advisor, Sir H. Grattan Bushe, declared that indirect rule was doomed. 'My own belief is that given sufficient inertia the system will, sooner in one place and later in another, come to an end.' He implied neglect in the colonial service, where, except in the Gold Coast 'where conditions have passed the possibilities of pretence, serious criticism by any District Officer of the theory or practice of Indirect Rule is not a thing which is done.' 'On the other side of the picture there appears in an ever growing progression the educated African, and he views with extreme distaste the primitive, inefficient and in many cases corrupt institutions of indirect rule. If, like the white man, he need do no more than worship them he might be content. Unfortunately, however, he finds that, unlike the white man, he has to subject himself to them.'[9] The assistant under-secretary, Sir Arthur Dawe, normally staid and conservative, agreed:

> 'I think that the truth of Sir G. Bushe's remarks . . . is becoming increasingly realised. It is absurd to erect what is an ephemeral expedient into a sacrosanct principle. Things are moving so fast in Africa that the doctrinaire adherents of the indirect rule principle may find themselves out-moded much quicker than anyone would have thought possible a few years ago.'[10]

Beneath these criticisms there were fundamental sociological assumptions which indicated a profound change in attitudes. The preservation of pre-colonial culture was no longer a basic goal (although a minister might still genu-flect publicly to the ideal of 'preserving all that is best'[11]). 'Detribalization' ceased to be a ghost, and became an Angel of Progress. 'Classes', whether bourgeois or proletarian, were now to be seen as harbingers of a bright future, fermenting centres of enlightenment in their urban settings, whatever problems this might pose. The business of colonial policy was now the business of social change and the emergence of social classes should be welcomed, not feared or resisted. Everywhere in the colonial empire, Macdonald proudly proclaimed to a Commons Committee, the local populations were

> 'producing more and more of their own doctors and nurses, their own school teachers and agricultural officers, their own civil servants and lawyers, their own leaders in every walk of life. More and more, also, they are producing their own legislators and their own executive officers and that ultimately is the crux of the matter.'[12]

These assumptions that social classes would gradually replace 'tribal'

---

9.   CO 847/13/47091/2 Min. by Bushe, January 1939.
10.   *Ibid*. Min. by A.J.D. 19 January 1939.
11.   As did Malcolm Macdonald in the House of Commons Committee on Supply on 7 June 1939, quickly following this with a reference to the need to train colonial peoples in modern science, 'social progress' and 'political thought' so as to become 'full citizens of the modern world'.
12.   The quotation is from the same speech as footnote 11 and may be found in CO 847/20/47139.

institutions were not confined to the urban setting; detribalization should be watched and controlled in the very rockbed of rural Africa.   Here, it should be noted, it does appear that the British deliberately set their face against the cultivation of rural compradors.   The assumption was that British policy must prevent the transformation of traditional chiefs into a great landlord class controlling cash crop exports.   At the end of July 1938 J. A. Calder drew attention to what he regarded as the danger of this development, already apparent in Buganda, spreading throughout British Africa in the absence of a firm policy on land use and land law.   Calder simply assumed that the aim must be the creation of smallholding agriculture in individual peasant tenure.   He pressed for a full-scale study of the problem.   Hailey's *Survey* had made the same point.   Macdonald took up the suggestion with enthusiasm, held full scale meetings on the question, which he chaired, and sent a circular despatch to all the African colonies two months after the war began, announcing that such a study would be commenced.   He stressed that land was the basis of African social structure and that it was 'closely intertwined with issues of future political and economic development'. The matter, he insisted, was urgent, and the British had no policy.   African traditions were eroding and governments must intervene.   The war would increase the speed of change.   'I am not disposed to adopt a fatalistic attitude of *laissez faire*' and he was ready to use law to fight against peasant indebtedness, while the costs of this would be met from British and not colonial funds.[13]

This commitment to support an independent peasantry and the strong theoretical hostility to the development of an African landlord class is a theme which raises fundamental doubt about the neocolonial interpretation.   A mass of peasants, holding legal title to their lands, would hardly appear fertile ground, in the long run, for a class interested 'in sustaining the colonial economic relationships' (to use Colin Leys phrase again) into a post-colonial period.   Support for the creation of a powerful landlord class, interested in profits from cash export crops, especially if that class, as in Buganda, could be seen as a 'modernized' and 'enlightened' chiefly élite, would surely have been a better posture, promising the emergence of a conservative yet capitalistic class in command of its mass tenantry and well able to offset any tendencies towards urban radicalism.[14]   A further difficulty is presented by the

13.   CO 847/12/4708. Mem. by Calder, 23 July 1938; extract of meeting in the S. of S.'s room 27 June 1939; minutes of meeting chaired by Macdonald, 9 October 1939 and F.29, Macdonald to all African governors, 29 November 1939.   Hailey's *African Survey* extracts were listed on pp. 3–9 of Calder's memorandum.   The great inquiry into land law and policy was a casualty of the period after the end of the 'phoney war' and never materialized.   The whole subject of land, land law and land utilization after 1939 and its relationship to political change in Africa is one which well merits serious study.

14.   This argument can be applied even more forcefully to white settlers in Africa, who were of course the ideal comprador class (and performed this role historically in Latin America).   A truly rigorous neocolonial policy would have seen decolonization to this group throughout east and central Africa, with the concession of responsible government to the Kenya settlers (perhaps forcing them into co-operation with the Indian immigrants and the Baganda elite), an east African federation

Footnote 14 continued on next page

evident strain in London-based thinking, both inside and outside the Colonial Office, which assumed, often with considerable naiveté, that a strong peasantry would prove to be the backbone of a genuine democracy in Africa. The assumption that a democratic system would be the goal of colonial reform was apparently there from the first, was hardly ever discussed in principle, and simply 'emerged' in detailed comment.[15]

The period of the late 1930s also forms a watershed in official attitudes towards the urban African working class, which for the first time began to be recognized not just as requiring official stimulation and protection. Not only was adequate trade union legislation written into the Colonial Development and Welfare Act of 1940 as a condition for the granting of funds, but trade union advisors, generally with British union experience, soon began to make their appearance in the colonies. *Dependentista* theorists have tended to stress the machiavellian aspects of this latter device, and appear to agree with liberal-nationalists in emphasizing that its purpose was to prevent, if possible, the emergence of a 'natural' nationalism among the 'masses'. But if the policy was directed towards the handing over of powers to a comprador bourgeoisie, one is left wondering why the British were at all concerned to prevent the nascent trade unions from falling under the control of politically motivated clerks and literati, or why the trade union advisers stressed the concept of a stable, resident working class and the need for 'economistic' goals, neither of which appeared to serve the interests of international capitalism. The less sophisticated explanation, that the British now wished to foster a stable proletariat, capable eventually of articulation of its economic needs, appears to be more in conformity with the evidence and fits in with the new attitudes to the peasantry and the professional and salaried classes. Colonial Office opinion

centred on Nairobi, the linking of this with a central African settler controlled federation, the welcoming of South African ambitions in 'the north', perhaps leading eventually to a 'United States of South and East Africa'. All these ambitions were strenuously, both covertly and overtly, fought for by the white settlers between 1938 and 1947, and in general were supported by the colonial service personel, especially in Kenya. In 1942–3 the Kenya settlers, with the support of Governor Sir Henry Moore, in effect tried to carry through by stealth the *de facto* creation of a unitary state of British East Africa. British economic and military power was eclipsed by that of South Africa during the war in east Africa, yet the Colonial Office fought, from a weak base, with great skill and effectiveness against all these settler and South African ambitions. In east Africa none of them were realized. Even the Central African Federation, a product of the era in which the colonial reform planning of the 1940s was demonstrably collapsing and leading to decolonization, was so set up as an experiment in decolonization to white settlers that Britain was able eventually to unscramble Malawi and Zambia. As for South Afirca, it came to be regarded as a dangerous rival sub-imperial power, whose influence needed to be resisted. I have dealt with these themes, which are highly complicated and much misunderstood, in a number of unpublished papers which may see print eventually, including 'The Colonial Office and the South African "Menace", 1940–1943'; 'Last Chance for the White Man's Country; constitutional plans for Kenya and East Africa, 1938–43', Parts I and II; and 'Nazi Plans for the repartition of Africa, 1940'.

15. The question of what was meant by 'democracy', on the other hand, was a source of bitter discussion and recrimination from the colonial service side, which constantly attacked the concept of the secret ballot and the Westminster model, regarded as potential instruments for demogagy, corruption and exploitation by rootless parvenu professional politicians. The dire and Jeremiad prophecies bear a striking resemblance to the picture of 'wasteful, corrupt and reactionary comprador regimes' (Baran, *op. cit.*, p. 218) so beloved by *dependentista* writers.

21

had come to accept with some enthusiasm that formation of 'classes' in Africa was taking place, and that consequent 'detribalisation'[16] was inevitable, ought to be encouraged, and was 'progressive'.

Given these new assumptions about the inevitability and desirability of social change, had the time come to consider whether these might 'render direct rule by the metropolitan power unnecessary'?

It was Malcolm Macdonald who began to consider these implications. Throughout 1938 and 1939 Macdonald, in public and private, began hammering out a doctrine for an overall and consistent definition of British colonial policy.   He was not prepared to defend an implicitly racist position that there could be one policy for the white dominions and another for the colonies.[17] The most articulate statement of what this policy meant was made when Macdonald addressed the summer school on colonial administration at Oxford University on 27 June 1938:

'What is the main purpose of the British Empire? I think it is the gradual spread of freedom amongst all His Majesty's subjects, in whatever part of the earth they live . . . .

'The spread of freedom in British countries overseas is a slow—sometimes a painful—evolutionary process [which had already resulted in the Dominions evolving as "completely free" and "fully sovereign nations"] . . .

'The same spirit guides our administration of the Colonial Empire.   Even amongst the most backward races of Africa our main effort is to teach those peoples to stand always a little more securely on their own feet . . . the trend is towards the ultimate establishment of the various colonial communities as self-supporting and self-reliant members of a great commonwealth of free peoples and nations.   The objective will be reached in different places at different times and by many different paths.   Before it is reached there may be re-arrangements of political divisions; units at present separate may be combined, others may be split up into component parts.   The important thing is to ensure so far as is possible that whatever changes are necessary should be so effected as to be in harmony with the general aim.'[18]

This was the first occasion on which self-government for British African

16.   It would be tedious to cite the numerous uses of this concept.   I will argue elsewhere that it was fundamentally an erroneous view of social developments which were taking place.   That it existed was generally simply assumed by almost all commentators, official or unofficial, African and non-African, at this time.   The concept was closely linked to ideas about class formation. For an example see Godfrey Wilson, *The Economics of Detribalization in Northern Rhodesia*, Rhodes Livingstone Institute, 1941, which argued strongly against migrant labour, and for government to follow policy which would recognize and stabilise a permanent urban African working class.
17.   *Hansard*, H. C. 30 November 1939, Debate on the Address—'there is no division of imperial policy.   We cannot have one policy for the Dominions and a totally different policy for the Colonies.   The fundamental principle is the same.   They are equal . . . at any given time the peoples of the Colonial Empire shall enjoy the maximum, practicable amount of freedom.'
18.   CO 847/20/47139 at folio 1, and CO 323/1868 Pt II/9057 1A.

colonies had been proclaimed as a central purpose of colonial policy.[19]   These objectives were announced publicly, though in more guarded terms, in the House of Commons on 7 December 1938.[20]   A few days later, in a speech to the Constitutional Club, Macdonald referred to the end of an imperialism which could be seen as 'duping and domineering of weaker people' and proclaimed a 'new imperialism ... the gradual spread of liberty in every part of the colonial empire'.

By mid-1939 Macdonald was linking the idea of political advance with social and economic development by state action.   British colonial rule had as its 'main purpose to enable her subjects throughout the Colonies and Protectorates to partake in ever larger measure of the benefits of modern education, of economic well-being, of education, of health and of a full enjoyment of life.   We must repay their loyalty by giving back to them the best that lay in our power, the gift of self-government and freedom.' Further speeches in the Commons in June and November reiterated this position.[21]

The Colonial Secretary had evidently begun to contemplate what Leys calls 'the replacement of direct colonial authority by 'independent' governments'. Macdonald would likewise have put 'independent' in quotation marks.   Did Macdonald proceed from this to consider which might be the 'local strata and classes' who might eventually man such governments?

Indeed, as we shall see, he did.   But put in its *dependentista* jargon the question is naive, crude and conceals some of the most fascinating aspects of the problem.

In effect the disillusionment with indirect rule had pre-empted a choice which had never been a real choice anyway.   Some colonial officers continued to argue that 'self-government' would amount to the restoration of sovereignty to precolonial states, but now they were sat upon firmly not only by the Colonial Office, but by governors such as Sir Bernard Bourdillon in Nigeria.[22] The most extreme advocate of this position was Sir Theodore Adams, Chief Commissioner of Northern Nigeria, who maintained that Emirs had 'subjects', that there was 'separate Emirate nationality', tried to insist that emirates

19.   Professor Reginald Coupland, who attended the lecture, immediately noticed this, and stressed the point when pumping Macdonald's hand after the lecture.   One could, by assiduous scholarship, find earlier references to an ultimate goal of 'self-government' in the writings of colonial servants in Africa, but these are hardly in the line of Macdonald's thought; rather, such writers are considering self-administration of future units which might be considered as protected states, and assume that power would rest in the hands of traditional rulers.   It is interesting that Macdonald's words quoted above are almost a paraphrase of the last paragraph of the conclusion to Coupland's chapter on 'The Meaning of Empire' in his book *The Empire in These Days*, Macmillan, 1935, pp. 179–180.
20.   *Hansard*, H. C., 7 December 1938.
21.   The quotation is from a speech to the British Empire Society given on Empire Day in May 1939, CO 847/20/47139.   The Commons speeches are in *Hansard*, H.C., 7 June 1939 and 30 November 1939.
22.   Bourdillon, like Sir Alan Burns in the Gold Coast, was, however, hardly typical of the contemporary colonial governor, being much closer to the reforming movement in Britain.   For his views on Nigerian politics and constitution plans see my article, 'Governor *versus* Colonial Office: An Anatomy of the Richards Constitution for Nigeria, 1939 to 1945', *Historical Papers/ Communications historiques*, Canadian Historical Association, 1981, pp. 125–132 and *passim*.

had the right to all their revenues, argued that they were 'protected states' and asserted that 'The policy of a central African Government is incompatible with the Emirate system. One or other must be discarded.' Bourdillon firmly rejected these claims, which presented 'a grave danger of seriously compromising future political developments . . . If the Emirs cannot learn to see beyond the end of their own noses they are doomed'.[23]

Even given a willingness on the part of the chiefly élites to come together in federations, they could hardly be considered as a strata or class to whom power might ultimately be transferred.[24]   Hailey's *Survey* had brought this out clearly.   If social change were to be fostered by government action, the 'native administrations' seemed inappropriate and incompetant to undertake such functions so long as they remained under chiefly control.   Their maintenance, according to Hailey, was in any case not 'an end in itself' and it was 'not unlikely' that they might even collapse and colonial governments be forced to undertake their functions by direct rule.   Hailey raised the question of whether 'native administration' was 'incompatible with the growth of a large educated urban population?'   Would the educated African tolerate 'orders from his inferiors in civilization?'   He would insist on a system which guaranteed him 'British justice'.   There seemed to be few prospects of absorbing the educated African into a chief-dominated system.[25]

It could be argued therefore that the class which would inherit colonial sovereignty—the comprador strata—had been identified beyond doubt as early as 1938.[26]   It could only be the English-speaking literate professional group; only they could function in a 'national' setting and command the skills needed to manage a process of social change in a 'modern' state.   This being so, following the logic of the neocolonial school, it should have been followed by a restructuring of policy designed to strengthen the bourgeoisie and prepare for the transfer of power.   An obvious direction for such change would have been the extension of the elective principle to more urban centres, increasing the number of elected representatives in legislative councils, perhaps supported by the creation of numerous urban governments, elected on a property and educational franchise, and measures to transform 'native administrations' into local government bodies representative of these new elements.   The existing West African voting franchise, restricted by property and education

23.   CO 847/21/47100/1 *Comments . . . by . . . Bourdillon on Lord Hailey's Report*, Government Printer, Lagos, 1981, Confidential.
24.   Unless, of course, British policy had been firmly neocolonial, and had taken active steps to transform the chiefly elite into a comprador landholding class, with sufficient western and technical education to run a neocolonial structure, as in Buganda.
25.   Hailey, *African Survey*, pp. 538–42.
26.   Always assuming, of course, that the British, for reasons which the *dependentista* thesis seems to be unable to explain, were unwilling to transfer power to existing settler compradors, perhaps with Indian immigrants coopted (an ambition of the East African Indian National Congress, for which they had bitterly fought since its early days) in East Africa, and the transformation of chiefly elites in West Africa, on the Buganda analogy.

qualification, even perhaps liberalized cautiously while excluding rabble, would have admirably suited the purpose of extending the power of a comprador bourgeoisie. At this time no serious critic of imperialism contemplated universal suffrage for African voters, so on that ground such moves would hardly have attracted criticism, but would have been hailed, even by foreign critics, as liberal reforms.[27]

From the documentary evidence, however, it is obvious that not a single person in the colonial establishment, and very few in Britain outside it,[28] were prepared even to consider such a course. Hailey's *Survey* shied away from decisive recommendations, arguing that the problem of 'native administration' needed extensive research and evaluation, but tentatively suggested the development of groupings of native administrations into regional councils which might serve as electoral colleges for central quasi-parliaments. Macdonald, in private discussions with Hailey, pointed out the inconsistency of developing indirect rule further and capping it with a parliamentary body. Hailey, ever cautious and never a man to be impressed with mere logic 'admitted the apparent inconsistency but said that he felt sure that every territory connected with Great Britain would turn towards the Parliamentary model, and that whether Parliamentary institutions were suitable to the country or not, they represented the most educative phase of political development— one through which every country must pass before it can find the political form best suited to its needs'.[29]

These were the desperate times between Munich and the outbreak of war, but in the Colonial Office Macdonald continued to press on with reform. His priority was to implement Moyne's report and pass a colonial development and welfare act, which was quickly drafted. Delayed by Munich and the Treasury Macdonald continued to press for it, successfully intervening with the Prime Minister and arguing, once the war broke out, that it would help to rally

27. Even in Britain universal suffrage was by no means clear until after 1945 in the sense of 'one (wo)man one vote'. Some persons could still not vote because they lacked householder (or housewife) status, and many property owners, as well as university graduates, held more than one vote. In the United States, of course, many states, by legal or other means, prevented blacks from registering as electors. The proposition that illiterates should not be permitted to vote was almost universally regarded as common sense, for in a system of secret ballot with voting papers which listed merely the candidates names without any system for permitting the listing of party symbols, it was not practical for an illiterate to vote. In all the areas of British non-self-governing territory where elective systems were established, literacy was a qualification for voting, with the striking exception of Ceylon, where universal suffrage had been introduced after 1931, with provision to assist illiterates in voting.
28. Coupland pressed the Colonial Office in September 1939 to begin constitutional advances in West Africa, arguing that the urban professionals 'could provide a quota of reasonably competent and public-spirited politicians'. His *The Empire in These Days*, p. 234–238 contains the first serious suggestions for parliamentary self-government in West Africa.
29. CO 847/13/47097. F2 Record of discussions between S. of S. and Lord Hailey, 6 December 1938. This is perhaps the first reference to an interesting concept which constantly reappears later. From the first it was the British who considered that African territories would need to work out specific African forms of 'democracy' and the Westminster model would probably not provide a suitable permanent constitution. Nationalists resisted this firmly. It can be said with some confidence that the emergence of the Westminster model was the result of nationalist insistance and not of imperial imposition.

colonial support for the war effort.[30]   Africa, however, remained high on the
agenda.   As early as February 1939 officials were discussing ways to plan political change.   By an almost sacred tradition colonial governors should have
been consulted, but several officials were anxious to by-pass gubernatorial
opinion.[31]   O. G. R. Williams, head of the West African department, wanted
to ask for the views of colonial governors, but opposed any idea of a governors'
conference.   Planning, in his view, was urgent.   Britain should initiate change
before Africans began to demand it 'rather than allow ourselves to be forced
into the position of making concessions to the 'clamour of demagogues'[32]   This
was a theme that would constantly reoccur in future planning discussions.
Meanwhile Hailey's *Survey* was mined as a blueprint for change.[33]

The contradiction between the policy of 'native administration' and the
development of legislative councils (which in neo-colonial terms may be seen
as the attempt to identify the 'local strata and classes' to whom power might
be transferred) had clearly emerged as the central issue of African policy
discussion throughout 1939.   It was the theme of the interesting attempt to
consult university opinion at a meeting in the Carlton Hotel on 6 October 1939,
which revealed the surprising strength of the 'indirect rulers', with only
Coupland pressing for constitutional advance on parliamentary lines.   If the
'nationalists' were to be wooed, it was evident that the courtship would fall
short of any possibility of breach of promise.[34]

What lay behind this reluctance to identify the 'new strata' to which power
could be handed over as part of the colonial reform strategy, given that common
sense appeared to have defined the western educated elite as the only acceptable candidate in the long term?   There were two major difficulties, one
severely practical, the other theoretical but no less significant.

The practical problem was that in 1939 a 'national' bourgeoisie capable of
running a colonial state simply did not exist.   This was literally the case in

30.   I hope to develop this point further elsewhere.
31.   e.g. CO 847/13/47100, Min. by Preston 23 February 1939 strongly resisting any consultation
with governors, and referring to governors who were 'lacking the necessary leisure or intelligence,
or both' to make sensible comments, while chances were 'remote' that they would have views 'of
significance or value'.
32.   *Ibid.* Min. by Williams, 7.3.39.
33.   Over 150 extracts were made into separate files of problems for discussion and solution.
34.   This meeting deserves rather more extensive treatment than space permits here.   Besides
Macdonald and his senior officials, Hailey and Lugard attended.   That Lugard, the conqueror of
northern Nigeria should have been present at the first serious discussion of planning for self-
government, is indeed a historical curiosity.   It also is noteworthy that of the academics, all but
one, the biologist Julian Huxley, were historians.   Coupland's was the most liberal academic view,
and it was sharply contested by his junior colleague from Oxford, Margery Perham, who strongly
defended Lugard's demand for regional councils of native administrations, arguing that 'the plane
of the tribes' was the African reality, and not the 'plane of our big state system imposed artificially
from above ... the intelligentsia are very rapidly acquiring political consciousness and naturally
wish to capture the big state system.   We shall probably give in to them too soon.'   In minutes
afterwards Perham was condemned as reactionary and representative of the kind of people who
had caused much of the trouble in India.   CO 847/17/47135, Record of a discussion held at the
Carlton Hotel, 6 October 1939, Minutes by Mahew, 2 November 1939; Keith 3 November 1939;
Bushe 7 November 1939 and Seal 11 November 1939.

the eastern and central African territories (unless the British were prepared
to accept the white settlers, Indians and Baganda chiefs as such).   In West
Africa such a bourgeoisie had begun to make its appearance and to articulate
a 'nationalist' political philosophy, which was of course essential if the integrity
of the colonial political unit and its economy were to be preserved, but it was
far too small to be considered capable of manning the administrative system.
Much more statistical work needs to be done before we can estimate numbers
of the professionally educated with any degree of accuracy, but it is clear that
these were extremely small.   In the Gold Coast, with the largest educated
group in proportion to population of any African colony, there were only 1,000
children in secondary education in 1939, and only 31 at Achimota College, most
of whom were preparing for London intermediate BA exams.[35]   Only 3,000
electors could qualify for the £100 franchise in Nigeria, and of these it is likely
that less than one-third were educated at secondary level.[36]   There were a few
dozen Africans attending universities in Britain, fewer in the USA, where we
know there were twelve university students from Nigeria when war broke
out.[37]   West Africa alone, therefore, could offer precursors of a coming bourgeoisie, but not a viable class capable of assuming power.   The discussion had
merely identified a *future* class to which power could *eventually* be transferred.

The way forward was clearly to create such a viable class and this was
indeed planned and executed even during the war.   The Advisory Committee
on Education (ACEC), responding to the reluctance of the West African
Governors' Conference to endorse such a development in 1939, made a
vigorous counter-attack demanding the immediate establishment of planning
for African universities.   Their stance was almost completely political; 'a
university which fully trains graduates to occupy positions of responsibility'
was 'essential to any complete development' and 'progress will be gravely
embarrassed unless the essential preliminary steps towards the creation of a
university are taken in the immediate future'.[38]   This initiative led directly to
the creation of the Asquith and Elliot Commissions and resulted eventually
in the creation of the university colleges at Legon, Ibadan, Makerere and
Khartoum, as well as in the West Indies.   Paradoxically, the University of
London was given an educational colonial empire as part of the road to
decolonization.[39]

35.   CO 847/16/47122/1 F8, Minutes of 94th meeting of the Advisory Committee on Education,
18.5.39, comments of Miss Oakden.
36.   The property franchise enable many traders to qualify.   In Lagos the strong Muslim role in
elective politics after 1923 is evidence that the electorate was hardly coterminous with the western
educated élite, as many scholars once assumed.   See R. Sklar, *Nigeria Political Parties*, Princeton,
1963, p. 46.   Sklar is in error when he writes on p. 52 that only 792 voted in the Lagos town council
elections of 1938; some 1,500 did so.
37.   Sklar, *op. cit.*, p. 73.
38.   CO 847/18/47029.   Report of the sub-committee of ACEC... 4.12.1940, quotations from
Part II, pp. 50–1.
39.   Secretary of State Stanley's letter to the Vice Chancellor of London University, confidential,
of 29 May 1943, soliciting co-operation in the plan, put this paradox very consciously.   Stanley
Footnote 39 continued on next page

The ardent neocolonial theorist, at this point, may be tempted to shout 'Eureka!' Having identified their ideal compradors, and finding them lacking in quantity, the British proceeded to create more of them. This is indeed the planning of neocolonialism.

Such a conclusion ignores the other strain of thought which lay behind the reluctance to begin reform along parliamentary lines, the theoretical issue which was referred to earlier. The British were not, in fact, gifted with machiavellian skills and prophetic insights (or their colonial reform movement would not have degenerated into rapid constitutional advance in the 1950s or the scramble for decolonization of the 1960s). They appear to have had no aspirations whatsoever for the role of puppet-masters. A question of the legitimacy of political authority lay beneath all these discussions. From the international perspective Macdonald's statements implied that colonial rule could only be legitimized if its purpose was eventual self-government.[40] Hailey's writings had thoroughly undermined the assumptions of earlier times that indirect rule was self-evidently legitimate, because it was 'traditionally African' and run through 'natural rulers', by insisting that native administrations needed popular acceptance before they could be considered viable. The 'new strata' might well be able, with expansion of their numbers, to run a post-colonial state—but where was their legitimacy? Certainly not in the property and educational franchise, which ensured oligarchy. Nor, as yet, in universal suffrage, which, in the absence of an educated electorate, would produce something worse, oligarchy compounded by demagogy and corruption. The British were indeed looking for inheritors, 'leaders', 'nationalists' and the like, but unless these could be used to develop self-government they could not be made legitimate. At the end of 1939 G. Seel commented that if the time was near for 'Africans who would take part in the deliberations of a national assembly' they must be 'sufficiently representative of the great mass of their fellow Africans... the method of selection will require the most careful

urged the British universities to do their patriotic duty and transform their links with Empire. In the past they had trained and nourished pro-consuls and imperial administrators, now their task would be 'no less vital by taking the form of assistance in the development of Colonial Universities which will rear the local leaders of the future.' The letter is quoted in Eric Ashby, *Universities, British, Indian, and African: a study in the ecology of higher education*, Harvard, 1966, pp. 211–212.
40. There was a strong awareness of the point, which is nowadays discarded into a limbo, that self-government is a much deeper and more fundamentally important principle than sovereign independence of the state. One colonial office official, in a minute resisting American pressure for colonial 'independence', commented that the word independence was 'a political catchword which has no real meaning apart from economics. The Americans are quite ready to make their dependencies politically 'independent' while economically bound hand and foot to them and see no inconsistency in this', CO 323/1858/9057B Min. By Eastwood, 21 April 1943, quoted in W.R. Louis, *Imperialism at Bay*, p. 247. The documents could hardly be mined to find a clearer rejection of neocolonial planning, though many statements along these lines could be found. At the same time Eastwood's futures were wrong; the Americans subsequently did not move to grant independence to their colonial possessions after the war, except in the Phillipines, but integrated them more intensely into the USA, Alaska, Hawaii and Puerto Rico developed self-government and not independence, while as it turned out British Africa in the main ended up with independence but not self-government.

consideration'.   It could be 'taken for granted that anything in the shape of direct election ... will be out of the question for some time to come.'[41]   The implications of this kind of thinking were that Britain could not decolonize to mere compradors; the new elite would have to demonstrate that it had genuine support from the masses at large.   Ultimately the African elite would discover that this principle was their key to success; by confronting Britain with organized mass nationalist parties the entire house of cards of colonial reform planning could be brought to the ground after 1948.

Thus, in the months before and just after the outbreak of the second world war, a revolution of attitudes had taken place and a mood of colonial reform taken hold.   In the economic sphere the doctrine of *laissez faire* had been breached with the Colonial Development and Welfare Act.   But in the political sphere, though self-government was now the goal of planning, nothing practical had been decided.   The old compradors of settlers and chiefs were losing centre stage, and new 'classes' or peasants, proletarians and professionals being written into the script.   But the plot was far from clear.   The situation called for the intervention of a *deus ex machina*, and as usual Lord Hailey was expected to fulfill that role.[42]

Towards the end of 1939 Macdonald decided to commission Hailey to undertake a comprehensive study in Africa, and to make fundamental policy recommendations, especially as to how the 'native administration' policy could be harmonized with development of the legislative councils and parliamentary forms.   In   discussing   the   task   with   Hailey   Macdonald   outlined virtually all the major questions of African policy:

'It was time that we got our minds clearer as to the objects of our native policy in Africa.   What exactly were we driving at in our policy of 'indirect rule'?   What was the next step in advance after we had set up efficient *local* native administrations?

'[Where there was] ... a considerable European minority, how was govern-

41.   CO 847/13/47100/f7 Mem., no title, date or signature, but written by Seel sometime before 2 December 1939, on which date he sent it to Boyd.

42.   Lord Hailey's rise to an extraordinary position of prominence in Colonial Office influence has yet to be explained.   Despite his great age, the fact that his experience was entirely in India as a practical administrator, and that he held only *ad hoc* and advisory positions in the Office, Hailey's was the single most powerful influence on the shaping of policy from 1938 to 1945, after which he became eclipsed by Sir Andrew Cohen.   Probably his Indian experience was considered an important asset, for the Colonial Office constantly held the view that British policy in India, and especially relations with the nationalist movement, had been mismanaged beyond repair, and that these mistakes must be avoided in Africa.   The lack of systematic and organized research in Africa also gave the *African Survey* an enormous prestige, for there was no other comparable work of reference.   Above all, however, Hailey's temperament and attitudes, combining progressive thought and caution, experience and experiment with a sense that 'sound' history could be made by evolutionary stages which tried to keep economics, social change, educational and scientific progress all in tune with each other, admirably suited the mood of the times in Britain, where the idea of 'sound planning' was taking deep root after 1938.   His influence on colonial policy can be compared with that of Lord Beveridge in domestic social policy.

ment to be organized *ultimately* so that native interests were not sub-
ordinated to European interests and vice versa?[43]

Without general objectives, Macdonald asserted, there was a real danger of
taking *ad hoc* steps which could not later be reversed.   In addition, Hailey was
asked to visit Southern Rhodesia, to see if any measures could be taken to bring
that country's 'native policy' into some kind of harmony with British policy,
without which 'Amalgamation (with Nyasaland and Northern Rhodesia) was
impossible.'   All the political aspects of his mission would be kept secret;
ostensibly it would be announced that he was making further studies of
'native administration'.[44]   The political aspects were made crystal clear in
Macdonald's request for Treasury funds for the mission:

> 'The war is likely to create a demand in Africa for a quickening in the pace
> of development towards self-governing institutions ... we shall be wise to
> anticipate this demand (with) ... carefully thought out plans.   ... we should
> pursue a slowly but surely developing policy of training Africans to look
> after many of their own affairs.'

The problem of the future of indirect rule and how it could be harmonized
with the aspirations of 'detribalized natives' was urgent.[45]

Hailey's 1940 visit to Africa was perhaps the last of the epic and eccentric
'travels in Africa' genre, though this frail old man's adventures were in rickety
aeroplanes rather than picturesque canoes and steamboats.   In the midst of his
inquiries he undertook a brilliantly successful mission to bring the Belgians in
the Congo into line with the British cause after the surrender of their
King.   His report took a year to complete and was submitted to the Colonial
Office in February 1941.[46]   Here only the fundamental lines of the report can
be addressed.   From present-day perspectives it is difficult to assess; had it
been published in the mid-1950s it would have been condemned by African
nationalists as reactionary, but a present generation of young Africans may be
tempted to see it as deep and subtle, full of forebodings and warnings of the
future.

At the outset of his report Hailey made basic recommendations which were
to form axioms of planning for both the Coalition and the Labour governments

---

43.   The underlined words were inserted into the draft record of the conversation in Macdonald's
handwriting.
44.   CO 847/16/47100/1/F1 Mem. by S. of S. of a conversation with Lord Hailey, 5 September
1939.
45.   *Ibid.* Macdonald to Sir John Simon, draft at F2.
46.   The original, from which the summary and comments below are taken, is to be found in CO
847/21/47100/1.   This version was published as a C.O. Confidential Reprint for the use of the
colonial service as *Native Administration and Political Development in British Tropical Africa* in
1944, but several important passages were omitted from the printed version as a result of governors'
objections, especially from Kenya.   It is this version which is republished recently, with an
excellent introduction, by A. Kirk-Greene, F. Cass and Co., 1980.

until the collapse of colonial reform after 1948.   Economic and social development must form the base for, and take precedence over, political advance.
The former must be regarded as the essence and foundation of reform, while
political change was a superstructure which could only reflect the more
fundamental changes, and must be in tune with them.   This point was constantly hammered home throughout the report in almost every detailed
recommendation in every region.   Hailey saw no problem in reconciling the
two so long as, from the first stages, Africans took part in planning and
execution of the social and economic developments.   This would entail the
transformation of 'native administration' into local government by 'a resolute
development of local institutions combined with the progressive admission of
Africans to all branches of the government services.'   At the same time this
brand of what might be called socio-economic decolonization implied an
Indian summer of imperial control, 'until experience has shown us under what
constitutional forms the dependencies can move most securely towards the final
stages of self-government.'

Hailey then proceeded to endorse all the candidates for the inheritance of
imperial power, while doubting the fitness or legitimacy of any.   The Native
Authorities were not the 'natural heirs' and he rejected the view that they had
inherent rights from traditional African legitimacy.   A future self-governing
central government could not be simply a federation of Native Authorities,
which were not representative of many facets of African societies, certainly not
of the urban areas, and not of some rural areas where indirect rule could not
be based on traditional society.   Native Authorities could be used, especially
in the 'earlier stages of political development' as electoral colleges for a central
legislature and also to form 'regional conferences' to discuss issues before
legislative council meetings.   But similar functions could also be allotted to the
pan-tribal Unions which had made their appearance in the 1930s, to the urban
municipalities and even to professional associations.

The 'intelligentsia' must also be absorbed into the 'advanced institutions
of central government' by increased representation in legislative Council,
admission to the civil service, and being given extensive experience in urban
government, taxation and provision of social services.   Hailey saw the
difficulties which would come from the response to such moves by the educated
elements, 'unable to read the future in any other terms than the expansion of
parliamentary institutions of the normal type', but they must be resisted, for
advance along parliamentary lines was irrevocable, while experimentation with
other forms was not.   Perhaps by such trial and error experiments in representation, 'full powers' could later be transferred to a legislature 'not constituted
in the nomral way'.   Such a body might well be more stable, more truly
representative of Africans and more effective than the alien Westminster model.

Hailey's report became a kind of organic blueprint for the colonial reform
movement.   Almost every plan, and all the schemes for constitutional

31

advance[47] until the Accra Riots of 1948, bore the stamp of Hailey's ideas. Even the much-trumpeted local government despatch circularized by Creech Jones in 1947 merely carried out the democratization of indirect rule which Hailey would have wished to see inaugurated by stages in 1941. Throughout 1941–2 Hailey in effect became the Grand Panjandrum of colonial planning in his capacity as Chairman of the Colonial Office Committee on Postwar Reconstruction in the Colonies, seen self-consciously as uniquely forward-looking and ahead of other Ministries, and soon simply referred to as 'the Hailey Committee'. No one with objectivity who has read the voluminous papers of this committee could leave them and continue to maintain the belief that the British were planning the development of underdevelopment.[48] By April 1942 the committee had prepared a list of fifty subjects requiring action, or further research and decision. This document represented no less than a total planning base for a massive scheme of colonial reform in which each item, however detailed, could be planned in an integrated and inter-related fashion.[49]

By this time, however, the British were being forced by American pressures, starting after the signature of the Atlantic Charter but intensifying after America's belated entry into the war, to concentrate not so much on detailed planning, but on public definition of policy and propaganda needs. This phase

47.　It is true that Burns and Bourdillon, governors of the Gold Coast and Nigeria respectively, forced through, against the opposition of the Colonial Office and Hailey, the admission of Africans as members of the Executive Councils in 1942, but the councillors were nominated and the effect was not so fundamental as it might appear.

48.　Indeed, a surprising amount of *dependentista* theory, in different jargon, seems embedded in the committee's papers, especially those dealing with economic problems. The 'development of underdevelopment' several times seems to be outlined as the dire and probable consequence if the committees plans should *not* be implemented. As with present-day radical commentators, there was great euphoria, characteristic of all war-time planning, that the boom and slump conditions affecting primary producers would be eliminated by international price planning, state marketing and rigid price controls. This would form the base for capital formation for industrialization, and the flow of inward imports would also have to be controlled and planned, with rigid fixing of interest rates. Planned self-sufficiency in food production was essential. Long range planning had the general objective of 'raising the standard of life in the Colonial Empire itself'. CO 967/13, Mem. by Clauson on the 'Colonial Economic Problems in the Reconstruction Period'. 31 May 1941. There were numerous discussions of industrialization in the colonies, in great detail, and careful identification of lobbies which would oppose it. The Committee finally recorded that it agreed as a matter of principle, the development of secondary industry in the colonies should be encouraged in spite of opposition on the part of United Kingdom manufacturers whose interests might be affected.

49.　CO 961/13 is the collection of the papers of the Hailey Committee. The 50 point list is contained in 'Schedule of subjects for consideration of actions taken', 7 April 1942. Subjects covered included external relations, a long list of economic matters including marketing, quotas, tariffs, food production, industrialization, financial policy, soil conservation, railway finance, etc. Constitutional and political change occupied several categories, with individual memoranda on each colony, and was linked to questions of the reorganization of African boundaries, the creation of larger units, future relations with the UK, other Dominions and foreign countries. Other broad categories, often broken down into detailed problems, included social change, broadcasting, airways, land reform, demobilisation, education, health (with a strong plea for priority to the financing of preventive medicine at the expense of curative facilities), the colonial service, the role of women, town and country planning, legislation against racial descrimination (to be introduced in the UK also), the prison system, trade unions, forest problems, and long range speculations on the ultimate objectives of reform. Only the last item, '50. Eugenics' was not taken seriously; this, it was recommended, 'should be left entirely to unofficial agencies'.

has been dealt with in great detail in Louis's *Imperialism at Bay*. In the practical sphere the effects of the American intervention were negative, diverting energy to abstract considerations and creating resentment which helped to stiffen conservative attitudes in the Colonial Office, while tipping the scales again towards the indirect rulers in the colonial service. For policy definition, however, the effects were positive (though the result was far from American desires). Churchill's insistence in September 1941 that the Atlantic Charter had no application to the British Empire opened up the field for Labour Party pressure by exposing the absence of well-defined public statements on the goals of colonial reform. Creech Jones, the future architect of West African decolonization, was enlisted to tour the USA and recruited (or infiltrated like the good Fabian he was) important Colonial Office committees on welfare, social and economic development, and education. He and Attlee played an important part in dealing with the Americans, and thus in defining policy.[50] The colonial reform movement had, since 1938, in effect pulled the goals of colonial policy in Africa close to the Labour Party's traditional colonial demands for protection of African labour, encouragement of trade unions, emphasis on social and economic development for Africans, more higher education for Africans, and the building of friendly relations with the educated elite.[51] Such emphases were, in any case, the only sound basis on which to resist American demands. This eventually bore fruit in the public statement which Creech Jones had continued to demand since 1941, when Colonial Secretary Oliver Stanley in July 1943, formally defined the objectives of British colonial policy and declared in the House of Commons that 'we are pledged to guide colonial peoples along the road to self-government within the framework of the British Empire'. This was firmly linked to the obligation 'to build up their social and economic institutions' in harness with an educational policy designed so that 'as quickly as possible people are trained and equipped for eventual self-government'. Economic and social development, and education, would thus parallel political change granting 'further and future responsibilities.'[52] A bi-partisan policy of colonial planning and reform had emerged, and would remain in effect until it foundered in Central African problems in the 1950s.

It soon became clear that this consensus included the West African nationalists as well. As Stanley was delivering his speech, the British Council, prompted by the Colonial Office, was preparing invitations for a West

---

50. In January 1943 formal negotiations began for an Anglo-American Declaration on the future of colonies, with Attlee handling the British end. His draft expressed the essentials of what would become Labour's policy after 1945, stressing the concept that social and economic development, coupled with an educational drive, must first create viable independent economies with just societies, which would be able to assume a real independence 'without danger to themselves and others'. CO 323/1858 Pt II/9057B. War Cabinet paper draft by Attlee, 1 January 1943; sent to US 8 January 1943, final draft to British ambassador in Washington, 1 January 1943.
51. P. S. Gupta, *Imperialism and the British Labour Movement, 1914–1964*, London, 1975 is the best overall treatment of Labour's colonial attitudes.
52. *Hansard*, 13 July 1943 House of Commons.

33

African delegation of newspaper editors to visit Britain.   Given the almost
non-existent state of any formal nationalist organizations in West Africa at
the time there seemed no other means of contacting the potential nationalist
leadership.   Nnamde Azikiwe, the future first president of Nigeria, himself
drafted the position paper which the editors presented to the Colonial Office—
'The Atlantic Charter and British West Africa'.   It was a remarkable document, consistent in all respects but one with the British plan of colonial reform.
It stressed 'social equality and communal welfare' and presented a detailed
series of demands for social and economic development to form a base for
future constitutional development along lines of democratic advance in rural,
municipal and central government.   This, they agreed, must be planned,
gradual and evolutionary.   In one respect only did their demands differ significantly from Colonial Office thinking; they boldly suggested a time-
table.   There should be unofficial majorities in the legislative councils as
soon as practicable, and this should be followed by ten years of 'representative government', to be succeeded by five years of 'responsible government'
after which each territory should become a Dominion.[53]   This was not a
bad margin of error, as political prophecies go, even when they are of the
self-fulfilling variety.

If such a consensus was achieved as early as 1943, why then was the colonial
reform movement in Africa such a colossal failure?   For failure it was.
Decolonization did not, except in a merely cosmetic sense, proceed by orderly
evolutionary stages.   It was not a process of finely tuning constitutional
arrangements upon a base of fundamental economic and social change.   It did
not reflect growing self-consciousness of viable 'classes', peasantry, proletarians and bourgeoisie, balancing themselves in a democratic political
evolution.   No solid bases of rural and urban institutions emerged.   The
economies did not become sophisticated and self-sustaining.   Independence,
rather than self-government, triumphed in the end, as did the Westminster
model and not a specific unique African form of democracy.[54]   The parliamentary British model served only as a temporary expedient, generally collapsing within a few years of independence.   In most of Africa the result
of decolonization has been to entrench oligarchic government, whether this
be military, one party or simple autocracy, in precisely the way which colonial
reform planning sought so strenuously to avoid.

To answer this question satisfactorily will need a full monograph on the
period from 1945 to 1951.   But a number of tentative answers may be

53.   N. Azikiwe, *The Atlantic Charter and British West Africa*, Lagos, n.d. (but printed late in
1943).   The document was reproduced in the *Pilot*, 13 Sept 1943.   It was delivered to Stanley
on 1 August 1943.   CO 554/133/33732 has the memorandum, and the minutes.
54.   The recent constitutional changes in Nigeria may turn out to be an exception to this
generalization.   Though the new model of federalism is clearly the American constitution, the
attempt to reconcile and harmonize precolonial nationalities with Nigerian nationality by the
creation of states on ethnic lines displays some interesting and original ideas which do appear to
be attempts to create 'freedom' and liberal institutions which could be rooted in an African reality.

suggested.   Fundamentally the whole notion of planning to create nations is profoundly imperialistic.   Its smacks of the *tabula rasa* attitudes towards the humanity of Africa so prevalent in the days of partition.   It is perhaps impossible to forecast human reactions to introduced change, and to herd men like cattle through the gates of a planned history.   Hailey was aware of this in his insistence that Africans should participate in their own planning from the first.

The plan was also over-ambitious, and characteristic of wartime euphoria and confidence.[55]   It assumed a post-war economic and financial capability which Britain did not possess.   British indebtedness and the dollar problem led to the exploitation of colonial export earnings, hoarding of their sterling balances, and reduced real African earnings, which the loyal nationalists were ready to bear in wartime, but which erupted in wide-spread strikes, riots and disturbances after 1945 and formed fertile soil for the transformation of elite reformism into mass nationalism on challenging and not the cooperative lines envisaged by the plan.   In the end this forced a policy of political decolonization to replace that of colonial reform.

London also gravely underestimated the power of resistance in the colonial service, and the difficulties of recruiting new cadres after the war.   Hailey's gradualism, and concept of working upwards by democratization of Native Administration, through regional bodies, to secure representation of 'the masses' at the centre could easily be manipulated into a rearguard action for the preservation of chiefly comprador elites.[56]   Local resistance meant that Africanization of the administrative service in the colonies proceeded at a snail's pace, with only a handful of Africans in service by 1945, despite an acute shortage of personnel.   Racism, officially condemned in London and in governors' circulars to district officers, remained rife and seriously compromised social cooperation with the educated elite.   Even at independence, white churches, schools, clubs, residential areas and beaches were still operating in West Africa.

The social thought which underlay the planning was also deeply in error.   The entire edifice was based on the concept of 'detribalization' and the assumption that class formation was inevitably replacing precolonial ethnicity in Africa.   This, it was believed, would lead inevitably to the politics of social welfare.   Instead, the challenge which the British threw down to the educated elite, that they must demonstrate their legitimacy with the support of the people, led not to leftist and rightist groupings, but to the politics of ethnic reality.   This was perhaps the fundamental flaw, for even had the British, after 1945, possessed the means to undertake a vast scheme of economic and social regeneration, the evidence would now suggest that this would have intensified ethnic consciousness even further.

55. Paul Addison's *The Road to 1945*, Quartet Books, London, 1977 (first published by Cape, 1975) brilliantly conveys this spirit for British domestic history in the period.
56. This point is examined in detail in my article, 'Governor *versus* Colonial Office...' cited in footnote 22.

Journal of African History, 31 (1990), pp. 393–421
Printed in Great Britain

MAU MAUS OF THE MIND:
MAKING MAU MAU AND REMAKING KENYA[1]

BY JOHN LONSDALE
Trinity College, Cambridge

WHY was Mau Mau believed to be so evil?[2] The horror story of Britain's empire in the 1950s, it was less of a threat but thought to be more atrocious than either the Communists in Malaya or the Cypriot EOKA. It has lived in British memory as a symbol of African savagery, and modern Kenyans are divided by its images, militant nationalism or tribalist thuggery. This essay explores some of these Mau Maus of the mind.

[1] An earlier version of this essay was read to the Royal Historical Society in December 1989 and will appear in the society's *Transactions*. Much of my material is derived from a research project on 'Explaining Mau Mau' shared with Bruce Berman of Queen's University, Ontario. Some of my ideas are also his, but I have been unable to test on him this particular approach, which is preliminary to our larger work, and cannot ask him to share the blame. The classic study of the Kenya whites' imaginative construction of Mau Mau is Carl G. Rosberg and John Nottingham, *The Myth of 'Mau Mau': Nationalism in Kenya* (New York and London, 1966); this essay is part of the revision to which this work is now subject with the availability of archival material. Four other colleagues to whom I am also grateful for help in understanding the European constructions of Mau Mau are: Frederick Cooper, 'Mau Mau and the discourses of decolonization', *J. Afr. Hist.*, XXIX (1988), 313–20; Dane Kennedy, 'The political mythology of Mau Mau', paper presented to the American Historical Association, December 1989; David W. Throup, *Economic and Social Origins of Mau Mau* (London, 1987); Luise White, 'Separating the men from the boys: constructions of gender, sexuality and terrorism in central Kenya, 1939–1959', *Int. J. Afr. Hist. Studies*, XXIII (1990), 1–27. I also see myself as revising the 'Euro-African myth' presented in Robert Buijtenhuijs, *Mau Mau Twenty Years After: The Myth and the Survivors* (The Hague, 1973), 49–62, which has no consideration of Kikuyu political thought. For this I lean heavily on the unpublished work of Great Kershaw and on Tabitha Kanogo, *Squatters and the Roots of Mau Mau* (London, 1987). Richard Waller has commented wisely. Finally, I must thank those who were there at the time and who have shared their thoughts over the years, especially: Tom Askwith, Peter Bostock, Dick Cashmore, Thomas Colchester, Terence Gavaghan, Richard Hennings, Harry Hilton, Cyril Hooper, Elspeth Huxley, Frank Loyd, Desmond O'Hagan, Tommy Thompson, and Dick Turnbull. They bear no responsibility for my conclusions, which I hope they will find not too distorted by hindsight.
[2] I was unable to give a satisfactory answer when John Dunn put this question at a Cambridge University African Studies Centre seminar; this essay is a second attempt. But I end with the same question, put to me in 1988 by Justus Ndung'u Thiong'o. Much of the impact of 'Mau Mau' on the mind lay in its name; many different origins have been proposed for it. The most plausible comes from Thomas Colchester, lately of the Kenya administration: in Swahili *ka* is a diminutive prefix, *ma* an amplifying one, enhanced by repetition. *Mau* would thus connote something larger than *Kau* (the colloquial form of the Kenya African Union). The beauty of this explanation is that it needs no originator, merely a common play on words.

War and freedom

The colonial government first knew of the movement in 1948, with the renewal of unrest among Kikuyu labour tenants on white settler farms. 250,000 of these squatters lived on the 'White Highlands', a quarter of the Kikuyu people and half the farm labour force. Mau Mau was banned in 1950. In 1952 violence flared on the farms, where restraints on squatter cultivation and grazing rights were more sternly enforced in the interest of farm capital and resisted in the cause of peasant clientage;[3] in the slums of Nairobi where crime offered more than employment; and in the Kikuyu reserve where Mau Mau's opponents, 'the resistance' as whites first called them, were killed, often by fire and with their kin's assent, a form of execution once reserved for sorcerers.[4] A new governor, Sir Evelyn Baring, declared an emergency in October. Jomo Kenyatta, alleged to be the manager of mayhem, was arrested with 180 others. Mau Mau did not, as expected, collapse in terminal frenzy; after months of phoney war it was transformed into a formidable guerrilla force. The British did not win the initiative until early 1954. Their army was then a full infantry division with six King's African Rifles (KAR) battalions and five British, backed by Royal Air Force bombers. The police had multiplied threefold, and the Kikuyu 'resistance' had become a patchwork private militia, the Kikuyu Guard, over 20,000 strong. The army was withdrawn from operations in late 1956, after a four-year war.[5]

The causal relationship between the containment of Mau Mau and the concession of majority rule has yet to be unravelled, but its intimacy can be suggested by citing three coincidences. Over white protest, the first African was appointed minister in 1954, in a reform of government designed to quicken the war; two months later the army cleared Mau Mau, and thousands of Kikuyu, from Nairobi. Then the first African general election was held in March 1957, barely a month after Mau Mau's forest leader, Field-Marshal Sir Dedan Kimathi as he entitled himself, was hanged. Finally, the emergency ended in January 1960 as delegates went to London for a conference which promised African rule. The right-wing settler leader, Group-Captain Briggs, called this remaking of Kenya 'a victory for Mau Mau'.[6] His supporters felt overcome by the evil out of which they had imaginatively made the rising. In a suitably Biblical gesture one of them threw thirty pieces of silver at the feet of Michael Blundell, whose liberalism they believed had betrayed white supremacy.[7]

[3] Kanogo, *Squatters*, 129–37; Frank Furedi, *The Mau Mau War in Perspective* (London, 1989), chapters 3 and 4.

[4] Willoughby ('Tommy') Thompson, Kandara division (Fort Hall) handing over report, 1 March 1955: Rhodes House, Oxford, [RH] Mss. Afr. s. 839 (1); Jomo Kenyatta, *Facing Mount Kenya* (London, 1938), 304.

[5] For a brief outline of the war, see Anthony Clayton, *Counter-insurgency in Kenya 1952–60* (Nairobi, 1976). My research student Mr Randall W. Heather, whose Ph.D. thesis on the intelligence war is nearing completion, has been generous with material and ideas.

[6] George Bennett and Carl Rosberg, *The Kenyatta Election: Kenya 1960–1961* (London, 1961), 22.

[7] Sir Michael Blundell, *So Rough a Wind* (London, 1964), 283; similar symbolism was used by white demonstrators in Pretoria on 10 February 1990, the day before the release of Nelson Mandela.

Ignorance and imagination

This essay tries to explain neither Mau Mau nor its connexions with decolonisation. It addresses the prior question of how to read the evidence. We must know how Mau Mau was intellectually constructed before we can decide what it was and how it may have changed history. Behind the surface solidarities of war, myths of Mau Mau were more disputed than has been thought, with Africans as divided as whites. This should not surprise us. The future of Kenya was more anxiously contested after the second world war than at any time in its stormy past, behind rival dreams of social order; the social authorisation of murderous violence is an anxious issue in any culture; and all contenders were ignorant of their situation. True of any political conflict, this was true twice over of Mau Mau. It was mainly, but not entirely, a Kikuyu movement, and whites knew little of Kikuyu society. Few spoke Kikuyu. Most were content to know 'what everybody knew', the stereotypes that explained the daily uncertainties of Africa. The ignorance of whites was therefore structured. To them the Kikuyu were a 'tribe', but already an unusual and unsettling one. Mau Mau then fundamentally challenged the imaginative structures of race and tribe which underwrote the colonial order, forcing whites to choose between punishing a tribe and dissolving race as strategies of survival.

Kikuyu were just as ignorant, and as uncertain how to maintain or recreate social order. Always a fragmented set of parochial societies whose ruling principle was 'local government run mad',[8] they were, increasingly, a divided and mutually hostile people. Their oaths of political allegiance reflected both periods of this history. Most remained mundane rituals of initiation which imposed on aspirants the costs which promised seriousness of open, public purpose in a small community. But some now demanded hidden, factional loyalty to persons often unknown, outside the immediate locality, on pain of death. For Mau Mau emerged as the militant wing in a struggle for allegiance in which, as will be shown, authority and energy were ill matched. That is the tragedy which, when carried to extremes, marks all contexts of political terror. Mutually apprehensive ignorance ruled. Competition was secret, not public, since the main issue was not social honour but effective action. In any case, the obvious political vehicle, the Kikuyu Central Association (KCA), was already banned. As subject people, further, Kikuyu were under pressure to cloak real divisions under an invented common front. Political purpose could not be freely debated. Divided loyalties could not be openly recorded. A leader's public authority could with impunity be whisperingly invoked in his followers' private interest. Lies and intrigue flourished. Secrecy exacts that price.

Once battle was joined, ignorance and imagination were poor guides to action. As the enemy had to be better known, allies courted, and decisions faced, so four mutually incompatible meanings of Mau Mau occupied white minds, conservative, liberal, revivalist and military. These divisions were clouded by a common assumption of white superiority and that tacit evasion of dispute which survival demands in horrific times. Whites preserved a united front of counter-insurgency by damning what all saw as Mau Mau's

[8] W. S. and K. Routledge, *With a Prehistoric People* (London, 1910), 195.

savagery which, all agreed, had to be destroyed. But they divided over its
civil remedies, which governed their view of its causes. Their debates
sometimes forced their way furiously to the surface. The ostensible issues of
dissension were generally military, over rules of engagement and interrogation, how clean or dirty, and surrender talks, whether Mau Mau
should be offered them at all. But the conduct of war was disputed, as always,
with an eye to the construction of peace. As peace neared and the future had
once more to be faced directly, so the coalition fell apart. This was because
the war had only doubtfully been won. Briggs was soon to say it had been
lost. For the settlers had become dependent upon dubious allies with diverse
Kenyas in mind: the British government, the leaders of 'loyal tribes' which
had furnished police and troops, and, above all and most ominously, the
'loyalist' Kikuyu guard (KG).[9]

While whites negotiated unity, it seems that the Kikuyu were forced into
it by the first fury of repression. An official enquiry secretly admitted as
much. Mau Mau members generally had one set of enemies. Their opponents
often had two, 'Mau Mau on the one hand and the forces of law and order
on the other'. Many Kikuyu, who had welcomed the emergency as a defence
against terror, 'became disillusioned' when all Kikuyu were treated as
rebels.[10] Kingsley Martin, visiting Kenya, reported the same effect of 'Black-
and-Tannery'. This caused bitter hatred of whites among Kikuyu, of whom
'only a very small section' had supported Mau Mau a few weeks earlier.[11]
These views were part of the liberal construction of the movement; it was a
product of its environment. But many settlers believed that up to 80 per cent
of Kikuyu had taken the first oath of initiation by October 1952, in agreement
with or out of fear of their fellows, not from fear of whites.[12] This reflected
the conservative view, that terror was inherent in Kikuyu society. Estimates
of the movement's growth were political claims on the future. The more
initiates there were before the emergency, the more the entire tribe was a
criminal gang which had forfeited all prospective liberties. The very limited
data available from the screening teams, which certified people's loyalties,
support the liberal view. They suggest that half the Kikuyu men on white
farms or in Nairobi had been oathed before Kenyatta's arrest, and under
20 per cent in the Kiambu district of the reserve. This last figure more
than doubled in the first five months of the emergency.[13] If one were treated
as Mau Mau by police, it looks as if it seemed prudent to become one.

[9] From his upcountry retirement, former governor Mitchell warned settlers that
'loyalists' would expect fundamental change after the war: Sir Philip Mitchell, *African
Afterthoughts* (London, 1954), 268.
[10] 'Report on the sociological causes underlying Mau Mau with some proposals on the
means of ending it' (mimeograph, 21 April 1954, seen by courtesy of Greet Kershaw),
paras. 2 and 34.
[11] Kingsley Martin, 'Kenya report', *New Statesman and Nation* (London),
15 November 1952.
[12] Rob Buijtenhuijs, *Essays on Mau Mau* (Leiden, 1982), 35–6, discusses Mau Mau
recruitment rates.
[13] Figures seen by courtesy of Greet Kershaw; full discussion must await her own
publication, but some of her evidence suggests that many joined Mau Mau during
Kenyatta's trial in late 1952 and early 1953. They both wished to support Kenyatta and
were reassured that Mau Mau could not have been as dreadful as they imagined if he had,
after all, been in charge of it.

Even while Kikuyu were being lumped into Mau Mau by casual white violence, the government anxiously split them more sharply between Mau Mau and 'loyalist' resistance, by arming chiefs and tribal policemen. These latter suffered terribly in the first year of war, with a death rate of around 10 per cent,[14] perhaps because they had what Mau Mau needed most, guns. Chiefs then enlisted among waverers and those who had joined Mau Mau under duress, creating the KG by a similar mix of threat and persuasion. Recruits had to prove themselves with public confession and a traditional oath of cleansing.[15] Most KG units had substantial numbers of ex-Mau Mau. The insurgents also used these early months to gather their forces, with larger units and stronger oaths.[16] A Kikuyu civil war was being prepared. But many on both sides tried to evade the barbed invitation to fight the wider battle by local feud. While the KG killed more Mau Mau than any other formation and in some places acquired a grisly reputation,[17] some units conspired with insurgents to keep the local peace. Conversely, Mau Mau leaders claimed to subjugate violence to the social audit of local communities which would have to live with the aftermath of murder.[18] And Mau Mau warriors, like any soldiers in battle, displaced their guilt and fear on to gangs other than their own.[19] Like Kikuyu society it was a parochial war, obsessed with parochial honour. When the war was over, many were obsessed with its shame.

These blurred distinctions on both sides, in which the divided opinions of peace were compromised by the tactical agreements of war, have been insufficiently recognised. The evidence must be read with these tensions in mind. The white conventional wisdoms of the day glossed over them, skimming with care the fragile surface of racial solidarity. They only begin to address the question of evil. But one has to start with them before one can follow the divisions, white and black, which lead one down to the roots of social dread.

Conventional wisdom and private doubt

What then did whites at the time say publicly about the Mau Mau evil? Many thought it uniquely depraved, even in the dirty annals of modern terror and partisan war. There were three parts to the conventional answer, its leader's treachery, the bestiality of its ritual, and its savage method of killing. Kenyatta, who had enjoyed the best that Britain could offer, study at

[14] S. H. Fazan, *History of the Loyalists* (Nairobi, 1961), 78.

[15] *Ibid.* 12–16.

[16] Donald L. Barnett and Karari Njama, *Mau Mau from Within* (London, 1966), 153–97.

[17] For some details, see, D. Macpherson (Criminal Investigation Department) to Commissioner of Police, 23 December 1954: Arthur Young papers, RH Mss. Brit. Emp. s. 486 (3), seen by courtesy of Mr Heather; Judgement by Acting Judge Cram, Supreme Court of Kenya, criminal case No. 428 of 1954 ('the Ruthagathi case'), given on 10 December 1954, and published as a 33-page mimeo by the Federal Independence Party, under the title 'Kenya's Belsen?'; more generally: Clayton, *Counter-insurgency*, 46–7.

[18] Barnett and Njama, *Mau Mau from Within*, 138–9, 142, 155, 193–5; 'Interrogation of Waruhiu s/o Itote, alias "General China"' (Kenya Police Special Branch, Nairobi, 26 January 1954), para. 219: privately held.

[19] This point is briefly developed at the end of the essay, with reference to the *komerera*.

the London School of Economics (LSE) and the love of an English wife, was the probable artificer of the oaths.[20] British propaganda found it easy to present these as utterly debased and degrading. Mau Mau oaths produced Mau Mau murders. Like most conventional answers they say more about the interpreter than the matter 'explained'. It will be convenient to take the murder and magic first, leaving the making of Mau Mau's manager till later.

In a big book twice reprinted, which probably introduced more western readers to modern Africa than any other, the American journalist John Gunther remarked that Mau Mau killings were, 'as everybody knows, peculiarly atrocious'. Victims might be 'chopped to bits', partly for security's sake; all gang members had to join in and share the guilt. They might also remove a corpse's accusing eyes, for Kikuyu, after all, were 'profoundly superstitious'.[21] Perhaps some reporters were too superstitious of what 'everybody knew'; for another, Graham Greene, thought that a Bren gun wounded as savagely as a *panga*, the heavy farm knife used by Mau Mau, as the British pointedly demonstrated by exposing guerrilla corpses.[22] There was also scandal over the army's habit of severing the hands of insurgents killed in action, to save the labour of carrying their bodies away to be identified by finger print.[23] The only systematic survey of Mau Mau victims suggests that chopping up on the other side was in fact rare. Dr Wilkinson examined 210 dead. Yes, many had multiple wounds. But these were generally superficial. The fatal ones were commonly six blows to the head, almost as if insurgents had been trained to make 'a quick and certain death for their victims'.[24]

Total casualty figures also suggest a picture different to Gunther's. The disparity in death is striking. On official data, Mau Mau (or Africans so described) lost 12,590 dead in action or by hanging over the four most active years of war; 164 troops or police died in the same period, most of them Africans. Mau Mau killed 1,880 civilians, nearly a third of them KG and all but 58 of them black.[25] This is a tragic total, but it may be thought to be not large when one considers how vulnerable their targets were at night, dispersed in broken country without light, guns, or wire until the villagisation programme of mid-1954. Settlers believed that all Kikuyu domestic and farm servants had taken at least one oath;[26] yet very few felt impelled to kill their masters. Mau Mau killing looks on the whole to have been rather restrained, at less than one sixth of their own dead, as if it was indeed under some social control. Against this, it should be said that insurgent attacks were largely confined to the first two years of war, and to specific battle zones in the districts of Nyeri and Fort Hall (Murang'a). Again, it was a parochial war

[20] To use the language of Bishop L. J. Beecher, 'Christian counter-revolution to Mau Mau', in F. S. Joelson (ed.), *Rhodesia and East Africa* (London, 1958), 82.

[21] John Gunther, *Inside Africa* (New York, 1953, 1954, 1955), 361.

[22] Graham Greene to editor, *The Times* (London) 1 December 1953, under the heading 'A nation's conscience'.   [23] Clayton, *Counter-insurgency*, 42, n. 84.

[24] J. Wilkinson, 'The Mau Mau movement: some general and medical aspects', *East Africa Medical J.*, xxxi (July, 1954), 309–10.

[25] Statistics from Colonial Office, *Historical Survey of the Origins and Growth of Mau Mau* (Cmnd. 1930, May 1960), 316 (hereafter cited as *Corfield report*), and Clayton, *Counter-insurgency*, 53.

[26] As in Nellie Grant to Elspeth Huxley, 20 Oct. 1952, in Elspeth Huxley (ed.), *Nellie : Letters from Africa* (London, 1980), 179.

and on both sides, in some places, dirty and bloody, with local peasant
conflicts driving on the bitterness as much as wider political frustration.[27]

As to the oaths, they made sensational reading which official sources and
journalists exploited with a coyness which titillates while it repels. It was
reliably reported that recruits committed their lives to the cause in swallowing
a stew of mutton or goat, vegetables and cereals, sprinkled with soil,
marinated in goat's blood, watched by uprooted sheep's eyes transfixed on
thorns. All this was cruel, not bestial.[28] But that was just the beginning of
horror. For it was reported, possibly less reliably in some respects, that oaths
became more ghastly as the war dragged on and insurgents despaired. Many
writers left the details unsaid and readers' imaginations free to range in
fascinated self-disgust. Police interrogators, rather less delicately, may have
invited their prisoners to invent some more.[29] Other authors adopted a
formula which claimed to deny the reader 'the full details' but then gave
specifics which one could scarcely bear to think of as less than complete. If
it was enough to say, with Blundell, that they included 'masturbation in
public, the drinking of menstrual blood, unnatural acts with animals, and
even the penis of dead men', then even a dirty mind must shrink from
exploring further.[30] A parliamentary delegation thought the rituals too
beastly to lay before the British public. They were hidden in an appendix to
their report, privately available only in the House of Commons library.[31]
Similarly, while fresh British troops were given a booklet, *The Kenya
Picture*, to prime them against the enemy, the account of the 'advanced' oaths
was inserted on a loose sheet of paper. This had to be returned after being
read, a charming protection for wives and girlfriends in the days before the
photocopier.[32] Yet, in spite of everything, many whites continued to employ
Kikuyu. They badgered officials to waive emergency rules in respect of their
employees.[33] Whatever they said in public, whites acted in private as if cross-
racial trust and the wage relation were stronger than any oath, however
bestial.[34]

---

[27] Compare Terence Ranger, 'Bandits and guerrillas: the case of Zimbabwe', in
Donald Crummey (ed.), *Banditry, Rebellion and Social Protest in Africa* (London, 1986),
373–96; Norma Kriger, 'The Zimbabwean war of liberation: struggles within the struggle',
J. Southern Afr. Studies, XIV (1988), 304–22.

[28] All this is to be found not only in white narratives and Mau Mau memoirs but also
in a scholarly Kikuyu account: R. M. Githige, 'The religious factor in Mau Mau with
particular reference to Mau Mau oaths' (M.A. thesis, University of Nairobi, 1978). The
attitude of most Europeans to the oaths can conveniently be found in *Corfield report*,
163–70.

[29] As suggested by Josiah M. Kariuki, '*Mau Mau' Detainee* (London, 1963), 33.

[30] Blundell, *Wind*, 168; one must be thankful that the British popular press did not
then include *The Sun*.

[31] *Report to the Secretary of State for the Colonies by the Parliamentary Delegation to
Kenya January 1954* (Colonial Office: Cmd. 9081, 1954), 1. Nellie Grant provided her
usual back-handed sanity, remarking that in the first world war some Australian troops
billeted in Wiltshire were said to have given some polo ponies venereal disease 'and no
one worried much.' Huxley, *Nellie*, 299 (letter of 28 February 1954).

[32] Clayton, *Counter-insurgency*, 7, n. 12.

[33] R. D. F. Ryland (Officer-in-charge, Nairobi extra-provincial district) to R. G.
Turnbull (Minister for African Affairs), 23 December 1954: Kenya National Archives,
Nairobi [KNA], MAA. 9/930.

[34] KNA, Rift Valley Province annual report (1953), 2, 16, reporting the systematic

43

Boundaries and infiltrators

After this public horror it is instructive to remember that the principal white
authority on Mau Mau, Dr Louis Leakey, said absolutely nothing about
their ritual in his initial explication of the oaths. Their malign power lay,
rather, in combining a heightened tradition with its deliberate violation. The
initiates' deeds did not offend custom; in any culture legal oaths were strong
meat. It was the sociology of oathing which, he thought, subverted Kikuyu
values. Customary oaths-at-law were voluntary acts of responsible adults,
taken in the open, before witnesses and by agreement with relatives who
risked magical harm in the event of a litigant's perjury. Mau Mau oaths, by
contrast, were often taken under duress, at night, in unlit huts, in the
presence of persons unknown, without consent of kin. Worse still, in order
to tie their proverbially loose tongues, Mau Mau officers oathed legal minors,
women and children, on whom such heavy moral demands ought not to be
made.[35] While Leakey did briefly mention the Mau Mau cocktail in his
second book, nearly two years later, he again stressed something different,
the morally liminal status of initiates. These had to undergo for a second,
customarily unthinkable, time the passage between careless youth and tested
adulthood, by crawling through the circumcision arch of sugar cane and
banana leaves before taking the oath. Leakey believed that enforced and
unexpected re-entry into this fluid state must cause intense shock.[36] Blundell
thought that oathing sowed a 'mind-destroying disease'.[37]

Leakey was no disinterested expert; he was committed to the fight against
Mau Mau, as Kikuyu elder first and settler second. From his accounts one
can infer an explanation of the evil imputed to Mau Mau not only deeper
than any mere drinking of a devil's brew, but one to which many Kikuyu also
subscribed.[38] What disturbed Leakey was the mixing of moral and social

screening of the remaining Kikuyu farmworkers after large-scale repatriation to the
reserve in early 1953: while 95 per cent were shown to have been oathed, no less than 80
per cent were allowed to remain at work. Much evidence could be cited which casts doubt
on the factual details of the 'advanced' oaths other than in the minds of some
interrogators. But there is no reason to doubt the public masturbation (mentioned also by
Frank Kitson, below). See, L. S. B. Leakey, *The Southern Kikuyu before 1903* (London,
1977), vol. 1, 24; vol. 2, 691–2; and H. E. Lambert, *Kikuyu Social and Political
Institutions* (London, 1956), 53–4, for the ceremonial group rape-cum-masturbation
performed by circumcision initiates in the past, to symbolise the ending of adolescent
restrictions. Leakey's material was collected in 1937, Lambert's in the 1930s and '40s.
[35] L. S. B. Leakey, *Mau Mau and the Kikuyu* (London, 1952), 98ff.; but the social
horror of women's oathing in the minds of Leakey's informants may be part of the
Kikuyu male imagination of Mau Mau. Larger numbers of women took the oath (on
Kershaw's data) and played a more active role than can be explained by their men's
reluctant induction of them; see also Cora Presley, 'Kikuyu women and their nationalism'
(Ph.D. thesis, Stanford University, 1986).
[36] L. S. B. Leakey, *Defeating Mau Mau* (London, 1954), 77–81.
[37] Blundell, *Wind*, 171.
[38] See Ngugi wa Thiong'o, *Weep not Child* (London, 1964), 83–4, where the elderly
Ngotho saw no harm in Mau Mau oaths but was shocked that they were administered
by his son. Also, B. A. Ogot, 'Revolt of the elders', in B. A. Ogot (ed.), *Hadith 4: Politics
and Nationalism in Colonial Kenya* (Nairobi, 1972). Born in 1903 in Kikuyuland, Leakey
was an initiated first-grade elder by his early thirties: L. S. B. Leakey, *Kenya, Contrasts
and Problems* (London, 1936), vii. The other white Kikuyu expert, superintendent Ian

categories which Kikuyu culture had previously separated in creating order. This was to take the liberal view, that Mau Mau was a product of cultural decay; the more common preoccupation with the paraphernalia of the oaths reflected the conservative position, that Kikuyu were savages. But Leakey may also have come close to portraying the horror with which Kikuyu faced the problem of violence far more intense and internal than could be controlled by conventional ritual means.[39] Mau Mau's offence lay in its confusion between persons of hitherto distinct legal status, gender and generation; its subversion of morally responsible legal tests, which resolved disputes, into coerced submission to unknown wills; and its inversion of actions proper to the day, social time, into the deeds of anti-social time, of darkness visible and spiritual.

Disease enters society, body and mind by subverting order or infiltrating boundaries, natural or socially constructed. This was the internal Kikuyu evil of which Leakey warned, with the elders. But Mau Mau presented whites with a violent concentration of all the dangers to which their own Kenya was also exposed, seemingly suddenly since the second world war. The essence of treason was social dissolution, twice over. If tribes were tottering, could white supremacy survive?

Before the war the colonial world had rested on a mental construction of social separations. Rulers and ruled were distinguished, and differentially valued, by race. Different subjects, otherwise anonymous, were recognised by tribe. Tribal authority and the extended family underpinned control. It was believed, even by sympathetic observers, that tribal character was inherited in a mystic union protected from neighbours by cultural isolation, 'like a fragile orchid, native of some windless forest'.[40] Africans had never enjoyed that secret of British progress, a vigorous commerce of ideas and social conflict. Nor did tribes produce workers. Colonial rule, cash and Christianity, in creating 'useful citizens' and 'industrious assets',[41] must come as a whirlwind of change which uprooted communal fences, especially around the fields of labour and learning. Here Africans invaded the white world[42] and injured their own. 'Detribalised' and 'semi-educated', they were failures in themselves and a reproach to whites, as well as a threat. To profit by Africans it seemed that whites must subvert them. On entering Kenya, therefore, settlers also entered a nineteenth-century South African debate on how to construct political security and morality on shifting sands. It was never resolved, whether in white opinion or in the priorities of the colonial state. Conservatives thought Africans inherently primitive, liberals that they were retarded children who promised well as modern men. The former thought order lay in 'adaptation', propping up reformed tribal authorities against the gale in segregated local governments; the latter trusted in 'assimilation' to replace external controls with the self-disciplines

---

Henderson, gave as flat an account of the oaths as Leakey in his prosecution evidence at Kenyatta's trial, when one might have expected him to be more colourful: Montagu Slater, *The Kenyatta Trial* (London, 1955), 95–6.

[39] Leakey, *Southern Kikuyu*, vol. 3, 1037–48, 1056–67, 1234, 1238, 1269–70, 1276, for the customary controls on violence.

[40] Norman Leys, *Kenya* (London, 1924), 303.

[41] *Ibid.* 305–6, quoting an *East African Standard* editorial of February 1924.

[42] The metaphor is John Gunther's: *Inside Africa*, 9.

of educated Africans, westernised men. Similarly, some reckoned the answer to African unrest was repression, others that cooptation was cheaper and even safer in the end.[43] Africans were similarly divided. More tried to link the imperial and household civilising missions within invented ethnic nationalisms than in a still more imaginary 'Kenya'.

After 1945 these border issues became ever more complex. The segmentary domains of political control were subject to trespass by competing economic interests seeking access to the centre, Nairobi.[44] Conflict wracked all political levels. At the centre, the watchword of cooptation was 'multiracialism'. The first African was nominated to the legislature in 1944: Eliud Mathu, witchdoctor's son and Balliol man. But settler obduracy denied Mathu's moderate supporters, the Kenya African Union (KAU), the political resources which might have secured their effective cooperation. The governor, Sir Philip Mitchell, combined belief in education as a cultural bridge between the races[45] with contempt for the idea that African nationalism might creatively purge the confusions of communal identity.[46] In the segregated reserves the local politics of control rested on the growing powers of African councils. Officials promoted progress but distrusted its twin foundations, peasants who exhausted the soil and 'progressives' not in chiefs' uniform, the egotists and agitators. In the deeper politics of work, the labour department struggled to open gateways of industrial relations through the emerging fences of class, against the opposition of both capitalists and workers, neither of whom saw themselves in such exclusive terms. Farmers refused, and urban employers were reluctant, to recognise trades unions; most workers preferred general to craft organisations. Yet white paternalists and anonymous black townsmen personified conflict, not control.[47] The deepest politics of all opposed labour and land on the White Highlands. The Maasai had formerly grazed most of this area. Little more than one per cent – but the richest part – had been Kikuyu land. Settlers claimed sole right to the land by virtue of treaty and achievement; it was their one sure footing in uncertain times. Their squatters claimed a share. They had given two generations of labour to taming the land and had made it ritually home by

[13] For the debate in Kenya see, Robert G. Gregory, *Sidney Webb and East Africa* (Berkeley and Los Angeles, 1962); B. E. Kipkorir, 'The Alliance High School and the origins of the Kenya African elite' (Ph.D. thesis, Cambridge University, 1969); Kenneth J. King, *Pan-Africanism and Education* (Oxford, 1961); Bruce Berman, *The Dialectics of Domination* (London, 1990); and in South Africa for the same period, Saul Dubow, *Racial Segregation and the Origins of Apartheid in South Africa 1919–36* (Basingstoke, 1989).

[14] Throup, *Origins*; Berman, *Dialectics*. For the pre-war origins of conflict between segmentary and centralised politics see my 'The depression and the second world war in the transformation of Kenya', in David Killingray and Richard Rathbone (eds.), *Africa and the Second World War* (Basingstoke, 1986), 97–142.

[15] An idea which he seems to have first adumbrated in 1938 when governor of Uganda: Margaret Macpherson, *They Built for the Future* (Cambridge, 1964), 26.

[16] Governor Mitchell to Secretary of State Creech Jones, confidential despatch 16, 30 May 1947; KNA, African Affairs file ii (reference noted in 1965 but not checked since the revision of the archives classification).

[17] Anthony Clayton and Donald C. Savage, *Government and Labour in Kenya 1895–1963* (London, 1974), 265–346; Sharon B. Stichter, 'Workers, trade unions and the Mau Mau rebellion', *Canadian J. Afr. Studies*, IX (1975), 259–75; Frederick Cooper, *On the African Waterfront* (New Haven and London, 1987), 78–203.

initiating their young and burying their dead on white farms.[48] White farmers no longer wanted a tenantry, and squatters had no wish to become free labour. Settlers called in the police, squatters called on what they now saw as a tribe. Here was a thicket of cross-cutting boundaries indeed. The conflict between settler and squatter, capital and labour, class and tribe, was the most bitterly complex border dispute in all the unfinished business of Kenya.[49]

Mau Mau blew indecision apart. It outraged tribal elders and household authority at the foundations of control. Kikuyu militance also subverted, fractured and then seemed to dominate the pan-ethnic urban elite in the KAU, the only possible basis of African co-optation. Mau Mau thus destroyed past and blasted future images of social control, communal segregation and a multi-racial state. Policy could no longer wait on events. It had to be made. But a scapegoat must also be found for the catastrophe of confusion, an infiltrator-in-chief. It could only be the culture-rustler, Kenyatta.

Most whites feared and loathed Kenyatta, probably more for his English marriage than his trips to Moscow.[50] District officers resented the way in which his oratory had broken the politics of progress in Kikuyuland, when women downed hoes and refused to terrace hills against erosion.[51] Missionaries, who may once have nursed him back to life, feared him.[52] After his return home in 1946, Kenyatta presided over the Teachers' Training College at Githunguri, the apex of the Kikuyu independent school system which competed with the missions; he was also said to attack the Christianity which had saved him.[53] Settlers blamed him for stirring up squatters.[54] Governor Mitchell must have included him in his scorn for the manufacturers of premature nationalisms.[55] The rise of Mau Mau then proved Kenyatta, the enemy of tribal progress, to be a tribalist traitor to the African elite. Only he was thought clever enough to invent the oaths, perhaps from his reading in the LSE where, it was guessed, his anthropology had covered European

[48] The earliest reference I have seen to squatters seeing the 'White Highlands' as their own (other than that small portion which was once Kikuyu) comes from Kenyatta in June 1932: *Kenya Land Commission Evidence*, vol. 1 (Nairobi, 1933), 430. Something more than an old retainer's loyalty brought former headman Njombo back to Nellie Grant's farm to die in 1947; eighteen years later his heirs were among those who bought her out in a syndicate called Mataguri ('we have been here a long time') Farm: Huxley, *Nellie*, 165, 270.

[49] Kanogo, *Squatters*; Furedi, *Mau Mau War*; Throup, *Origins*, chapter 5.

[50] Kikuyu politicians must have distrusted Kenyatta as much as whites; before his departure for England they had sworn him against going with white women. Conversely, it seems that Kenyatta was more terrified by Moscow than inspired; see, Robin Cohen, editor's 'Introduction' to A. T. Nzula et al., *Forced Labour in Colonial Africa* ([Moscow 1933] London, 1979), 15. I owe this reference to David Throup.

[51] Throup, *Origins*, 152–64, shows that the administration little understood Kenyatta's position in this heavily politicised 'terrace war'.

[52] Jeremy Murray-Brown, *Kenyatta* (London, 1972), 45, reports how the young Kenyatta was nursed through phthisis by Scots missionaries in 1910; by 1951 phthisis had become 'some spine disease', an operation for which saved his life: see W. O. Tait, memorandum, May 1951, in press cutting file on Kenyatta with *The Standard*, Nairobi.

[53] M. G. Capon, 'Kikuyu 1948, a working answer', September 1948: KNA, DC/MUR. 3/4/21.

[54] Throup, *Origins*, 129–30.   [55] As in footnote 46 above.

witchcraft.[56] He also had charisma. His campaign tours in early 1952 had everywhere been followed by, and must therefore have instigated, spates of Mau Mau oaths and murder. He had got Kikuyu to boycott bottled beer. Yet his denunciations of Mau Mau, at government request, were ineffective; his heart therefore cannot have been in them. This was the chief supporting evidence in Baring's request to call an emergency.[57] The presumed back-wardness and conformity of tribes did not admit of any other than a sorcerous origin for the cunning and internecine ferocity of Mau Mau.

To deconstruct the evil of Mau Mau is to reconstruct past boundaries of morally valid knowledge and power. To summarise the rest of the argument, it is to find not that Mau Mau was an official invention, as the British left thought, an alibi for suppressing legitimate African politics, but dreadful reality, a pathological image of the right social group relations which ought to order colonial life. These relations were in any case in disarray, between the myth of what once had been and the mirage of what they might become. In the several Mau Maus of their minds whites negotiated fresh African stereotypes, to bring new order out of confusion.[58] In simpler times the white model of African cultural transition had been a linear, compensating, process of loss and gain in which small, tribal identities were diluted into a larger, civilised one; educated natives might agitate the untouched, but each could be calmed by a combination of adaptation and assimilation. Mau Mau smashed that innocent picture. Transition now looked like trauma. Loss of identity seemed to stir somnolent savagery. Education did not lead modern men out of the past; it made amoral men who manipulated its darkest fears. With a linear, if always subversive, model of progress now challenged by a movement which suggested that modernity could recreate savagery, whites had to rethink their ideas of social explanation. Mau Mau was bound to be made in divergent ways.

Two ideas competed to control the conduct of war, with different border trespass in mind. Conservatives stressed the unchanging danger of the primitive. Race was the most obvious boundary under threat and was simplest defended by hardening the polemical frontier between white civilisation and black savagery. They demanded an end to the liberal imperial promises which had aroused primitive envy. But if that had been Mau Mau's only border outrage, it could never have been punished with such cost and brutality in a just war by the decolonising Empire of the 1950s. After all, Kwame Nkrumah was already the Queen's chief minister in the Gold Coast. The compelling construction of Mau Mau, which won the whites the right

[56] Carothers, *Psychology*, 16, is cautious on this point; Beecher 'Christian counter-revolution', 82, much less so, comparing him with Marx and Engels in the British Museum. This accusation lingered long after it was understood that there was nothing exotic about the oaths, which merely reworked Kikuyu symbols of dangerous power: the strongest white attack on Kenyatta on this point was also the last; see, *Corfield report*, 169–70.

[57] Baring, top secret telegram to Lyttelton, 10 Oct. 1952: PRO, CO 822/443, and reproduced in Charles Douglas-Home, *Evelyn Baring, the Last Proconsul* (London, 1978), 227–8. That a beer boycott and Mau Mau should be thought to be of equal existential weight is an extraordinary indication of the assumption of African malleability. See also, Kingsley Martin's reports in *New Statesman*, 22 November 1952, 'The case against Jomo Kenyatta'; and 6 December 1952, 'The African point of view'.

[58] I am grateful to Malcolm Ruel for urging me to clarify my thoughts at this juncture.

to fight the war, was more subtle and of wider application. Liberals saw border unrest within the African soul, on its psychic frontier between tradition and modernity, community and society, past tribe and future nation. Racial repression might have sharpened the conflict, but was not its cause. This lay in the trauma of transition. Mau Mau had to be destroyed, of course. But while diehards fought to keep the Kikuyu on the far bank of the river of transition – *The river between* as Ngugi the Kikuyu novelist had it[59] – white liberals knew it had to be crossed. Peace would come only when Kikuyu society was on the modern side. The need for wartime allies, local Africans and the home government, nerved the liberal imagination as never before to convert this conventional wisdom into government action. Whites thus failed to agree on a fresh African stereotype; Mau Mau split their previous indecisions into opposite camps. They fought the war on different premises. Privately, many thought any means tolerable for punishing ancient savagery; publicly, government strove to force the modern transition.

This public, liberal construction of the issue did not, however, win the peace. Nor did its Christian subtext of spiritual conversion. Measures of modernity, education and loyalty were, it is true, used to ration out the franchise for the first African general elections in 1957. This was seen as a precondition for a colour-blind common electoral roll in due time, in which white 'standards' would be safe. But this liberal control over the future had no future. It was blocked by African parliamentary boycotts and then killed by the deaths of eleven Mau Mau detainees at Hola camp in early 1959. At the Lancaster House conference in 1960, the modernizing liberal mission gave way to hard political bargaining. The ideas which cleared the way for, and then controlled, this longer future were held by those who fought the war and who were, under any circumstances, bound to outlast it, the British army and members of Kikuyu agrarian society. Generals asked not how one modernised Africans but who would hold power. They were part of the British establishment; Tory ministers, their civil partners, finally accepted the army's view of the war. Mau Mau fighters, on the other hand, were not privy to Kikuyu authority; they called themselves its *itungati*, its warrior servants. Their seniors, most of them 'loyalists', begrudged their service but enjoyed its rewards.

Settlers and supremacy

The iconography of the war was horrible, with pictures of hamstrung cattle grotesquely knelt upon the grass and burned black babies lying decapitated in the ashes of their homes. It looked very like a war between savagery and civilisation. On the side of order blond youths in slouch hats, backed by honest spearmen in blankets, represented the finest examples of their race, each in their proper place. African troops were also shown with guns, starched into civilisation by the creases in their khaki. On the side of chaos crouched wild-eyed men in rags and ringlets, just out of the trees.[60] A local publisher toasted the 'emergency alliance of men and women of all races and

---

[59] (James) Ngugi (wa Thiong'o), London, 1965.
[60] Two illustrated accounts of Mau Mau are Granville Roberts, *The Mau Mau in Kenya* (London, 1954), and anon, *Mau Mau, a Pictorial Record* (Nairobi, nd., ?1954).

49

tribes' which gave hope for the future.[61] That was too simple. The ambiguities of adaptation and assimilation were now armed. Spearmen in blankets were politically sound but militarily doubtful. Trousered gunmen were essential in war but rivals in peace.

Mau Mau's horror united whites in demanding its forcible suppression. But the ambiguities of security, based on adapting African authorities or assimilating black individuals, divided them over the sort of power to which force must answer. Conservatives demanded a return to white supremacy and tribal discipline. Liberals thought that white control would be more surely preserved if Mau Mau were isolated in African opinion. This must mean some sharing of power between the races, as represented by their educated individuals. Divided contemplation of the future invited new appropriations of the past. White Kenyans wrote history now as never before, their own and that of the African peoples.[62] One cannot reduce their mutual differences to class interest, between, say, liberal businessmen and hardline farmers. Theirs was too small a community for that, too closely tied by marriage, church and club. Nonetheless, the insecurity of farming on a mortgage was probably the closest that Europeans came to living out a personal analogy of their community as a whole, an experience which put 'firmness' foremost in race relations.

The highland farm mocked white supremacy in its daily confusion of categories. A tribute to middle class English effort, it was also the site of black peasant expansion. In hock to the banks, whites had made the 'untouched land of Africa' into farms, 'with all that a farm implies'.[63] Farms meant civilisation; farms pleased. They were fenced against the bush; water glinted in their dams; windbreaks marched straight over the horizon; lawns were greener than any 'at home'. Farms also satisfied. They supported not only a white family but dozens of black ones too. Only the ignorant or malevolent could talk of 'stolen lands'. Most of the Highlands had been wastefully grazed by a few Maasai in the past; even a Fabian critic said so.[64] African farm families were immigrant strangers too, other than on the coffee estates of Kiambu. To employ resident labourers was an act of generosity. Colonial rule had brought peace, health and rising population; some settlers added to these general benefits the paternal care of black communities who owed them the reciprocal duty of loyal service. But that was the problem; farms also unsettled. Squatters were not a dependent class, tied by a moral community of protection and service. They were not a conquered people who had lost the right to liberty. They were a fifth column, a menace. They created their own communities in hidden corners of white estates. They reintroduced the African bush within the fences of the farm. Nobody knew how many there were. Part of white domestic life and yet unknowable, the

[61] *Ibid.* Foreword.

[62] For histories of white settler achievement, see J. F. Lipscomb, *White Africans* (London, 1955) and *We Built a Country* (London, 1956); M. F. Hill, *Cream Country* (Nairobi, 1965); there were farm memoirs too. For works which contrasted this with African stagnation or worse, see C. J. Wilson, *Before the Dawn in Kenya* (Nairobi, October and December 1952, January 1953) and *Kenya's Warning* (Nairobi, 1954); C. T. Stoneham, *Out of Barbarism* (London, 1955). The only work sympathetic to African civilization was Leakey's *Mau Mau and the Kikuyu.*

[63] Lipscomb, *White Africans*, 82; Wilson, *Kenya's Warning*, 13.

[64] Kingsley Martin, 'The settler case', *New Statesman*, 29 November, 1952.

sullenness of race undid the duty of class.[65] Worse still, after the war farms
began to accuse. The tensions of the squatter relationship broke into conflict.
White district councils enacted orders to restrict squatter rights to cultivation
and pasture, and to require of them more labour. Settlers squeezed their
dependants' livelihood partly because wartime profits enabled them to farm
intensively, using more capital than labour. But the political consolidation of
civilisation was still more urgent. The highland achievement must become
unequivocally white, and farmworkers' claims be met with a wage alone, not
land. Squatters resisted the new contracts, muttering among themselves of
settler 'sin' and 'hypocrisy'. Even white officials used the language of 'moral
entitlement' on behalf of labour.[66] Many settlers refused or failed to
repudiate their squatters' rights. Nonetheless, squatter resistance had to be
deprived of legitimacy. Some settlers regained the moral ground by
infantilising their workers. One district council urged that 'the African',
'still a savage and a child', would respond to 'firmness' with a new 'respect'
for whites who removed his freedoms.[67] It is difficult not to conclude that
white guilt was assuaged by racial contempt. Africans ought not to make
their masters behave so badly.

Most whites knew Mau Mau as the squatter armed. The frontline was at
home, between supper and bedtime. Tools became weapons. The man with
one's cast-off trilby fingered his panga.[68] Mau Mau was an ungrateful stab in
the back, 'a revolt of the domestic staff... It was as though Jeeves had taken
to the jungle'.[69] Two of the first settlers murdered were doctors, known for
giving free treatment to squatter families;[70] the six year-old son of one of
them was also killed; the press pictured his bloodstained bed, with chamber
pot and clockwork train-set on the floor. And what must, alas, be the best
known account of Mau Mau, Ruark's oft-reprinted novel *Something of Value*,
centres on the friendship between the settler's son Peter and the squatter's
son Kimani. Kimani grew up in Nairobi's slums to become Mau Mau.
Friend was now beast. In a blood-curdling book, the most chilling sentence
for its settler readers must have been Ruark's statement of Kimani's purpose
when he left the forest, gun in hand and murder in mind: 'This time Kimani
was going home.'[71]

The conservative response was the settler alarmed. It had six strands,
entwined in a circular argument. The first related grievance and terror.
Kikuyu had no grievance; white settlement had allowed them to colonise

[65] Among the useful phrases for settler wives to learn in Swahili or Kikuyu, in the
Kenya Settler's Cookbook (Nairobi, 1959), was the injunction 'it is better not be sulky'.
[66] Kanogo, *Squatters*, 45, 65, 72.
[67] Uasin Gishu district council resolution, April 1947, quoted in Furedi, *Mau Mau
War*, 35–6.
[68] Pictured on the blood-red dustcover of Wilson, *Kenya's Warning*.
[69] Graham Greene, *Ways of Escape* (London, 1980), 188; I owe this reference to David
Throup.
[70] Wilson, *Kenya's Warning*, 56.
[71] Robert Ruark, *Something of Value*, (London, 1955), 368. For Kimani's earlier
appreciation of settler hospitality to Kikuyu squatters on Maasai land, see *ibid.* 272–4. It
was one of the ironies of Mau Mau, as Richard Waller has reminded me, that the squatters
shared the settler view that they had cultivated civilisation on Maasailand's transhumant
pastures: see Mugo Gatheru's reflections on his squatter childhood, *Child of Two Worlds*
(London, 1964), 7–8.

Maasailand. Since Mau Mau could not appeal against wrong, it had to impose by fear.[72] Then why had it emerged? Since 1945, in Kenya as elsewhere, 'the spineless policies of the rulers seemed to encourage the revolt of their subjects'.[73] Savages respected firmness. Talk of democracy showed weakness, which invited questions. Once privilege was questioned, envy stirred; if not, then agitators were free to stir it. Thirdly, democracy was a 'fantastic idea'[74] for people whose recent history showed them unfitted to exercise it. Settlers were prepared to accept that Africans were potentially equal; but they were observedly different, improvident, incurious, ungrateful, superstitious and slothful. Search their history and one found alternating autocracy and anarchy. Mau Mau warned how thin was the modern veneer; it foreshadowed an African self-rule as bloody as the court of Kabaka Mutesa, not a century before. Fourth, western education had not improved Africans; Kenyatta's career suggested the reverse. Islam might be better than Christianity; it neither demanded nor promised so much. Fifthly, as for the squatters, so for Africans generally, firmness, even force, was the language they understood. This was especially true of the Kikuyu, once terrorised by a secret council of wizards, from which Mau Mau was perhaps descended.[75] Finally, the answer was plain. European dominance must be restored. In centuries to come, white discipline might have shaped African potential. For the moment, they must respect whites more than they feared Mau Mau. The chief instrument of correction ought to be, not blundering British battalions, but an expanded KAR 'drawn largely from tribes inimical to the Kikuyu', officered by settlers 'experienced in dealing with black men'.[76] If all this was too much for Whitehall, lately ruled by woolly minded socialists, then the settlers knew where to find friends, further south in Africa.[77]

For many whites the emergency offered, more simply, the prospect of revenge. That was why Baring had to reinforce its declaration with airlifted British troops. He feared that settlers would otherwise supply, privately and without restraint, any violence the state appeared to lack.[78] From the start,

[72] Most succinctly put by Wilson, *Kenya's Warning*, 59.

[73] Stoneham, *Barbarism*, 105.

[74] 'The voice of the settler', anonymous correspondent to *New Statesman*, 4 October 1952, 378.

[75] In April 1952 the director of intelligence and security submitted a memorandum on Mau Mau (KNA, GO. 3/2/72) which, while comparing the movement to Nkrumah's Convention People's Party in the Gold Coast (whence the director had recently been posted), traced it back to a supposed 'Supreme Council of Elders', all 'experts in witchcraft' who in days past had specialised in cursing wealthy upstarts. This information was said to have been supplied by 'a well known authority', but nothing remotely like it can be found in the obvious sources, Routledges, *Prehistoric people*; C. W. Hobley, *Bantu Beliefs and Magic* (London, 1922); and C. Cagnolo, *The Akikuyu* (Turin, 1933). Neither Lambert's nor Leakey's works were then available (see footnote 34 above), nor do they support the idea of a wizard's council. It is possible that it was derived from one of the earliest Kiambu settlers, W. O. Tait, an amateur historian who claimed to have been a member of the council (Stoneham, *Barbarism*, 112–13), and who twenty years earlier had spoken of 'a secret society among the Kikuyu which nobody ever gets to know much about': *Kenya Land Commission Evidence*, vol. 1, 590.

[76] Stoneham, *Barbarism*, 122.

[77] This composite picture is drawn from *ibid.*; and Wilson, *Before the Dawn* and *Kenya's Warning*.

[78] Baring to Lyttelton, 9 October 1952: PRO, CO 822/443.

the governor was determined not to fight a racial war. In the empire of 1952 that would in any case have been impossible.

Liberals and transitionals

Conservatives said what they meant. Liberals dissembled. This was partly because ignorance and panic made them share conservative views. It also preserved a united front. On his first visit to Nairobi, Lyttelton, colonial secretary, maintained that Mau Mau was not the child of economic pressure.[79] That was to calm the settlers; he himself knew better. Two months earlier his officials had considered reforms which might meet 'any legitimate grievance of law-abiding Africans' and raised them with Baring before he flew to Kenya. They had discussed housing schemes, civil service promotion, crop prices, even the question of African farming on the White Highlands. Baring called reform his 'second prong', to make his first, repression, look presentable. It was also an essential tactic of war. The government must stop driving moderate Africans into the arms of the extremists and, instead, split the KAU. Baring might well have to decide 'either to "bust" or "buy" Kenyatta'.[80] Events precluded that. But London had to buy the settlers or they might bust the government. Some cried 'appeasement' when Baring revealed the second prong. If he was to keep the settlers at heel he would have to mind his tongue.[81] Official statements followed the conservative line.[82]

Official action was different, and action remade Mau Mau in many official minds. Policy steered between two rocks of disaster. First, the settlers must be allowed no increase in influence; the precedents of two world wars were ominous in that respect. Nor must they be stampeded into a ferment which could be calmed only by concession. Yet the state had to answer African grievances, despite white fears of betrayal. For the second need was to prevent Mau Mau 'infecting' other African peoples; there was anxious evidence that it might. Brutal repression of their fellows was stirring angry passions.[83] The deputy head of the colonial office, Sir Charles Jeffries, squared the circle with some dog-eared official wisdom. 'The only sound line', he believed, was to 'build up a substantial "middle class" of all races to be the backbone of the country.'[84] He did not know how it should be done; nobody did, but it was

[79] Lyttelton, radio broadcast from Nairobi, 4 November 1952 (transcript in KNA, CD. 5/173); and repeated in his statement to parliament: House of Commons Debates, 5th series, vol. 507 (7 November 1952), col. 459.

[80] W. Gorell Barnes to Baring, 10 September 1952; note of a meeting with Baring, 23 September 1952: PRO, CO 822/544. The KAU was already split; official belief in its unity, in thrall to Mau Mau, caused it to be banned early in 1953.

[81] I have adopted Kingsley Martin's reading of the situation: New Statesman, 8 November 1952.

[82] For instance, official press handout no. 70 of 19 April 1953, purporting to show a Mau Mau central committee circular, omitted all its references to 'peace' and 'freedom'; Baring to Lyttelton, 19 April 1953: PRO, CO 822/440. Wilson, Kenya's Warning, 63, made much play with what was made public, including threats to drink the blood of enemies and to castrate and decapitate anybody who helped the government.

[83] Rogers, minute to Gorell Barnes, 24 October 1952; Rogers, minute to Sir Charles Jeffries, 16 February 1953; Lyttelton to Baring, 5 March 1953: PRO, CO.822/440.

[84] Jeffries, minute to Lloyd, 17 February 1953 (original emphasis): CO.822/440.

by now the standard magical spell for conjuring new order out of colonial confusion. Racial barriers must melt into class coalitions. Meanwhile a war had to be fought, and its methods were hardly middle class. Yet most of Kenya was at peace and must so remain. African rural ambitions must be satisfied, urban discontents relieved and, more urgently, tens of thousands of Kikuyu in detention weaned from Mau Mau. An awful war needed a beastly enemy. A solid peace needed radical reform. An ideology which joined the two in causal sequence emerged from the daily discourse of harassed men.

This liberal doctrine adopted as its subject a new stereotype, 'the African in transition'. It diagnosed Mau Mau as a disease which demanded as cure none other than the government's best intentions of the postwar years. It was offered by Dr Colin Carothers, who had been a local medical officer for twenty years and now practised psychiatry in England. He had been asked back to reassure the commissioner for community development, Askwith, that his approach to rehabilitating Mau Mau detainees was on the right lines.[85] He assumed that they were possessed by evil and must be cleansed by public confession as performed in Kikuyu law, paid manual labour, literacy classes, instruction in the beneficent colonial history of Kenya and, if they chose, by Christian witness.[86] It was a working theory of a guided transition. Carothers was asked to comment on the ideas of practical men; his doctrine was dug from experience, theirs and his. He himself was a self-taught psychiatrist.[87] But he did much more.

Carothers' contribution to constructing Mau Mau was to theorise the detention camps' commonsense concept of a crisis in modernisation, a war for the soul of transitional man. He had just published a general treatment of the liberal approach to African psychiatry, which stressed the influence of environment rather than heredity on mental capacity. The preliterate tribal personality, he had argued, was moulded from outside by the conformity of the community. Literate western man was inner-directed, disciplined by the competition of society. This general work neither mentioned Mau Mau nor forecast any unusual psychiatric problems for 'the African in transition'.[88] But when he came to investigate, he found that Mau Mau was, in part, a reaction to psychic insecurity. Transitional men would have lost many cultural supports while still dreading the power of external, magical 'wills'. Their grievances would tell them that whites controlled a richer store of these than they did themselves. Here lay the cunning of Mau Mau; its oaths promised redress of the magical balance.[89]

Carothers has often been misinterpreted, perhaps because he allowed his understanding to change as he wrote, without then revising earlier passages, 'an approach which held the writer in as much suspense as any of his readers'.[90] It is remembered that he thought that the Kikuyu, as secretive

[85] T. G. Askwith, typescript memoirs, chapter on 'Mau Mau', p. 8, seen by courtesy of the author.
[86] Colony and Protectorate of Kenya [CPK], *Community Development Organization Annual Report 1953* (Nairobi, 1954), 2–3; CPK, *Annual Report of the Department of Community Development and Rehabilitation 1954* (Nairobi, 1955), 21–33.
[87] Dr J. C. Carothers, in conversation, 26 July 1989.
[88] J. C. Carothers, *The African Mind in Health and Disease* (World Health Organization, Geneva, 1953), 54–5, 130–3.
[89] CPK: J. C. Carothers, *The Psychology of Mau Mau* (Nairobi, 1954), 6–18.
[90] J. C. Carothers, 'The nature-nurture controversy', *Psychiatry : J. for the Study of Interpersonal Processes*, XVIII (1953), 303; this was in response to critics of his WHO

forest-dwellers with little of the music of social cohesion in their souls (he was badly advised on both counts), unusually ill-fitted for the transition. It is forgotten that his report concluded with a call for deliberate modernisation. If Mau Mau abused the inner bewilderment of transitional man, Africans must be given the self-assurance of modernity. Confusion of category must cease, especially in the family. Disorder reigned where the river of transition separated traditional woman from modern man.[91] New boundaries of order must be drawn around modern genders. Again, this was the view of practical men. Askwith believed that recovery from Mau Mau was confirmed only by regular employment and the companionship of family life. Other senior officials had long called for a similar remedy for wider ills.

Post-war British colonial policy assumed that neither peasant economy nor unskilled urban labour could sustain social order much longer, let alone provide for development and improved welfare. Neither side of African life was self-sufficient; each was debilitated by what connected them, the oscillation of male wage labour. As Carothers fitted Mau Mau into his concept of transition, officials did likewise. Their transitional man was flesh and blood in the migrant worker. Mau Mau had travelled home with him. The slum had infected the countryside with the incessant movement between them.[92] Two government plans and unprecedented sums of public finance were now devoted to separating them. The labour department pressed for improved wages and conditions, to create a new basis for society, the urban African family, where before Nairobi had accommodated loose atoms, labour units, bachelor workers.[93] The department of agriculture embraced a freehold revolution in land tenure to produce the rural mirror image, the peasant family able to earn a rapidly increasing income on its own land by its own labour, neither subsidising bachelor sons in town nor yet needing their monthly remittances. The conflicting bundles of rights which confused customary land tenure, fragmented holdings, the constant drain of litigation, must be swept aside with registration, consolidation, fencing, contour-ploughing and tree-crops.[94] Disorder would give way to cadastral survey and straight lines. Both departments seized on the emergency to argue, with a conviction which more than a decade of frustrated persuasion had sharpened, that the risks of pushing African communities through the transition to market society were as nothing to leaving them hanging betwixt and between. If Mau Mau was a disorder of the beginnings of progress the cure must be to bring progress to a successful end. Moreover, and this was

---

monograph, but the same method was openly employed in his pamphlet on Mau Mau. See, *Psychology*, 20–1: 'assessments of other people must continually be based on re-assessments of oneself.' The first half of the pamphlet described the Kikuyu in admittedly 'derogatory' terms; the second half turned the tables on the whites; for Kikuyu were, of Kenya's African peoples, 'the most like ourselves'.

[91] Carothers, *Psychology*, 22–4; a message to which I have been alerted by the work of Luise White.

[92] The best summary statement of the district commissioner's view is in Margery Perham, 'Struggle against Mau Mau II: seeking the causes and the remedies', *The Times* (London), 23 April 1953; while reprinted in her *Colonial Sequence 1949 to 1969* (London, 1970), 112–15, it has been given the disastrously wrong date of 1955.

[93] CPK, *Report of the Committee on African Wages* (Nairobi, 1954).

[94] CPK, *A Plan to Intensify the Development of African Agriculture in Kenya* (Nairobi, 1954).

vital, they could not be accused of appeasing Mau Mau; to the contrary, they were disciplining with individual obligation the collective disorders of transitional society. Each talked openly of class as the basis of order and power.

Missionaries had a not dissimilar idea of progress. While the two 'established' British missions, Anglican and Presbyterian, publicly supported the multi-racial aim of the former governor, Mitchell, to 'evolve from components at present heterogeneous, a harmonious and organic society',[95] their private history taught them that their particular role in the war against Mau Mau was to transform individuals. They had reason to hate the movement. Their congregations and school enrolments withered in mid-1952; pastors and teachers could not be paid. Some Christians were martyred. The missionary sense of history almost welcomed the catastrophe. For this was the second great test for the young Kikuyu churches, purging them of nominal believers to reveal the faithful remnant of rebirth. Presbyterians in particular had suffered similar persecution in 1929, in the 'female circumcision crisis'. The KCA had led the resistance to their teaching against clitoridectomy and then spawned independent churches and schools which were thought to have inspired the new savagery of Mau Mau.[96] Their origin in a backsliding defence of an 'old, cruel and degrading practice'[97] showed their dark potential. Moreover, just as the earlier opposition had followed on an unprecedented period of church growth, so Mau Mau seemed to have been galvanised to defeat the new challenge of Revival. This largely lay movement, potentially anti-clerical and schismatic, challenged missionary authority with the priesthood of all 'saved' believers.[98] It took much missionary humility, racial and clerical, to avoid schism. Having demolished their own defences, missionaries saw Mau Mau as a counter revival, to rescue Kikuyu belief for nationalist ends, to break racial comity once more.[99]

Missions willingly assisted the government's rehabilitation work in the *gulag* of detention, which in 1954 housed one-third of Kikuyu men and not

[95] For Mitchell's statement, see Church Missionary Society [CMS], *Mau Mau, What is it?* (London, 1952), 8; and Church of Scotland Foreign Missions Committee [CSM], *Mau Mau and the Church* (Edinburgh, 1953), 4, where 'organic' is rendered, in a splendidly illustrative slip, as 'organised'.

[96] The colony's director of education conducted a survey of the first detainees to investigate the sources of their schooling and discovered that they showed no significant difference from other Kikuyu; there was thus no solid evidence for the general suspicion of the independent schools, another private doubt which did not sway the conventional wisdom: CPK, *Education Department Annual Report 1953* (Nairobi, 1955), 39–40.

[97] CMS, *Mau Mau*, 5. An indication of the aroused imaginations of the time is given on the same page, where the difficulty of obtaining evidence against Mau Mau is compared with the fruitless enquiry into the murder and sexual mutilation of a woman missionary in 1930. Yet there was never any suggestion that Mau Mau murders involved circumcision – or, indeed, rape.

[98] For two Kikuyu accounts, see E. N. Wanyoike, *An African Pastor* (Nairobi, 1974), 151–68; Obadiah Kariuki, *A Bishop facing Mount Kenya* (Nairobi, 1985), 46–59, 78–9; Kariuki gives a glimpse of his relations with Kenyatta, his brother-in-law, *ibid.* 79–81.

[99] CSM, *Mau Mau and the Church*, 5. For Kikuyu comparisons between Revival and Mau Mau see, Wanyoike, *African Pastor*, 175, 180–85, 195f. By contrast, Githige, 'Religious factor', arguing from oral reminiscence, is doubtful of Christianity's influence on Mau Mau, whether as inspiration or antagonist.

a few women. Confession of sin and Christian teaching could restore dead souls. Thus far Christians agreed; like everybody else they then divided. Most thought that individual conversion was all they could properly pray for, but a few came close to a concept of structural sin. The first approach, to which fundamentalist belief attracted most missionaries, got more publicity. Its limitations were, nonetheless, well appreciated at the time.[100] The best known attempt to resolve political conflict by confession of racial brotherhood, at the Athi River camp, was the work of Moral Rearmament, thanks to the private interest of a senior prison official. The Christian Council of Kenya (CCK), which represented the Protestant missions, never approved; and the experiment was soon abandoned.[101] The CCK had humbler hopes of conversion. Guided by their secretary, Stanley Morrison, who had come from working with Palestinian refugees, they understood Mau Mau to be a complex phenomenon, political, economic, and social as well as spiritual. Individual conversion could thus be only an adjunct to political change, not a substitute for it. Moreover, the churches faced a particular disability, the nature of Revival. Hitherto it had produced men and women so convinced of the power of Christ that they often chose martyrdom by, rather than armed resistance to Mau Mau. District officers so mistrusted their pacifism that they refused them the 'loyalty certificates' which allowed free movement.[102] Conversely, the churches despaired of using such private conviction in social action.[103] Christianity could work its miracle of reconciliation only if justice had been created by other means. That, too, was conventional Christian wisdom, at least in the liberal theology of the CCK. Its separate members, the locally rooted missionary churches, had little interest in a theology of power or, therefore, in political reform.[104] Neither fundamentalists nor liberals exercised the influence which has been attributed to Christian rehabilitation as a whole.

Liberal beliefs, reinforced by pragmatic action, helped officials to fight the war of transition with a clear conscience and to bring to justice some at least of their subordinates who fought a different, dirty, racial war. But this construction of Mau Mau failed to provide a foundation for peace. Two men at the centre of the bid for liberal authority warned explicitly that it would not. The forgotten part of Carothers' report on Mau Mau psychology argued

[100] Which may not be sufficiently clear from the brief treatment in Rosberg and Nottingham, *Myth*, 340.

[101] CPK, *Annual Report of the Department of Community Development 1954*, 26.

[102] The one notable exception to Christian pacifism was shown by the independent Africa Christian Church in Murang'a, whose headquarters at Kinyona was so bellicose that Mau Mau fighters christened it 'Berlin': 'A book of forest history' recovered by Willougby Thompson in December 1953: RH.Mss.Afr.s.1534. See also, David P. Sandgren, *Christianity and the Kikuyu : Religious Divisions and Social Conflict* (New York, 1989), 158.

[103] T. F. C. Bewes, *Kikuyu Conflict : Mau Mau and the Christian Witness* (London, 1953), 41–2, 68.

[104] As in all other aspects of this essay, there is a deeper history to be told; this analysis is derived principally from S. A. Morrison, 'What does rehabilitation mean?', 5 June 1954, seen by courtesy of Greet Kershaw who was employed by the CCK in the 1950s. For an indication of a wider approach see, John Lonsdale, with Stanley Booth-Clibborn and Andrew Hake, 'The emerging pattern of church and state co-operation in Kenya', in Edward Fashole-Luke *et al.* (ed.), *Christianity in Independent Africa* (London, 1978), 267–84. (My two co-authors were also CCK employees in the 1950s).

that it was futile to try to remake the Kikuyu in the individualist English image unless they were given the chance to exercise the responsibility of power. Rehabilitation would be complete only with some kind of democracy, however that was defined.[105] Askwith conducted rehabilitation on the same assumption. The first was only an adviser, the second was sacked for not forcing the pace, when in 1957 the African elections demanded altogether more urgency, and the administration decided that persuasion must be stiffened with 'compelling force'.[106] The views of the army were quite a different matter. It trusted neither in controlled reform nor in compelling force.

Soldiers and politics

The army fought against Mau Mau's military confusions. These were very different from those which haunted the liberal myth of modernisation. General Erskine, commander during the critical first part of the war, took a simple soldierly view of the oaths which so disturbed the understanding of most observers. He recognised that Mau Mau had grievances and an aim, to eject Europeans. The connexion between strategic end and nauseating means was crisply rational.

Secrecy was necessary, hence oaths were administered. Money was necessary, hence the oath had to be paid for. The whole tribe had to act as one, hence oaths were administered forcibly. Discipline was necessary, hence judges and stranglers became part of the organisation. It was perfectly clear from the nature of the oaths that violence was intended. Oaths became more and more binding and bestial.[107]

Cooling the mind the better to know the enemy was carried still further by the soldier who had the best Mau Mau war and later became a theorist of similar 'low intensity operations', the then Captain Kitson. He found the conservative obsession with savagery bad for tactical intelligence. 'Looked at over one's shoulder the oath was a frightful business, suffused in evil.' If one looked at it straight, what was left?

A cat hung on a stick; poor pussy. An arch of thorns with goat's eyes impaled on them: a silly scarecrow to frighten the feeble...what next? The initiates are abusing themselves into a bowl of blood – prep school stuff...The whole business when looked at carefully is no more than the antics of naughty schoolboys.[108]

Kitson made his sense of Mau Mau by assimilating it to his own experience, more lurid than that of many of his compatriots one might think, even of those who had endured boarding school. At a more workaday level, he recognised the guerrillas as army types, skivers and time-servers whose kindred spirits once swarmed over base areas in the second world war.[109]

The colonial secretary, Oliver Lyttelton, was struck by a nobler likeness

[105] Carothers, *Psychology*, 19–20, 28–9.

[106] T. G. Askwith, in conversation, 27 July 1989; Terence Gavaghan, in conversation over the years.

[107] General Sir George Erskine, despatch, 'The Kenya emergency June 1953–May 1955', 2 May 1955: PRO, WO 236/18 (seen by courtesy of Mr Heather).

[108] Frank Kitson, *Gangs and Counter-gangs* (London, 1960), 131.

[109] *Ibid.* 158; for his later thoughts, see his *Low Intensity Operations: Subversion, Insurgency and Peacekeeping* (London, 1971).

between forest fighter and British soldier. A veteran of the Great War, he respected men who, contrary to their 'tribal reputation', had 'more than once pressed home attacks against wire, and in the face of hot fire, and heavy casualties.' He had asked no more of his Grenadiers. If Mau Mau gallantry was explained by 'dutch courage...doped with hemp', had he not too, like others in his war, braced himself with rum before battle?[110] Such recognition of equivalence, so contrary both to the racialism which denied a common humanity and the liberalism which pitied dupes, was politically important. On a visit to London, Blundell (whose own respect for Africans came from commanding them in war), was shocked to find that Churchill thought the 'fibre, ability and steel' of the Kikuyu deserved to be acknowledged by an offer of terms.[111]

Erskine thought like Churchill. The settlers never trusted him after his statement that Mau Mau required a political rather than military solution.[112] But that was a soldier's reaction to guerrilla war, the most difficult of all wars to fight. It poses the keenest moral problems for its participants, on both sides of the hill. It blurs the distinction between military and civil and so too, more than other wars, between victory and massacre, gallantry and crime.[113] Insurgents can win political battles by an underhand refusal to fight open, soldierly, ones; they muddy the aims and reputation of security forces by denying them the clean tactical objective of a 'fair target' or 'fair fight'.[114] After clearing the army of the political confusions created by others, Erskine then strove to restore proper distinctions to the battlefield itself. Forest and mountain became prohibited areas, where troops could operate on a 'straight forward [sic] war basis knowing that anybody they met must be an enemy.' He reserved these zones of simplicity to the army, leaving to the police the inhabited areas where 'pressure and persuasion' had their murkier role. White settlers were as messy as Mau Mau. Erskine's compulsory evacuation of elderly and isolated white farmers from the front line, to avoid dissipating his forces as scattered farm guards, was almost his most unpopular act.[115]

Erskine angered whites most with his successive surrender offers to the forest fighters. These thwarted the lust for revenge. Negotiation also denied two fundamental beliefs of the conservative myth, that the obscenities of the oath turned men into beasts and that Mau Mau lacked rational aims.[116] Even Kenyan-born white police found that Mau Mau commanded their respect. After sixty-eight hours of interrogating the captured 'General China', superintendent Ian Henderson, the boys' own hero of the settlers' war, concluded that his prisoner was 'a complete fanatic'. Was he then mentally ill? Not at all. China had 'a good brain and a remarkable memory'. He knew

---

[110] Lyttelton, secret and personal telegram to prime minister Churchill, 18 May 1953: PRO, CO 822/440; Oliver Lyttelton, *The memoirs of Lord Chandos* (London, 1962), 41, 59.

[111] Blundell, *Wind*, chapter 4 and p. 184.

[112] James Cameron, 'Bombers? Kenya needs ideas', *News Chronicle* (London), 15 Nov. 1953.

[113] Michael Walzer, *Just and Unjust Wars* (Harmondsworth, 1980), chapter 11.

[114] The quoted phrases come from Erskine's despatch of 2 May 1955, para. 17: PRO, WO 236/18; and Kitson, *Gangs*, 46.

[115] Erskine's despatch, 2 May 1955, paras. 15, 17, 40, 74.

[116] For settler outrage see, Blundell, *Wind*, 189–92, but discussion of the surrender offers must await Mr Heather's findings.

why he was fighting; 'his sole wish was to expound his political testament before Legislative Council and then walk to the gallows without trial.'[117] When he too was captured, China's successor in Mount Kenya's forests, General Kaleba, outlined his objective as

the achievement of more land and power of self-determination. They do not consider this will be achieved by violence alone, but they firmly believe that those who are sympthetic to their cause can only succeed if Mau Mau continue to fight.[118]

The opposing generals understood each other. Each acknowledged their limitations in a political war. They could only exert the military pressure needed to force a political peace.

It took the tragedy of Hola camp, when eleven 'hard core' detainees were beaten to death in the name of modernisation, to bring the British government round to the military view. As Margery Perham put it, the hard core were determined to prove that they 'were not in the grip of some remedial obsession but pursuing logical and irrevocable political aims'.[119] The detainees might have put it differently. The immediate issue was work and its refusal. Their case was simple. They were political prisoners, not criminals. To work to order would be to admit to wrong. Work was a proper demonstration of responsibility for free men; under any other condition it was slavery.[120] The colonial government did not agree, but that was no longer relevant. The liberal campaign for westernisation, as both the bridge of transition and condition of political rights on a qualified franchise, could no longer govern policy. Political change could not wait on repentance and the development of a politically responsible (that is, guilt-conscious) middle class. Britain could not continue to remake Kenya by force when other European powers were abandoning attempts to remodel colonial rule for the moral high ground of informal empire.[121] A political war must be ended by political means. Civilisation had to be gambled on concession and agreement,

---

[117] 'Interrogation of "General China"', para. 14.

[118] 'Flash Report No. 1 – Interrogation of Kaleba', Special Branch headquarters, 28 Oct. 1954, para. 37: KNA, DC/NYK.3/12/24 (by courtesy of Mr Heather). This statement accurately summarises two themes of guerrilla doctrine. They called their movement '*ithaka na wiathi*', which is better rendered as 'land and moral responsibility' or 'freedom through land', the highest civic virtue of Kikuyu elderhood, rather than the more common 'land and freedom' which invites the retrospective connotation of 'land and national independence'. The 'power of self-determination' by which *wiathi* is rather well translated in this police report was essentially moral and individual. Secondly they called themselves *itungati*, a reserve of seasoned warriors who neither commanded nor attacked on raids but acted as bodyguard to the leaders and then beat off counter-attacks as a successful raiding party withdrew. For these former military tactics see, Jomo Kenyatta, *Facing Mount Kenya* (London, 1938), 206; Lambert, *Kikuyu Institutions*, 7of.; Leakey, *Southern Kikuyu*, vol. 3, 1051–3.

[119] Foreword to Kariuki, '*Mau Mau*' *Detainee*, xv.

[120] Gakaara wa Wanjau's prison diary, published as *Mwandiki wa Mau Mau ithaamirio-ini* (Nairobi, 1983) and *Mau Mau Author in Detention* (Nairobi 1988), is driven by such reasoning. Wanjau's father, a Presbyterian minister, was killed at the outset of the war; he himself was a noted political songwriter and pamphleteer.

[121] As argued by John Darwin, *Britain and Decolonisation : the Retreat from Empire in the Post-war World* (London, 1988), 244–69.

not enforced by the tyranny of good intentions and warders' truncheons. Within months of Hola came Lancaster House and the prospect of majority rule.

Freedom and crime

The remaking of civilisation in Kenya, then, had to be a political creation, not a confessional crusade. But whose? The man who won the peace was the man found guilty of causing the war, Kenyatta. The government had charged him with imposing evil on the Kikuyu. But Mau Mau could never have been a simple imposition. There were too many Mau Maus for that. They were the product of deep political conflict within Kikuyu society. Their militants were inspired by Kenyatta, of that there is no doubt. But his exhortations were overtaken by their compulsions.[122]

On the surface, Mau Mau was an anti-colonial revolt to recover Kikuyu land and to press the claim to much of the remainder of the White Highlands which had been lodged by two generations of squatter labour.[123] But what gave the revolt its shape and inner meaning was its junior status in a long struggle for patriotic virtue within Kikuyuland. Kikuyu virtue lay in the labour of agrarian civilisation, directed by household heads. Honour lay in wealth, the proud fruit of burning back the forest and taming the wild, clearing a cultivated space in which industrious dependents too might establish themselves in self-respecting independence; the possibility of working one's own salvation was the subject of more Kikuyu proverbs than any other.[124] But by the 1940s this myth of civic virtue began to mock the majority rather than inspire. Big men no longer welcomed dependents, they expropriated them. Wages fell behind prices, whether of food, housing, land, or marriage transfers. Young men asked if they would ever earn enough to marry and mature.[125] Those who had most cause to fight colonial rule had the least chance to merit responsibility. Those whose deeds might deliver power would have no right to enjoy it. That was the Kikuyu tragedy, a struggle over the moralities of class formation, not mental derangement.

Kikuyu were engaged in a struggle about class, not in class struggle. They were not yet morally divided, however much their material chances diverged. They argued within one myth of virtue. A Mau Mau leader recalled how the trade unionist Makhan Singh taught him that the Kikuyu were once communist; but he meant a communalist society, in which 'the community took care of everyone and his family.'[126] Nobody had a socialist

---

[122] As African leaders complained to Kingsley Martin: 'The case against Jomo Kenyatta', *New Statesman*, 22 November 1952.

[123] As Governor Mitchell almost said in retirement: *Afterthoughts*, 268.

[124] G. Barra, *1000 Kikuyu Proverbs* (Nairobi, 1974, first edition 1939); Ngumbu Njururi, *Gikuyu Proverbs* (Nairobi, 1983). What follows is a too brief sketch of Kikuyu political thought which I intend to develop elsewhere.

[125] See, Meja Mwangi's novel, *Kill me Quick* (Nairobi, 1973).

[126] 'Classification report no. 3468: John Michael Mungai', (17 May 1956), 9–10: RH, Mss.Afr.s.1534; the only direct indication I have found of Makhan Singh's thought on pre-colonial Kenya is in his *History of Kenya's Trade Union Movement, to 1952* (Nairobi, 1969), 1–2, from which the quotation comes.

Mau Mau in mind.[127] The right to force political change was contested between the men of authority like Kenyatta, who was the son-in-law of not one but two official chiefs, and the dispossessed, legal minors. The reputable, it began to appear, could not win power except at the appalling price of owing its achievement to men they despised. These latter, the hard men of Nairobi, took over the oath of respectable unity which Kenyatta knew and pressed it, by force, deception, and persuasion on those who hoped that desperate deeds, *ngero*, would earn them what they needed, the adulthood which would entitle them to share the fruits of victory. These were the men and women whom Kikuyu knew as Mau Mau, not all those who had taken the oath of unity but the few who had taken the second, fighting oath.[128] But, however much Kikuyu may have denounced Mau Mau within, few were so careless of communal solidarity or their own lives that they betrayed it without. Europeans mistook this fear and solidarity for tribal unity, a mystic force. This myth of tribal unity found Kenyatta guilty. If he was the tribal leader he was responsible for everything done in his name.

Throughout his career, with sustained consistency over fifty years, Kenyatta taught that authority was earned by the self-discipline of labour, as he had learned from his grandparents. In 1928 he had warned of the fate of native Australians, whom the British 'found were decreasing by reason of their sloth...and so they got pushed to the bad parts of the land'. Kikuyu ought to follow the Maori example. The British had found them 'to be a very diligent people. And now they are permitted to select four men to represent them in the Big Council...'.[129] This simple contrast summed up all his later political thought. On numerous occasions, between his return from England in 1946 and his arrest in 1952, Kenyatta publicly denounced those who no longer worked their land as the enemies of political advance: 'if we use our hands we shall be men; if we don't we shall be worthless.' Among the vast crowds who listened, those who no longer had land did not thank him for this sermon.[130]

So Kenyatta also made a meaning for Mau Mau. In front of a huge crowd at Nyeri in July 1952 he compared it with theft and drunkenness. Henderson, the police observer, thought he equivocated; and the provincial com-

[127] Kingsley Martin studied extracts of the vernacular press and found there only liberal nationalism, not Marxism: 'Kenya report', *New Statesman*, 15 November 1952. The most likely source for any Mau Mau class ideology would be Kaggia, *Roots of Freedom 1921–63* (Nairobi, 1975), but the nearest he comes to that is syndicalism; no memoir of Mau Mau initiation suggests that the political education given to recruits referred to class struggle; conversely, a 'typical notice' of a Mau Mau initiation contained, as its sole programmatic statement, a threat to 'all those who try to stop us selling our goods where and when we want': *Corfield report*, 164. Maina wa Kinyatti (ed.), *Thunder from the Mountains, Mau Mau Patriotic Songs* (London, 1980), gives a retrospective, socialist, twist to insurgent thought.

[128] Rosberg and Nottingham, *Myth*, 234–76; Kaggia, *Roots*, 78–115, 193–5; M. Tamarkin, 'Mau Mau in Nakuru', *J. Afr. Hist.*, XVII (1976), 119–34; John Spencer, *KAU, the Kenya African Union* (London, 1985), 202–49.

[129] Editor (Kenyatta), 'Conditions in other countries', *Muiguithania*, i, 3 (July 1928), translation by A. R. Barlow of the CSM. KNA, DC/MKS.10B/13.1.

[130] Profile of Jomo Kenyatta in *The Observer* (London), 2 November 1952, doubtless by Colin Legum. The *Corfield report*, 301–8: Appendix F, (Assistant Superintendent Henderson's report on KAU mass meeting at Nyeri on 26 July 1952, with 25,000 estimated present) shows the difficulty Kenyatta could have in controlling a crowd.

missioner believed this meeting marked a turning point in the swing of opinion towards Mau Mau.[131] But Henderson also reported Kenyatta as asking the crowd to 'join hands for freedom and freedom means abolishing criminality'.[132] That may not be an obvious point for a nationalist orator to make, but precisely what one would expect of a Kikuyu elder.[133] Freedom and criminality were at opposite poles in Kikuyu thought. Freedom was *wiathi*; this enjoined not only independence from others but also self-mastery. It came from disciplined effort, whether as herdboy, warrior, dependent worker, or household head. Criminality was *umaramari* or *ngero*. The former term derived adult delinquency from childhood disobedience; the latter carried connotations of failing a test.[134] Kenyatta was not alone in making a delinquent Mau Mau in the mind. A former Mau Mau fighter has called it a council of *ngero*.[135] Even the chairman of its central committee or *kiama kia wiathi*, Eliud Mutonyi, would have not demurred. A self-made businessman himself, he regretted that in the Nairobi slums, from which Mau Mau recruited so many fighters, 'poverty knows no patriotism',[136] a modern rendering of the old, dismissive proverb, 'poverty has no responsibilities'. The path of crime, *umaramari*, could never lead to its opposite, self-rule, *wiathi*.[137]

In the forests the struggle for respectability was as fierce as the fight for freedom. Guerrillas remembered in song what Kenyatta had said at Nyeri: 'Vagrancy and laziness do not produce benefits for our country.'[138] Perhaps also revealing their own anxieties about socially unauthorised killing, they anathematised ill-disciplined gangs, always the ones over the next hill, as *komerera*, an appellation which pairs the concepts of idleness and concealment, mere thugs who perpetrated anti-social violence and refused to cook for their leaders. They personified the nightmares not only of military

---

[131] KNA: Edward Windley, Central Province annual report (1952). This was certainly true of at least one future forest leader: see, Barnett and Njama, *Mau Mau from Within*, 73–80.

[132] *Corfield report*, 305.

[133] I assume that Kenyatta spoke Kikuyu at this point, as remembered by Henderson a few months later at his trial (Slater, *Trial*, 93), and as recalled for me by one who was there as a schoolboy, Professor Godfrey Muriuki (in a letter of 7 February 1990); elsewhere, Kenyatta's Swahili was translated into Kikuyu by the KCA leader Jesse Kariuki.

[134] For these and other translations I depend on T. G. Benson (ed.), *Kikuyu-English Dictionary* (Oxford, 1964), and on help from friends, especially John Karanja, Tabitha Kanogo, Mungai Mbayah, Henry Muoria Mwaniki, Godfrey Muriuki (both of whom advised Benson), and George K. Waruhiu. Both *ngero* and *umaramari* have Maasai forms, on which Richard Waller has advised.

[135] Joram Wamweya, *Freedom Fighter* (Nairobi, 1971), 52.

[136] Eliud Mutonyi, 'Mau Mau chairman', undated typescript, copy in author's possession.

[137] This Kikuyu political logic is strong ground for thinking that Kenyatta was sincere in his denunciations of Mau Mau; if he did equivocate, he had good reason to do so in the threats made on his life by the Nairobi militants: evidence of Fred Kubai for Granada Television's 'End of Empire', screened 1 July 1985. While Wilson (*Kenya's Warning*, 54) made much of the mass Nyeri meeting of 26 July 1952, quoting long extracts from the *East African Standard*'s record of the other speakers, he passed over Kenyatta in half a sentence, as if his pieties were indeed difficult to square with his demonic reputation.

[138] Barnett and Njama, *Mau Mau from Within*, 180.

discipline but also of civic virtue.[139] Forest fighters also argued out the question of gender and the social order. They divided between literates, who assumed the adult status required to form a household, and illiterates, the 'Kenya *riigi*', who saw themselves as a warrior age-set below the age of marriage, for whom sexual relations were more free.[140] Even in the forest, to outsiders the very fount of evil, literacy was becoming associated with respectable class formation, threatened by the illiteracy of a junior generation, in which one can dimly discern the emerging contradiction of a lower class. Mau Mau faced within itself the confusions of the rest of Kenya.

But while Nairobi's hooligans crawled under the arch of Mau Mau circumcision in search of the responsible 'spirit of manhood' and then persevered in the forests to earn their right to land,[141] they did not win. The remaking of Kenya and their place in it were decided by others. The agrarian revolution of the war of modernisation had gone on without them. On emerging from forest or detention they were landless still, indeed more so than before in a rural world now realigned by land consolidation and freehold title. They remained debarred from the creation of order, outside its boundary fence. And on his release back to political life in 1961 Kenyatta took up his old refrain. His government would not be hooligan rule; Mau Mau had no moral claim on power. He no doubt intended to calm white farmers and foreign investors. But he had a still more anxious audience to reassure, with nowhere else to go. Most Kenyans, certainly all household heads, were relieved to discover that Kenyatta was on the side of domestic order, after all. Their traditional civilising mission had now become a modern ruling ideology. By criminalising Mau Mau once more in the public mind, as he had tried a decade earlier, Kenyatta reasserted his authority to remake Kenya.[142]

There are therefore many answers to the question I was asked two years ago by a landless taxi-driver. As a schoolboy he had taken General Matenjagwo – General matted hair – his last bowl of beans before he met his death in action. His mother had lost their land rights to the senior wife during land-consolidation. 'Why', he asked in some indignation, 'why did they call us *imaramari?*' They still do. White conservatives and liberals may have gone, and the regiments departed. Household heads, many of them now reinforced with fundamentalist Christianity, remain.

SUMMARY

This article explores the imaginative meanings of Mau Mau which white and black protagonists invented out of their fearful ambitions for the future of Kenya. Within

[139] *Ibid.* 213, 221, 293–5, 376, 390, 397, 479, 498; Waruhiu Itote (General China), *Mau Mau General* (Nairobi, 1967), 139–41.

[140] Barnett and Njama, *Mau Mau from Within*, 471–8; Itote, *Mau Mau General*, 78, 127–38. White, 'Separating the men from the boys', has much more on all this.

[141] The full title of Gakaara wa Wanjau's 1952 pamphlet was 'The spirit of manhood and perseverance for Africans', as translated in an appendix in *Mau Mau Author*, 227–43.

[142] Jomo Kenyatta, *Suffering without Bitterness* (Nairobi, 1968), 124, 146, 147, 154, 159, 161, 163–8, 183, 189, 204. My view of Kenyatta's attitude to Mau Mau at this time is thus entirely different to that proposed by Buijtenhuijs, *Mau Mau Twenty Years After*, 49–61, and is supported by the picture facing page 57 in this book, showing ex-Mau Mau in 1971 with the slogan 'Mau Mau is still alive: we don't want revolution in Kenya'.

the general assumptions of white superiority and the need to destroy Mau Mau savagery, four mutually incompatible European myths can be picked out. Conservatives argued that Mau Mau revealed the latent terror-laden primitivism in all Africans, the Kikuyu especially. This reversion had been stimulated by the dangerous freedoms offered by too liberal a colonialism in the post-war world. The answer must be an unapologetic reimposition of white power. Liberals blamed Mau Mau on the bewildering psychological effects of rapid social change and the collapse of orderly tribal values. Africans must be brought more decisively through the period of transition from tribal conformity to competitive society, to play a full part in a multi-racial future dominated by western culture; this would entail radical economic reforms. Christian fundamentalists saw Mau Mau as collective sin, to be overcome by individual confession and conversion. More has been read into their rehabilitating mission in the detention camps than is warranted, since they had no theology of power. The whites with decisive power were the British military. They saw the emergency as a political war which needed political solutions, for which repression, social improvement and spiritual revival were no substitute. They, and the 'hard-core' Mau Mau detainees at Hola camp who thought like them, cleared the way for the peace. This was won not by any of the white constructions of the rising but by Kenyatta's Kikuyu political thought, which inspired yet criminalised Mau Mau.

The Road to Independence in French Tropical Africa[1]

'Ladipo Adamolekun[1]
Institute of Administration
University of Ife

The most significant event in twentieth century African History was the attainment of independence by the overwhelming majority of African States after more than six decades of European domination. The purpose of this article is to examine how independence was achieved in the territories under French colonial rule in Africa, south of the Sahara. These territories are collectively referred to as French Tropical Africa. In all, we shall be concerned with two federations (French West Africa and French Equatorial Africa), one island (Madagascar) and two United Nations Trust Territories (Togo and Cameroun).

Except in Madagascar, the word 'independence' was unheard of in the public vocabulary of leading African politicians in these territories until after the Second World War (as late as 1958 in French West Africa!). However as early as December 1915 the *Vy Vato Sakelika* (VVS),[2] a student movement formed in Madagascar in 1912, resolved to 'throw the French out of Madagascar'. The movement was mercilessly suppressed and its leaders sentenced to various terms of imprisonment. This incident was an exception in French Tropical Africa and it was not until after the Second World War that nationalist movements launched the struggle against French colonial rule. What factors contributed to the launching of the struggle and how was it prosecuted?

The Reforms of 1944–47

The period 1944–47 witnessed important changes of attitude, as well as constitutional and institutional changes, in French colonial administration in Africa. The Brazzaville Conference of January 30 to February 8, 1944, was the starting point. It was summoned partly in acknowledgement of the debt Free France owed to the colonies in her struggle against the Germans and partly in response to growing international criticism of colonialism. Although its recommendations showed some liberalisation in France's attitudes towards her colonies, there was nothing radical about it. The Con-

---

[1] I am grateful to Professor Michael Crowder for assistance with this article and for freely letting me use his paper on 'Independence as a Goal in French West African Politics: 1944–60'. W. Lewis ed. *French Speaking Africa—The Search for Identity*, New York 1965.
[2] All abbreviations are given in full in the glossary on page 84. For map of the area see Michael Crowder's article, page 59.

ference recommended administrative decentralisation as a policy and political assimilation as a goal and declared that 'The ends of France's civilising achievements in the colonies eliminate any idea of autonomy: all possibility of evolution outside the framework of the French Empire, (and) the eventual establishment, even in the distant future, of self-governments in the colonies, is to be dismissed.' In pursuance of its assimilationist aims, the Conference advocated the abolition of both the *corvée* (forced labour) and the *indigénat* (summary administrative justice). With them they also abolished the humiliating status of *sujet* (subject) under which the vast majority of Africans were classified. *Sujets*, as distinct from citizens, were subject to the *corvée* and *indigénat*. Further, the Conference advocated greatly increased economic development in the colonies, as well as the extension of education, which, true to assimilation, was to be exclusively in the French language. All colonials were to be granted citizenship and, at the same time, to retain their *statut personnel*, meaning that they were not required to accept French civil law as a prerequisite of citizenship but in civil matters could follow customary or Muslim law. What in effect was being proposed was a new type of French citizenship, that of a Greater France, a citizenship different from that in Metropolitan France, which was automatically accompanied by voting rights.

Neither of the two Constituent Assemblies (1945 and 1946) held to decide the constitution of the Fourth Republic in France followed faithfully the political recommendations of Brazzaville. The 1945 Assembly which had a left-wing majority was the nearer of the two to the spirit of Brazzaville. Africans voted massively for its constitutional project but it was rejected by the majority of metropolitan voters. The project of 1946 which was less liberal than the first in its provisions for France's colonies was accepted and it became the Constitution of the French Fourth Republic. According to its provisions, African territories became members of the French Union which had its own Assembly and an executive called the High Council. Forty-one members of the French National Assembly were to come from the overseas territories as the colonies were now termed and of this number, thirty-two were to come from the African territories. In the Council of the Republic (i.e. the Senate) fifty of the 320 senators represented overseas constituencies of which thirty-four were to come from the African territories. Local representative assemblies were created and suffrage was extended, though not to all adults, who nevertheless were now recognised as citizens of the French Union by the *Loi Lamine Guèye* of May 9, 1946. During the two years 1946–47, laws were passed to put into effect many of the social, constitutional and institutional reforms recommended at Brazzaville and written into the 1946 Constitution. The *corvée* and the *indigénat* were abolished and Territorial Assemblies were set up for each colony. *Grands Conseils* (Great Councils) were established for the two French African federations of West and Equatorial Africa at Dakar and Brazzaville respectively. Elections were held for the French National Assembly and Senate.

These reforms had serious limitations. First, the dual electoral rolls in force in all the territories (except in Senegal) meant that Frenchmen occupied roughly 2/5 (and sometimes 1/3) of all elective posts since the 'first college', comprising French citizens as distinct from citizens of the Union, was largely dominated by them. A second limitation was the small powers of the local representative assemblies. (The Representative Assemblies in Togo and Cameroun were more powerful. We shall explain why this was so later.) African politicians were well aware of this limitation and until the establishment of the *Loi Cadre* Governments in 1957 they were more interested in seats in the powerful National Assembly in Paris than in the Territorial Assemblies or the *Grands Conseils*. Finally suffrage was not extended to all 'new' citizens. It was another decade before these limitations were removed through the provisions of the *Loi Cadre*.

First Phase of Political Activity 1946–1956

Whatever the limitations of the 1944–47 reforms, they had important consequences for the growth of political activity in providing the constitutional and institutional framework for political action. Before the Second World War the only formal outlets for political activity had been the elections to the Colonial Council and the four municipal councils of Dakar, Rufisque, Gorée and Saint Louis in Senegal and the election of the Senegalese deputy to the National Assembly. Besides its contribution to the reforms, the Second World War also produced a number of other factors that stimulated political activity. First, the defeat and occupation of France by the Germans shattered the myth of imperial impregnability. Second, African soldiers who had witnessed the atrocities perpetuated by white men and had killed white men on the battlefield returned with reservations about the so-called French 'civilising mission' in Africa. Finally, these soldiers for the most part returned to the towns and cities where they provided raw materials for political mobilisation.

The first form of political activity which eventually dominated political life in these territories was the formation of political parties, groups and movements. Hitherto only in Senegal had there been political parties. The most important of these new parties was the *Rassemblement Démocratique Africain* (RDA) launched in Bamako in October 1946. Although it was formed by politicians from the French West African Federation, its influence extended to the whole of French Tropical Africa. Between 1946 and 1956 parties were created in large numbers but the majority were either branches of the RDA or affiliated to it. Although an African party, the RDA was affiliated to the French Communist Party (PCF) and its organisation was greatly influenced by Communist theory. This affiliation to a metropolitan party, unknown in British West Africa, was the general practice throughout French Tropical Africa. Thus, all the major French political parties, from the extreme right to the extreme left, sought allies among African politicians. The explanation of course lies in the representation granted to these territories in metropolitan institutions by the reforms we

The French National Assembly—focal point of French-speaking African politics, 1944–60

have just examined. Because of the instability of French governments in the Fourth Republic, depending as they did on coalitions of parties, and with very small majorities, the thirty-two votes of the African deputies were of the greatest importance.

Political action during this period had a threefold dimension: mobilisation of the masses to join the parties, competition in elections to the local and metropolitan assemblies and the defence of African rights against the oppression and victimisation of colonial administrators. The parties were not alone in performing these functions but were joined by two other important groups: Trade Union Associations and Student Organisations. The first two activities largely involved internal competition among rival African groups. Although the branches of the RDA had a national character in many territories, adherence to it was partly through ethnic groups and it was not surprising to find internal party rivalries reflecting ethnic competition. For example, this was the situation in Guinea until 1951. The intrusion of Europeans into African political activity was another side to the internal struggles and this was particularly noticeable in French Equatorial Africa. There, Europeans working for partisan or economic interests exploited personal and ethnic divisions among the Africans. Perhaps the commonest sources of party rivalry were the personality clashes among African politicians. This accounted for the numerous parties that sprang up in most of these territories, notably in Madagascar and Cameroun.

More important than the clashes of personality was the confrontation between African nationalist movements (Parties, Trade Union Associations and Student Organisations all combined) and the colonial administration. The best known of these was the Madagascar Revolt of 1947. No satisfactory explanation of this revolt has so far been put forward. A French scholar, Dr. Manoni, argues that it was caused by freedom (granted by the Post Brazzaville reforms) without adequate preparation, which led to irresponsibility.

Against this view is the argument that Brazzaville granted 'too little, too late', that the expectations raised by 'the spirit of Brazzaville' were frustrated by the French administration in Tananarive. It has also been argued that the French provoked the revolt. Although a full and truly objective report has as yet to be written, three points stand out clearly. First, if the French did not provoke the revolt they did nothing to prevent it though they had foreknowledge of it. Secondly, the exploitation of the Malagasy under the *Service de la Main-d'oeuvre pour les Travaux d'Interest Général* (SMOTIG)[3] led to great resentment and protest. Finally, there was a general under-estimation of the nationalist zeal of the Malagasy. The revolt was concentrated in the north-east and south-east of the country. European settlers were beaten and some were killed. Hundreds of pro-French Malagasy and converts to Christianity were tortured and murdered, and some churches were razed to the ground.

If the 1916 repression was merciless, no word can adequately describe French reprisals which lasted for over a year. An entire trainload of prisoners was massacred, while many 'rebels' incarcerated in prisons were executed in the courtyards without trial. Madagascar lost more than 1% of her total population in the revolt.

Another example of bloody confrontation between French colonial administration and nationalist movements was in the Ivory Coast (1949–51).

Although the repression here was much less brutal than in Madagascar, many Ivorian leaders were imprisoned and several militants lost their lives. The only political bloodshed in French Equatorial Africa was connected with the territorial elections of 1952 when several dozen Africans were killed in Chad by French-led troops during clashes that resulted between rival political parties.

Another method of resistance to French rule took the form of strikes. These were expressions of African resentment of, and resistance to, the exploitation and discrimination that characterised the colonial economic system. This was a regular occurrence between 1946 and 1956 and was largely the work of trade union associations which provided a focus for airing economic grievances. Perhaps the most important of them was the 60-day strike in Guinea under the leadership of Sékou Touré. In the end the administration gave in. It was a great victory for Guinean democratic forces. Although the immediate years after the revolt led to a period of

---

[3] SMOTIG was the cover for forced and compulsory labour in Malagasy.

political lull in Madagascar, it recorded the greatest number of strikes of any French African colony within this period, forty in all.

The decade after the War witnessed important political activities in most parts of French Tropical Africa. Bloody confrontations occurred in Madagascar and in some parts of French West and Equatorial Africa while strikes were becoming increasingly commonplace. Student Organisations, notably the *Fédération des Etudiants d'Afrique Noire en France* (FEANF), based in Paris, carried on constant verbal and printed denunciation of French colonial rule. These activities and parallel developments in other colonial territories in Africa and Asia heralded the second phase of political activity in French Tropical Africa.

Before considering what happened during this second phase, we shall look briefly at development in Togo and the Cameroun whose special status as United Nations' trust territories guaranteed their different treatment from other French territories in Tropical Africa. The post-war reforms granted each territory a Representative Assembly with more powers over local matters than those of the other African territories. Furthermore, under the Trusteeship Agreement of 1950, France undertook to ensure the local inhabitants a share in the administration of the territory through the development of representative democratic bodies. Above all, the Trusteeship Agreement included an obligation to promote 'progressive development towards self-government or independence'. This obligation which sharply contradicted the principle established at Brazzaville in 1944 meant that for the French the objectives of political development in these territories had to be different from those for the other African territories.

Thus, while the word 'independence' was on the lips of only a few radicals in French West Africa it was a commonplace in party programmes in these two territories. The *Union des Populations du Cameroun* (UPC), the official Cameroun section of the RDA, championed the struggle against French rule in that territory. Between 1955 and 1957 it resorted to violence three times. It was dissolved after the first incidents but nevertheless for the next five years it dominated Cameroun political life through its clandestine organisations and from its bases abroad. Political life in Togo was more peaceful and in October 1956 it obtained a large degree of self-government as an autonomous republic within the French Union, a status it retained until independence in 1960. Cameroun followed in February 1957 and in 1958 it asked for independence which it obtained in 1960.

The Second Phase of Political Activity 1956–1960

Swift suppression of revolts and strikes by the French together with a general African acceptance of the post-war constitutional and institutional framework laid down by France were responsible for the absence of radical nationalist demands in the early fifties. This was true of all the territories in French Tropical Africa except the trust territories whose special status we have already examined. Thus, while Ghana and Nigeria were demanding *independence* from the British, French Tropical African territories demanded only concessions from the French. One such concession was the passage of the Labour Code in 1952, which accorded African workers many of the benefits enjoyed by their French counterparts.

Developments in British West Africa and in other colonial territories however contributed to the growing demand by French speaking African leaders for a greater measure of local self-government. Paradoxically, the French themselves virtually initiated the new reforms that came to be known as the *Loi Cadre* of 1956. Although pressure by African nationalist leaders influenced the French decision, the *Loi Cadre* was introduced by the French as much in response to the changing international situation and the disintegration of the rest of the French Empire. Indo-China had become independent after a bloody war, Morocco and Tunisia had just gained independence after prolonged struggles against the French and the Algerian Revolution was in full swing. The principle of autonomy had been conceded to Togo. Nearby Ghana and Nigeria were making progress towards self-government and ultimate independence, and independence was demanded by most shades of political opinion in the Cameroun. As the French Minister for Overseas Territories, Gaston Deferre, rightly remarked in his speech on the *Loi Cadre*, French territories in Tropical Africa could not be isolated from developments in the world at large.

Like the recommendations of the Brazzaville Conference, the basic principle of the *Loi Cadre* was conservative. Its reforms were designed 'to maintain and reinforce for many years to come the necessary union between Metropolitan France and the peoples of the overseas territories.' In spite of its conservatism, the *Loi Cadre* made large concessions to African desires for autonomy in local affairs. All African territories were given the elements of responsible democratic government, with legislative power over internal matters such as agriculture, health, customary law and the civil service. In each territorial Council of Government (*Conseil de Gouvernement*), the Governor was the President of the territorial Council of Ministers while the effective Prime Minister was to be the Vice-President, who was the political leader who could command a majority in the Assembly. Other provisions of the *Loi Cadre* included the abolition of the double electoral college and the introduction of universal suffrage, thus removing the shortcomings of the 1944–47 reforms.

One important question that demanded an urgent answer after the introduction of the *Loi Cadre* concerned the fate of the federations of West and Equatorial Africa. The effect of the provisions of the *Loi Cadre* was to weaken the government-general of the federations, much of whose power was devolved on the territories. Did France consciously decide to abolish the federations? What were the views of African leaders on the continued existence of federations?

These are questions that still arouse passion in French speaking Africa today and we can only try to suggest some answers to them.

Although both *L'Afrique Occidentale Française* (AOF) and *L'Afrique Equatoriale Française* (AEF) were affected by the provisions of the *Loi Cadre*, the issue of federation posed no immediate problems in the latter except as a result of decisions by the RDA leadership. In general there was relatively less political activity in AEF than in AOF and developments in the latter tended to dictate those in the former. Federation had been under discussion in AOF since 1953 and the new reforms only made

Félix Houphouët-Boigny, Ivory Coast   Léopold Sédar Senghor, Senegal

the issue more urgent. The chief protagonists of federation were members of a Parliamentary group in the French National Assembly known as the *Indépendants d'Outre-Mer* (IOM). They wanted the French Union to become a federal republic of which the federations of West and Equatorial Africa would be members. Such federations would be strong enough to counterbalance the dominant influence of France in the French Union. When the *Loi Cadre*, instead of strengthening the *Grand Conseils* of the federations, weakened them by giving a large measure of autonomy to the constituent territories, the federalists denounced it as balkanizing Africa. In the words of their leader, Léopold Sédar Senghor of Senegal:

'La Loi Cadre est une régression dans la mesure où elle balkanise les fédérations d'Afrique Noire.' [4]

Of course not all African politicians belonged to the IOM. In fact, the RDA Parliamentary group was much larger and the views of its leaders on federation were therefore crucial to the future of West Africa. At the RDA Congress at Bamako in September 1957, it was clear that the leader-

[4] 'The Loi Cadre is a backward movement in as much as it balkanizes the federations of Black Africa.'

ship of the RDA was divided on the issue. The Ivory Coast, under its leader, Houphouët-Boigny, who was also President of the RDA, wanted direct association with France instead of remaining in the federation. He wanted to avoid the Ivory Coast having to subsidize a political federation as she was subsidizing the administrative federation; secondly, he feared that a federation with responsible government would be dominated by radicals, who would become increasingly hostile to the more conservative policies he and the Ivory Coast section of the RDA were following. Sékou Touré of Guinea was the spokesman for those who supported the federa-

Sékou Touré, Guinea

tion. The only support given to the Ivoirian plan of direct association came from Gabon, whose political and economic position in Equatorial Africa was not dissimilar from that of the Ivory Coast in West Africa. The compromise resolution passed at the end of the Congress evaded solving the issue of federation versus direct association in any clear manner.

Some have claimed that France had in fact rejected the federal arguments by passing the *Loi Cadre*. The opposition of Houphouët to federation is often quoted in support of this, for Houphouët was a Minister without port-folio in the French Government and greatly influenced the *Loi Cadre* in its final shape. Another explanation for the French decision to dissolve the federation is that by dividing powers, she hoped to be able to weaken African unity and secure her control over the economy of the individual territories. It however remains a fact that the reforms introduced by the *Loi Cadre* granted important concessions to African politicians. The question whether France was motivated by liberal ideas or by a desire to balkanize Africa still needs further investigation. What is true is that the *Loi Cadre* heralded the end of the unity of AOF and AEF which had been nurtured by France for nearly sixty years.

Another question that was raised after 1956 was that of independence. We have seen how developments in other parts of the world contributed to the introduction of the *Loi Cadre* reforms. By 1957, with Ghana fully independent and with prospects for independence rising in Nigeria and Togo, the issue of independence could no longer be excluded from discussion in French West Africa. The important trade union association, the *Union Général des Travailleurs d'Afrique Noire* (UGTAN) and the students of FEANF championed the demand for independence. They supported the federalist thesis and urged the political leaders to demand independence. Thus, it was a FEANF representative who introduced the question of independence to the 1957 Bamako Congress of the RDA. Although no definite stand on the question was taken at the Congress, it was clear that some politicians covertly supported the demand; the march to independence could no more be halted.

This was the situation when De Gaulle came to power in 1958. The French dilemma in Algeria was the immediate and perhaps the most important factor responsible for De Gaulle's assumption of power and it was not surprising that one of his first actions was to reshape France's relationship with her overseas territories. He then introduced the idea of a Franco-African Community that would link France directly with the individual African territories as Houphouët had proposed. These territories were to be transformed into autonomous republics. The alternative to this was for African territories to take total independence outside the Community. No African leader was readily able to make up his mind and, sensing their indecision, De Gaulle decided to visit each territory in order to sell them the Community idea.

Before De Gaulle's historic tour, extensive discussion had taken place among African leaders and the various nationalist groups. The small Marxist-oriented *Parti Africain de L'Indépendence*, the FEANF and its Dakar-based section as well as the UGTAN openly agitated for independence. They obtained tangible if temporary support for their demand from the *Parti du Regroupement Africain* (a coalition of progressive and some moderate parties all over French West Africa) which at its Cotonou Conference in July 1958 demanded immediate and total independence.

At the end of De Gaulle's marathon tour, most African leaders were still unable to make up their minds and this dilemma was succinctly put by the Malagasy leader, Philibert Tsiranana who, in connection with De Gaulle's visit to Tananarive said: 'when I let my heart talk, I am a partisan of total and immediate independence; when I make my reason speak, I

French aid to Africa: President Tsirinana in a helicopter given to Madagascar by France

realize that it is impossible'. 'Reason' of course refers to economic realities, since independence outside the Community would mean loss of the very substantial financial assistance France had given to her African territories since the war. For some other African leaders, like Senghor of Senegal, their 'hearts' were not for independence outside the Community because its cultural dimension was nearly as important to them as its economic advantages.

The referendum on the Community was held in September 1958 and only Guinea rejected it, preferring, in the words of its leader, 'poverty in freedom to riches in slavery'. Within two years, the Franco-African Community collapsed and all its African members became independent sovereign states. Guinea's independence and the increased stature of its dynamic President, Sékou Touré, provoked radicals in other territories to demand immediate independence and more important still, it provoked the jealousy of other African leaders. Thus, in November 1959, Tsiranana of Malagasy (new name for Madagascar after 1958) flew to New York in company of Houphouët-Boigny to counter the growing prestige of independent Guinea in the United States.

In any case, we can see that the movement towards independence had become irreversible and France finally had to accept the situation. In December 1959, at the instance of the Mali Federation (made up of Senegal and the Soudan), France agreed to grant independence within the Community to any of her remaining African territories that might ask for it. The Mali Federation represented a final effort to keep alive the idea of federation in French West and French Equatorial Africa. Federalists from Senegal, Soudan, Upper Volta and Dahomey, with observers from Mauritania had met at Bamako in December 1958 to plan the Federation of Mali. France together with the Ivory Coast successfully brought pressure to bear on Upper Volta and Dahomey to withdraw from the federation and only Soudan and Senegal remained to constitute the Mali Federation in January 1959.

In French Equatorial Africa, more progress was made towards the continuation of the federal structure. A charter for a Union of Republics of Central Africa (URAC) was also drawn up and it was hoped that independence would be achieved for the URAC rather than for its component territories. Gabon declined to participate (in keeping with what the Gabonese RDA representatives had supported at Bamako in 1957) leaving the three other republics, Congo-Brazzaville, Chad and the Central African Republic (known as Oubangi-Chari until 1958) to sign the charter at Fort Lamy in May 1960.

Congo-Brazzaville's membership of URAC lasted for only about three months. Political developments in neighbouring Congo-Kinshasa which Patrice Lumumba led into independence in June pushed her to search for separate sovereignty. The two Congos are not only neighbours but they also have some common ethnic groups and a sort of rivalry had developed between the respective leaderships. In the circumstance, the Congo-Brazzaville leadership felt that a separate diplomatic representation and membership in the United Nations were indispensable and this led to the withdrawal of Congo-Brazzaville from the URAC in July. By August, URAC had collapsed and the four republics became independent and separate.

The trust territories, Cameroun and Togo, were the first to achieve independence, the former in January 1960 and the latter in April. The Republic of Malagasy and the Mali Federation became independent in June and the other republics followed suit in the remaining months of 1960. By August 1960, the Mali Federation had collapsed because of the differences in political outlook between moderate Senegal and radical Soudan. Soudan took up the name of the Federation in September after Senegal had proclaimed its separate independence. The only form of inter-state grouping that survived independence was the *Conseil de l'Entente* (the Council of Understanding) made up of the Ivory Coast, Upper Volta, Dahomey and Niger (and since 1965 Togo) and sponsored by Houphouët-Boigny.

This is understandable since Houphouët's Ivory Coast was able to dominate these poor territories, two of which, Upper Volta and Niger, supplied her with her labour force, whereas she could not have dominated Soudan and Senegal. Needless to say, the *Conseil de l'Entente* enjoyed (and still enjoys) French active support and encouragement.

Conclusion

In this article we have highlighted some of the major events in the progress towards independence in French Tropical Africa. One of the striking points in our account is the uniformity in French policy, a uniformity that was unknown in British West Africa. The reforms of 1944–47, the *Loi Cadre* of 1956 and the Franco-African Community proposals all applied throughout French Tropical Africa (except in the Trust Territories which followed separate lines after 1950). This uniformity in French colonial policy was paralleled by striking resemblances among African nationalist movements. Thus, the RDA had influence in most territories and until the independence of Guinea, the UGTAN grouped most of the trade unions in these territories.

France until the very end believed that the 'umbilical cord' tying her African territories to herself must never be broken. This explains why one form of association was tried after the other. In 1946 it was the French Union and it was succeeded by the Franco-African Community idea in 1958. When Guinea dared opt for independence in 1958, she was heavily punished for it (the famous withdrawal of all movable French property in the country!) and it was not until December 1959 that France agreed to concede independence without Guinea-style consequences. Cartesian reasoning proved most inadequate for dealing with colonial problems. By her eleventh-hour consent to grant independence to her African territories, France merely confirmed a permanent characteristic of her colonial policy, lateness to concede reforms. In the end French desire to maintain continued association has not failed; today, eight years after independence, the 'umbilical cord' still attaches most of the former French Tropical African States to 'mother' France culturally, politically and economically.

Notes

> *Indigénat*—A judicial system imported from Algeria reserved for Africans with the status of '*sujet*'. Under it, they were subjected to imprisonment without trial by the French administration.
>
> *Corvée*—Forced labour.
>
> *Sujet*—This was the status of most Africans until 1946. The term is used in contrast to a '*citoyen*' (citizen). The *sujet* had no rights and was subjected to both the *indigénat* and the *corvée*.
>
> AEF—*L'Afrique Equatoriale Française.*
>
> AOF—*L'Afrique Occidentale Française.*
>
> FEANF—*Fédération des Etudiants d'Afrique Noire en France.*
>
> IOM—*Indépendants d'outre-Mer.*
>
> PCF—The French Communist Party.
>
> RDA—*Rassemblement Democratique Africain.*
>
> SMOTIG—*Service de la Main-d'oeuvre pour les Travaux d'Interest-Général.*
>
> UGTAN—*Union Général des Travailleurs d'Afrique Noire.*
>
> UPC—*Union des Populations du Cameroun* (official Cameroun Section of RDA).
>
> URAC—Union of Republics of Central Africa.
>
> VVS—*Vy Vato Sakelika.*

Further Reading

HODGKIN, T., *Nationalism in Colonial Africa*, London, 1956. (Covers the period up to 1956.)

CROWDER, M., 'Independence as a Goal in French West African Politics: 1944–60'. W. Lewis ed. *French Speaking Africa—The Search for Identity*, New York, 1965.

The Path to Independence in French Africa: Recent Historiography

David E. Gardinier
Marquette University

INTRODUCTION

A quarter of a century has now passed since the territories of French West Africa, French Equatorial Africa, Cameroon, and Togo achieved their independence from France. Whereas scholars at that time and shortly thereafter looked at the period of decolonization[1] (roughly from 1940 to 1960) in relation to the colonial period which preceded it, the scholars of the late 1970s and 1980s have had the additional advantage of being able to view that era in relation to the period of national independence or neo-colonialism which has followed it. In general, it is the post-independence perspective far more than the availability of additional archival materials or other new sources, such as the memoirs of participants and observers, that has informed the bulk of the research and writing of the past decade. For independence has turned out to be, in most cases, largely formal and limited to the political sphere.

This should not be surprising in the light of the policies France followed in the era after the Second World War. Independence, even in the long term, was not the goal towards which France directed its territories; rather it sought to promote the advancement of the Africans within a constitutional framework that ruled out the possibility of independence and left Frenchmen dominant for the foreseeable future. At the same time the intensified efforts towards the economic and financial integration of these territories within the Fourth French Republic and the cultural assimilation of their elites not merely perpetuated but actually increased their dependence on France. In addition, the process by which independence ultimately took place involved the dismantling of the federations of French West Africa and French Equatorial Africa; the transfer of power to the individual territories which composed them, while satisfying the wishes of some of their leaders, further contributed to making their independence a formality and continuing dependence upon France the reality.

This article reviews some of the more important scholarship of the late

1970s and 1980s which contributes to an understanding of decolonization in the French territories in general, and of the path to independence in particular. Readers who are interested in critiques of the previous scholarship on these subjects should consult the author's historiographical essays in two volumes edited by Prosser Gifford and Wm. Roger Louis, *France and Britain in Africa* (1971) and *Transfer of Power in Africa* (1982).[2] They may wish later to refer to a forthcoming volume of case studies of decolonization and transfer of power in Africa, by the same editors, in which I am responsible for an annotated bibliography on the territories of French Africa.

THE BRAZZAVILLE CONFERENCE AND CONSTITUTION-MAKING (1945–1946)

Very little new research has occurred on the Brazzaville Conference of January–February 1944 at which the Free French government formulated new colonial policies for the postwar era. The reason may well be that these matters have been so thoroughly and carefully covered in the penetrating analysis by D. Bruce Marshall, *The French Colonial Myth and Constitution-Making in the Fourth Republic* (1973). Laurent Gbagbo's *Réflexions sur la Conférénce de Brazzaville* (1978) contains documents preceded by a brief essay. Gbagbo composed the latter in order to correct the misconception of Ivorian students that the conference was called in order to plan the decolonization of the French Empire. In reality, it was organized to reform colonial rule in Black Africa in order to make continued French dominance acceptable to the populations who had contributed much to the success of the Free French movement and the war effort.

Gbagbo uses only the published documentation from the conference and a very limited range of secondary works in French in composing his essay. He does not employ archival materials or such standard studies as Bruce Marshall's. He puts forth the thesis that the conference was part of a French tradition of seeking to deal with a national crisis by mobilizing colonial resources. Just as the conference of 1917 responded to wartime needs and the economic conference of December 1934–April 1935 to the problems of the world depression, Brazzaville was a response to the problems of the Second World War. France therein sought to reform the colonial regime to the extent necessary to mobilize African resources to aid French recovery and to maintain the French position as a world power. While Gbagbo may be correct in seeing the conference as part of a French tradition, it was shaped in a very real sense by the very different circumstances of the Second World War and has far greater importance for the French role in Africa than its predecessors.

René Pleven, who served Free France as commissioner of the colonies, has presented a valuable *témoignage* (1980) on the conference. Pleven points out that the immense sacrifices of the Africans during the war ruled out the possibility of returning to the pre-war colonial order. Furthermore, the war brought immense psychological changes among the colonized that necessitated political changes. Pleven saw the need, without waiting for the end of the war, not only to plan for these changes but also to be prepared immediately at the liberation of France to educate the metropolitan populations, who had been cut off from contacts with Black Africa, about the necessity for fundamental revisions.

At the conference itself, questions of economic and social progress were important. But it was the need for the Africans to participate in the management of their own affairs and in the formulation of the postwar constitutional arrangements that took primacy. De Gaulle endorsed Pleven's proposals, which he had drafted after consultation with the territorial governors and the top officials of the provisional government at Algiers. Though only French citizens, mainly functionaries, participated in the formal discussions of the draft texts, African évolués made written statements and dialogued with the participants after the sessions. The views of canton chief Fily Dabo Sissoko, a schoolteacher from the French Sudan (Mali), and Jean-Rémy Ayouné of Gabon were particularly influential.

The question of the mode of political participation by the Africans found the French officials divided. While some were prepared to grant them political autonomy, others feared that such arrangements might be a step along the path to independence and separation from France, a destination that they all rejected.

Circumstances saw Pleven transferred in November 1944 from the Overseas Ministry to the Ministry of Finances so that he personally was unable to guide the Brazzaville proposals through the constituent assemblies. He was disappointed that the Africans received only token representation in the decision-making bodies of the French Union. He further regretted that the constitution makers did not make the Assembly of the French Union a genuine colonial parliament with decision-making powers; instead, it was only a consultative body. Both metropolitan and colonial matters were decided in the National Assembly and the Council of the Republic (Senate), into which the Second Constituent Assembly had integrated the overseas territories. By effectively preventing their movement towards distinct political entities, these arrangements very much limited their options for future political evolution.

POLITICAL EVOLUTION

Joseph-Roger de Benoist served in the 1950s as the editor of *Afrique Nouvelle,* a Catholic newspaper in Dakar that was sympathetic to African aspirations for liberation from colonial rule. Products of his subsequent training as a historian at the University of Paris are two works, *La Balkanisation de l'A.O.F.* (1979) and *L'A.O.F. de 1944 à 1960* (1982).

The subjects which the author treats were already dealt with rather thoroughly in the late 1950s and early 1960s in both journalistic and academic works. But he gives some aspects of them new authenticity because of his contacts with both the African and colonial French participants at the time and in later years. He seems particularly close to two Senegalese, Lépold Sédar Senghor and Doudou Guèye, leader of the portion of the interterritorial R.D.A. which followed Houphouët in his break with the French Communist Party in 1950. De Benoist also had access to a wealth of political ephemera. He utilizes the existing literature in English, which some French scholars and even more Francophone Africans still omit from their researches.

While his sections in the second work on the evolution of the labor unions and education frequently cite records of the colonial government, his more extensive sections on political evolution in both works rarely do. Thus the eventual opening of the metropolitan archives and the complete colonial ones, both of the government-general at Dakar and of the individual territories in their capitals, may reveal additional details or new information and ultimately lead to further precisions and some clarifications. Until then, these two works, which are extremely detailed for political questions, provide useful accounts from the perspective of one writing two decades after the events of which he was an active observer.

Balkanisation[3] reviews the formation of the colonial federation of French West Africa, its structure, and its functioning from 1895 to 1957. It discusses the factors favorable to the maintenance of federal ties and those unfavorable to such unity. It looks at the criticisms of the government-general by settlers, officials, and African politicians along with the various projects for reorganization put forth during the Fourth Republic. The most original section of the book deals with the origins of the Loi-Cadre of June 23, 1956, and the decrees of 1957 implementing it, which dismantled the federation and established decision-making institutions at the territorial level. One sees the debates at three levels—metropolitan, federal, and territorial—and within the executive and legislative bodies at each level, and their various interactions.

De Benoist states that the decision to dismantle the federations (French Equatorial Africa as well as French West Africa) as taken by Overseas Minister Gaston Defferre and by Félix Houphouët-Boigny of the Ivory Coast, who was also a minister in the government headed by Socialist Guy Mollet. Defferre had originally favored retention of an economic federation but ultimately supported the proposal of his predecessor, Pierre-Henri Teitgen of the Mouvement Républicain Populaire, for outright suppression of the government-general and federation. Senghor, by contrast, while supporting the Loi-Cadre's establishment of executive and legislative institutions, wanted comparable federal structures created also. But Senghor could not convince Houphouët and most other African leaders other than Sékou Touré of Guinea that the absence of a federation directed by Africans would mean the strengthening of the metropolitan government's role in each territory. Though the territorial assemblies of Senegal, Guinea, Sudan (Mali), and Dahomey (Benin) opposed ending all federal ties, they were unable to prevent the replacement of the federation by a "group of territories" or to secure its reconstitution.

The study then turns to detailed yet clear description and analysis of the regrouping of the political parties and movements in French West Africa in the light of the issues of federation and future political evolution. It shows how the antifederation forces led by Houphouët proved stronger than the profederation ones led by Senghor.

The collapse of the Fourth Republic and the birth of the Fifth Republic gave the partisans of federation a new chance to reestablish ties. Their failure, especially in the absence of support from de Gaulle's regime, is ably related, as is the creation of the Mali Federation and its breakup, and the organization of the Ivorian-dominated Conseil de l'Entente.

Ultimately de Benoist holds the Socialist Party and the M.R.P. responsible for practicing a policy of divide-and-rule which prevented the kind of African unity in 1946 and after that would have promoted interterritorial cooperation. It was deputies from these two parties who headed the overseas ministry during the Fourth Republic. He seems to hold the metropolitan parties more responsible for the breakup of the federation than such intra-African rivalries as those between Senghor and Houphouët. He questions whether Sékou Touré would have rejected membership in the French Community in September 1958 if a federation had been maintained.

The second and larger work by de Benoist reviews the evolution of French West Africa from 1944 to 1960. It contains practically no discussion of the impact of the Second World War or the reactions of the Africans to Vichy and later Free French rule or of the rivalries between the two competitors. Instead the narrative begins with the Brazzaville Conference as the point of departure for a reformed colonial order and then turns to the two constituent assemblies and their reforms.[4]

The rest of the story from 1946 to 1960 is a rather familiar one. Just two points require commentary. Following Doudou Guèye (1975), de Benoist explains Houphouëts termination of R.D.A. parliamentary ties with the Communist Party in October 1950 and his subsequent compromises with the colonial administration and local French interests as an abandonment of an abstract anti-imperialist, anticolonialist ideology that did not serve African interests. By refraining from indicating what those interests were, de Benoist fails to provide a complete and therefore accurate account of this important turning point in Ivorian and West African history.

In his conclusion, echoing Henri Brunschwig (1963), de Benoist sees the African elite as having passed through three stages of awakening between 1944 and 1959: (1) the acquisition of a consciousness of their status as colonial persons; (2) the utilization of the possibilities which the "semi-assimilation" of the 1946 constitution offered them to gain the maximum of rights; (3) the conviction that only political independence would permit them to reconquer and affirm their Negro-African identity. The third stage of this description applies to Senghor, Sékou Touré, and others, but not to Houphouët. Given the latter's emphasis on self-liberation through economic advancement and his subsequent attitudes towards African languages and culture, this seems very wrong. The essays in the collection edited by Fauré and Médard (1982) on state and society in independent Ivory Coast provide much contradictory evidence as do the writings of Yves Person, to be discussed below.

The volume, *Transfer of Power in Africa: Decolonization, 1940–1960*, edited by Prosser Gifford of the Woodrow Wilson Center in Washington and Wm. Roger Louis of the University of Texas, contains five chapters which deal entirely or partially with French Black Africa in the postwar period in the light of developments since independence. (By contrast, the essays on French Africa in *Decolonisation and After* [1980], edited by W. H. Morris-Jones and Georges Fischer, deal almost entirely with Franco-African relations since independence in light of the periods of decolonization and colonial rule.) The various authors refer to a common outline of questions about decolonization and transfer of power, which facilitates comparisons among the French territories and between them and the British, Belgian, and Portuguese.

Henri Brunschwig of the University of Paris in his chapter contends that just as French colonization in Black Africa was able to succeed, on the whole, because of African acceptance or collaboration, so decolonization had to take place when the most advanced Africans opposed the continuation of French dominance and requested independence.[5]

Until 1956 France was resolved not to decolonize but to reform colonial rule. The African elite worked within this framework until they could clearly see that it would never permit them to make the basic decisions about their own affairs. At the same time, they noticed that other African countries, no more or even less advanced than they, were moving towards self-rule. Decolonization thus began, as a result of African pressures, in the mid-1950s with the passage of the Loi-Cadre, which was the work of the leading African politicians in the French National Assembly as much as of Gaston Defferre and the government. In most territories power at this point was transferred to the very same political elite who had been collaborating with the French since the Second World War.

While Defferre and the government sided with Houphouët on the question of the breakup of the French West Africa federation, it is by no means clear in Brunschwig's view that the government was thereby opting for a divide-and-rule principle. He argues that it might have been easier to influence a single federal government than many territorial ones. Benefiting from the independence which ultimately resulted from the direction taken in the Loi-Cadre were those new states which now received greater means from abroad for their economic development and those foreign powers, whether capitalist or socialist, that furnished these means and expanded their political influence. "Decolonization," in Brunschwig's view, "has engendered a neo-colonialism under the aegis of the former collaborators," (p. 223), Guinea, of course, being an exception.

Brunschwig's major thesis that decolonization came above all because of the pressures from the Africans seems basically sound. It did not arise, as was the case of some of the British and Dutch territories, because of international pressures such as those exerted by the United States. But Brunschwig's contention that "contrary to experience elsewhere, even that of France in other theaters such as Indochina and the Maghreb, colonization and decolonization took place within a watertight compartment" (p. 223) needs some qualification. The willingness of the government in Paris to accede to African pressures was enhanced by its experience in Indo-China and the colonial war in Algeria. It was evident to its ministers that French interests could very likely be safeguarded despite the granting of independence because of the willingness of the Africans to make cooperation agreements in the economic, military, and cultural areas.

Yves Person (d. 1982) of the University of Paris was a Breton nationalist and a member of the Comité Directeur of the Socialist Party. Both of these orientations influenced his scholarship on Black Africa where he served as a colonial administrator. His chapter takes its chief importance from its interpretations, in part drawn from the perspectives of the two decades after the events it describes.

For Person as for others the postwar period is divided into two uneven portions, 1945–1946, the era of renovated colonialism, and 1956–1960, the era of real decolonization which led to independence. 1945–1956 is itself divided at 1950, the moment at which the R.D.A. abandoned its links with the Communist Party and thereafter cooperated or sought accommodations with the colonial administration. Person's interpretation of the conduct of Houphouët in this process is close to that of Tony Smith as expressed in another chapter in the Gifford-Louis volume and in *Pattern of Imperialism* (1981), and different from that of de Benoist. In Person's opinion Houphouët's alliance with the Communist Party was always a tactical one, not an ideological one. It was a product of the anti-colonialist struggle forged at Bamako in 1946 with the organization of the Rassemblement Démocratique Africain in response to the renewed activity of French colonial interests. Person contends that Houphouët was fearful of the African masses; he felt, as a traditional chief and head of the African planters organization, that bourgeois interests could be better pursued by close alliance with France. Person credits François Mitterand for convincing Houphouët of the folly of maintaining Communist ties and of the wisdom of forging new ones with moderate socialist elements such as his Union Démocratique et Sociale de la Résistance instead. Moreover, Houphouët and the leadership of the R.D.A. in the Ivory Coast had embraced the values of French civilization and had rejected an African identity. In Person's view Houphouët later rejected the continuation of the federation of French West Africa not merely to serve the Ivory Coast's economic interests but to avoid becoming tied to a federal regime that might be dominated by revolutionary radicals from other territories. De Gaulle's government made Houphouët the architect of the chapters on the Community in the constitution of 1958, which hindered independence and made federation exremely difficult. Later Houphouët himself unintentionally set off the movement to independence by his successful efforts to restrict the Mali Federation to only Senegal and the Sudan and to create the Conseil de l'Entente.

Going back to 1945–1946, Person blames the Socialist minister for Overseas France, Marius Moutet, and his party for destroying inter-African unity at Bamako by pressuring the Senegalese Socialists to stay away. This action helped Senghor to see that the nationalist ideology of the Socialist Party blocked both the restoration of an African identity and political liberation. Thereafter he created his own territorial socialist party, the Bloc Démocratique Senegalais, based on rural areas, and captured power from Lamine Guèye's Senegalese section of the French Socialist Party, which preserved links with the parent body despite its positions.

Person has interesting comments on the Loi-Cadre, some of them based on conversations with Gaston Defferre. Person claims that it was the independence of the Gold Coast (Ghana) that was decisive in promoting a desire for independence among French West Africa's leaders. While Defferre was personally opposed to Balkanisation of the federation, he did not fight to keep it. At the same time the colonial administration strongly supported fragmentation. The Loi-Cadre, which created embryonic executives and legislatures in the individual territories, left open the question of federation. Person points out that the Loi-Cadre, which was at odds with the French tradition of centralization and really violated the constitution, was a "cunningly evolutionary document." (p. 162).

Person contends that General de Gaulle is wrongly credited as a great decolonizer.[6] As late as the drafting of the 1958 Constitution, the general thought that political independence lay in an unspecified future; he expected, however, that strengthened economic and cultural ties along with the French military presence would serve to protect French interests whenever independence did arrive.

A most important aspect of Person's chapter is the cultural question. Whereas Senghor and the Senegalese saw the necessity of revaluating an African identity, which French colonialism had made an exceptional effort to negate and destroy, Houphouët and the Ivorians did not. In fact, they have pursued policies which ignore and therefore further weaken the traditional culture and indigenous languages. They thereby have created an even larger cleavage between the Gallicized ruling class and the masses of people with disastrous consequences for the development of the country. They have perpetuated and intensified those aspects of the colonial system which reduced the masses to the level of marginal exploited objects while they themselves pursue self-enrichment through obtaining a larger share of profits from the global economic system.

Person pursues the cultural question in greater detail in an article "Colonisation et Decolonisation en Côte d'Ivoire" (1981).[7] The findings of Y. A. Fauré & J.-F. Medard, eds., *État et bourgeoisie en Côte d'Ivoire* (1982), for the most part substantiate the views of Person. The authors in this collection examine political and economic developments since independence in the light of earlier periods. The chapter by D. S. Bach on post-1960 foreign relations reviews the political developments from 1956 to 1960 in order to show the remarkable continuities in relations with France under Houphouët.

Elikia M'Bokolo, a Zairian who teaches at the University of Paris, is the first to deal comprehensively with French policy in the four countries of French Equatorial Africa in the postwar period. French Equatorial Africa was smaller in population and far less advanced than French West Africa. In M'Bokolo's view, it was the domain of brutal economic exploitation and uncompromising political domination before the Second World War. The general lines of French policy from 1945 were the same in both French West Africa and French Equatorial Africa but the chronology and pace of events were different. As in French West Africa, 1946–1956 was the era of the transformation of the colonial regime in order better to perpetuate it, while 1956–1960 saw gradual French resignation to the granting of independence. Among the differences in French Equatorial Africa were the absence of continuity in the governor-general's policy and instability of personnel. French colonial policy was decided at different times in Brazzaville and in Paris but the immobilism of the territorial governors and the hostility of French economic interests braked the centrally-decided reforms.

The first initiatives that changed the course of French policy came from Félix Éboué, the Free French governor-general from 1940 to 1944. It was Éboué's ideas that subsequently provided the guidelines for the Brazzaville Conference. Éboué's reforms were achieved more at the doctrinal level than at the practical level. Éboué focused more on the renovation of traditional society and institutions, including the chiefs, than on urban society and the educated elites who would become the more important collaborators of the postwar period. Nevertheless he tried to improve the status of the *évolués* and to give them a role in municipal government at the same time that he helped the masses by ending forced labor. He greatly expanded educational opportunities, now including the advanced or post-primary level, and enlisted the help of the missions to this end through greater subsidies.

From 1944 to 1952, in M'Bokolo's view, the intitiatives for change came from the metropolitan level with the various reforms of the Fourth Republic. The First Plan accelerated economic integration with the metropolis and accentuated the outward direction of the local economy. Then in the period 1952–1956/57 initiatives passed back to the federation to implement the reforms. Governor-General Paul Chauvet (1951–1958) sought to eliminate colonialism while preparing the Africans for self-rule. He sought to satisfy the aspirations of the masses and to involve the elite in government. Public employment for the educated elite isolated them from the masses and conditioned them to come to terms with the French. Thus it was easy for the French to transfer power to them between 1956–57 and 1960, in another era of metropolitan initiatives. Just a few trade unionists and intellectuals wanted independence. Only when neighboring territories began to move towards independence did the Equatorial African leaders also seek it. Neocolonial cooperation agreements resulted both from the French determination to preserve their interests and the Africans' desire for a privileged relationship. The process of decolonization from 1956 to 1960 was controlled by Paris because the political elite did not challenge the colonial regime in any important way. The African elite conceived of independence as the obtaining of powerful positions without change in society's structure or in the relationship with France. This is why neocolonialism replaced colonialism.

In a related article (1981) M'Bokolo tries to explain the socio-economic bases for the absence of an anticolonial movement among the most politically advanced elements during the period 1940–1960.

M'Bokolo's sources are exclusively published documents and secondary materials. No interviews are listed and no archives cited. Further modifications of his interpretations are therefore possible if not too likely.

Gaston Defferre has presented a brief but revealing *témoignage* (1980) on his role in formulating the Loi-Cadre and the decrees implementing it. He states that he was always opposed to the policy of integration embodied in the October 1946 constitution. He declares that the autonomy granted in 1956–57 was intended to be a step on the way to independence, peacefully and with the continued aid of France. While for him it might have been, it is clear that for others the concessions of the Loi-Cadre were a means of delaying or preventing independence. According to Defferre the dismantling of the federations of French West Africa and French Equatorial Africa and the granting of autonomy at the territorial level corresponded to the national aspirations of the overseas representatives. The Loi-Cadre also sought to accelerate the economic evolution in order to raise living standards and to promote fruitful relations between them and France.

There are a number of works on individual countries that should be mentioned. Philippe Decraene, long-time *Le Monde* correspondent and now head of the Centre des Hautes Études Administratives Modernes in Paris, has devoted more than half of his introductory work on Mali (1980) to the political and economic evolution since 1945. Also authoritative because of their authors' long association with the countries about which they write are the chapters on the periods since 1940 in Jean Chappelle, *Le Peuple Tchadien* (1980), and Marcel Soret, *Histoire du Congo, capitale Brazzaville* (1978). Jean-François Bayart, *L'État au Cameroun* (1979) includes a detailed discussion of the political evolution of Cameroon in the late 1950s and the French role in instilling the pliant regime headed by Ahmadou Ahidjo after they had crushed the U.P.C. nationalists by force. Laurent Gbagbo (1982) focuses upon the role of Houphouët and the well-to-do African planter class in the political evolution of the Ivory Coast from 1944 to 1960. He contends that once these elements had achieved security for their economic interests, they were content to compromise with French colonialism and later to accept a neocolonialist relationship. The work's greatest originality lies in its sections on the economic aspects of the Second World War in relation to the political mobilization of the African planters. Its greatest merit is its careful documentation of the evolution of the R.D.A. leadership's positions, which support the interpretations of Person cited above.

Finn Fuglestad's history of Niger (1983) has a fine chapter on the period 1945–1960. The implementation of the institutions of the Fourth Republic brought into being a new socio-economic group, an urban bureaucracy, to whom the French would transfer power between 1957 and 1960. This group would ruthlessly exploit the rural masses while maintaining a close privileged relationship with France after 1960. Neither the reforms of 1945–1946 nor the decolonization of 1957–1960 resulted from pressures within Niger but from external factors. In 1960 France exchanged a formal empire for an informal one. Nationalism, to the extent it has existed in Niger, has postdated independence rather than preceding it.

Frederick Pedler, a British colonial official and later Unilever executive, in *Main Currents of West African History, 1940–1978* includes clear summaries on the evolution of the French territories. They have usefulness for those who do not read French and desire an introduction mainly to the political and economic aspects. This work must be used with some caution, however, because of the author's faulty understanding of the French constitutional and institutional settings.

Finally, recent years have seen the appearance of some important research on the history of trade unions in French West Africa, including their role in the political emancipation of the territories from colonial rule. George Martens, an American scholar, used interviews and labor publications for a general account on all of French West Africa (1980–1981) and a specific one on just Senegal (1983). Philippe Dewitte (1981) has treated the largest trade union, the Confédération Générale du Travail, between 1945 and 1957. His criticisms of French syndicalist leaders provoked a response from Paul Delanoue and a reply by Dewitte (1983). Delanoue was an active member of the Communist-linked C.G.T. teachers' union in Senegal in the late 1940s as was Jean-Suret Canale, the author of a general article on union protests (1977) and a specific one on the important railway workers strike of 1947–1948 (1978). Taken as a whole, these studies have provided a much more authoritative and carefully nuanced description and analysis of the political dimension than heretofore available.

Considerations of space prevent a setting forth of most of their important findings or interpretations. But two points may be noted. First of all, the recent research tends in general to support the revisionist position of Christopher Allen of the University of Edinburgh in his "Union-Party Relationships in Francophone West Africa: A Critique of 'Téléguidage' Interpretations" (1975). Therein he attacked the generally held view that the unions' actions in such major developments as the 1947–48 railway workers strike and the formation of an autonomous confederation in 1955–56 were controlled *(téléguidé)* by certain French and African parties. In his reply to Delanoue, Dewitte argues that the failure of the French leaders of the C.G.T. in France and West Africa to understand the African desire for autonomy delayed its achievement to the point that the unions could no longer play a key role in maintaining the federation of French West Africa or in obtaining independence. Union weakness and disunity allowed the conclusion of arrangements favorable to French interests as well as a politically and economically catastrophic Balkanization. A strong Pan-

Africanist movement, if organized earlier, might have helped to block such a harmful evolution.

ECONOMIC EVOLUTION

This section is concerned with the ways in which the economic evolution influenced the course of the various territories towards independence. An important article by Jean-Claude Barthélémy (1980) deals with the evolution of the economies of French West Africa and Togo from 1946 to 1960. It is based on the available published literature—statistics, government documents, and secondary works. Taken as a whole, it shows that French policy provided the coastal territories, in particular, with an infrastructure which permitted greater production of primary materials (coffee, cocoa, palm products, groundnuts, bananas, woods). The costs of constructing, maintaining, and operating this infrastructure, which also included health and educational facilities, created severe financial problems for the territories. Only with French aid, both before and after independence, could they keep such an infrastructure functioning.

The increased exports, while providing greater revenues, further integrated the West African economy into the French economy (and after 1957, into the Common Market's as well) and made it much more vulnerable to variations in world market and climatic conditions. By 1960, the nine countries were far more economically and financially dependent upon France and the outside world than they had been previously. Furthermore, 44 percent of the expenditures for infrastructure went to just two territories (Senegal [25 percent] and the Ivory Coast [19 percent]), while the Sahelian territories of Mauritania, Sudan (Mali), and Niger received very little. Most of the facilities were concentrated in urban areas, thus contributing to the rural exodus and the growth of the coastal cities. The dismantling of the federation in 1957 and after would require the establishment or expansion of various administrative services in the particular territories, at further continuing cost to their already overloaded budgets. Only the Ivory Coast proved capable of continued prosperity in the 1960s on the basis of the postwar system; Senegal, by contrast, stagnated.

The volume of essays on Senegal edited by Rita Cruise O'Brien (1979) of the Institute of Development Studies of the University of Sussex deals with the entire modern period of the economic history of Senegal. The authors seek to understand the precise reasons for the stagnation of the economy growing out of the country's dependent relationship with France. In her chapter Mrs. Cruise O'Brien contends that the French and Lebanese presence effectively barred the growth of an African capitalist class during the colonial period. Further, the poor quality of African manpower training in the colonial context, especially between the Second

World War and independence, reinforced reliance on a substantial French labor force with limited skills and training while blocking the advancement of Senegalese workers. The economy at independence could only function with the continued presence of French personnel, including those in the government departments responsible for planning and directing the economy and finances. In her essay in Morris-Jones and Fischer, "Factors of Dependence: Senegal and Kenya" (1980), Cruise O'Brien provides further insights into the findings of her group of scholars by comparing them with those of Colin Leys on Kenya in the same period.

Jean Suret-Canale, a Marxist economic geographer, is well-known for his detailed history of French colonialism in Africa. In an important chapter in Gifford and Louis (1982), he deals with the economic evolution of the French territories from 1945 to 1960, in part in light of post-independence developments. He concludes that decolonization did not occur in the economic sphere nor was there an economic transfer of power that paralleled the process leading to political independence. Rather, what took place in the economic field in the postwar period was an accentuation of colonialist features, namely the much increased integration of the French territories into the western capitalist economy and particularly an intensified subordination to the profit objectives and exploitative aims of their large companies.

The chapter is particularly valuable because it describes the mechanisms of the colonial economy with both precision and detail. It deals perceptively with the changes that took place as a result of greater state involvement in new sectors. It assesses the impact of the FIDES-CCFOM loans and grants under the various four-year plans. The bulk of the investments went to infrastructure, which permitted the expansion of production of export crops and the further development of mining. Mining and such import-substitution industries as food products, textiles, and construction materials showed the greatest expansion in the secondary sector. The most radical innovations in the economy during these fifteen years were the rise of extractive industries and the often related use of hydroelectric resources. Given the fact that part of the investment credits of the French state was spent directly in France and another part repatriated in profits, only an estimated fifteen percent of the investments of the First Four-Year Plan actually remained in Africa. While the French state provided approximately 70 percent of the total public investments during the period 1946–1960 (569.8 billion CFA francs out of 820.9), it required the African territories to contribute the remaining 30 percent (251.1 billion), some of which clearly benefited French interests more than African ones. (An article by Abdoulaye Diallo (1980) shows that the road network in the Ivory Coast financed by the plans was designed primarily to benefit local French interests rather than Ivorian ones.)

Suret-Canale also deals with those aspects of the social and political evolution that were linked to the economic developments. The postwar period saw the appearance of a much larger African bureaucracy with better educated elements and a greatly enlarged salaried working class. Both of them would play important roles in political emancipation. Two smaller bourgeois groups also increased in size and influence: African merchants and freight carriers, on the one hand, and an African planter class employing African labor, on the other. The latter was the most numerous in the Ivory Coast where it became the backbone of the R.D.A. and the anticolonialist struggle. For Suret-Canale, it was a struggle with only anticolonialist and democratic objectives until 1957, at which time the question of independence began to be raised. In his view the Loi-Cadre and the overseas provisions of the 1958 Constitution were French concessions intended to obstruct independence rather than stages preparatory to it. Evidence for his position is the treatment meted out to Guinea, which in 1958 opted for an independence that in 1960 had to be given to all territories on much better terms.

Independence saw the emergence of internal conflicts of interest that had been submerged during the struggle for political emancipation. In French Black Africa the agrarian bourgeoisie and commercial strata, which have been so politically important elsewhere in the Third World, have not played strong postindependence political roles. The outstanding feature of this era has been the emergence of the bureaucratic stratum, which replaced the European functionaries and now manages the state for the benefit of foreign interests and its own personal financial advantage. Thus while direct political domination has ended, the economic realities have remained much the same. Even in Guinea, where a socialist regime totally nationalized commerce, banking, industry, and infrastructure, the principal enterprises in the mining sector, the sources of the greatest revenues for the state, are still partially owned and completely operated by foreign capitalists.

The question of the creation of dependency through the institutional structures of the postwar period and of its perpetuation after independence has been studied in the case of one of the least advanced territories by a British scholar, Richard Higgott. In "Structural Dependency and Decolonisation in a West African Landlocked State: Niger" (1980), he poses two questions: (1) to what extent and in what ways did French colonialism create a situation of structural dependence? (2) to what extent have the relationships created in the colonial period been modified by the decolonization process?

During the postwar period Niger's economy was based on exports of groundnuts and cotton directed overseas. Although Niger received little aid from the plans, its infrastructural and administrative services grew two to three times as fast as the material of the economy. Between 1957 and 1960 France transferred power to the Parti Progressiste Nigérien whom the chiefs and French administrators saw as better preserving their interests than Djibo Bakary's more radical Sawaba alternative. According to Higgott, "if to decolonise a state is to dismantle the politico-administrative, cultural, financial, economic, judicial and educational procedures of the colonial period, then clearly decolonisation in Niger did not accompany the accession to formal independence." (p. 48). The ruling class, "intellectuals, bureaucrats, and managers of the coercive apparatus of the state", sought to preserve French links while increasing its range of international partners. Top P.P.N. politicians and Frenchmen have held the key positions in the thirteen parastatals which are the backbone of the economic infrastructure. For ten years after independence Niger received budgetary support from France to replace the subsidies to infrastructural and administrative expenses that had come from the French West Africa federation. The reliance of the regime on external supports led to unresponsiveness to internal inequities and the demands of the exploited agricultural producers. Only with the development of uranium, in part with West German and Italian capital, did the country achieve budgetary autonomy, but unfortunately not economic autonomy.

Two pioneering works, one a history of Niger by the Norwegian historian, Finn Fuglestad (1983), and the economic history of central Niger by Stephen Baier (1982), who teaches at Boston University, provide further information and insights into the economic evolution of Niger in the postwar period. Their analyses support the main conclusions of Higgott.

Another brief but important article, "The Political Economy of Mauritania: Imperialism and Class Struggle," by Mahfoud Bennoune (1980) deals in similar terms as Higgott with another of the poorer states of West Africa. It discusses the brutal consequences for a large portion of the Mauritanian people of French-sponsored mining development undertaken in cooperation with the regime headed by the now deposed Ould Daddah.

Finally, for the economic evolution, one should refer to some of the publications of a Guinean scholar, Aguibou Yan Yansané. His chapter "Decolonization, Dependency, and Development in Africa: the Theory Revisited" (1980), is more a descriptive catalogue of the various theories of recent decades than a comparative analysis. The several hundred citations nevertheless provide a useful introduction to the major sources for studying the colonial and neocolonial economic relationships. Another chapter, "Political Economy of Decolonization and Dependency of African States of French Colonial Legacy" (1980) is also short on analysis. Its value lies in its clear descriptions of the economic and financial institutions of French Black Africa from 1945 to 1960 and post-independence efforts at decolonization. In 1984 Yansané published *Decolonization in West Af-*

rican States with French Colonial Legacy. The two long chapters on the period 1945–60, which make up the first quarter of the study, contain little material that is not already found in his earlier publications. Like his earlier studies, they have useful data and good bibliographies but show weakness in construction and analysis.

EDUCATIONAL EVOLUTION

The bulk of the recent research on the development of western education in French Black Africa has continued to center upon the periods before 1945, for which archival records are available, or after 1960. The role of education in preparing the Africans for self-government and independence during the postwar period has been very little studied. An exception is my own chapter, "Schooling in Cameroun under the French Trusteeship" (1982), which examines to what extent and in what ways French education promoted the goals of the U.N. trusteeship system, including self-government or independence. Through the records of the Cameroonian Territorial Assembly it documents the support that African representatives gave to the introduction of the metropolitan educational system (structure, programs, diplomas) in order to achieve full equality with Frenchmen. It discusses the consequences of the extension and expansion of the French system to the point that the bulk of the children of primary school age outside the North were enrolled while secondary and technical education became well established. Although the system was beginning to produce an elite capable of taking over direction of the country and staffing its lower and middle-level administration, it did not educate either effectively or efficiently the great mass of individuals, who attended only the first one to three grades. At all levels it produced school-leavers and dropouts who were fitted neither to work in the modern sector nor to reinsert themselves in the traditional environment. Thus at independence Cameroon's leaders found an educational system that was so extensively developed that it could only be modified, not basically changed. Efforts better to adapt education to the needs of the independent nation would have to take place within the framework of the French-derived system and, as it has turned out, with the help of France.

Another chapter in the same collection by a Canadian historian, Claude Marchand (1982), deals with the efforts to develop institutions for agricultural education in Cameroon within the framework of the French-derived system. The primary school program of the postwar era saw manual agricultural and artisan skills virtually eliminated, even in the rural areas. The program in general contributed to detaching the pupils from rural life rather than integrating them more meaningfully. Thus not only did it not aid the kind of economic development that might render the country independent in food production, it further served to promote a destructive kind of social dislocation. A third chapter in the collection by the French sociologist, Jean-Yves Martin (1982), discusses the reasons for the relative backwardness of the North (the savanna and sahelian areas). His chapter makes an indirect contribution to understanding the role of the northern representatives in the political evolution of the country. For it was to a regime headed by a northern leader, Ahmadou Ahidjo, and heavily based on northern deputies to whom France transferred power between 1958 and 1960.

My article, "Education in French Equatorial Africa" (1978) includes a discussion of the educational policies of Félix Éboué as Free French governor-general of French Equatorial Africa between 1940 and 1944. Éboué initiated an educational expansion by quadrupling the funds given for the schools. In addition, he enlisted the assistance of the Christian missions, whose schools had previously received only infinitesimal sums from the colonial government. The Fourth Republic would generalize Éboué's policy to the other Black African territories rather than reverting to the anti-Christian, anti-clerical policy of the Third Republic. How this worked out in Cameroon is discussed in detail in my chapter above (1982). Finally, another of my articles, "The Impact of French Education in Africa" (1980) summarizes the main policies and practices in all the Black African territories from 1945 to 1960. It indicates that the main lines of educational development experienced in Cameroon were common to all the territories under French rule.

In a provocative yet stimulating chapter, "Education and Class Conflict" (1979), a Belgian economist and development specialist, Olivier LeBrun, discusses the history of French education in Senegal, with special reference to the period from 1946 to the present. He claims that in the period 1900–1946 education was primarily a function for preparing the population for the labor force. Then from 1946 to 1972 it was a force for ideological conditioning; since then it has served once more to prepare the labor force. In the aftermath of the Second World War France sought to create a genuine elite, a new social class capable of eventual transformation into a ruling class should political emancipation come to Africa. The school programs of 1946–1960 with their western bourgeois humanist values led to the growth of an anticolonialist consciousness among this new elite but to an even greater cultural dependency and alienation from the masses of people than had occurred among educated Senegalese in earlier periods. Though France agreed to independence in 1960, it has been able to maintain a community of interests with the elite based on a common culture. Even though the ruling class came to favor a more functional type of education for the masses, the teachers have resisting diluting the strong French cultural content of the programs of which they are the products.

G. Wesley Johnson of the University of California at Santa Barbara, well known for his study of elite politics in the Senegalese communes, has written on "Cultural Dependency in Senegal" (1980). He ably places the origins and development of the urban elite's attachment to France, the French language and culture within a historical perspective extending back to 1659. He rightly predicted that Senegal, after the departure of Leopold Sédar Senghor, might begin to lessen its cultural attachment despite its continued close political and economic ties with France.[8]

William Bosworth, a political scientist at C.U.N.Y. (1981), examines the phenomenon of cultural dependency of which the foundations were both deepened and broadened during the period 1946–1960. He contends that the lack of local cultural unity and of the wealth necessary to prepare for instruction in local languages inhibits a change away from French, even in the elementary grades. Even Guinea, which began using local languages in the elementary grades after its break with France in 1958, has retained the French language at the secondary and higher levels. To do so, it begins teaching French as a second language in the fourth grade.

NOTES

1. Decolonization may be defined in a restricted sense as the process by which the Asians and Africans gained self-government and independence from their colonial rulers. It may be defined in a broad sense as the process by which they remove all vestiges of external control at the economic, cultural, and psychological levels as well as the political level. For a brief introduction to the historical evolution of the concept, see my article, "Decolonization," in Joseph Dunner, ed., *Handbook of World History* (New York, 1967), pp. 268–72.
2. A bibliography of the works cited in this essay is found at the end.
3. The term *Balkanization* was apparently coined by Leopold Sedar Senghor to describe the breakup of the federations of French West Africa and French Equatorial Africa. He was referring to the earlier breakup of the Ottoman Empire in the Balkans into several small, economically weak national states.
4. For a discussion of recent research and writing on the impact of the Second World War on French West Africa and Togo, see my forthcoming article in the *Proceedings of the Tenth Meeting of the French Colonial Historical Society* (1984), edited by Philip Boucher.
5. Brunschwig develops the thesis that French colonization was able to succeed because of African collaboration in his recent work, *Noirs et Blancs dans L'Afrique Noire Française ou comment le colonisé devient colonisateur (1870–1914)* (Paris, 1983).
6. The most thorough and best argued case for de Gaulle as a generous and perspicacious decolonizer is Dorothy Shipley White, *Black Africa and De Gaulle: From the Empire to Independence* (University Park, Pa., 1979). There is a sizeable literature developing on de Gaulle's role in African decolonization, including from 1960 to 1969. Among the most important works are: Robert Bourgi, *Le Général de Gaulle et l'Afrique Noire, 1940–1969* (Paris, 1980); D.

Lavroff, Ed., *La Politique africaine du Général de Gaulle, 1958–1969* (Paris, 1981); and *"Colloque franco-africain; Le Général de Gaulle et la décolonisation,"* *Études gaulliennes,* v. 6 (April–July 1978), pp. 7–179.

7. Further elaboration of Person's views on the linguistic dimension of the cultural question are found in two publications: "Langues africaines et décolonisation," in *Colóquio sobre educação e ciências humanas na Africa de lingua portuguesa, 20–22 Janeiro de 1975* (Lisbon: Fundação Calouste Gulbenkian, 1979), pp. 307–19; "Langue et pouvoir," in Y. Mignot-Lefebvre and J. M. Mignon, eds., *Éducation en Afrique: alternatives* (Toulouse, 1980), pp. 21–32.

8. For the educational and cultural changes since the resignation of President Senghor and under the rule of President Abdou Diouf since January 1981, see Sheldon Gellar, *Senegal: An African Nation Between Islam and the West* (Boulder, 1982), pp. 117–19.

BIBLIOGRAPHY

Allen, Christopher. "Union-Party Relationships in Francophone West Africa: A Critique of "Téléguidage' Interpretations," in Richard Sandbrook and Robin Cohen, eds., *The Development of an African Working Class* (Toronto, 1975), pp. 99–125.

Bach, D. "L'insertion ivoirienne dans les rapports internationaux," in Y. A. Fauré and J.-F. Médard, eds. (1982), pp. 89–121.

Baier, Stephen. *An Economic History of Central Niger* (Oxford, 1980).

Barthélémy, Jean-Claude. "L'économie de l'A.O.F. et du Togo, 1946–1960," *Revue Française d'Histoire d'Outre-Mer,* v. 67 (no. 3–4, 1980), pp. 301–38.

Bayart, Jean-François. *L'État au Cameroun* (Paris, 1979).

Bennoune, Mahfoud. "The Political Economy of Mauritania: Imperialism & Class Struggle," *Review of African Political Economy* (May–August 1978), pp. 31–52.

Bosworth, William. "The Rigid Embrace of Dependency: France and Black African Education since 1960," *Contemporary French Civilization,* v. 5 (Spring 1981), pp. 327–46.

Brunschwig, Henri. *L'Avènement de l'Afrique Noire, du XIXᵉ siècle à nos jours* (Paris, 1963).

———. "The Decolonization of Black Africa," in P. Gifford and William Roger Louis, eds. (1982), pp. 211–24.

Chappelle, Jean. *Le peuple tchadien, ses racines et sa vie quotidienne* (Paris, 1980).

De Benoist, Joseph-Roger. *La Balkanisation de l'A.O.F.* (Dakar, 1979).

———. *L'A.O.F. de 1944 à 1960* (Dakar, 1982).

Decraene, Philippe. *Le Mali* (Paris, 1980).

Defferre, Gaston. "La Loi-Cadre," *Revue Juridique et Politique,* v. 34 (no. 4, 1980), pp. 767–70.

Delanoue, Paul. "La C.G.T. et les syndicats de l'Afrique Noire de colonisation française de la Deuxième Guerre Mondiale aux indépendances," *Le Mouvement Social* (January–March 1983), pp. 103–16.

Dewitte, Philippe. "La C.G.T. et les syndicats d'A.O.F. (1945–1957," *Le Mouvement Social* (December 1981), pp. 3–32.

———. "Réponse à Paul Delanoue," *Le Mouvement Social* (January–March 1983), pp. 117–21.

Diallo, Abdoulaye. "Financement de l'infrastructure routière en Côte d'Ivoire, 1946–1953," *Annales de l'Université d'Abidjan, Série I: Histoire,* v. 8 (1980), pp. 257–82.

Fauré, Y. A., and Médard, J.-F., eds., *L'État et la bourgeoisie en Côte d'Ivoire* (Paris, 1982).

Fuglestad, Finn. *A History of Niger, 1850–1960* (Cambridge, 1983).

Gardinier, David E. "Decolonization in French, Belgian, and Portuguese Africa: A Bibliographical Essay," in P. Gifford and William Roger Louis, eds. (1982), pp. 515–66.

———. "Education in French Equatorial Africa, 1842–1945", *Proceedings of the French Colonial Historical Society,* v. 3 (1978), pp. 121–37.

———. "French Colonial Rule in Africa: A Bibliographical Essay," in P. Gifford William Roger and Louis, eds. (1971), pp. 787–902.

———. "The Impact of French Education on Africa, 1817–1960," *Proceedings of the French Colonial Historical Society,* v. 5 (1980), pp. 70–82.

———. "Schooling in Cameroun under the French Trusteeship," in Santerre and Mercier-Tremblay, eds. (1982), pp. 454–82.

Gbagbo, Laurent. *La Côte d'Ivoire. Économie et société à la veille de l'indépendance (1940–1960)* (Paris, 1982).

————. *Réflexions sur la Conference de Brazzaville* (Yaoundé, 1978).

Gifford, Prosser, and William Roger Louis, eds., *France and Britain in Africa* (New Haven, 1971).

————, and Wm. Roger Louis, eds. *The Transfer of Power in Africa: Decolonization, 1940–1960* (New Haven, 1982).

Guèye, Doudou. *Sur les sentiers du Temple; ma rencontre avec Félix Houphouët-Boigny* (Ventabren, 1975).

Higgott, Richard. "Structural Dependency and Decolonisation in a West African Landlocked State: Niger," *Review of African Political Economy* (January–April 1980), pp. 43–59.

Johnson, G. Wesley. "Cultural Dependency in Senegal" in A. Y. Yansané, ed. (1980), pp. 101–12.

Le Brun, Olivier, "Education and Class Conflict", in R. Cruise O'Brien, ed. (1979), pp. 175–207.

Marchand, Claude. "Tentatives d'adaptation de l'enseignement aux réalités camerounaises: l'enseignement agricole, 1921–1970," in R. Santerre and C. Mercier-Tremblay, eds. (1982), pp. 483–504.

Marshall, D. Bruce. *The French Colonial Myth and Constitution-Making in the Fourth Republic* (New Haven, 1973).

Martens, George. "Révolution ou participation: syndicats et partis politiques au Sénégal," *Le Mois en Afrique* (February–March 1983), pp. 72–79, 97–113; (June–July 1983), pp. 78–80, 97–109.

————. "Le Syndicalisme en Afrique Occidentale d'expression française de 1945 à 1960," *Le Mois En Afrique* (October–November 1980), pp. 74–97; (December 1980–January 1981), pp. 53–64, 81–92; (February–March 1981), pp. 52–64, 81–83.

Martin, Jean-Yves. "Inégalités régionales et inégalités sociales: l'enseignement secondaire au Cameroun septentrional," in Santerre and Mercier-Tremblay, eds. (1982), pp. 616–44.

M'Bokolo, Elikia. "Forces sociales et idéologies dans la décolonisation de l'A.E.F.," *Journal of African History*, v. 22 (no. 3, 1981), pp. 393–408.

————. "French Colonial Policy in Equatorial Africa in the 1940s and 1950s," in P. Gifford and Wm. Roger Louis, eds. (1982), pp. 173–210.

Morris-Jones, W. H., and Georges Fischer, eds. *Decolonisation and After* (London, 1980).

O'Brien, Rita Cruise. "Factors of Dependence: Senegal and Kenya," in W. H. Morris-Jones and Georges Fischer, eds. (1980), pp. 283–309.

———. "Foreign Ascendancy in the Economy and State," in Rita Cruise O'Brien, ed. (1979), pp. 100–25.

———. *The Political Economy of Underdevelopment: Dependence in Senegal* (Beverly Hills, 1979).

Pedler, Frederick. *Main Currents of West African History, 1940–1978* (London, 1979).

Person, Yves. "Colonisation et décolonisation en Côte d'Ivoire," *Le Mois en Afrique* (August–September 1981), pp. 15–30.

———. "French West Africa and Decolonization," in P. Gifford and Wm. Roger Louis, eds. (1982), pp. 141–72.

Pleven, René. "La Conférence de Brazzaville," *Revue Juridique et Politique*, v. 34 (no. 4, 1980), pp. 749–66.

Santerre, Renaud, and Mercier-Tremblay, eds. *La Quête du savoir: Essais pour une anthropologie de l'éducation camerounaise* (Montreal, 1982).

Smith, Tony. *The Pattern of Imperialism: The United States, Great Britain, and the Late-Industrializing World since 1815* (Cambridge, 1981).

———. "Patterns in the Transfer of Power: A Comparative Study of French and British Decolonization," in P. Gifford and Wm. Roger Louis, eds. (1982), pp. 87–116.

Soret, Marcel. *Histoire du Congo, capitale Brazzaville* (Paris, 1978).

Suret-Canale, Jean. "The French West African Railway Workers' Strike," in Peter Gutkind et al., eds, *African Labor History* (Beverly Hills, 1978), pp. 129–54. [Tr. "La grève des cheminots africains d'AOF (1947–1948)," *Cahiers de l'Institut Maurice Thorez* (no. 28, 1978)].

———. "From Colonization to Independence in French Tropical Africa: The Economic Background," in P. Gifford and Wm. Roger Louis, eds. (1982), pp. 445–82.

———. "Strike Movements as Part of the Anti-Colonial Struggle in French West Africa," *Tarikh*, v. 5, no. 3, (1977), pp. 44–56.

Yansané, Agibou Yan, ed. *Decolonization and Dependency: Problems of Development in African Societies* (Westport, 1980).

————. "Decolonization, Dependency, and Development in Africa: The Theory Revisited," in A. Y. Yansané, ed. (1980), pp. 3–51.

————. *Decolonization in West African States with French Colonial Legacy: Comparison and Contrast: Development in Guinea, The Ivory Coast, and Senegal, 1945–1980* (Cambridge, Mass., 1984).

————. "Political Economy of Decolonization and Dependency of African States of French Colonial Legacy, 1945–1975," in A. Y. Yansané, ed. (1980), pp. 113–44.

Strike Movements as Part of the Anticolonial Struggle in French West Africa

J. Suret-Canale

In French West Africa, as in all other territories subjected to colonial rule, strikes were one of the ways of protesting against colonial domination and its effects. As a form of action, strikes presuppose the existence of relatively large work-forces, which are likely to down tools at a given time. Any form of exploitation, such as slavery or forced labour, can give rise to strikes, but in such cases strikes are generally mistaken for rebellions and are rapidly and violently suppressed. Strikes as a specific means of action can only be brought about when there is a substantial category of permanent paid workers, even if this category, by virtue of its restricted development, cannot as yet be called a working class.

This first point explains why strike action was used only occasionally and was limited in form in French West Africa during the period of colonial rule proper, that is until the end of the 1930s. However, when this form of action did take place and there was a simultaneous increase in paid work, a strike within the colonial context took on a significance notably different from that in other social contexts, especially in 'developed' capitalist countries.

As a general rule, the employer of paid labour became identified with the colonial exploiter or oppressor. Within African society, paid work—almost unheard of in pre-colonial times—was extremely restricted and operated under a more or less patriarchal system. The only employers of paid labour on a large scale were the colonists or colonial European companies on the one hand and the colonial government itself on the other, which, in French West Africa, employed the largest bodies of permanent wage-earners (in the ports, railways, public works, post office, etc.).

Consequently, a strike was nearly always a protest against the colonial regime and against the colonisers, and it took on a definite political dimension which was felt by both sides, African and European.

With these two linked considerations as our starting point, we may distinguish three periods in the history of French West Africa: from the colonial conquest to 1936, during which period strikes played only a sporadic role in view of the absence of a sizable wage-earning force; from 1936 to 1939, the pre-history period of the labour movement in these territories; and 1944 to 1948, the origin of the first impetus of the labour movement.

A third point should be made. To date, as far as this period in particular is concerned, no systematic or detailed study has been carried out on the history of the labour and strike movement in French West Africa. It is only during the last few years that historians—especially African historians—have begun to carry out studies on the most important movements. This essay will therefore be

44

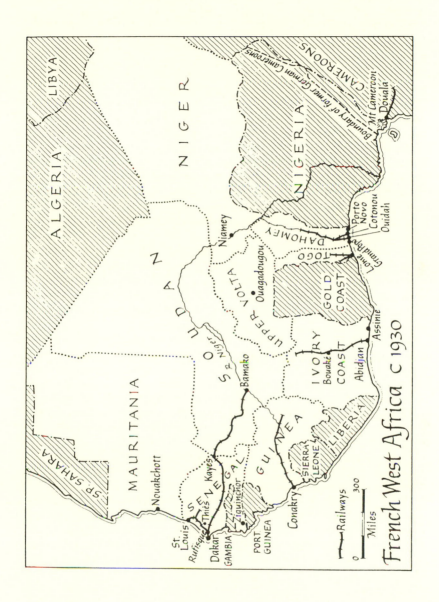

French West Africa c 1930

incomplete and provisional. It should be considered only as a preliminary approach and will certainly have to be completed and rectified by future studies.

From the colonial conquest to the thirties

During this period, the dominant feature of French West Africa was the persistence of the most retrogressive methods of colonial exploitation, summarised by the term 'économie de traite' (mercantile economy).

Occupied mainly for political and strategic reasons—in order to compete with other colonial powers, notably Britain—French West Africa was of little interest to the leading capitalists of France. Practically no investment was made in the region which was left 'in reserve'. Only a few commercial companies, mainly from Bordeaux and Marseilles, which were already interested in trading on the African coast, decided to establish trading posts in Africa. They were more interested in making large profits than in investing large sums of capital, and created monopolies using government pressure so that they had charge of all local agricultural products that were of interest to the European market. They bought the 'raw products' very cheaply and sold for very high prices imported products such as gewgaws, textiles and hardware. The low prices imposed for the delivery of local products—for example, Senegalese peanuts—prevented the development of a white farming community as in South Africa or Algeria. Even though badly paid, the labour used in capitalist-type agricultural enterprises would impose higher cost prices than those paid to the indigenous farmers.

Because of lack of demand, the development of the communications infrastructure was kept to a minimum: a few railway tracks with a one-metre gauge, completed only during the years immediately preceding the first world war and whose original purpose was more strategic (transport of troops) than commercial: only two ports, Dakar and Conakry (the latter of tiny capacity), and elsewhere only wharfs. Industry was virtually non-existent, consisting of a few repair workshops, a small textile factory established in 1916 at Bouaké in the Ivory Coast, and a few small oil mills dating back to the twenties.

There was no working class. Skilled workers (carpenters, metal workers, mechanics), nearly all of whom were Senegalese or occasionally Gabonese from Libreville, were mainly employed by the government. These were spread over a large area, strangers to the peoples among whom they worked, relatively well paid and, enjoying the advantage of job-security by virtue of their status as civil servants, they were scarcely likely to take part in collective disputes. The only exceptions were the railwaymen, who were relatively concentrated and rapidly acquired a feeling of corporate solidarity. It should also be pointed out that, numerically, the majority of workers employed on the railways, especially for track construction and maintenance, as well as the dockers and public works labourers such as roadworkers, were not permanent workers; they were either recruits supplied by forced labour, or temporary workers from rural areas who intended to return there. It was among this category, however, that the largest movements arose, in the form of a rebellion against their intolerable working

46

Dakar in the early 'thirties: the port (above) and the fish market (below)

conditions, and were crushed by the colonial authorities with the help of the armed forces.

Government and foreign trading post clerks, educated at government schools or the religious missions, did not usually get involved in such movements. The ambiguity of their condition meant that they were both despised by the colonisers who used their services and hated by the people in whose eyes they appeared to form part of the colonial system, sharing in its advantages. Considering themselves privileged, they were too scared of losing their position; if they were dismissed they could rarely get back into the administration and they would be blacklisted by the trading houses.

47

Not surprisingly, then, there were only a few significant strike movements during this period, of which the earliest, at the end of the nineteenth century, were quite alien to the labour movement as such.

Government documents mention, in 1890, at the time of the take-over by Archinard of Segou (the capital of Ahmadu, successor of al-Hajj Umar) a strike by railway workers on the Dakar-St Louis line and by St Louis traders. The government feared a general rebellion. We have no further information on the movement—the form it took, how long it lasted, how widespread it was. It would make a fine research topic for a Senegalese historian, for there is very likely to be more information in the Senegalese and French archives. However, it would appear that the motives behind such a movement were essentially religious. A large number of Senegalese Muslims had become affiliated to the brotherhood founded in West Africa by al-hajj Umar; his immediate successor Ahmadu was the caliph of the brotherhood, and the aggression against his state and occupation of his capital were regarded as sacrilege by the members of the brotherhood. It goes almost without saying that this protest took on an anti-colonial and anti-French complexion. But in our present state of knowledge we cannot say more.

We must now leave French West Africa and go to the Cameroons, then under German rule, to find a second example of strike movements, which also took the form of a rebellion, so characteristic of the early colonisation period. This was the strike of Dahomeyan women employed on the German plantations of Mount Cameroon and the revolt of their policemen husbands. The circumstances were as follows: In 1891 (before Dahomey was conquered by the French) the German consul at Ouidah bought hundreds of slaves, men and women, who were 'exported' to the Cameroons. Two years later, approximately two thirds had died; those who survived were employed by the local police, according to current colonial practice which considered it safer to use non-indigenes for such duties. But on the pretext that these men had been 'liberated', the German authorities claimed that they should withhold from their pay the money spent on buying them two years previously. Furthermore, they demanded that the men's wives, also bought as slaves, should work for nothing on the plantations and should be at the disposal of the German officers for 'evening entertainment.' When the Dahomeyans protested, the German authorities reduced their rations. The women employed on the coffee plantations then came out on strike. The Chancellor of the German administration, Leist, ordered them to be whipped naked in the presence of their husbands. Under the shock of this outrage, the Dahomeyan policemen, on the night of 15 and 16 December 1893, seized the armoury, took the German officers by surprise and killed one of them; the others managed to take refuge on the ships anchored in the Douala estuary. From this point, the Germans launched a counter-attack which succeeded on 23 December; all the Dahomeyans taken prisoner were hanged, their wives were condemned to forced labour and they were supplied as free labour to the plantations. Subsequently Leist was convicted for maltreating and abusing the women prisoners, and was sentenced, for 'failure in the service', to be transferred to an equivalent position elsewhere but with a loss of seniority.

48

The first significant movements that we can trace after this period came immediately after the 1914–1918 war. The war put West Africa under great strain; the 'war effort' was interpreted as a drive for increased production and increased taxes, the repression of various uprisings, and the recruitment of soldiers to send to the trenches in Europe (see Osuntokun's article). The revolutionary wave that swept Europe from 1918 onwards had repercussions in West Africa. In this respect an important part was played by the repatriated African servicemen who had witnessed and even participated in revolutionary uprisings that had taken place in Europe. Thus African sailors called up into the French war fleet participated in the Black Sea mutiny when sailors refused to take part in the war against the new Soviet Republic.

In 1919 the first strike took place by dockers at the port of Conakry in Guinea. In 1925 the railwaymen on the Dakar–St Louis line went on strike; this was certainly not the first movement to take place on this network (we have already mentioned the strike of 1890) nor the last, but a study has yet to be carried out on strike movements among railway workers.

During the same year, 1925, there was unrest among the Bambara 'conscripts' used for building the Dakar–Kayes railway track, probably caused by their ill treatment and poor food. The administration had three ringleaders arrested and flogged. A general strike immediately erupted. The troops, among whom there were many Bambara, refused to intervene, and in order to put an end to the strike, the administration was forced to free the prisoners and give some consideration to the workers' demands.

In Dahomey there were stoppages of work in 1918–1919 among the Cotonou and Grand Popo paddlers, who had an old corporate tradition supported by a certain ethnic homogeneity: from the nineteenth century and probably before, they were responsible for transport from the beach to the ships in the roads, which involved the difficult and dangerous crossing of the surf.

In February 1923, the Cotonou dockers came out on strike, followed by employees in the private sector (mainly commerce) each making their own claims. This was during the passive resistance movement against taxation (the establishment of new market dues) at Porto Novo and Cotonou. The instigators of this movement belonged on the one hand to the radical intellectuals, such as teacher and journalist Louis Hunkanrin, and on the other to the traditional elite such as Prince Sognigbé Mêkpon, of the branch of the royal family of Porto Novo dethroned by the French administration.

The Benin-Niger railwaymen (about a thousand men with the Cotonou dockers who were answerable to the same government) came out on strike several times during the twenties, the last time being in 1929.

The political aspect of the strikes was far more in evidence at the time of the Lomé incidents in Togo, in January-February 1933, than in the Porto-Novo incidents of 1923. The dispute resulted in a petition being drawn up by traditional 'notables'—the heads of the Lomé districts and canton—against a tax increase which they rejected on the grounds that the economic crisis of the Great Depression had considerably diminished the revenue. The administration had two leading citizens, both agents of foreign companies, arrested as 'ringleaders'.

49

A general strike followed and a demonstration was held in front of the offices of the Lomé *cercle*, which forced the distracted government to release the prisoners. Several days later, military repression was imposed by troops brought in from the Ivory Coast, and large-scale arrests followed.

From this rather fragmented picture one conclusion stands out: the nature of strike movements recorded during the course of this period was extremely varied. Certainly one can see the beginnings of labour protest movements, notably among railwaymen and dockers; several other movements, on the other hand, fall into a different social context, occasionally linked to 'traditional' resistance movements. Whether the aims or motives of the movements were strictly a protest or politically based, colonial exploitation or oppression was at the root of the grievances and the colonial administration, for whom all protests and strikes were 'subversive' and 'anti-French', gave all these movements an 'anti-colonial' context.

From the Popular Front to the Second World War (1936–1939)

From 1919 to the thirties, the very slow development of the economy, coupled with the political awakening brought about by recruiting soldiers to fight in Europe during the war, led to the tentative beginnings of a proper labour movement. The consequences of the advent of the Popular Front government (supported by Socialists and Communists) in France in 1936 cannot be regarded as having the impact on local social life in French West Africa of purely external events. But certainly the advent of a left-wing government in France, supported by the working class, was to contribute to the surge forward of a movement which had been slowly maturing for a long time.

True, the colonial government was still in control. Most of the colonial administrators and still more of the private colonial sector were violently opposed to the Popular Front, and many of them sympathised openly with Fascist regimes in which they saw the ideal of 'government by force', the glorifying of the hierarchical system and the racialist views which they shared. This explains why there were very limited changes in the colonies as a result of the Popular Front. But limited does not mean insignificant.

First of all there was the infectiousness of example. The large-scale strike movements in France, the drawing-up of collective bargaining agreements and the recognition of trade unions as legal spokesmen were not without repercussions in French West Africa. French sailors, notably those from Marseilles, who worked on African routes, had for a long time nurtured a nucleus of the extreme left-wing, influenced by the French Communist Party and the CGTU (Confédération Générale du Travail Unitaire, or United Labour Confederation) affiliated to the Red international trade union in Moscow. Several of them, immediately after the First World War, made contact with African sympathisers, principally by ensuring the transport of revolutionary literature, in the form of newspapers and leaflets, banned by the colonial authorities. Their contact, and even their example, had a certain effect. The colonist Marcel Homet related the 'deplorable' example of sailors from a French vessel, who while at their port of call at Assinie, urged the Krumen to insist on their rights; the latter were

50

subjugated *manu militari* (by military means) by the local administration, but the French crew came out on strike and the Krumen obtained satisfaction.

On the other hand, pressure from the French left wing forced the government to take certain liberal measures. The Régnier Rollin decrees of 1935, which stipulated that any political demonstrator could be sent to prison, were annulled; two decrees, dated 11 and 20 March 1937, made conditions of the French Work Code regarding trades unions applicable to the colonies, and introduced collective bargaining agreements and the election of personnel representatives in companies employing more than ten paid staff.

Actually, the conditions of the first decree were singularly restrictive. For French West Africa permission to form a trade union was granted only to those who could not only speak, read and write fluent French but also offer a certificate of primary education or its equivalent issued by the governor. In the eyes of the bureaucrats of the Ministry of Colonies, this meant restricting trade union rights to Europeans or to those who had been 'Europeanised'.

In fact, before these decrees were even published, from May 1936—under the influence of the social movement which was taking place in France—the trade unions were established. European trade unions in the first instance, but also African trade unions, not always in accordance with legal custom, which would have made it virtually impossible for them to exist. The aforementioned colonist Homet indignantly denounced the constitution of a trade union at Ziguinchor, in Casamance, Senegal, by 'fetishist cooks and chauffeurs' (*sic*) who demanded that a collective agreement be drawn up.

The existence of separate European and African trade unions—the European unions being made up of 'small-minded whites' who often revealed themselves as extreme racialists, more concerned with safeguarding their 'privileges' over their African colleagues than with joining them in protest—made it difficult to establish a united trade union movement. The ill-will of the European unions resulted in the failure in 1937 of the first attempt to establish in Dakar a united trade union affiliated to the CGT (Confédération Générale du Travail, or General Labour Confederation). Not until 1938 were the unions of the Dakar district united, and then only the African unions. The most important unions were the Dakar-Niger Railwaymen's Union and the Seamen's Union.

However, unlike what occurred in France, there was to be no large-scale and prolonged strike movement in Africa. The only significant strike of this period was that of the Thiès and Dakar railwaymen (27 September–1 October 1938). This took place at a time when France's social movement was on the decline; the Popular Front had had its day; even in France, the strike of October 1938 against the decrees of the Daladier government was to end in failure and in the dismissal of those responsible as well as militant trade unionists. The Colonial Secretary was no longer the Socialist Moutet but Georges Mandel, Clémenceau's former secretary, who was reputed to govern 'with an iron hand'.

The railwaymen's strike, sparked off by the arbitrary removal of an auxiliary or non-regular railwayman and the plight of 'auxiliaries' who were more numerous than, but did not have the advantages of, the regular railwaymen as far as guarantees were concerned, was spontaneous and not prompted by trade

51

113

union intervention. The strike led to bloodshed: at Thiès the *commandant de cercle* brought in the troops and several people were killed and wounded. The next day, 29 September, the whole network came out on strike. The following day an agreement was signed between the workers' representatives and the Government General which excluded any sanction, and the union ordered 'vork to resume on 1 October. The Governor-General, accused of weakness, was dismissed.

Birth of the labour movement: 1944–1948

There was a temporary lull in the labour movement brought about by the return to an authoritarian colonial regime under Georges Mandel, followed by the war and the installation of the Vichy regime under Governor-General Pierre Boisson in 1940 which lasted till 1942. It was succeeded by the equally authoritarian Free French regime concerned up to 1944 only with pursuing the 'war effort'.

But from 1943 the elimination of the Vichy administration (which after the Allied landing in North Africa had belatedly 'rallied' to the Allies' cause) induced a leaning towards the left from the French Committee for National Liberation which, despite the aversion of de Gaulle and his immediate entourage, had become the provisional government of the French Republic.

The left-wing militants, who had had to knuckle under during Boisson's strict rule, hastened to re-establish the trade union organisations. Consequently the union of munitions workers at Dakar was reconstituted in June 1943, grouping together African and European workers. But this remained an isolated example;

Governor-General Boisson (right) in Dakar during the Vichy regime, with General Weygand

52

elsewhere the trade unions were re-established as before the war on a racial basis, especially in Dakar. And despite the vigorous intervention from 1945 of the CGT—which as soon as contacts were resumed opposed any 'racial' trade union movement and threatened to ban the 'European' unions—the various regulations were so devised that certain unions, especially those concerned with public office, were *de facto* made up of one colour. However, they all came together under the same united trade unions affiliated to the CGT. The Christian CFTC (Confédération Fédérale de Travilleurs Croyants) had yet to be established, in 1948, with the arrival of the ministers of the MRP (Mouvement Républicain Populaire, or Christian Democrats) at the Ministry of French Overseas Territories. On the other hand, in numerous territories left-wing Europeans played a decisive role in the constitution of African trade unions: for instance, Pierre Morlet, a teacher, and Fayette, a postal official, in the French Soudan, Jean Rigo in the Ivory Coast and Donnat in the Cameroons.

The rise of the trade union movement was particularly shown by the expansion of trade unionism beyond the categories which had already been organised for a long time (railwaymen, seamen, dockers). Trade unions were now formed at Dakar by industrial workers as there had been appreciable industrial development as a result of the war. They were also formed by civil servants who had previously relied on a corporate 'friendly association', not daring to establish a union.

This increase in trade union organisations was to be at the root of strike movements on a much larger scale in the years 1945–1946. During the war, wages had been frozen, while prices steadily increased. In France wages were increased from the time of the liberation, but in Africa they remained frozen or were raised only inadequately. This situation is what was behind the large-scale strike movements in 1945 and 1946 at Douala and Dakar.

The September 1945 strike at Douala was sparked off by non-regular railwaymen, outside and even contrary to the wishes of the union. The reason for the protest was a savage increase in the price of *macabo*, the people's basic foodstuff. However, it must be acknowledged that there was additional provocation. The colonial element was in fact launching an extremely violent campaign against the trade unions and was seeking a pretext to justify their repression. A peaceful demonstration provided just such a pretext. With the approval of the government the colonists armed themselves and rushed about the streets shooting at anyone who was black. The European secretary of the railwaymen's union was attacked at his home with a machine gun and had to defend himself with a revolver, killing one of his aggressors. To 'protect' them, the governor arrested and expelled the trade union leaders, three Europeans and three Cameroonians.

The Dakar strike of December 1945–January 1946 was on a far bigger scale and better organised. The political opportunity which would allow labour claims to be made was created by the municipal elections in April–May 1945 in the communes of Senegal, Dakar, Rufisque and St. Louis, and the victory of the left wing at the first Constituent Assembly in the autumn. In the face of the govern-

53

began in December 1945 with a strike by European teachers at the Dakar lycée, demanding the salary increase that had been promised six months previously but never granted. This quickly gained support from Dakar's industrial workers who set up a 'Labour Inter-Trade Union' within the United Trade Union. The commercial employees joined in and finally the auxiliaries (non-regular personnel) of the Government General. The strikes went on until January 1946 and also affected Guinea, Ivory Coast, the Cameroons and the French Congo.

Besides the increase in wages—which was generally obtained—the strikers everywhere claimed *equal* wages with European workers holding the same qualifications, exclusive of the bonus paid to expatriates.

From then on, strikes were resorted to more and more frequently, with permanent inflation causing constant claims for wage increases. The strikes were to become more and more anti-colonial in demanding the suppression of racial discrimination in matters relating to salaries and work legislation. The most extensive of these movements was the general strike of 1952 for the passing of the Overseas Work Code, which had been blocked by the opposition of those in colonial affairs circles since 1946.

The anti-colonial aspect was also noticeable in the most significant movement of this period: the strike of French West African railwaymen. The Federation of African Railwaymen united the African trade unions of the various 'networks': Dakar–Niger, Conakry–Niger, Abidjan–Niger, Benin–Niger. It was autonomous, i.e. not affiliated to the CGT, although some of its unions were local members of the CGT's territorial unions.

The railwaymen's main demand was the setting up of a *cadre unique*, a 'single framework' without discrimination on the basis of colour. This was opposed by the European railwaymen, who belonged to a separate union with a racial bias. Other demands were the integration of 'auxiliaries' or non-regular workers, who comprised the bulk of the staff but were not entitled to statutory guarantees, and an end to dismissals (a management programme envisaged 3,000 dismissals out of a work force of 18,000 railwaymen).

The first strike, lasting 24 hours, took place on 19 April 1947 and was ended by a protocol agreement which led the African railwaymen to believe that their demands would be met; this acknowledged 'the need to establish a single framework for French West African railwaymen as soon as possible'.

But it was not long before the railwaymen realised they had been tricked. In the meantime the removal in France of the communist ministers had accentuated the colonialist tendency of the government; the 'committee' in charge of executing the 'single framework' were unable to do so in the face of opposition from the European railwaymen and the management.

In these conditions the men began an unlimited strike on 10 October 1947; it was to last for more than five months, until 19 March 1948. The government used every kind of pressure to combat the strike: legal proceedings against the unions responsible and the strikers themselves (the strike was declared 'illegal' because the strikers did not resort to the arbitration procedure stipulated by law); dismissals; recruitment of blacklegs. But the European railwaymen, for the most part *petits blancs* recruited to represent authority but without any professional skill, and the blacklegs could not make the trains run.

Obviously such a long strike can only take place if there is a feeling of solidarity, not only of the workers but of the African population as a whole. Thanks to this popular solidarity, the strikers and their families were fed and helped. The African and French CGT unions also gave support which led to the establishment of bonds of collaboration between the CGT and the autonomous Federation of Railwaymen. Other local trade unions also gave their support.

Léopold Sédar Senghor in the 1940s

55

There was only one weak link in the chain of African solidarity: the African planters in the Ivory Coast whose harvest was held up by the strike, pressed for a return to work and the strike ended in the Ivory Coast on 5 January 1948.

The protocol agreement which ended the strike did not satisfy the railwaymen except for one point: giving up the legal proceedings and withdrawing the sanctions resulting from a strike. But the workers were not paid for the days they were on strike and many auxiliaries were dismissed on the grounds of 'reduction of manpower'.

It only remains to point out that some historians seem completely to have misinterpreted the significance of the strike. They appear to have reproduced the version given them by the colonial authorities before an enquiry was held, and to have failed to interview African strikers or consulted the relevant documents. According to these historians, the French Communist Party (PCF) and the CGT which were engaged at the end of 1947 in 'insurrectional' strikes 'forced' the African railwaymen to strike for five months without any real motive relating to their own working conditions. And at the end of this strike the African railwaymen left the CGT. This not uncommon version of a 'plot' does not stand up to any close examination and seems quite preposterous. Who could imagine that African workers would come out on strike for a period of five months without any reason of their own simply at a request made from overseas? Besides, the Federation of African Railwaymen was not affiliated to the CGT and moreover was directed at that time by political friends of Léopold Sédar Senghor, who definitely had nothing to do with the Communists.

This essay has shown how important strikes in French West Africa were—however sporadic they may have been—as means of protest against the colonial situation. From 1952, and especially after 1954, strikes were to become more and more frequent and to play an important part in the movement which was to lead first to the semi-autonomy granted France's Overseas Territories in 1957 and their ultimate independence in 1960. But this is the subject for another essay.

For further reading

MORTIMER, EDWARD, *France and the Africans 1944–1960*, Faber and Faber, 1969.

OUSMANE, SEMBENE, *God's Bits of Wood*, London, 1970 (a novel about the Dakar railway strike).

SURET-CANALE, J., *Colonialism in French Tropical Africa, 1900–1945*, Hurst, 1971.

56

SEKOU TOURÉ AND THE GUINEAN REVOLUTION

by R. W. JOHNSON
Magdalen College, Oxford

PRESIDENT AHMED SEKOU TOURÉ of Guinea is indisputably Africa's senior radical leader still in power. But, for a number of reasons, both the man and his ideas remain somewhat obscure, particularly in the non-francophone world. We still have no biography of the man and only a few dated and fragmentary articles considering his early *idées majeurs*.[1] It must be admitted at once that to fill this gap is a task much larger than can be performed by this article.

The period up to independence (1958)

First, a few biographical details. Touré was born in Faranah (Haute-Guinée) in 1922 of peasant parents. He is a Malinké and is of the same clan as the great Samory Touré who for so long led pre-colonial resistance to the French.[2] In the 1930s he came to Conakry to study at the Ecole Professionelle. Academically this was to represent the summit of his career; he did not go on to receive a post-primary, secondary, or university education. He is very largely a self-made and self-taught man—something which is virtually unique among the members of the political élites which have ruled West Africa in the last decade. On leaving school he held several lowly positions in the French Administration before becoming involved in the trade union movement (the *Conféderation Générale da Travail*, CGT) which he, virtually alone, founded in 1945-6 and which he dominated and led for the next 12 years.[3] He also was a founder-member of the *Parti Démocratique de Guinée* (PDG), the Guinean section of the *Rassemblement Démocratique Africain* (RDA), within which he played a second-echelon role until 1952 when he took over the Party's leadership. The PDG's period of political and electoral ' take-off ' really dates from his accession to power within it, and well before independence was achieved in 1958 Touré had emerged as indisputably the dominant personality in Guinea, his position bolstered by a degree of popular and organizational support perhaps unique in West Africa.

The author is a Fellow in Politics and Sociology of Magdalen College, Oxford. He is working on a study of politics and social change in Guinea, where he spent six months in 1968. He is grateful to the Social Science Research Council for the research grant which made this visit possible.

1. The best of which is I. Wallerstein, ' The Political Ideology of the PDG ', *Présence Afrıcaine*, **12**, (First Quarter 1962), pp. 30–41.
2. The belief that Touré is a direct descendant of Samory, widely current outside Guinea, is believed by nobody within the country.
3. The best general background study of Guinean political history in this period is to be found in R. S. Morgenthau, *Political Parties in French-Speaking West Africa* (Oxford, 1964). The best existing biographical sketch of Touré—though it does contain some errors—is in J. Lacouture, *Cinq hommes et la France* (Paris, 1961).

350

In order to understand Touré's personal and ideological development we must first examine his period of trade union leadership. As Secretary-General of the Guinean CGT, Touré was in continual contact with the French CGT (he attended a Paris Congress of the CGT as early as 1946). It is undoubtedly to this source that we must trace Touré's acquaintance with marxist theory and communist organizational practice. Moreover, his later strong rejection of all forms of racism, including theories of negritude, is probably also partially a product of the sympathy and support which he received from the French metropolitan Left in this period.[4] But Touré's trade union experience was of a more general importance as well. It was in this movement that he learnt most of all that he still knows; this phase stands at the very centre of his auto-didactic career. One long quotation from the Touré of this period will have to stand for a total impression. The subject is the duties of trade union leadership:

' First of all you must thoroughly familiarize yourself with the *Code du Travail* and all other social legislation. *Responsable*, your bedside reading is the *Code du Travail* which you can never study enough. Its French, this beautiful language, has a finesse that will escape even those who suckled it with their maternal milk. *Responsable*, you have the duty of educating the masses; in order to educate them you must first educate yourself. That's why you must know all the rules and decisions which rule the world of work. You must be able at any moment to reply to the questions of comrades, even if they appear completely anodine to you .... A lot of your comrades are illiterate. You must always read and explain social legislation and the trade union press to them.

' You must never believe that ability resides solely in the so-called ' *évolué* ' element. In fact some of our best leaders are illiterates. Moreover, you will have noticed that they are the most able to sustain a discussion and can defend a cause or a thesis with rare aptitude. Notice too that they are seldom tricked for they often recognise a sincere man from his very first words. You must always take account of the opinions of illiterate comrades whatever their branch of professional activity. The majority of them have experienced concrete situations and their observations on them may well be highly consequential. The trade union leader who is most apt, best advised and the most *évolué* in every meaning of that word, is he who puts things at the level of all, so as to make better understood the aspirations of the masses with whose guidance he is charged. He must concretise the cause which he defends in all his actions and words so as to facilitate the workers' understanding of it.

' We are all more or less presumptuous, more or less proud: we all believe

4. It is important to stress that the French Left which Touré has known is that which resides in Saint-Denis rather than on the Boulevard Saint-Michel. Interestingly, some of Touré's earliest major articles for the RDA paper, *Reveil*, consisted of primitive but bitter attacks on Sartre and the doctrines of existentialism—then a reigning mode of the intellectual Left and the bête-noire of the French Communist Party.

ourselves already important. But pride and presumption are two vices that kill trust, esteem and sympathy . . . . We must struggle against these internal enemies in order to deserve the trust of the workers . . . . Our struggle does not consist solely in material demands, but also in raising the workers morally and professionally, in stimulating emulation and professional conscience, and in helping them struggle against their own weaknesses. The trade union leader is, then, a defender, a guide and an educator of the masses. He must always bear in mind the fact that one false manoeuvre, one imprudent word, one gesture in a moment of anger and, moreover, every unreasoned act, compromises the whole of the movement which he represents.

' It is in order to overcome these weaknesses in himself so that he may become a fit leader of others, that the trade union leader must frequently and in a spirit of fraternal comradeship accept and even provoke criticism and self-criticism, correcting his own weaknesses and those of his comrades.'[5]

Several themes which have continued to mark Touré's thought are already present here, notably his consciousness and populist rejection of the élitist presumptions of the educated *évolué* group constituting the political Establishment, Right and Left, against which he was ranged. Touré's stress on remaining in close sympathy and contact with the masses is merely the obverse side of his hatred of the group who made their possession, and his own lack, of French cultural finesse a reason for consigning him for many years to humiliatingly second-rank positions. The fact that in Guinea—uniquely in francophone West Africa—the independence ' inheritance ' élite was *not* composed of men with a secondary or higher education was due to the fact that once Touré and the *petit-fonctionnaire* trade union-based group around him had attained power within the PDG, they were able to exercise a number of social controls to keep it. ' Keeping power ' in this context meant either preventing altogether the otherwise inevitable yeast-like rise of educated *évolué* elements within the movement, or making their tenancy of power depend on a fairly explicit acceptance of these social controls.[6]

What were these social controls ? The story of Touré's political career in the 1950s could really be summarized by saying that in the course of it he learnt, perhaps even over-learnt, two things. The first was that he could transform a political and even a social situation by the enthusiastic mobilization of large numbers of people. In particular this involved his encouragement and harnessing of the seething peasant discontent which provided the real motor of the PDG's development, eliciting mass response from the peasants to the Party's loose ideological definitions of their situation. Secondly, Touré learnt the virtues and power of organization: organization to sustain this mobilization and

5. *L'Ouvrier* (a Guinean CGT paper edited by Touré), No. 37, July 17, 1953.
6. For an account of how Touré exerted control in a critical situation see R. W. Johnson, ' The PDG and the Mamou " Deviation " ' in C. H. Allen and R. W. Johnson (eds.), *African Perspectives* (Cambridge, 1970 forthcoming).

give direction to the movement thus created; and organization to institutionalize and bolster the power of personal leadership. In the period between 1946 and 1952 when the PDG had been led and run by *évolué* intellectuals, organizational coherence and discipline were at a discount. After 1952, under Touré, they were at a premium. Touré and the *petit fonctionnaire* group around him exploited their organizational position, not only in the normal sense of enforcing discipline on men more educated than themselves, but also in order to multiply their organizational bases. Plural office-holding, indeed, became perhaps the most striking characteristic of Touré's group.[7] Thus when the 'intellectuals' again became important in the PDG in the later 1950s, they did so subject to the constraints of both organizational and ideological discipline. They had not only to accept but even to enunciate a populist rhetoric which explicitly devalued their own status as intellectuals.[8] By 1958 Touré had fairly thoroughly subjugated all possible rivals and established an apparently unchallengeable position of personal leadership.

Examination of Touré's role in pre-independence politics reveals a personal and ideological development of complex proportions. After an obscure early period (1945?–1948?) in which he held apparently orthodox marxist views, he moved towards a more *ouvrieriste* position, concentrating almost solely on trade union questions to the neglect of more overtly political ones. With his assumption of the PDG's leadership he veered towards a position that is perhaps best described as that of a radical populist-reformist, with his original marxist and even trade union background increasingly diluted and obscured. In the light of Touré's current stance—and of the PDG's re-writing of the 1950s period—it is as well to emphasize that Touré, as is clear in dozens of articles and hundreds of speeches, never seriously envisaged the possibility of violent revolutionary action in this period. Rather, his aim was to achieve power by whatever means were both possible and necessary, always acting within or on the margin of the institutional context provided by the French. He had, after all, no wish to see the PDG go the same way as the UPC (*Union des Populations du Cameroun*) in Cameroun.[9] On the other hand, he clearly aimed to achieve power while preserving as radical a party and policy as the situation would allow, thus hoping to retain the option of effecting radical change by the use of the power so achieved. This classic reformist tactic which just occasionally, due to the more militant attitude of the grass roots rank and file, seemed to be based on an

7. On the political importance of this plural office-holding see *ibid.*, pp. 368–9.
8. Since independence Touré's use of ideology as an agency of social control has taken on an entirely new dimension with his stress on the rediscovery of the African past. The continual public exaltation of Alfa Yaya and Samory Touré rather than, say, sophisticated café-society theories of negritude, or a technocratic stress on modernity and efficiency, allocates value to the heroic militancy of a popular past for which intellectuals feel the least affinity. The (by and large historically accurate) aspersions cast on these past heroes by contemporary Guinean intellectuals are not academic quibbles; they are a questioning of the hegemonic PDG ideology which has outflanked and displaced them.
9. Here a radical popular movement adopted armed guerilla tactics and was bloodily crushed by the French. See '*Union des Populations du Cameroun* (UPC) in Cameroun Politics, 1948–55', R. A. Jospeh, unpublished B. Phil. thesis, Oxford, 1969.

implicit revolutionary threat, actually succeeded in Guinea; though this was largely because of the sheer historical accident of the quite unexpected abruptness with which independence was achieved.[10]

From independence to 1964

Given Touré's central personal position, the evolution of his ideas since independence conflates ineluctably with the evolution of official PDG policy in this period.   Here it is important to take note of the emphasis laid officially— that is, by Touré himself—on the watershed of the *loi-cadre* of 8 November 1964.[11]   Up to 1964, so runs the official view, the PDG followed an essentially reformist path, albeit a radical one, while since 1964 the Party has been trans- forming itself into a truly revolutionary *avant-garde* movement and it has become possible to speak of the ' Guinean revolution '.   This distinction carries with it its own implied self-criticism, since the pre-1964 period was itself amply decked out in revolutionary phraseology and claims to revolutionary status and ambitions.

Nevertheless, an examination of Sekou Touré's writings—which have now reached seventeen volumes[12]—does support the view that, in the realm of ideology at least, there has been a marked change since 1964.   Gradually the forms of Touré's earlier radicalism have re-emerged; some ambiguous elements, such as the ' African personality ', have virtually disappeared from view; and the marxist element has become more pronounced—though, as we shall see, Touré is still some distance from any of the various marxist-leninist orthodoxies.

There was little hint of such development in the first four volumes of Touré's *Works*.   Indeed, the fact that these are the most widely known of his writings has itself become a source of confusion since they are so unrepresentative of Touré's contemporary position.   In this early period attention is focussed primarily on the meaning of independence.   As early as March 1959, Touré had termed Guinea's acquisition of independence a ' revolution '.   Apparently sensitive to Fanonist criticism, he denies that political violence is more than one of several possible revolutionary forms: the gaining of independence has resulted in a fundamental transformation of such proportions as to place Guinea in an objectively revolutionary situation (*Tome 3*, pp. 209–10).   On the other hand he is concerned to emphasize the continuing nature of the anti-colonial struggle, not only in the sense of the completion of Africa's liberation but also in the sense of a still ongoing struggle in Guinea itself against the ' inherited structures of colonial domination '.   In sharp contradistinction to those African leaders who saw independence as the fruit of a completed struggle, Touré insisted that

10.   See G. Chaffard, *Les Carnets Secrets de la Decolonisation, Vol. II*, (Paris 1967), pp. 165–268, esp. pp. 179–216.
11.   A. S. Touré, *8 Novembre* 1964, Imprimerie Patrice Lumumba, Conakry, 1965.   The texts of the declarations on the *loi-cadre* are also reprinted in Tome 14 of Touré's *Works*.
12.   See the bibliography at the end of this article.   Further references, as given in the text and in footnotes, will be simply to the volume number of each of the *Works*, which may be checked against the specific titles in the bibliography.

independence was a purely instrumental acquisition.   So, too, were democracy and national unity; to make them ends in themselves was as barren a doctrine as 'art for art's sake.'   They were merely means towards social progress, towards the destruction of the old colonial ' structures of domination ' and, above all, towards the decolonization of the minds, habits and attitudes of the people, without which other forms of progress were impossible or illusory.   A great effort of education, at once civic, moral, ideological and national, must be launched in order to accelerate the normal course of history in Guinea.   Yet the object of this enormous effort is still rather vaguely conceived as ' social progress '.   The aim of socialism is entirely absent at this stage.[13]

The extent to which Touré's earlier marxism had been diluted and compromised is clearest when the question of social class in African society is considered.   This question, indeed, provides a convenient touchstone for the measurement and evaluation of radicalism in Africa particularly in the early 1960s.   One may use it to place all African ideologists within a four-point scale :[14]

(i) the Know-Nothing stage involving an attempt to deny the existence of significant social differentiation in African societies.   Attempted by some political leaders in the early 1960s, it is clearly untenable for long;

(ii) a second stage in which it is acknowledged that a process of social differentiation and stratification has begun but in which it is insisted that the social conflicts thus occasioned are of a second order pressure group variety which may, indeed must, be reconciled in the interests of national unity or some other long-term goal;

(iii) a third stage in which it is frankly acknowledged that social classes proper with fundamentally opposed interests exist, but in which it is asserted that such conflicts, however bitter, may be due to the merely temporary strains of a particular historical period of, say, intensive ' modernization '.

There is, it is claimed, both the tactical possibility and the strategic necessity of a pragmatic alliance of classes.   Normally it has been the trade unions that have been asked or compelled to subordinate their class interests, but they may be asked to do this under either right or left wing regimes, for technocratic, developmentalist reasons, or in the name of ' scientific socialism ';

(iv) a fourth stage in which it is acknowledged that the social conflicts between different strata are of a fundamental nature, incapable of resolution. This necessitates the implicit or explicit taking of sides—theoretically, at least —for some groups and against others.

Briefly, the development of Touré's thought in the 1960s sees him move from

13.   See p. 359.
14.   The scale is conceived for heuristic rather than historical purposes and the stages are set out more discretely than they may ever be in fact.   In particular, stages (ii) and (iii) are frequently conflated, as they are for example in much Western contemporary pluralist ideology.

(ii) through (iii) to (iv) though, to say the least, his thinking has moved a great deal faster than its political implementation.   Thus when in 1959–60 Touré talked of the ' internal contradictions ' within Guinean society, the contradictions with which he was concerned were idealist rather than social, sins of individual behaviour—' egoism ', ' individualism ' and ' opportunism '.   It is hardly surprising that we should find that these sins are particularly liable to be committed by *déraciné* intellectuals with a ' superiority complex ' (*Tome 1–2*, p. 554, and *Tome 3*, pp. 161–8).   Touré admits that social conflict is possible between the different ' *couches sociales* ', between, for example, peasants and traders on the question of free trade in rice; he warns *fonctionnaires* that resources are scarce; and he speaks of the danger that the fruits of independence will be confiscated by the few.   But greed and selfishness, not class interests, are the true villains of the piece, and cultural and intellectual decolonisation is the remedy.

It is, naturally, on the delicate subject of trade unionism that Touré makes his assumptions and position most explicit :

' In Africa, where class antagonism does not exist, where an identity of interest dominates merely occupational-functional diversity . . . the labouring masses must accordingly quickly comprehend the particularities of their situation as against that of the European working class.   For them trade unionism must not be an instrument of class struggle but an instrument for harmonious evolution and rapid emancipation ' (*Tome 1–2*, pp. 419–20).

Indeed,

' . . . while marxism is applied in its doctrinal integrity by the international working class insofar as the class struggle is concerned, so we have amputated that element of it so that all the African *couches sociales* may work together in the general anti-colonialist struggle ' (*Ibid.*, p. 420).

On the other side of the coin he is equally clear, even to a trade unionist audience :

' The financial support of capitalism for which we appeal does not in any way compromise the mastery of the situation which we have acquired politically . . . . We launch this appeal to Capital so that those who possess it may also, with complete solidarity, enter into collaboration with us ' (*Ibid.*, p. 426).

Even at this stage, however, the marxist origins of Touré's basic ideas are always evident.   Indeed, there is always the suggestion that it is with a pragmatic reluctance that he abandons a more purely marxist approach.   In time such an approach may become more clearly relevant, but in a sense the task is to prevent it from becoming relevant by halting social differentiation.   At other times Touré appears to doubt whether such preventive action can be successful. And ultimately this more historicist view is dominant :

' Certainly, as our society develops, so it has a tendency to fragment itself into a more and more differentiated hierarchy. The scale runs from the plebeian element to the élite and the result is the dissociation of each element from that which precedes it and that which follows it, on the basis of the more or less accentuated contradiction between their interests. In the face of this hierarchical deployment there is a great temptation for each distinct *couche sociale* to act in a ' cellular ' manner—pursuing its own narrow interests rather than the common interest. Already (1959) one must observe—and one must deplore—that a very clear tendency towards crystallisation is manifesting itself among the various layers of society. This egocentric phenomenon will of necessity continue, accentuating itself so that at least the most urgent of these (particularist) demands may be met, for it is undeniable that the man who is himself deprived is deaf and blind to the misery of others. There is in this tendency a social aspect which threatens to condition the political situation.

' Thus one may fear, with justification, that this social mutation will have as its corollary the formation of a bourgeoisie, of a sort of aristocratic feudalism, the danger of which it is unnecessary to underline. As we have said, we reject the principle of class struggle, less through philosophical conviction than through the desire to save African solidarity at any price. For this [African solidarity] alone can lead us along our destined path, this alone is capable of preserving our originality and of imposing on the world a respect for African Man ' (*Ibid.*, pp. 411–12).

The ' teachers' plot ' and subsequent strikes of 1961 served to confirm Touré's ideas on these points even to the point of claiming that:

' Should the class struggle appear in the Republic of Guinea—if we were to give leeway to egoistic interest groups, even trade union ones, they would form a reactionary class of a bourgeois sort ' (*Tome 8*, p. 296).

Indeed, he went even further, insisting that it was only counter-revolutionaries and the ' anti-Party group ' who tried to substitute the notion of social classes for that of social differentiation endemic in all societies (*Ibid.*, p. 309). Only anarcho-syndicalists, he claimed, could believe that the principal contradictions facing Guinea were internal rather than those of the external struggle against imperialism (*Ibid.*, pp. 318–19). The fact was that colonialism had prevented the growth of a national capitalism or a national bourgeoisie in Guinea, and accordingly there could be no class struggle (*Ibid.*, p. 326).

At this point it appeared that Touré was moving clearly to the Right—there is little to separate the statements quoted above from positions later adopted by Mboya or Senghor. But in fact the long-term effect of the ' plot ' was rather to dissipate the euphoria of the early independence period. As other real or imagined plots followed, the Guinean political climate tautened considerably, and the foundations of a formidable police and intelligence *apparat* were laid in place. Meanwhile Guinea's isolation within Africa and internationally deepened at the same time that the economy, labouring under an over-valued currency, hasty nationalizations[15], inefficiency, corruption and smuggling on a massive scale, plunged into ever more desperate straits. In the face of the first real signs of political disaffection and mounting apathy Touré's position hardened noticeably. He had always insisted, from independence on, that ' bourgeois democracy ' was not applicable in Guinea, which was a *république populaire* (People's Republic), a democratic dictatorship. He now began to lay greater stress on the specifically revolutionary role of the PDG; disaffection must be expected and fought since ' every revolution creates its own counter-revolution. ' The time for sentimentalism was gone—now was the time for ' la fermeté révolutionnaire '. ' L'ennemi de la fermeté révolutionnaire, c'est le liberalisme qui, de compromis en compromis, fait tomber un parti dans la compromission et l'anarchie ' (*Tome 9*, pp. 144–7 and p. 151).

In some ways the period from 1961 to 1963 saw disaffection reach its height, particularly among intellectuals. Many French *progressistes* and foreign Africans who had come to Guinea after independence, full of enthusiasm for the new state and its regime, left in this period, disgruntled and despairing.[16] Many Guineans left as well, not only intellectuals but many thousands of peasants too, flooding into Abidjan and Dakar. Touré appeared to be building a regime of iron—and of smuggled cigarettes; an inefficient dictatorship in which austerity and corruption combined to provide the worst of both worlds. Such a view is, of course, still held by many.[17]

The *loi-cadre* of November 8, 1964 was essentially an attempt by Touré to halt this political and economic slide. Draconian new measures were introduced to curb corruption and to regulate commerce; in Conakry licences to deal in commerce were to be cut back by 80 per cent; all state and Party officials were to be submitted to examination of the sources of their income and possessions; all private import and export trade was outlawed; the PDG was entirely re-organized with work-place organization and a slimmed-down membership. Excluded from all Party responsibilities were all merchants and all those convicted since 1958 of theft, corruption, fraud, subversion or racism. There followed a whole series of further decrees aimed at corruption among civil servants. Henceforth even the most senior Minister would have to prove his revolutionary militancy and vigilance in word and deed under pain of the most severe sanctions.[18]

15. Nationalization, which was always justified in radical-democrat rather than socialist terms, was in almost all cases followed by a steep fall in output. The great bauxite mining complex at Fria has not been nationalised and its continuing economic success remains crucial to the regime's solvency and, probably, its stability as well.
16. This mood of despair is best expressed in B. Ameillon's *Guinée—bilan d'une indé-pendance* (Paris, 1963), a Fanonist-Maoist critique—which Touré has doubtless read.
17. There are several anti-Touré front movements based in Senegal and the Ivory Coast and a significant Guinean intellectual emigré group in Paris. These opposition groups are generally badly split—the Parisian group has a Maoist splinter. *Perspectives Nouvelles*, the organ of the main Paris-based group, is a source of interesting though unverifiable information on contemporary Guinea.
18. See *Tome 14*, pp. 331–408 for the relevant tests and the supplementary reform decrees of later weeks. A comparison of 8 November 1964 and other sudden turns to the Left in Africa—Nkrumah's ' Dawn Broadcast ', and the Arusha and Mulungushi Declarations—would be a worthwhile subject for future research.

This sharp turn to the Left is reflected in *Tome 13, L'Afrique et la Révolution*. Using the same analytic base that he had earlier employed in his attack on the ' teachers' plot ', Touré claimed that the measures were necessary to prevent a Guinean compradore bourgeoisie from becoming a full-blown national bourgeoisie:

' In Africa colonial intervention occurred during a feudal period which was still profoundly marked by a ' communocratic ' spirit. The organization of the modes of production was still neither of the slave-based type, nor assimilable to the so-called ' Asiatic ' mode. The despotism which characterizes feudalism only appeared after the colonial intervention and at its behest. *A fortiori* there was no bourgeoisie at all. In the absence of a national bourgeoisie one could not have a capitalist society. Moreover, colonialism, by its take-over of both land and men as means of production, hindered the formation of a bourgeois class. While a privileged social category (feudal chiefs, civil servants and merchants) did appear under this omnipotent reign, it did so only very late and still possessed none of the means necessary for primitive capital accumulation, for these means were in the hands of colonialism or, at least, under its direct control. It is quite evident that this privileged national category was using our independence as a cover for transforming itself into a national bourgeoisie ' (*Tome 13*, pp. 110–11).

Guinea had moved from the stage of People's Democracy to that of National Democracy, by which was meant a regime intent upon preventing the emergence of antagonistic social classes by crushing the national bourgeoisie at the moment of its emergence (*Ibid.*, pp. 115–16).

For the first time Guinea's socialist option was affirmed, though Touré made it clear that he had doubts as to the applicability of the term. And, although *Tome 13* concludes with an academic discussion of dialectical materialism, Touré's conception of socialism remained essentially idealist.

' Since the creation of the PDG we have always made clear, without hesitation or complexes, the aims of our actions. But we have always used the words ' socialist ' and ' socialism ' as little as possible. Often at (PDG) Congresses comrades have brought up the question and we have always replied that our basic philosophy of history did not allow us to consider capitalism or socialism as finalities. This being so, our revolutionary option has aimed only at the well-being of the people . . . . The question of our socialist perspectives is poorly framed. In every country there are capitalist and socialist perspectives which develop conjointly or separately . . . . One may well ask whether it is possible to ' build socialism ' in the conditions of an agricultural economy issuing from colonial mercantilism . . . . We opt for the socialist system, that is to say that we devoutly desire the continued progress of social justice . . . . The socialist Revolution is first and foremost a heightened consciousness, a willing determination to see the good of all, a firm courage ' (*Ibid.*, pp. 171–3).

Here it may be as well to note that Touré's writings on semi-philosophical subjects such as this descend all too easily into self-repetitious generality and out-right mystification.   One must always remember that his printed word is merely transcribed platform oratory.   He is at his best and clearest when he defines his positions in contradistinction to those of others; as when he analyses and condemns the concept of negritude as racist mystification,[19] or when he is analysing the incomplete and satellitic nature of ' independence ' in so many African states.   His often scathing clarity frequently deserts him when faced with the problem of conceptualising or analysing original or purely Guinean phenomena.

The period since 1964

The major swing to the Left of 1964 has been followed in succeeding years less by important original ideological departures than by a process of continuous expansion, elucidation and intensification of the 1964 theses.   1964 also marks a landmark, however, in the use of ideology as a form of social control.   Hitherto, as we have seen, the dominant position of Touré's ideology had been used to disadvantage members of certain social groups in their public and political activities.   Since 1964 ideology has increasingly become an instrument of control over *individuals* rather than groups.   This has happened for several reasons.

The *loi-cadre* reforms of 1964 have never been fully or properly carried out, as Touré himself acknowledges.   Since 1964 the disjuncture between what Touré says and what actually happens in Guinea has grown increasingly radical and severe—indeed, one has the impression that Touré has long ago run up against the outside limits of all that organisation and exhortation to mass mobilis-ation can achieve.   At the same time Guinea's isolation within Africa has increased enormously with the fall of the friendly Sierra Leonean, Malian, Ghanaian, and Algerian regimes and the weakened position of the UAR since the war with Israel.   This isolation has, in turn, predictably intensified the domestic climate of tension and suspicion in Guinea.[20]   This climate and the fact that Touré's ideology has far outrun both popular understanding and concrete every-day Guinean realities produce a situation in which hardly anyone

19.   *Tome 13*, pp. 191–3.   One of the declared aims of the 8 November *tournant* was a relentless struggle against all forms of mystification—which included sorcery, witchcraft, maraboutism and racial versions of pan-Africanism and pan-Arabism. ' *Technocratisme* ' has been more recently added.   This campaign was coupled with a massive literacy campaign, with a stress on literacy in the mother tongue (Soussou, Pular, Guerzé, Malinké etc.)   The de-mystification campaign has been more successful than most, the literacy drive less so.
20.   The impact of the Ghanaian and Malian coups was particularly great.   Much of *Tome 15* is taken up with considerations issuing from these coups.   The attempted coup in Guinea in April 1969 saw the first official death sentences for political crimes meted out in Guinea since independence.

in any position can feel safe from denunciation for ideological crimes such as the harbouring of counter-revolutionary sentiments. This is particularly so since Touré has continued to coin new watch-words so that ' what was progressive in 1964 may cease to be so in 1965 ' (*Tome 13*, p. 127). The need for vigilance is absolute since subversion is literally everywhere :

> ' . . . subversion is not a material fact that one can show people. It is not an objective thing, it only has objective results. Subversion is part of one and it is in all of us, beginning with the Secretary General of the PDG down to the last militant who joins the Party as he strolls out of a meeting. Subversion inhabits every heart . . . ' (*Tome 15*, p. 39).

Naturally, the enemy has the sense to stay hidden :

> ' Embourgeoisement continues to make progress. Of course, a cadre will never say that he has become a bourgeois. But it is easy to detect it in his manner of speaking, in the way he discusses future possibilities, in the way he interprets facts, in the way he takes on a job, in the way he behaves himself in regard to the people. Of course, all this denounces him without his realising ' (*Ibid.*, pp. 46–7).

If this sounds like a ' conspiracy theory of history ' one ought to add that there are, indeed, many real enough conspiracies.

Implicitly, though not explicitly, the 1964 *tournant* revoked all Touré's earlier denials of the existence of social classes and of class struggle; the Party was summoned to revolutionary struggle against the bourgeois class. Since 1964 the principle of class struggle has been increasingly emphasized, particularly since the 8th PDG Congress in 1967. Moreover, Touré has made it clear that he views the problem of class struggle in both a national and an international context.

Domestically the lines of division have been somewhat clarified :

> ' The interest of the labouring masses . . . demands that the working class, the peasantry and sincerely progressive elements effectively direct and control all the vital sectors of the national life and that the reactionary elements of the bourgeoisie, of the bureaucracy and of capitalism, even national capitalism, be thrown from all positions of influence, decision and control . . . . The class struggle hereby becomes the political form of practical explanation . . . The class struggle is a universal reality and a historic necessity . . . . Political organization, political and ideological education of the people, are the principal weapons in the struggle against the class enemy. '[21]

Touré characterises the ' class enemy ' in several ways :

> ' Undoubtedly in these last few years a bureaucratic bourgeoisie has installed itself within the Party and in public administration and the State

21. A. S. Touré, ' Rapport politique et de doctrine ', *8ème Congrès National du PDG, Conakry 25 septembre–2 octobre 1967*, pp. 22–3.

enterprises. It has spawned about itself a ' clientele ' of merchants, *transporteurs* and rural land proprietors—an embryonic national bourgeoisie—all as its dependants ' (*Tome 13*, p. 115).

But the real problem is a cultural one, of bourgeois and petit-bourgeois aspirations :

'. . . there are some who, victims of colonial petit-bourgeois ideology, owing to their training as servants of colonialism, have never been able to regain their self-possession but have retained their old expectations, waiting for new masters able to provide them with the neo-colonialist crumbs to which they aspired during the colonial period and of which they have since been deprived . . . . It is a petit-bourgeoisie with an aberrant mentality, incapable of any creative or serious effort, while the European bourgeoisie, for example, was and still is tough-minded and ready for work. It is a petit-bourgeoisie which has resigned itself, which is slothful, which is ready to sell the Nation to any imperialist power that presents itself, which is hypocritical and treacherous . . . it is a corrupted petit-bourgeoisie . . . in fact a lumpen-bourgeoisie. '[22]

Internationally Touré has moved towards a more ' Cuban ' position. In several diplomatically explosive passages of his *Rapport Politique* to the 8th PDG Congress he declared that *tiers monde* countries were now in the forefront of the struggle against imperialism. Not only could one no longer believe that imperialism and capitalism would fall of themselves, but one could not rely either upon the Socialist great powers. It was, for example, not true that ' the British worker can wait upon the USSR or China to see the end of the exploitation to which he is submitted. '[23] Moreover, the Socialist powers were guilty of helping to uphold an international primary products price-system which merely institutionalized *tiers monde* exploitation.[24] The doctrine of peaceful coexistence was a reactionary and unacceptable compromise for it helped to freeze a world situation in which imperialism was still rampant.[25] Fruitful relationships between *tiers monde* countries and capitalist-imperialist ones were simply impossible—and, consistently, Touré gives a list of extremely restrictive conditions under which Guinea will be prepared to accept foreign aid.[26]

Although Touré's continuing exhortations to ' wage the class struggle to the death ' and to ' deepen and radicalize the Revolution '—the general currency of

22. Touré, ' Rapport politique et de doctrine ', *loc. cit.* p. 85.
23. *Ibid.*, p. 44. Touré's ' Rapport politique ' was, as originally published, a diplomatically explosive document which led to protests from both the USSR and China. The official account of the 8th Congress was accordingly withdrawn from circulation and the account of it provided in *Tome 16* omits all the more controversial passages.
24. *Ibid.*, p. 57.
25. *Ibid.*, pp. 45–48. Touré also denounces the Sino-Soviet split as a near-criminal irrelevance. Guinea sides with the Vietnamese against the USA and the NLF is normally cited as a paradigm model for anti-imperialist struggle. Characteristically and in company with China and Cuba, Guinea has refused to sign the Test-ban Treaty.
26. *Ibid.*, pp. 55–6.

his speeches since 1967—amount to little more than appeals for the execution of long-declared policy aims, there have been several ideological and organizational innovations in this latter period.   Most notably these have included the declaration of a Socialist Cultural Revolution, the creation of a Popular Militia, the greater role given to the PDG Youth, the JRDA (*Jeunesse de la Révolution Démocratique Africaine*), and the institution of Local Revolutionary Power (PRL—*Pouvoir Révolutionnaire Locale*).

These innovations should not be allowed to obscure the continuities in Touré's thought.   The counter-revolutionary bourgeoisie is still continually depicted in terms of armchair intellectuals with superiority complexes: ' The counter-revolution has installed itself in armchairs.   It no longer lives in the (chiefs') huts from which it has fled.   Now it lives in villas and civil service apartments . . . ' (*Tome 15*, p. 45).   Touré's marxism also still contains a strong voluntaristic element, only partially derived from occasional imitation of Chinese models.[27]   The counter-revolution *is* counter-revolutionary for the same old ' raisons de comportement individuel '—' egoism ', ' individualism ', and so on. The Cultural Revolution, a massive campaign of orchestrated education and indoctrination, aims at changing the hearts and minds of the people in an entirely voluntaristic fashion.   It is the same combination of education and organization, and continual re-organization, on which Touré has always relied. These factors were enough to bring him political success in the 1950s and to achieve independence in 1958—when an aroused and militant population, impressively organized and disciplined within the PDG, voted ' NON '—and the walls of Jericho came tumbling down.   One may legitimately doubt whether the barriers of poverty and corruption will fall in the same way.

Touré is doubtless aware of these considerations and there is an element of despair in these recent innovations. The Cultural Revolution is aimed particularly at the young through sweeping changes in the educational system which stress —to borrow the obvious Chinese analogy—the qualities of being ' red rather than expert '.   It may well be that Touré has written off the present generation of office-holders and civil servants as irredeemably corrupted by colonialist ideology; hope lies with the younger generation who have come to maturity in the twelve years since independence.[28]   Touré has certainly laid increasing

27.   The extent to which imitation is conscious is a matter for debate, but one might list as possible subjects for such comparison *investissement humaine*, the de-mystification and literacy campaigns, Touré's conceptions of National Democracy and the compradore bourgeoisie and the Cultural Revolution.   (One might also instance, more frivolously, Touré's budding ambition as a poet—most of the later *Tomes* include a number of his poems and some of them have been collected and published under the title *Poèmes Militants* (Conakry, 1969).   Unlike Mao's poetry, however, Touré's is exclusively political in content.)   The regime has tolerated but not encouraged conscious popular imitation of Chinese models—Mao jackets, Mao buttons and so forth.   Touré has refused an initiative to have a little Red Book of his quotations published.
28.   The first graduates of the Conakry Institut Polytechnique—the *Promotion Lénine*— were all made deputy-directors of State enterprises on graduation.   Only students in advanced technical subjects such as engineering are now allowed to study abroad and even they must compulsorily work for one year in a factory as part of their course.   Guinea is likely to have the first home-grown intelligentsia in Africa.

stress on the role of youth in the revolutionary bloc of peasants and workers though of late there has been increasing stress on the vanguard nature of the working class—and the JRDA is now more in evidence in the streets of Conakry (performing police functions, for example) than is the Party proper.   Similarly, the creation of the *Milice Populaire* (restricted to 20–30 years-olds) tends to assume that the Army is ultimately unreliable too.   The PRL program, aimed at transferring a whole range of administrative functions from the State to local village Party committees, would, if successful, greatly reduce the power of the civil service bureaucracy which Touré has quite patently in large part written off.[29]

It is to be expected that, as with so many other of Touré's plans, projects and slogans, these latest innovations will be at best partially fulfilled, particularly since enormous vested interests are at stake.   It is difficult, however, to see what other course Touré could follow within the ideological limts he has set himself.   The only obvious alternative would be to use openly stalinist means to attain his objectives: the heightened and systematized use of discriminatory rationing, police and intelligence repression, and forced mobilization of labour. And he can rely neither on sufficient personal popularity nor an efficient enough repressive *apparat* to make this work for long.

At the moment he does seem to remain popular—impressionistically one feels he could probably win a free election easily enough, though not without signi-ficant opposition.   This is no inconsiderable achievement for a radical leader in Africa who has already been in power for 13 years and who—it should be remembered—is still only 48.   Provided that Touré retains his formidable health and physical strength, and his agility in thwarting both intra- and extra-Party challenges, it is conceivable—despite his currently critical situation—that he could remain in power for many years yet.   But he has already taught us a good deal about the limits of the radical and the possible in contemporary Africa.

29.   On PRL see *Tome 16*, esp. pp. 46–109.   On the Cultural Revolution see *Tome 17*, esp. pp. 210–309.

BIBLIOGRAPHY OF THE WORKS OF SEKOU TOURÉ TO 1969

Unless otherwise indicated all of the *Works* referred to were published in Conakry at the Imprimerie Patrice Lumumba.

TOME 1: *L'Action politique du PDG pour l'émancipation africaine*, (1958). 206pp.
TOME 2: *L'Action politique du PDG pour l'émancipation africaine*, (1959). 320pp.

These two volumes were published together in 1962 by Présence Africaine (Paris) with a preface by Aimé Césaire, under the title *Expérience guinéenne et unité africaine*, 566pp.   This is the version which I have used above.
TOME: 3 *L'Action politique* . . . . *etc*, (1960). 269pp.

Except for 20 pages this volume has been reprinted by Présence Africaine under the title of *La Guinée et l'émancipation africaine* (1959), 249pp.   This is the version which I have used above.
TOME 4: *La Lutte du PDG pour l'émancipation africaine*, 2nd ed. (1960). 390pp.

TOME 5: *L'Action politique du PDG: la planification économique*, (1960). 438pp.
TOME 6: *L'Action politique du PDG (as Tomes 1 and 2)* (1961). 562pp.
A special edition of this volume was published in Conakry in 1962 under the title *La Révolution guinéenne et le progres social*. 644pp. It is this enlarged version that I have used above.
TOME 7: *La Politique internationale du PDG* (n.d. 1961?). 278pp.
TOME 8: *L'Action politique du PDG en faveur de l'émancipation de la jeunesse guinéenne* (1962). 368pp.
TOME 9: ' *Au Nom de la Révolution* ': *conférences hebdomadaires* (1962). 248pp.
TOME 10: *L'Afrique en marche* (4th ed., 1967). 694pp.
TOME 11: *Apprendre . . . savoir . . . pouvoir* (1965). 376pp.
TOME 12: *Concevoir—analyser—réaliser* (1965?). 391pp.
TOME 13: *L'Afrique et la Révolution* (1965?). 398pp. (Also reprinted in Switzerland by Présence Africaine and in Cairo in Arabic.)
TOME 14: *Plan Septennal* 1964–71 (1967). 443pp.
TOME 15: *Défendre la Révolution* (1968?). 333pp.
TOME 16: *Le Pouvoir populaire* (1968). 454pp.
TOME 17: *La Révolution culturelle* (1969). 414pp.
The special edition of TOME 6 and TOMES 7 and 8 have been published in English title in Cairo.
Other major sources for the study of Touré's thought include:
Cinquième Congrès du PDG: rapport politique et de doctrine (1960). 112pp.
Textes des interviews accordées aux réprésentants de la presse (1959). 158pp.
Congrès Générale de l'UGTAN 15–18 *janvier* 1959 (Présence Africaine, Paris, 1959). An English version has also been published.
Confédération Nationale de Travailleurs de Guinée UGTAN-CNTG 2ème *Congrès National 7–9 juillet,* 1960 (1960). 114pp.
8ème *Congrès National du PDG* 25 *septembre*–2 *octobre* 1967 (1968). 325pp.

Journal of African History, XIV, 2 (1973), pp. 313–330
Printed in Great Britain

DJIBO BAKARY, THE FRENCH, AND THE
REFERENDUM OF 1958 IN NIGER

BY FINN FUGLESTAD

INTRODUCTION

WHAT happened in Niger between 1957 and 1958 has aroused little attention among scholars.[1] This is all the more astonishing, since the events that took place in Niger before, during and after the referendum of 1958, do not fit into a number of established patterns.

First of all, Niger was the only French African territory (*Territoire d'Outre-Mer*) in which General de Gaulle's new constitution was neither rejected nor approved by between 95 and 99 per cent of the electorate. Moreover it was the only territory where the voters did not support the official stand of their government, thereby provoking a cabinet crisis. And finally, the head of that government, Djibo Bakary, was a rare example of an African political leader whose strength was based on an ethnic group other than his own. All this happened in one of the most traditional and economically backward *Territoires d'Outre-Mer*, where the *per capita* GNP amounted to roughly 362 francs (compared with some 1,020 frs. in Senegal[2]).

What was at stake in the 1958 referendum was the new French constitution, de Gaulle's constitution, enacting the Fifth Republic. In Africa, however, voting for or against this constitution also implied something else, namely whether the Africans accepted the elevation of their territories as autonomous, self-governed but not independent republics, members of the French community, or whether they preferred independence straight away. It was understood that a negative vote would be followed by quick and complete French retreat.[3]

BACKGROUND TO THE CRISIS

In order to grasp what happened in Niger in 1957–8, it is necessary to go back to the early post-war years, when the reforms of 1946 radically

---

[1] Brilliant but not always accurate journalistic accounts are to be found in Georges Chaffard, *Histoire secrète de la Décolonisation*, II (Calmann-Lévy, Paris, 1967), and in Edward Mortimer, *France and the Africans 1944–60* (Faber and Faber Ltd., London, 1969). The author wishes to thank, among others, Michael Gerrard and J. D. Fage for help with his English text.

[2] Michèle Saint-Marc, *Décolonisation et zone franc* (SEDES, Paris, 1964), 19.

[3] The main bulk of information used in this article originates, where not otherwise stated, from interviews. These interviews were granted the author on the understanding that it would not be possible to trace any relevant information back to the man it came from. This is because the referendum of 1958 is still a 'hot' issue in Niger.

My sample comprises 16 Frenchmen who actually lived in Niger during and immediately before or after the referendum, namely 10 Colonial Administrators ('Administrateurs de la France d'Outre-Mer'), 3 Teachers, 2 Businessmen, and 1 Catholic priest.

altered the political scene in French West Africa. Political parties were for the first time allowed, local assemblies were set up, and seats were reserved for Africans (who suddenly became French citizens) in the various metropolitan parliamentary assemblies. In Niger, on 17 June 1946, low-ranking civil servants and, especially, school teachers (most of them being graduates of the famous Ecole Normale William Ponty in Dakar,[4] and belonging to ethnic groups from the west), established the *Parti Progressiste Nigérien*[5] (PPN), which later joined the Pan-African and eventually Communist-affiliated *Rassemblement Démocratique Africain* (RDA) of Félix Houphouët-Boigny. The PPN, having thus become the local branch of the RDA, pursued the same policy as the other RDA branches throughout Africa, namely one of extreme hostility towards the chiefs and the French Colonial Administration. It is not our purpose to determine whether this was a right policy or not. From a strategic viewpoint, however, it can be said that such a policy was conceivable in a territory like the Ivory Coast, where the chiefs were relatively weak, and where the indigenous planters, who made up the backbone of the *Parti Démocratique de la Côte d'Ivoire* (the local branch of the RDA), were financially independent of the French administration.[6] Pursuing the same policy in Niger, however, was close to folly, for two reasons. The society of Niger was and still is one of the most traditional in West Africa, with the chiefs firmly in the saddle. Secondly, there were very few *évolués*, and all of them were employed by, and therefore dependent upon, the very administration they denounced. The French responded by appointing the most turbulent of them to posts in

---

My sample of Africans comprises 34 persons: 16 Hausas, 11 Zerma/Sonrais, and 7 'others' (Fulanis, Kanuris, Mossis). Their background may be summarized in the following table:

	Hausas	Zerma/Sonrais	Others
Social background: Chiefs	2	1	1
Members of Chiefly families	6	4	1
Commoners	8	6	5
Education: William Ponty or higher	2	5	5
Other	14	6	2
Political itineraries: PPN/RDA–UCFA	6	5	3
UDN–MSA–Sawaba	2	0	2
UNIS–BNA–MSA–Sawaba	3	2	0
UNIS–BNA–MSA–Sawaba–UCFA	4	2	1
Others	1	0	1

Of the 14 Africans mentioned in the article, 6 have been interviewed; of the 13 Europeans, 8. (Notable exceptions: de Gaulle, Houphouët-Boigny, Senghor and Djibo Bakary.)

[4] According to my own calculations, there were by 1945 some 2,000 former William-Ponty pupils in West Africa. Only about 60 of these came from Niger.

[5] 'Territoire du Niger. Rapport Politique, année 1951', 62 (AP. Dosso).
Abbreviations:
AP: Archives of the 'Préfecture' of . . .
ASP: Archives of the 'Sous-Préfecture' of . . .
APR: Archives, Presidency of the Republic, Niamey.

[6] For politics in the Ivory Coast, see Ruth Schachter Morgenthau, *Political Parties in French-speaking West Africa* (Clarendon Press, Oxford, 1964).

distant regions, and in fact managed to dismantle the party organization. In short, the PPN/RDA lacked the means for succeeding with its policy, all the more so since, with the chiefs barring the way, it did not manage to become a real mass party. Furthermore, the PPN/RDA was dominated by Ponty-educated commoners from minority groups in the west (Zermas and Sonrais[7]), who tended to monopolize the party hierarchy for themselves.

Faced with an alliance between the chiefs, less-educated easterners (Hausas), *and* the colonial administration under its law-and-order governor Jean Toby,[8] the PPN/RDA had by 1952 lost all the seats it controlled in local, federal and metropolitan assemblies (according to the RDA, this was solely the result of fraudulent proceedings).[9] The sole gainer from these losses, was the *Union Nigérienne des Indépendants et Sympathisants* (UNIS), founded on 4 June 1948,[10] a typical 'patron' party and, as such, 'weakly articulated, comparatively indisciplined with little if any direct membership participation'.[11] Small wonder then, that the PPN/RDA leaders responsible felt a strong need for a change in policy. The same situation prevailed more or less in the other territories, and found its solution in the break with the Communist party in 1951. Inside the PPN/ RDA, two of its main figures, Djibrilla Maiga and Djibo Bakary, disagreed however with the official party line, and wanted to stick to the alliance with the French Communist Party (PCF).[12] Djibrilla Maiga finally joined UNIS, whereas Djibo Bakary, another Ponty-educated westerner of low birth and a cousin of the PPN/RDA-party chief Hamani Diori, remained faithful to his ideals and in 1954 set up a party of his own, the *Union Démocratique Nigérienne* (UDN). He claimed to represent the only true RDA line,[13] and maintained close ties with the PCF. But politics were far from being the only activity of Djibo Bakary, let alone the most important one. He launched himself into trade unionism, at a time when the first FIDES-sponsored[14] and financed public works were beginning, and so provoking the birth of an urban proletariat. Since the PPN/RDA appealed mainly to the *évolués* and UNIS to the rural and traditional world (whereas the staffs of the European trading houses were largely filled with Dahomeans who kept aloof from politics), Djibo was free to

[7] In 1964 the Hausas numbered 1,500,000 and the Zerma/Sonrais 650,000 out of a total population of 3,200,000. See Pierre Donaint, *Le Niger; Cours de géographie* (Ministère de l'Education nationale, Niamey), 148.

[8] Governor of Niger, 1942–52 and 1953–5.

[9] See interventions by Hamani Diori and M. Konaté in the French National Assembly 30 July 1949 and 21 August 1951.

[10] See note 5.

[11] Ruth Schachter Morgenthau, 'Single-Party Systems in West Africa', *American Political Science Review*, LV, no. 2 (June 1961), 294–307.

[12] 'Territ. du Niger. Rapp. pol. 1951', 12–14.

[13] On the new party's programme, see 'Procès-Verbal de l'Assemblée Générale Constituante de l'U.D.N. Comité Régional de Zinder', Zinder, 18 May 1954, 2 (AP. Zinder), and *Le Démocrate* (organ of the UDN) of 17 Nov. 1956.

[14] Fonds d'Investissement et de Développement Economique et Social.

build up a considerable following among the urban wage-earners.[15] In the
early fifties, a series of rather sucessful strikes[16] brought Djibo nationwide
attention. This was all the more deserved since, mainly thanks to his efforts,
an increase in salary of 33 per cent was agreed in 1952 by the French, who
had to admit that the workers were underpaid.[17] In short, Djibo singled
himself out to the French administration as the number one trouble-
maker. Backed by the French Communist-dominated *Confédération
Générale du Travail* (CGT), which provided him with a stable position as
member of the *Conseil Economique et Social* in Paris, Djibo (after having
resigned as a teacher in the late forties), along with his lieutenants, was
independent of the colonial administration, and therefore harder for the
French to tackle than were the PPN/RDA leaders.

In addition to his trade unionism and his party politics, Djibo also tried
to penetrate traditional youth movements—the *Samariats*—and women's
organizations (mainly the 'free women's' organizations), and where this
failed, he set up rival associations with considerable sucess.[18] The same
applies, although to a lesser degree, to the *Sanaa*, the traditional guilds of
craftsmen.[19]

By 1955 Djibo's position was however far from dominant in Niger. To
control the urban proletariat was all very well. But after all, in a country
where the towns were few and small (in 1956, the wage-earners numbered
only about 14,000 people, all categories included[20]), it was still the people
of the rural communities who decided who should hold seats in the different
assemblies, all the more so since the extension of suffrage favoured the
peasantry.[21] And rural Niger was still firmly controlled—or so it seemed—
by the chiefs and the French colonial administration. That year saw however the arrival of a new Governor, Jean Ramadier (son of the famous
French statesman, Paul Ramadier), who embarked upon a near reversal of
French policy in Niger. Contrary to his long-lasting predecessor, Jean
Toby, Ramadier, a staunch young socialist, had little respect for the chiefs.
Whereas Toby had earned a reputation as a 'know-all' governor, completely
at ease in the tortuous labyrinths of traditional African politics, Ramadier
was interested first and foremost in economic development and in pro-

---

[15] For an account of the trade union situation in 1954, see René Galinier, 'Rapport
Annuel, Cercle de Zinder, année 1954', 49–70 (AP. Zinder).

[16] 'Territ. du Niger. Rapp. pol. année 1953', 54 (AP. Zinder).

[17] 'Territ. du Niger. Rapp. pol. année 1952', 45 (AP. Zinder).

[18] See, for example, 'Lettre du Commissaire de Police de Maradi à M. le Chef des
Services de Police du Niger', Maradi, 5 Jan. 1956, 1–3 (AP. Maradi). For the role of the
'free women' see Colette Piault, *Contribution à l'étude de la vie quotidienne de la femme
mawri*, Etudes Nigériennes, no. 10 (IFAN/CNRS–Niamey/Paris, no date), 111.

[19] See Nicolas, Doumesche, Mouché, *Etude socio-économique de deux villages Hausas*,
Etudes Nigériennes, no. 22 (IFAN/CNRS–Niamey/Paris, 1968), 98.

[20] 'Territ. du Niger. Rapp. écon. année 1957', 38–9 (Centre de Documentation, Commissariat Général du Développement, Niamey).

[21] Before the introduction of general suffrage in 1956, Niger had 312,558 voters out
of 2,326,000 inhabitants. See A. Holleaux, 'Les élections aux Assemblées des T.O.M.',
Révue Juridique et Politique de l'Union Française (1956), 1–54.

moting education, both fields having been neglected by Toby.[22] Maintaining close links with prominent metropolitan politicians, he was able to obtain more funds for Niger than Toby had ever dreamt of, or perhaps even wanted.[23] More important to our purpose is Ramadier's attitude towards the tiny educated and 'westernized' local élite. Arguing that the future lay with these men, Ramadier felt he had little choice but to collaborate with the *évolués*. In Ramadier's view, continued French opposition to the most radical branch of this class, namely Djibo Bakary and his followers, could only lead to further radicalization.

It has been a fashionable viewpoint that Ramadier 'made' Djibo into what he became.[24] How true this is, is however virtually impossible to determine. What can be suggested is that both Ramadier and his sucessor—and fellow socialist—Paul Bordier (Governor 1956-8), tried to 'integrate' Djibo, probably promising him some kind of support if he eventually switched his party allegiance. However the same promises were very possibly extended also to the PPN/RDA leaders.

This change of attitude by the French, besides triggering off the first real economic development Niger had ever known, led to a bolstering of the 'modern' political parties, the PPN/RDA and the UDN, and found its expression in 1956 in the election of Hamani Diori as member of the French National Assembly (where he had already held a seat from 1946 to 1951) and in the near victory of Djibo Bakary. Out of the 307,515 votes cast for the candidates competing for the two seats, the list presented by the *Bloc Nigérien d'Action* (BNA—that is, UNIS renewed) received 126,673, the PPN/RDA list 82,437 (52,000 in the west alone), and the UDN list 74,063 (55,000 of these came from Hausaland, where the UDN took 45 per cent of all votes cast in the *cercle* of Maradi, and more than 50 per cent in the *cercle* of Zinder).[25] Finally the 'rump' UNIS list received 24,342 votes.[26]

[22] In 1953 Niger possessed *one* factory, that produced 200 tons of ground-nut oil (*Journal Officiel de la République Française, Avis et Rapports du Conseil Economique et Social*, 26 Mar. 1953). Regarding schools, these were in 1954 attended by some 7,703 pupils, that is 1·5 per cent of the population eligible for education (Jean Ramadier, 'Discours prononcé à la séance d'ouverture de la session ordinaire de l'Assemblée Territoriale du Niger', Niamey, 29 Mar. 1955, 4 (ASP. Magaria)). Moreover, Toby was not even capable of absorbing all the FIDES credits Niger was allocated (Ramadier, ibid. 4). Of the FIDES credits, of which Niger had received 322 million francs from 1949 to 1954, 36 millions had not been used ('Procès-Verbal de la Conférence des Commandants de Cercle', Niamey, 20–5 Apr. 1955, 10 (ASP. Madaoua)).

[23] In 1955–6 Ramadier, according to himself, was able to wrest out of the FIDES 1,450 millions instead of the 835 millions initially envisaged (Ramadier, op. cit. 5).

[24] Boubou Hama, 'Ramadier est le père du socialisme dans ce pays' ('Procès-Verbal des délibérations de l'Assemblée Territoriale du Niger. Séance du 18 May 1957') (ASP. Magaria). Djibo on the contrary accused Ramadier of having rescued the PPN/RDA from total oblivion. See 'Rapport Général, Congrès du MSA les 6 juillet et 8 mai 1957' cited in 'Synthèse Mensuelle, Direction des Services de Police du Niger' (henceforth SM. Police), Niamey, 31 May 1957, 8. (This periodical, only destined for the French Administration, is to be found in most archives in Niger).

[25] SM. Police, Nov. 1956, 3–10.

[26] Global results published in *Niger-Information* (Government newspaper), Niamey, 20 Jan. 1956, 2–3.

In short, less than 50 per cent voted for the 'traditionalists', compared with 85 per cent in 1951.[27]

Later that year, Djibo—having formally broken all ties with the PCF—was strong enough to force the BNA into a merger and to capture the newly established mayorship of Niamey. The new party became known as the local section of the *Mouvement Socialiste Africain* (MSA).

What had happened was simply that, embarking upon a series of forays into rural Hausaland, Djibo had proved himself to be a success among Hausa peasants, scaring the 'traditionalists', who were already appalled by Ramadier's and Bordier's attitudes. Fearing that they might fall between two stools, and at least encouraged by the French, the 'traditionalists' chose to join forces with Djibo after negotiations with the PPN/RDA had broken down. (The PPN/RDA in fact called the negotiations off, when they were well under way to success.[28]) In 1957, in the first elections to Niger's first autonomous Territorial Assembly, the MSA swept Hausaland, barely won (over independent candidates) in the far east (Kanuri country) and the north (Tuareg country), and left the west to the PPN/RDA. With a majority of 41 out of 60,[29] Djibo Bakary became Niger's first (and French Africa's only MSA) Deputy Prime Minister (*Vice-Président du Conseil des Ministres*).[30]

The important question is how Djibo could gain such strength in tradition-bound and very little politicized Hausaland, where the canton chiefs—the *Sarkis*—were supposed to wield unlimited power. Former BNA leaders claim today that *they*—together with Governors Ramadier and Bordier—'made' Djibo Bakary. Certainly, they added much strength to his power position. In fact the *Sarkis* became Djibo's uneasy allies. But in the 1956 election, that is *before* the UDN merged with the BNA to form the MSA, Djibo had made a very strong showing in the east, as we have seen. And it is by no means a wild assumption to state that, even alone, Djibo would have been able to win a substantial amount of the seats in the Territorial Assembly, although not perhaps anything like a majority. In other words, thanks to the *Sarkis*, Djibo emerged as the dominant factor in Niger politics. Without the chiefs, he would only have been one powerful factor among others.

As things stand, one can only guess at the reasons for the success of this Ponty-educated Zerma among the Hausa peasantry. It is true that Djibo

[27] SM. Police, 28 Jan. 1956, 3.
[28] 'Note d'Information. Direction des Services de Police', Niamey, 31 Oct. 1956 (ASP. Gaya).
[29] The MSA took 64·28 per cent of the votes, the PPN/RDA 30·57 per cent. The remaining 5·13 per cent went to independent candidates in the far east (*Cercle* of N'Guigmi, where the independents took 57 per cent of the vote) and in the north (*Cercle* of Agadès). The MSA had its highest scores in the Hausa *cercles* of Tahoua (86·81 per cent) and Madaoua (83·83 per cent), the PPN/RDA in the Hausa but western *cercle* of Dogond-outchi (79·34 per cent) and in the Zerma/Sonrai *cercles* of Tillabéry (73·14 per cent) and Dosso (63·70 per cent). See Bureau des Affaires Politiques et Administratives, 'Résultat des élections du 30 Mar. 1957' (ASP. Magaria).
[30] There was no Prime Minister, the Governor being legally the Head of Government.

Bakary was a charismatic leader in the strongest sense of the word. As one French administrator put it (in a conversation with the author): 'There was something in this nervous and feverish young man that reminded you of the toiling and sweating of the Sahel peasants'. In a less lyrical manner, Djibo's upbringing by his uncle in Tahoua, a typical Hausa town, must be recorded. There he learned to speak Hausa fluently and also became acquainted with the eastern peasants' mentality. There is also a possibility that the groundnut boom in the east after the war[31] provoked a political awakening among the Hausa peasantry, although there are few indications which would serve to bolster this theory.

'Tribal' rivalry between the Hausas and the westerners was perhaps the single most important factor, the Hausas strongly resenting the Zerma/Sonrai domination of the PPN/RDA and more especially of the civil service. This was all the more irritating for the easterners since—because of the groundnut boom—they paid substantially higher taxes than the westerners.[32] And although Djibo himself came from the west, he was—as we have pointed out—familiar with the Hausa mentality. In fact, the Hausas quite possibly looked upon him as one of their own. Moreover, although something like half of his most prominent lieutenants were natives of other parts of French West Africa, the highly organized party machinery was staffed with Hausas. These people, the trade unionist town dwellers, provided Djibo with a basis for forays into the rural environment. Many of them had only recently moved from the countryside, and still maintained close contacts with the folk at home. It was through these channels that Djibo's political message was conveyed, and conveyed in such a discreet way that the French did not even notice it till election day.[33] Moreover, Djibo, as a man closely linked with international, mainly communist-dominated, youth leagues and trade unions, disposed of a substantial amount of funds to distribute among his followers. His international connections also enabled him to reward faithful lieutenants with journeys to Moscow, Vienna and other far-off places.

Along with trade unionists, Djibo found his staunchest allies among the local traders and among the adherents of various Muslim brotherhoods, especially the Tijaniyya.[34] Such mobile and important people were naturally opposed to the reigning order represented by the chiefs.

[31] From 1947 to 1954 the sale of groundnuts from the *Cercle* of Zinder soared from 10,196 to 30,000 tons (René Galinier, 'Cercle de Zinder, Rapport Annuel 1953', 2 (AP. Zinder)). Nationwide the ground-nut *production* soared from 76,190 tons in 1953 to 193,000 in 1957, of which 92 per cent came out of Hausaland. See Ministère de l'Economie Rurale, Service de l'Agriculture, 'Rapport Annuel, année 1961, 1ère partie, Statistiques', 3 (AP. Zinder) and B.C.E.A.O., *L'Economie Ouest-Africaine*, no. 137, Feb. 1967.

[32] 'Compte-rendu de la séance du Conseil des Notables du Cercle de Maradi, le 11 juillet 1953', 4–6 (AP. Maradi).

[33] See, for instance, Noël Julien-Viéroz, 'Rapport sur le déroulement de la campagne électorale et des élections législatives du 2.1.1956 dans la Subdivision Centrale de Tahoua', Tahoua, 6 Jan. 1956, 1–2 (ASP. Birni N'Konni).

[34] See, for instance, P. Falgueirettes, 'Lettre du Commandant de Cercle, Konni, à M. le Gouverneur', Konni, 15 Nov. 1956 (ASP. Birni N'Konni).

When all is said and done, however, Djibo's party (or more precisely the
UDN wing of the MSA) was a long way from succeeding in organizing and
leading the peasantry as completely as, for instance, Sekou Touré's
Parti Démocratique Guinéen in Guinea. An attempt to establish Farmers'
Trade Unions in 1954 was unsuccessful[35] and not repeated. Hausaland
remained basically traditional in outlook and character.

FROM THE ELECTION OF 1957 TO THE REFERENDUM OF 1958

It is not our purpose to describe in detail the period between the elections
of 30 March 1957 and the referendum of 28 September 1958. Suffice it to
say that quite a few Frenchmen in official positions were favourably
impressed with the seriousness and industry of the African Ministers. It is
however interesting to note where these originated. Two were Frenchmen
(Robert Fréminé, a secondary school teacher, and Pierre Vidal, an
entrepreneur). Of the remaining eight (nine in 1958), only four were
natives of Niger, the others coming from Senegal, French Sudan and
Guinea. The same pattern is more or less true for the party. Among the ten
members of the Central Committee, only half were natives of Niger (and
among them, two westerners, Djibo himself, and Issoufou Seudou
Djermakoye, representing the BNA branch).[36]

This period is important from another angle, since it revealed Djibo
Bakary as a Pan-African leader with ambitions far exceeding the boundaries of Niger. He might even be accused of wanting to create a 'greater
Niger'. This is possibly the case with Djibo's frequent visits to Gao in
French Sudan, where he tried to build up a following among the local
Sonrais. In fact the *Parti Soudanais Progressiste* (the Sudanese branch of
the MSA) looked to Niamey for aid in its fight against the RDA.[37] This was
also quite probably the case in Dahomey, where Djibo backed the politicians fron the north, who threatened to secede and join Niger if the north
did not get a fairer share of the territorial budget. Whether this was a
serious threat to the unity of Dahomey, or whether the politicians from the
north simply used Djibo Bakary in order to scare Cotonou, is open to
debate. However, Djibo took the matter seriously enough to travel to
Parakou in Northern Dahomey and confer with local politicians.[38] This
journey sparked off a blast from Adamou Mayaki, one of the most prominent former BNA leaders. Denouncing what he thought looked liked
interference in another territory's internal matters, Mayaki—himself the
son of a chief—tried to persuade twelve Assembly members close to the
chiefs, or themselves chiefs, to overthrow Djibo Bakary, by resigning their
membership in the MSA and setting up a party of their own. If the

[35] 'Territ. du Niger. Révue des événements du 1er Trimestre 1954', 19 (AP. Zinder).
[36] SM. Police, 1 July 1957, 3.
[37] 'Territoire du Soudan Français. Délégation de la Boucle du Niger. Bulletin Mensuel
de Renseignements', Gao, 14 Nov. 1957, 4–8 (ASP. Tillabéry).
[38] SM. Police, 24 Nov. 1957, 12–15.

manoeuvre had succeeded, it would have left Djibo with a minority of twenty-eight assembly members out of sixty. In fact the twelve (thirteen with Mayaki) were more than willing, and even went so far as to hand their letters of resignation to the MSA. However, Djibo's homecoming and subsequent threats brought them all back to the fold again, except for Adamou Mayaki, who was officially excluded from the MSA.[39]

This episode should have been a warning to Djibo Bakary, since it showed clearly that the chiefs were even less trustworthy than expected. And if the chiefs could not be trusted, that meant that Djibo's whole power-base was far from being a solid one. As for the *évolués* (or rather the best-educated among them), solidly behind the PPN/RDA, they showed their strength in two nation-wide and highly successful strikes; the first one staged in November 1957 and concerning only the teachers, the other staged in February 1958 and leading to a walk-out of nearly 95 per cent of the civil service.[40]

Undaunted by these warnings, Djibo participated in the Cotonou congress in July 1958, where he won the day with a radical programme. This meeting in Cotonou was the constitutional congress of the new Pan-African Party, the *Parti du Regroupement Africain* (PRA), of which Djibo was already Secretary-General. This party united nearly all the local and federal parties that had remained outside the RDA. What came out of the Cotonou congress was a party programme stressing the necessity to stop the 'balkanization' of French Africa, by setting up federal executives in Dakar and Brazzaville, something the Deferre *loi-cadre* of 1956, granting limited autonomy to the French overseas territories, had not provided for. Furthermore, the Cotonou congress adopted a slogan of immediate and full independence.[41] This then was clearly something of a break with the previous political positions of prominent PRA politicians like Apithy, Senghor and Lamine Gueye. As far as Djibo is concerned, however, the Cotonou resolutions were not too much out of tune with his previous statements.[42] Nevertheless, on returning home, Djibo—along with the other PRA leaders—tried to soften the stand taken in Cotonou. His party, now having become the Niger branch of the PRA, changed its name to Sawaba, a Hausa word meaning quietness or tranquillity.[43]

The salient features of Djibo's personality and political credo were thus his personal ambitions and his Pan-African idealism. or more accurately, federalism. As a representative of one of the poorest territories in French West Africa, dependent on subsidies from Dakar,[44] Djibo's federalism

---

[39] SM. Police, 28 Dec. 1957, 9.

[40] SM. Police, Feb. 1958, 2.

[41] See *Afrique nouvelle* (newspaper, Dakar), 1 Aug. 1958.

[42] See, for instance, *Azalai, organe du MSA* (mimeographed newspaper, Niamey), 9 Apr. 1958 (ASP. Tessaoua).

[43] R. C. Abraham, *Dictionary of the Hausa language* (University of London Press, 1968), 791.

[44] Elliott Berg, 'The Economic Basis for Political Choice in French West Africa', *American Political Science Review*, LIV, no. 2 (June 1960), 391–405 (p. 403).

makes sense. All the more so since the subsidies received from Dakar were very far indeed from being sufficient. In fact, the people of Niger had to cope with the highest taxes in French West Africa.[45] Niger in short, needed the strongest possible federation, while Djibo needed it in order to satisfy his own personal ambitions.

TAKING POSITIONS

The intricate tale of political manoeuvres, meetings, alliances, journeys, interventions, etc., during the two months between the Cotonou congress and the referendum, has been told elsewhere,[46] and will not be repeated here. What will be discussed is: (1) Why Djibo finally decided to vote 'No' in the referendum, and how his decision affected his power-base. (2) How the French (and the PPN/RDA) reacted to Djibo's decision.

Clearly the decision to vote 'No' was not an easy one for Djibo and his followers to take. In fact during the two months we are concerned with here, they reversed their positions several times, going back and forth between 'Yes' and 'No'. It was only on 15 September, that is only fourteen days before the referendum and eight days *after* the opening of the electoral campaign, that the Sawaba party took its final and negative stand. Was this due to political ambition? Djibo Bakary *was* indeed a very ambitious politician, although the exact impact of his ambitions as a political factor is obviously impossible to ascertain. Can it be suggested that Djibo admired and was perhaps even jealous of Kwame Nkrumah, and that the rivalry between Djibo and Sékou Touré inside the Pan-African Trade Union (the UGTAN) must be a factor?

Did Djibo want independence in order to join with Nigeria? This is and was an opinion much favoured among his enemies, but clearly it cannot be true. There is absolutely no evidence whatsoever of any kind of close relations between Nigerian leaders and Djibo before the referendum. The one Northern Nigerian party close to Djibo's political credo, NEPU, was in a hopeless minority.[47] And it is hard to understand how a man like Djibo could be attracted by the society of Northern Nigeria, even more tradition-bound than that of Niger. (Regarding NEPU, there is evidence of contracts, not with Djibo, but with the PPN/RDA.[48]) The strange thing is that although from an economic viewpoint, the border between Niger and Nigeria does not seem to exist, politics in Nigeria have had absolutely no influence upon political evolution in Niger. There is, for instance, no reason to believe that the Hausas in Niger wanted to join with their brethren on the other side of the border to form one Hausa state. The

[45] In 1955, 635 francs in all *per capita*, as compared with 415 in Senegal and 303 in Mauritania ('PV de la Conférence des Commandants de Cercle', op. cit. 7).
[46] Chaffard and Mortimer, op. cit.
[47] See C. S. Whitaker Jr., *The Politics of Tradition. Continuity and Change in Northern Nigeria, 1946–66* (Princeton University Press, 1970).
[48] SM. Police, 27 Mar. 1958, 15.

great power concentrated in the hands of the Northern Nigerian chiefs quite simply repelled them. For that matter, the theory that Djibo wanted to join Ghana in a union, into which Togo and Dahomey were eventually going to be forced, sounds less impossible. It explains at least Djibo's interest in Dahomean affairs, *and* his long visit to Ghana in September, that is, right before he took his final stand. Everyone who approached Djibo immediately after his homecoming is witness to the fact that during his absence he changed radically.

The official Sawaba explanation is: (1) The new constitution was a step further towards the balkanization of Africa, and therefore contrary to the official stand of the PRA. (2) The new constitution did not stress in sufficiently clear terms the right of every autonomous republic to become independent whenever it chose to. (3) The French attitude, namely that a 'No' would lead not only to immediate independence, but would also be followed by a swift and complete French retreat leaving the infant state in a very difficult position, was blackmail and, as such, an insult to African dignity. (4) What Sawaba wanted was complete independence, not in order to secede, but in order to negotiate with France on *equal* terms the entry of Niger into the French Community, which was supposed to be a community of autonomous but not independent republics.[49] Would Djibo then relinquish his newly found independence? Some of Djibo's former lieutenants have hinted at this to the author. But there is very little evidence to support it. In fact, the impression remains that Djibo wanted his country to remain independent even inside the Community.[50] He called it 'indépendance dans l'union',[51] a rather wild and bewildering expression. Djibo, moreover, stressed time and again that his 'No' should not be considered as an act of hostility towards the French or even as a wish to secede.

To this official stand should be added another factor: Djibo as one of the leading trade unionists in West Africa could not overlook the fact that the federal trade union, presided over by Sékou Touré, the *Union Générale des Travailleurs de l'Afrique Noire* (UGTAN) had opted for 'No'.[52]

A delegation headed by the Minister of Health, Pierre Vidal—a Frenchman, and a not too highly esteemed Frenchman at that, at least in official circles—was sent to Paris in order to explain Djibo's rather ambiguous position to French officialdom. The French, however, who considered a 'No' to be a 'No', and did not want to indulge in subtleties, met him with closed doors. The French attitude cannot be dismissed as totally unsound, for it is difficult to avoid the impression that the discussion not only in Niger, but throughout the whole of French West Africa on French Africa's future was so heavily packed with legal subtleties that one had to be a law student in order to understand it all. Apart from showing how well some

[49] 'Lettre du Sawaba au Général de Gaulle', Niamey, 15 Sept. 1958 (ASP. Tessaoua).
[50] *Le Monde*, 17 Sept. 1958, 3.
[51] *Le Monde*, 31 Aug.–1 Sept. 1958, 2.
[52] *Afrique nouvelle*, 19 Sept. 1958, 3.

22   AH XIV

Africans had assimilated certain aspects of French culture, it was out of tune with those primarily concerned, the overriding mass of the African rural population.

As Mortimer says: 'One may reasonably wonder whether Djibo paid enough attention to local circumstances, in deciding to vote No.'[53] For one thing, Djibo must have known that a negative stand would lead to an almost immediate secession of chiefs from the Sawaba party, and would be fought by the French, for reasons that will be explained later. It was moreover evident that the west would be heavily behind the PPN/RDA, which decided to campaign for 'Yes', not so much out of sympathy with the French, but as a means to topple Djibo. The French could therefore count on as much help as they wanted from the African civil servants. As far as the Tuareg—the desert nomads—were concerned, they were opposed to *any* black government in Niamey, whatever its policy. Moreover it has already been stressed that Djibo's party (or rather the UDN branch of the Sawaba) was not sufficiently implanted in the rural areas, at least not sufficiently to wage an all-out war against both the chiefs and the French at the same time.

From the economic point of view, Djibo's decision does not make sense either. As we have seen, Niger badly needed all the subsidies it could get from richer French West African territories like Senegal and the Ivory Coast. In September 1958 it was abundantly clear that a negative vote in Niger would cut that country off from the rest of French West Africa. True, Djibo once stated that, if the French pulled out, he would turn to the people who had already promised to help him.[54] But this statement was probably first and foremost intended to scare the French. Besides, who could these helpers be? Russia or China? Among the African states, certainly not Nigeria; once more, Ghana would seem the likeliest possibility.

The question of why Djibo decided to vote 'No' still remains to be answered. Two more theories must be mentioned. First the fear that the *Organisation Commune des Régions Sahariennes* (OCRS) would eventually lead to the carving out of a separate Saharan *Territoire d'Outre-Mer*, comprising vast areas of Niger.[55] However it would seem that another theory deserves considerable attention, namely that Djibo's decision to vote 'No' was taken in desperation, as a last attempt to cling to a power that was fast eroding. From the election of 1956 to that of 1957, the combined votes for the UDN and the BNA in fact declined by 2 per cent.[56] After all not everbody was pleased with this unholy alliance between left-wing trade-unionists and chiefs. And the chiefs could be relied upon to secede at any time—Mayaki's attempt had been a near miss, and could well be re-

[53] Mortimer, op.cit. 321.   [54] *Afrique nouvelle*, 19 Sept. 1958, 3.
[55] On the O.C.R.S. see Marcel Chailley, *Histoire de l'Afrique Occidentale Française* (Berger-Levrault, Paris, 1968), 494–6.
[56] 'Rapport Général Congrès du MSA . . .', op. cit. 5.

peated in the future. It must also be borne in mind that Djibo came into power in an era when socialist governors were favourable to him. That era had clearly come to an end with de Gaulle's rise to power in France.

It must have been maddening for a man like Djibo, who had already risen to Pan-African prominence, to find that his own backyard was on the brink of revolt. Djibo in short needed the full command of the whole state machinery and, therefore, independence, in order to crush once and for all his enemies, among them first and foremost the chiefs. In other words, Djibo had the bad luck to believe in ideas and to stand for a policy for which there was no firm socio-economic basis in Niger. Perhaps by pulling out all the stops in a last all-out effort, he could secure the victory of a 'No' vote. Clearly he lacked the patience needed to build up a strong enough following at the grass-root level in such a tradition-bound country as Niger. And it is debatable whether his enemies, once in charge of an autonomous republic, would allow him to do so.

If this theory comes anywhere near the truth, it helps to explain a certain number of rather strange facts: first, Djibo's late announcement of his final stand, hoping perhaps to take his enemies by surprise; second, his desperate attempt to discredit and perhaps crush the chiefs (he revoked and suspended a total of twenty chiefs, among them such important figures as Abdou Salami Cissé, Alfaizé of Say, and Mohammed Dan Zambadi Bouzou, Sarkin Katsina of Maradi); third, his rather undignified way of trying to cling to power after he had lost in the referendum; fourth, his strange behaviour during the campaign (he was reportedly in contact with Gourmantché witch-doctors and often looked as if he was under the influence of drugs), which prompted one of his PRA colleagues (who was to become president in his homeland) to ask in private for the crushing of this 'rascal'; and, finally, his use of questionable arguments during the campaign, quite literally intended, as will be seen, to fool people into voting 'No'. Does all this indicate a man who was desperate and about to lose his grasp, or is this too speculative? One thing that must be admitted is that it still seems strange that Djibo should opt for 'No' in 1958, since it was so obviously the wrong thing to do, and stood in such blatant opposition to his federalist credo.

What was the French reaction to Djibo's attitude? If Guinea could be allowed to secede (some even murmured that de Gaulle wanted it that way, in order to show the world, and especially the Algerian nationalists, that he meant business), Niger was quite another matter. A negative vote in one *Territoire d'Outre Mer* was after all an honest result, a negative vote in *two* would involve a loss of prestige. There were however other compelling reasons of a geopolitical and perhaps also economic nature. The latter was that the French already knew that the desert contained huge deposits of uranium.[57] The geopolitical one can be put in two ways: first, the fear that

[57] *Niger* (Révue trimestrielle, Niamey), no. 10 (1970), 64.

an independent, isolated Niger would be swallowed up by Nigeria; second, that an independent left-wing governed Niger, serving as a base for the rebels in Algeria, had to be avoided. At *all* costs? There is reason to believe that the Minister of Overseas France, Bernard Cornut-Gentille (himself a former Governor-General of French West Africa) told Governor Louis Rollet of Niger just that when they met in Paris in July[58] (at a moment when the French authorities *suspected* that Djibo might finally opt for a negative vote). When Rollet refused to agree, the former Governor of Senegal, Don Jean Colombani, was sent to Niger, where he arrived exactly one month before the referendum. He came with no precise, written instructions from his superiors in Paris on how to tackle the situation; he was just told that 'things had to change'.

Colombani has been very ungallantly treated by narrators of the 1958 crisis in Niger.[59] The underlying assumption is that Djibo Bakary lost only because the French went out of their way to beat him. But we have tried to show that Djibo's power-base was so weak that very little pushing was in fact necessary. As for the chiefs, they had always been suspicious of Djibo; they were now all the more so since they found their power-base at home eroded by Djibo's support of the marabouts, youth leagues, village chiefs and rival dynasties, all of whom hoped to benefit from the chiefs' loss of power.[60] Djibo's removal, or intended removal, of twenty canton chiefs clearly showed his intention. If the chiefs had remained with Djibo it was because they wanted to be on the winning side, thereby hoping to retain at least part of their privileges. The chiefs, always a timid lot, were in fact only waiting for a sign from the French in order to break away. When that sign came (through the man who was both a French Minister and a leading African politician, Félix Houphouët-Boigny, who treated nearly all the revoked and threatened chiefs to journeys by air to Abidjan), Issoufou Seydou, of the family of the Zermakoye of Dosso, and unofficial leader of the chiefs, resigned his seat in the French Senate,[61] and led the chiefs out of the Sawaba party. (Houphouët-Boigny's interference with the domestic affairs of Niger also extended to the delivery to the 'Yes' supporters of a substantial amount of funds and of a great number of lorries, always a very important commodity at election time in such a huge and thinly populated country as Niger.)

Lastly Djibo had left in office a certain number of very seasoned and highly respected French administrators—survivors from the Toby era—who in 1958 held positions as District Officers (*Commandants de Cercle*) in such important places as Tahoua (Yves Riou, the *doyen* of the French in Niger), Filingué (Jean Espallargas), Maradi (Pierre Brachet) and Zinder (Francis Nicolas). Having been trained by that great master of traditional African politics, Jean Toby, 'they knew', in the words of one of the

[58] Chaffard, op. cit. 277.   [59] Ibid. 278–302, and Mortimer, op. cit. 322–4, 343.
[60] See, for example, 'Fiche de renseignement, Cercle de Gouré', 1 Nov. 1958 (Military archives of Zinder).   [61] *Le Monde*, 17 Sept. 1958, 3.

present Ministers in Niamey, who admittedly overdid his compliment, 'our society better than we will ever do'. This is however not to say that the French administration was solidly behind Colombani. On the contrary, many, particularly of the younger administrators, did not like the prospect of getting too deeply involved in a political battle ('ils ne voulaient pas se mouiller'), and tried to sit out the referendum upheaval by doing nothing. This was even more true of the Frenchmen who were active in business.[62]

Colombani did a number of things to harm Djibo. (1) He refused to sign a large number of requests for permission to carry arms that happened to come from Sawaba followers. (2) He reviewed the cases of the twenty chiefs, and decided that only two had been justly punished. The others were reinstated. (3) When on 15 September, Djibo requisitioned all the government-owned cars for his campaign, clearly an illegal step, Colombani ordered Djibo to return them. When Djibo failed to do so, Colombani used his constitutional powers to withdraw from Djibo and his ministers a substantial amount of their prerogatives. This was a perfectly legal thing to do, since according to the *loi-cadre* of 1956, the cabinet only governed by delegation from the French Governor.

The sight of chiefs ousted by Djibo being reinstalled by the French and of cars being taken away from the Sawaba followers dealt a dangerous blow to Djibo's prestige among the peasantry.

THE REFERENDUM CAMPAIGN AND ITS AFTERMATH

The French have been accused of not maintaining a neutral stand during the campaign, and of not playing a straight game. If this is true, the same can be said of the opposite side. Djibo and his lieutenants in fact used all available means to persuade their countrymen to vote 'No'. The marabouts forced people to swear on the Koran that they would actually do so. The Tuareg were told that a 'No' would mean no more schools, and an end to the freeing of the *bellahs*, whereas the latter were told the contrary. The peasants heard that a 'No' meant no more taxes and no more customs duties to be paid, and that it meant a refusal to let the French leave,[63] whereas a victory for 'Yes' would mean a break with France. So the French had no choice but to explain to the people what the referendum was all about: Djibo quite literally forced their hand. This is the background for the tour which Governor Colombani made of Niger, following closely in Djibo's footsteps, refuting his arguments. (The D.O.s did more or less the same thing, acting in many places through the chiefs.)

If Djibo felt compelled to use such arguments, one cannot avoid the reactionary conclusion that Djibo believed the people of Niger simply did

---

[62] See, for instance, 'Rapport sur le comportement des européens du Cercle de Tessaoua pendant le Referendum', no date, 3–4 (ASP. Tessaoua).

[63] 'Lettre, Commandant, Cercle de Tessaoua à M. le Chef du Territoire du Niger', Tessaoua, 1 Oct. 1958, 2 (ASP. Tessaoua). This information has been confirmed by many oral sources.

not want independence, especially if that independence meant a radical break with the French. This is not to say that the French colonial administration was—one hesitates to use the word—anything like popular among the peasants. What it does imply is that the French were probably less unwelcome in Hausaland than anywhere else. The French conquest of Hausaland had been swift and had met with very little opposition.[64] Being out of the way and having very little to offer, Hausaland had—contrary to the west—suffered lightly from forced labour before 1946. And the very small number of French administrators (and the near absence of tradesmen and missionaries), had led in fact to a partially indirect administration in Hausaland, the main preoccupation of which had been to curtail the chiefs' power. Another factor favouring the French in 1958 was the fear among peasants that a French withdrawal would leave the Tuareg free to sack the country as they had done before. Finally, the fear that the price of ground-nuts would sag (a fear kindled by the French) must have played a powerful role.

The referendum was, in the end, a cleaner affair than many had feared. With the exception of the *cercle* of Agadès—in other words, Tuareg country—where the military was still dominant,[65] there is no evidence of fraud, Djibo being too powerful after all to permit the French to indulge in such practices. No shots were fired, no riots were reported, nobody was killed (the only riot worthy of that name, took place in Niamey in April,[66] that is long before the referendum). What the French were accused of, and with reason, was of having campaigned openly for the 'Yes', instead of assuming their role as neutral onlookers. But then again, as we have seen, the French officials found themselves in a very awkward position (all the more so since the opposition party, the PPN/RDA, was incapable of waging an effective campaign in favour of 'Yes').

Many people maintain that had the French not intervened, Djibo would have won the day. This is possible, although one should bear in mind that the 'intervention' amounted, at the very most, to one short visit to the majority of villages. The important question is; whether in such circumstances a majority of 'No' votes would have meant that the people of Niger wanted independence straight away and were prepared to break away from the French Community?

In the event, 76 per cent of the votes cast were for 'Yes'. In certain regions of the east, there was, however, a majority of 'Noes' (close to 70 per cent in the Sawaba stronghold of Tessaoua).[67] That only 36 per cent of the voters cared to take part in the referendum—the lowest percentage in the whole of the AOF[68]—is due to the fact that it took place in September,

[64] See Yehoshua Rash, 'Un établissement colonial sans histoires. Les premières années françaises au Niger 1897–1906' (unpublished doctoral thesis, Paris, January 1972).
[65] Chaffard, op. cit. 294 and oral sources.   [66] *Marchés tropicaux*, 10 May 1958.
[67] 'Cercle de Tessaoua. Rapport Annuel 1958', 24 (AP. Zinder).
[68] Chailley, op. cit. 507.

when most people in Niger were tilling their land. It also reflects the fact that women rarely vote in a traditional Muslim society. Finally, it can be suggested that the low participation sounds much more plausible than the high ones enregistered in certain other *Territoires d'Outre-Mer*, and shows perhaps that the referendum in Niger was not too much rigged after all.

From the formal point of view, the referendum had shown that an opposition existed between the government in power and the people it was supposed to represent. However, on 6 October, the Sawaba party issued a declaration (signed by the remaining twenty-eight Sawaba members of the Territorial Assembly), to the effect that the party respected the results of the referendum, and was prepared to continue in power.[69] But among the French there was a widespread feeling that Djibo had lost all credibility, and that his stock of confidence among the people was dwindling away.

Much has been said about the way Colombani managed more or less to force Djibo to resign two weeks after the referendum, and how he was able, thanks to the resignation of thirty-two of its members (all the PPN/RDA members, and the Sawaba members who refused to sign the declaration of 6 October) to dissolve the Territorial Assembly.[70] One must however bear in mind that Djibo, as has been seen, no longer had a majority in the Territorial Assembly (only twenty-eight members out of sixty were still committed to him). It would therefore have been possible to topple Djibo in a parliamentary way, which was perhaps what the French should have tried to do. But Colombani was in a hurry and also wanted to clarify the situation.

The chiefs who by now had seceded from the Sawaba, and clearly were out to strengthen their position, did not join the PPN/RDA, but formed together with that party and with various smaller parties an electoral alliance called the *Union pour la Communauté Franco-Nigérienne* (UCFA). Before the elections, Governor Colombani issued two written orders, something unheard of in those tumultuous times, when higher French officials declined responsibility whenever they could. One stressed that complete neutrality was to be rigorously observed on behalf of the French administration[71]; the other that it was still forbidden to use official cars for any political purpose whatsoever.[72] That these orders were to a certain extent unheeded by many a D.O., eager to crush Djibo completely, is in little doubt. Nevertheless, although the country was once more in effervescence, no shot was fired, nobody was killed, no riots were reported, and very little detectable fraud was denounced. After all, the Sawaba was still able to win the day in the Hausa *cercles* of Tessaoua and Zinder, winning

[69] 'Communiqué du Parti Sawaba, Section Nigérienne du P.R.A.'. 6 Oct. 1958 (ASP. Tessaoua). [70] *Le Monde*, 21 Nov. 1958, 3.
[71] Don Jean Colombani, 'Circulaire à tous mes Commandants et Chefs de Subdivision', Niamey, 23 Nov. 1958 (ASP. Gaya).
[72] 'Télégramme-Lettre du Gouverneur au Chef de la Subdivision de Gaya', Niamey, 2 Dec. 1958 (ASP. Gaya).

eleven seats. Forty-eight seats went to the UCFA, and one to an independent candidate who won in the far east (*Cercle* of N'Guigmi), a region where both national parties fared badly as usual.[73]

That it was not too fraudulent an election should be attested by the fact that in the *Cercle* of Zinder, the Sawaba list, headed by Mamani Abdoulaye, the second man in the party, defeated—mostly thanks to Mahaman Dan Bouzoua and his work in Tanout—the UCFA list, headed by no less a political figure than Hamani Diori, the undisputed leader of the PPN/RDA. Nevertheless, Diori was appointed Prime Minister after the proclamation of the Republic of Niger on 18 December. Djibo—still mayor of Niamey—was beaten by his old foe, Adamou Mayaki, in Maradi.

The subsequent events, the invalidation of the elections in Tessaoua and Zinder made by the Assembly in the spring of 1959; Djibo's departure into exile and his attempts to overthrow the new government by force; the absorption of all political elements into the PPN/RDA, triggered by Djibo's threat; the outlawing of the Sawaba party; the harsh treatment of Sawaba stalwarts by the Minister of the Interior, Diamballa Yansambou Maïga; and the independence of the Republic, belong to another story, yet to be told, at least by a scholar.

SUMMARY

This article concentrates on the events of 1958 in Niger. It tries to show that Djibo Bakary's power-base was a very weak one. This could be the reason why Djibo decided to opt for 'No' at the Referendum, namely that he needed command of the whole state machinery in order to crush his enemies, especially the chiefs. The French were bent on thwarting Djibo for geo-political reasons (e.g. the nearness of Algeria), but did so in a rather lighthanded way. In fact, Djibo brought about his own downfall through a number of miscalculations and blunders.

[73] Complete results from the elections in 'Haut Commissariat de la République Française au Niger. Circulaire à tous Cercles et Subdivisions', Niamey, 22 Dec. 1958 (ASP. Tillabéry).

WOMEN IN NATIONALIST STRUGGLE:
TANU ACTIVISTS IN DAR ES SALAAM*

by Susan Geiger

> The Union has not forgotten women behind in its task of arousing national consciousness in the people. It now has 5,000 women members, the majority of whom enrolled during the past four months. Under the inspiration of Bibi Titi Mohamed, the women have organised a Women's Section of the Union with their own leaders. This Bibi Titi Mohamed is a very dynamic woman and is inspiring a revolution [in] the role of women in African society. Though only semi-literate, she is a dynamic and convincing speaker . . . she has already made extensive tours of the Eastern Province and is likely to lead all the women of Tanganyika in a revolution that is without precedent. The present and future [mothers] of Tanganyika have refused to be left behind and are flowing with the current alongside of their men-folk. The problem of the emancipation of women at a later date has, in this way, been disposed of . . . . We therefore look forward with confidence to a fully fledged women's organisation in the near future.[1]

Thus did the young Oscar Kambona capture the euphoria of an early moment in the popular mobilizing efforts of the Tanganyika African National Union (TANU). His heady enthusiasm for women's responsiveness, and his optimistic prediction that the process of nationalist mobilization would solve the "problem" of women's emancipation were not surprising. Nor was it surprising that he should be writing in such detail along these lines to the Fabian Society,

---

*Earlier versions of this paper were presented to the University of Dar es Salaam History Department Seminar, the Annual Meeting of the American Historical Association, and the African Studies Program Seminar at Northwestern University. I am grateful to a number of critical readers along the way, especially Allen Isaacman, Marjorie Mbilinyi, Margaret Strobel, Janet Spector, and Margaret Jean Hay. Generous support for my research came from the Social Science Research Council and from the University of Minnesota Graduate School and McMillan Travel Fund. I am also indebted to the University of Dar es Salaam for providing me with Research Associate status in the Department of History for five months in 1984, and to members of the Women's Research and Documentation Project at the University of Dar es Salaam for their critical interest and colleagial engagement during my stay. To the Chiume family, who provided me with a home in Dar es Salaam, and to M.W. Kanyama Chiume, for invaluable professional assistance, I am deeply grateful. But my greatest debt is to the women whose recollections of their participation in TANU provide the substance, heart and motivation for this work. Similarly, my greatest hope is that my interpretation is true to the words, memories, and self-reflections they shared with me.

[1]Oscar Kambona, Organizing Secretary-General of TANU, to Fabian Society, 18 October 1955, FCB papers 121, Rhodes House (RH).

International Journal of African Historical Studies, 20, 1 (1987)   1

since John Hatch, the Labour Party's Commonwealth Officer, had questioned a somewhat chagrined TANU Central Committee - all male - about the absence of women during his June 1955 visit of Dar es Salaam.[2]

Kambona and other TANU leaders therefore had good reason to be pleased with the significant results of their prompt attempt to rectify the situation Hatch observed by enlisting the aid of Bibi Titi Mohammed. In March 1955, TANU could claim only 2,000 card-carrying members among an urban African population of over 100,000. An increase of 5,000 between June and September 1955 not only enhanced the credibility of the Union's claims to represent popular aspirations, but as importantly, increased the coffers out of which subsistence salaries could be paid to the men like Julius Nyerere and Kambona, who had abandoned teaching jobs to work for TANU.[3]

Existing accounts of the growth of a nationalist movement in the former British Trust Territory of Tanganyika invariably allude, as does Kambona, to the importance of women's participation in TANU.[4] From these accounts we can surmise that responsibility for the extraordinary response documented above - a response that was to create a female majority in TANU membership by the end of 1955[5] - lay largely with the women themselves, led by one among them who was to emerge not only as leader of the women, but as a major TANU figure throughout the country. By the year of independence, 1961, Bibi Titi Mohamed, a Muslim Dar es Salaam townswoman with four years of primary school education, whose local popularity as lead singer in a women's dance group could scarcely have been regarded as a predicting factor in her rise to political prominence, was probably one of two TANU leaders known throughout the country.[6] Far more predictable indeed was the rise of the other widely known TANU leader, Julius Nyerere, the young, highly educated Catholic former school teacher turned politician, who led TANU and Tanganyika in the independence struggle of the 1950s and was to remain at the helm of state for nearly twenty-five years of political independence from December 1961 through October 1985.

---

[2]Judith Listowel, *The Making of Tanganyika* (London, 1965), 268.

[3]John Iliffe, *A Modern History of Tanganyika* (Cambridge, 1979), 517-518; John Hatch, *Tanzania* (New York, 1972), 115.

[4]In addition to Listowel, *Making of Tanzania*; Iliffe, *History*; and Hatch, *Tanzania*; see Henry Bienen, *Tanzania: Party Transformation and Economic Development* (Princeton, 1967); I.N. Kimambo and A.J. Temu, *A History of Tanzania* (Nairobi, 1969); Gabriel Ruhumbika, ed., *Towards Ujamaa: Twenty Years of TANU Leadership* (Dar es Salaam, 1974); Hugh Stephens, *The Political Transformation of Tanganyika: 1920-1967* (New York, 1968); William Tordoff, *Government and Politics in Tanzania* (Nairobi, 1967). Works published in Swahili by Tanzanians provide somewhat more detail on women's participation, and in some cases, refer by name to TANU women activists never mentioned in accounts in English. See, for example, E.B.M. Barongo, *Mkiki wa Siasa Tanganyika* (Dar es Salaam, 1966); S.A. Kandoro, *Mwito Wa Uhuru* (Dar es Salaam, 1961); D.Z. Mwaga, B.F. Mrina, and F.F. Lyimo, *Historia ya Chama cha TANU 1954 Hadi 1977* (Dar es Salaam, 1981); Ulotu Abubakar Ulotu, *Historia ya TANU* (Dar es Salaam, 1971).

[5]Hatch, *Tanzania*, 115.

[6]Iliffe, *History*, 572.

To date, and with a few important exceptions, scholars of African nationalist movements have devoted little more than passing mention to the presence of African women as conscious political actors in these struggles.[7] Nor has there been an attempt to assess the content of women's nationalist activities as expressions of or progress toward something called "emancipation," not just from colonial overrule, but from the socially prescribed gender roles and constraints attached to womanhood.

Of course, the "neglect of women" can be and frequently is rationalized on practical, historical and theoretical grounds. These grounds can be briefly summarized as follows. First, written records, whether colonial or African, are overwhelmingly androcentric. Research into these documents - minutes and reports of meetings, autobiographies of and interviews with (male) nationalist leaders, district and provincial reports, records of conferences, etc. - is necessarily research into what men have written, thought, and done. With a few notable exceptions, such documentation ignores women unless they cause trouble or constitute a problem.[8]

The historical reality which both reflects and flows from the androcentrism inherent in the written record is the predominance of and focus on men in state or national-level political leadership. As the focus shifts from the actions of men and women operating at the local or community level to the arena of national or state politics, one indeed finds mostly men. An absence of commentary on this readily observable phenomenon on the part of Africanist scholars suggests that this historical reality requires no examination or explanation; rather, it belongs in the realm of the "natural" or "inevitable."

Finally, at the level of theory, the neglect of women appears to be rationalized in two ways. First, gender is seen as an analytical category with relevance at the level of domestic, household, and community relations and economies, but not at the level of the nation or state. Although recent social science and development research now pays belated and still infrequent and uneven attention to women's work as a factor in the analysis of the contemporary agrarian crisis in Africa and in patterns of labor and labor migration, the neglect of gendered aspects of African political processes remains

---

[7]Although there are several important studies of women in African liberation movements, my focus here is on earlier sub-Saharan nationalist movements. I refer, in this context, to LaRay Denzer, "Towards a Study of the History of West African Women's Participation in Nationalist Politics: The Early Phase, 1935-1950," *Africana Research Bulletin* 6, 4 (1976), 65-85, and "Constance A. Cummings-John: Her Early Political Career in Freetown," *Tarikh* 7, 1 (1981), 20-32; Cheryl Johnson, "Grassroots Organizing: Women in Anti-Colonial Activity in Southwestern Nigeria," *African Studies Review*, 25, 2 (September 1982); Claude Rivière, "La Promotion de la Femme Guinéenne," *Cahiers d'études Africaines*, 8, 31 (1968), 406-427; Nina Mba, *Nigerian Women Mobilized: Women's Political Activity in Southern Nigeria, 1900-1965* (Berkeley, 1982); Filomina Chioma Steady, *Female Power in African Politics: The National Congress of Sierra Leone* (Pasadena, 1975).

[8]Three classic examples - the Igbo Women's War in eastern Nigeria 1929-1930, the Pare (Tanzania) Women's anti-tax protest of 1945, and the Kom (Cameroons) *anlu* protest of 1957 - are analyzed in my article "Anti-Colonial Protest in Africa: A Female Strategy Reconsidered," *Heresies*, 9, 3 (1980), 22-25.

pervasive.[9] Even in the context of a rapidly expanding literature focused on the lives of Tanzanian women, works which concern their political participation are scarce.[10]

Second, however, and equally apparent, gender is generally considered irrelevant to the analysis of the articulation of historical processes in a particular nation-state, such as Tanzania, within the capitalist world economy. At this level, where one is concerned with social relations of production, class struggle, the emergence of a bureaucratic bourgeoisie and/or "the state," one has superseded the realm of human agency - of men and women as actors - altogether. Here one finds forces and factors and conditions, not people.[11] Here, theories and research and historical analyses are especially disinclined to consider the extent to which gender assumptions, which can and do vary from society to society and change over time, permeated "imperialism's" penetration of Africa, "capital's" treatment of labor, or "Africa's" responses to the demands of imperialism or capitalism.[12]

In recent years, a number of scholars have successfully employed a variety of research methods, kinds of data, and alternative theoretical frameworks to overcome the problems of androcentric bias outlined above. Focused on diverse aspects, periods, issues and problems in African history, these works nevertheless share two essential features, namely, an understanding of the historical significance of gender differences, and a belief that determining how

---

[9]As Kathleen Staudt demonstrates in a comprehensive critique of recent mainstream agricultural development literature, however, the now substantial amount of research which documents women's crucial presence in African agriculture is all too frequently neglected by scholars purporting to analyze the general crisis. See Kathleen Staudt, "Rewriting Agricultural History: Women Farmers at the Center," paper for African Studies Association Annual Meetings, New Orleans, Louisiana, 23-26 November 1985. The particular neglect of women in studies of African resistance and nationalist movements is noted in Margaret Strobel's review essay, "African Women," *Signs* , 8, 1 (1982), 124. Joan Scott argues that scholars in women's history generally have not been able to transform or "rewrite" history because, at least in part, they have not paid sufficient attention to the relationship between women's experiences and politics, or the way "politics construct gender and gender constructs politics." Joan Scott, "Women in History, II, The Modern Period," *Past and Present*, 101 (November 1983), 156. I am indebted to Margaret Strobel for alerting me to Scott's article.

[10]See Ophelia Mascarenhas and Marjorie Mbilinyi, *Women in Tanzania: An Analytical Bibliography* (Uppsala, 1983).

[11]For a recent critique of this form of reductionist social science, see James Scott, *Weapons of the Weak: Everyday Forms of Peasant Resistance* (New Haven, 1985), 42-43.

[12]Belinda Bozzoli, "Marxism, Feminism, and South African Studies," *Journal of Southern African Studies*, 9, 2 (April 1983), 139-171, treats these issues thoroughly.

and why gender operates as it does in given historical situations requires access to women's views of their own lives and experiences.[13]

In the remainder of this essay, I intend to examine the origins and development of women's participation in TANU, using life history research and a feminist theoretical framework to explore women's conceptualization of the relationship between nationalist objectives and their own "emancipation," and to situate the history of their participation within the broader political history of TANU. The questions that have informed my research flow directly from what is left unstated or ambiguous in the quotation from Kambona which introduces this paper. They include questions about motive and intent behind women's mobilization, both on the part of the TANU leadership and on the part of the women involved; about the characteristics and organizational capabilities of the women who were most responsive and most active; about the relationship between issues of gender and nationalist consciousness as perceived by women activists; and about legal and/or customary constraints and gender ideology as these affected women's participation and "place" in nationalist struggle.[14]

Partial answers to questions involving laws, norms, and prescriptive literature governing women's behavior can be discerned through the examination of archival and secondary sources. But such sources will offer little if any access to the perceptions or views of the women under consideration - whether one is interested in accounts of personal motivation and action, or in women's assessments of the political process of which they were a part. The relative silence suggested here is familiar to women's historians generally; but the erasure is most evident and its impact most rapidly cumulative where illiteracy is the rule, as was the case for Tanganyikan women in general and Dar es Salaam women in particular in the 1950s.[15]

---

[13]See the useful bibliography in Margaret Jean Hay and Sharon Stichter, eds., *African Women South of the Sahara* (New York, 1984), 195-211. Marcia Wright, "Women in Peril: A Commentary on Life Stories of Captives in Nineteenth-Century East-Central Africa," *African Social Research,* 20 (December 1975), 800-819; Marcia Wright, "Bwanikwa: Consciousness and Protest among Slave Women in Central Africa, 1886-1911," in Claire C. Robertson and MArtin Klein, eds., *Women and Slavery in Africa* (Madison, 1983), 246-267; Edward Alpers, "The Story of Swema: A Note on Female Vulnerability in Nineteenth-Century East Africa," in Robertson and Klein, eds., *Women and Slavery,* 185-219; Claire Robertson, *Sharing the Same Bowl: A Socio-economic History of Women and Class in Accra, Ghana* (Bloomington, 1983); Margaret Strobel, *Muslim Women in Mombasa, 1890-1975* (New Haven, 1979); Stephanie Urdang, *Fighting Two Colonialisms: Women in Guinea-Bissau* (New York, 1979); Luise White, "Prostitution, Identity, and Class Consciousness in Nairobi during World War II," in *Signs,* 11, 2 (1986), 255-273; Luise White, "A Colonial State and An African Petty Bourgeoisie: Prostitution, Property, and Class Struggle in Nairobi, 1936-1940," in Frederick Cooper, ed., *Struggle for the City: Migrant Labor, Capital, and the State in Urban Africa* (Beverly Hills, 1983), 167-194.

[14]These questions are formulated in my preliminary research report, "Women in National Struggle: Dar es Salaam's TANU Activists," presented to the History Department Seminar, University of Dar es Salaam, 23 November 1984.

[15]See Marjorie Mbilinyi, "African Education in the British Colonial Period," in M. Kaniki, ed., *Tanzania Under Colonial Rule* (London, 1980), 267. Andrew Coulson, *Tanzania: A Political Economy* (Oxford, 1982), 86-90.

It is with these realities in mind, then, that both feminism and life history research become critical to historical reconstruction. As the "theory of women's point of view,"[16] feminism rejects the androcentric notion that there is, somewhere out these, a stance of "ungendered point-of-viewlessness" from which history gets objectively recorded. As a method which involves "the collective reconstitution of the meaning of women's social experience, as women live through it,"[17] feminism presupposes the value and significance of women's perceptions of their own experience. Under conditions where women either cannot or have not written about their lives, life history research provides necessary access. And it is here that recent critical insights into the importance of oral documentation complement those of feminism.

If one takes as the proper object of history not the past, but rather the past-present relationship, then life histories become significant as complex cultural products which reflect "interrelations . . . between past experiences and present situations."[18] Their subjective dimensions (memory, ideology and subconscious thought), though frequently treated as problems of weakness and unreliability, can more fruitfully and accurately be viewed as constituting important social facts.[19] Furthermore, the dimensions of personalization and selective recall equally characteristic of life history accounts, far from disguising social relations and larger structural causes, can illuminate these processes which operate, after all, through human action and experience.[20]

Life history accounts, then, are the product of social individuals speaking out of specific positions within the complex of social relations characteristic of their particular material/cultural conditions at particular points in time. As such, they "appropriate and make sense of salient features of social relations within which their authors have been implicated and within which they have acted and struggled."[21] It is these features of life history accounts which make them particularly relevant sources for the reconstruction of women's political mobilization in the nationalist movement.

An examination of archival and secondary sources for gender-specific documentation reveals two important aspects of colonial ideology of contextual relevance to an understanding of the lives of Tanganyikan women and, more specifically, the lives of the TANU activists of Dar es Salaam. First, this documentation provides significant evidence about the primary terrain of

---

[16]Catherine MacKinnon, "Feminism, Marxism, Method, and the State: An Agenda for Theory," *Signs*, 7, 3 (Spring 1982), 535.

[17]*Ibid.*, 543.

[18]Popular Memory Group, "Popular Memory, Theory, Politics, Method," in R. Johnson et al., *Making Histories: Studies in History Writing and Politics* (Minneapolis, 1982), 240-241.

[19]*Ibid.*, 226-227.

[20]*Ibid.*, 247.

[21]*Ibid.*, 234; James Scott, *Weapons*, 43.

struggle and focus of control issues with respect to colonized women. Control was, of course, the central feature in virtually all aspects of colonial treatment of the African population as a whole, as in the control of labor, cash-crop and food production, migration, settlement patterns, and political activity. Significantly, however, problems of control related to women, as raised in the few files or sections of files that treat women as a particular category of interest, are almost exclusively devoted to issues of sexuality and reproduction. Concretely, the "problem" is women's sexuality and the issue concerns the rights of particular males (fathers, husbands) either to regulate or to have exclusive access to women's sexual services and any attendant reproductive benefits.[22] Even when the issue is whether or not women should pay hut or poll tax, or the appropriate posting and differential pay scales of African women teachers, the rights, needs and responsibilities of men are the focus of concern against which the "problem of women" is posed.[23]

The structural situation within which Tanganyikan women operated was thus fundamentally affected by colonial interests in their sexuality and reproductive rights. But whereas specified colonial agents generally took responsibility for controlling male labor, migration, and cash-crop production, the control of women was invariably left to colonized men - to fathers, husbands, brothers or uncles - while its legal parameters were defined and redefined by colonial officials, including Native Authorities.[24]

The colonial state not only mediated men's interests in women and their offspring, it also established a framework for Tanganyikan women's development which, especially after World War II, was designed to promote their "domestication."[25] Beginning in 1945 with the creation of an African Women's

---

[22]Thus, one finds, in what might be called the "women's files" in the Tanzania National Archives (TNA), ponderous exchanges between colonial officers and reports of exchanges between officers and "native authorities" on the following subjects: adultery (seen as an injury, originally civil and later criminal, to the "owner-husband"), including whether and how severely women should be punished, forced to pay, or indeed imprisoned for their presumed complicity in an adulterous union (TNA 20411; 156/1/Vol. V); the monetization and/or increase of bride price, with almost exclusive attention to the consequences for men of the changing nature of the transaction (TNA A2/13; L5/7); the impregnation of unmarried girls, with a focus on the appropriate fine which a man should pay as punishment "for having stolen something to which he was not entitled" (Minutes of Dodoma District Council Meeting, 9 February 1953, TNA L5/7); marriage/divorce law and custom and appropriate court jurisdiction over same (TNA 29563); control of prostitutes, alleged or known (TNA 3/14, Vol. VIII); complaints, especially concerning the beating and/or desertion of wives by their husbands (TNA 16), but also desertion charges brought by husbands against wives. In the latter case, district officers appear to have assisted husbands in securing the return of wives on the sole grounds of a husband's request for help (DC, DSM to DC, Kilwa, 3/14/1326, 9 July 1955, TNA 3/14, Vol. VIII).

[23]TNA 10690 and TNA 1/8 concern hut and poll tax and the posting of women teachers respectively.

[24]For a thorough analysis of similar issues in colonial Zambia, see Martin Chanock, "Making Customary Law: Men, Women, and Courts in Colonial Northern Rhodesia," in Margaret Jean Hay and Marcia Wrights, eds., *African Women and the Law: Historical Perspectives* (Boston, 1982), 53-67; and Martin Chanock, *Law, Custom and Social Order: The Colonial Experience in Malawi and Zambia* (Cambridge, 1985), esp. 146-216.

[25]The use of this term is fully explained in Barbara Rogers, *The Domestication of Women* (London, 1981).

Welfare Section of the Women's Service League (founded 1926), and with the appointment of Tanganyika's first woman welfare officer at the end of 1948, the government envisioned a program for women that closely replicated the Western middle-class model of female domesticity. Thus it included basic literacy and math skills for more efficient marketing and household budget management; cookery, knitting, sewing, and other handicrafts deemed suitable for women; and the dissemination of information on health, hygiene, and childcare. By the early 1950s, in the hands of wives of colonial officers and women social development workers, this program had become institutionalized in the Tanganyika Council of Women (1951) and the "Women's Club Movement."[26]

The positive response of many Tanganyikan women to the opportunity to learn to read and write, sew and knit for personal family use as well as for sale indicated a strong desire to overcome the barriers to their development created by colonial educational and technical/vocational neglect.[27] The potential costs included indoctrination into Western women's bourgeois cultural and material ideology (including views of women as happy homemakers, efficient domestic managers, necessary moral restraints on their menfolk, consumers, and perhaps above all, "good" mothers) and direct exposure to the racist attitudes and assumptions of European women.[28] As an unnamed social worker with experience in Dar es Salaam put it, raising the level of the urban African woman's homelife and improving her self- and public esteem necessitated teaching her not only how to "do the arithmetic of housekeeping and the market place," but how to dress "in the mode and fashion of" and create homes which reflected "the tastes and standards of the advanced culture."[29]

By 1954, the year of TANU's formation, the government was actively using the Tanganyika Council of Women to unite women's groups and attract educated women of all races to promote domestic science through the establishment of branches throughout the countryside. "Big wives" and educated women made up the vast majority of branch members.[30]

A closer look at the lives of women in Dar es Salaam in the mid-1950s - at the moment of nationalist mobilization - enables us to examine the extent to which colonial ideology complemented or contradicted urban coastal Islamic cultural mores on matters of control over women's sexuality and reproduction and with respect to a Westernized version of domesticity as the appropriate goal

---

[26]Marjorie Mbilinyi, "Women's Role in the Historical Development of Tanzania," unpublished manuscript (1983), 102.

[27]See, for example, the 1951 report, "Progress in Pare," by social development officer H. Mason, in TNA 81/3.

[28]Evidence to support this generalization is amply provided in TNA 540 3/70; A/15; 540/A/14; 1/2/F; 81/3; 1/27/A III; 42226; 1/2/G. Vol. 1.

[29]Unsigned memo entitled "The Urban Way," n.d., TNA 540/A 14.

[30]Mbilinyi, "Women's Role," 102.

of women's "development."[31] At that time, the vast majority of women in Dar es Salaam between the ages of 16 and 45 were both Muslim (90 percent) and illiterate (88 percent), with literacy defined as "the ability to read and write a few words." Over half the women in this age group (57 percent) had been married once, while one-quarter had been married twice, 8 percent three times, and 2 percent more than three times.[32] Eleven percent were "single" or in a "free marriage" (*kinyumba* or *kimada*, in Swahili) relationship - a figure which corresponds closely to the 11.2 percent figure for female-headed households in the city. Women held titles to nearly a fifth (19 percent) of the 12,000 African-owned houses in the city, and in Kisutu, a predominately Manyema area where women constituted the largest percentage (38 percent) of female household heads, they also held titles to 45 percent of the houses.[33]

The houses in question, whether male- or female-owned, were invariably six-room "Swahili-type" dwellings in which the majority of Dar es Salaam's African population lived and still live. Families or single persons occupied a separate room, sharing a common passageway, courtyard, kitchen and toilet. In the 1950s, such houses were frequently over-crowded and without adequate sewage or water.[34] Yet for women residents, this style of housing provided ready-made female companionship and a central courtyard in which to socialize, take morning tea together, undertake various tasks, and share news and information. Such easy and comfortable access linked unrelated urban women to each other, while those who ventured into the streets daily to undertake one form of economic activity or another extended a network of relationships with other women similarly engaged.

------

[31] In summarizing women's situation in Dar es Salaam in the 1950s, I rely on the work of J.A.K. Leslie, a district officer who became acting commissioner for social development in Tanganyika in 1959. Leslie's *A Survey of Dar es Salaam* (London, 1963) first appeared as a lengthy report dated 29 December 1957. My references to this original report are so specified. Where I refer to *Survey*, my reference is to the book. Leslie's work is based on a questionnaire administered to 5 percent of a sample drawn from houses in predominantly African parts of Dar es Salaam during 1956. For all its shortcomings, this survey offers useful primary data on women's urban existence. (See Appendix C, 311, "Original Report," for Leslie's methodology.) Among these shortcomings is the familiar problem of androcentrism. With the exception of a special set of questions regarding marriage and children and a few "interludes" (short vignettes describing specific women), Leslie directed his survey to male respondents (e.g., "Do you live alone or with a wife?" "Who cooks for you?" "Did you leave your wife behind [when you came to Dar]?" Leslie, "Original Report," 313-317). Early sections on "the African" and why "he" comes to Dar es Salaam, etc., are uniformly androcentric. Nevertheless, one can piece together a tentative yet informative picture from both statistical and descriptive data.

[32] *Ibid.*, 260-261, 190.

[33] *Ibid.*, 221, 268, No. 9 of survey tables, 155. Leslie cautions that the 19 percent figure for woman-owned houses shouldn't be taken "literally," since "people" might apply to build a house in the name of a wife or daughter (p. 155). But he offers no evidence of this practice or its frequency, and in fact, explains how women could acquire houses through "lucrative small trades," inheritance from a deceased husband, parent or brother, from the proceeds from prostitution or as compensation for relocation (155, 227, 2H and 2I).

[34] See Marjorie Mbilinyi, "'City' and 'Countryside' in Colonial Tanganyika," *Economic and Political Weekly*, XX, 43, Review of Women's Studies (26 October 1985), 90.

For their part, the minority Christian population of Dar es Salaam shunned this form of housing, preferring to live separate from Muslims and "pagans" in the self-contained or semi-detached housing of the Mission Quarters. Here, they could protect their "reputation for more stable marriages" and reinforce their sense of themselves as a "class apart" by physical separation from less educated non-Christians, and especially, from the "immorality" of coastal women.[35] As one woman of this "professional class" explained:

> We prefer to live in Quarters rather than a Swahili house, because there is room to spread yourself, and you don't get into bad habits from the other women; there is no noise or jostling, and you can keep the place clean.[36]

It was primarily among this small, Christianized, and relatively better-educated group of urban dwellers that one found most of the few wage-earning or salaried women of Dar es Salaam - as school teachers, hospital workers, or employed in some aspect of social welfare directed at women. Although Muslim women householders probably enjoyed a monthly income from the rental of rooms that was a steady and perhaps more substantial than that of their wage-earning counterparts, the vast majority were limited in their economic activities to what is euphemistically called the informal sector. Here, women engaged in a range of occupations vital to urban existence. They purchased, fried, and sold fish; they made and sold cakes, fritters, beans, coconut ice and *pombe* (beer) - that is, affordable "fast food" for impoverished male workers; they split and sold firewood; and - though here the term "vital" is at best problematic - they engaged in prostitution. Of these enterprises, fish selling, beer brewing and prostitution appear to have been the most lucrative, at least for some women.[37]

Although a few women were probably well off and others made their lives substantially more secure through one or more income-producing activities, much of Dar es Salaam's African population lived in or precariously near the brink of poverty. During the late 1940s and early 1950s, male wage laborers had successfully struck for higher rates of pay in several areas. But Dar es Salaam municipality had no minimum wage law until 1956, and even then, when employers didn't ignore it (as many did) they persisted in paying lower wages to females than to males (30 percent lower, according to 1957 rates).[38] Given this reality, it is hardly necessary to idealize women's situation in the tenuous sphere of urban petty production and trade in order to understand why they might choose alternatives available in that sphere over wage and especially factory employment.

---

[35]Leslie, "Original Report," 260, 209.

[36]Leslie, *Survey*, 91.

[37]Leslie, "Original Report," 90, 227.

[38]Issa G. Shivji, "Development of Wage-Labour and Labour Laws in Tanzania: Circa 1920-1964" (Ph.D. thesis, University of Dar es Salaam, 1982), 268, 310-313.

Colonial officials of the period shared with urban African men an ambivalence toward urban women which is duly reflective of a shared gender ideology. On the one hand, urban wives were "economic liabilities" in contrast to rural wives "at home" who were "an investment" and an "economic asset."[39] On the other, they were hard-working, resourceful, and astute businesswomen, far more adept at saving and investing earnings than their male counterparts.[40] District Officer Leslie clearly sympathized with his male informants, who reported that they had to supply a "constant succession of new garments, ear-rings and plastic sandals" in order to keep their wives or female companions from the "smooth operators" or from simply leaving.[41]

At the root of urban men's stated preference for a wife "at home" who stayed there, as well as Leslie's ambivalent lapses into contradictory stereotypes, lay the issue of men's diminished control over an urban wife's labor or earnings. Thus, the real difference between the rural and urban wife had far less to do with relative productivity than with the increased control which the urban woman exercised over her own production and earnings, and hence, over her own life - with or without a particular husband.

In 1957, Senior Provincial Commissioner M.J.B. Molohan offered a class-specific solution to the "problem" of urban women wrenched from the hard-working rural life to which "they have always been accustomed" and left with "time on their hands."[42] In his refinement of the ideology of domestication already introduced, Molohan proposed domestic service training courses for the wives of wage laborers who could then replace men in "this unproductive sphere of employment for which [women] . . . are far better suited and equipped."[43] Even though the phenomenon of "houseboys" was a European colonial creation, Molohan felt it was "ludicrous" to have so many able-bodied men locked up in domestic work. Meanwhile, for the wives of "middle class Africans" in town, whose lack of education constituted "the greatest handicap" to the advancement of higher-paid clerical workers, small-scale entrepreneurs, or traders, he recommended "female education" on the model of the "foyer school" in Elizabethville, where women learned "sewing, simple domestic science, cooking, child welfare, etc."[44]

Breaking through the mists of colonial, capitalist, and patriarchal ideology shrouding the lives of Dar es Salaam's female population in the mid-1950s, it is possible to offer the following, albeit tentative, conclusions: Generally speaking, the range and flexibility of marital arrangements appear to have offered some women more choices and a greater degree of self-control in sexual as well as reproductive matters than could be exercised by their rural sisters. Although

---

[39]Leslie, *Survey*, 226.

[40]Leslie, "Original Report," 94.

[41]Leslie, *Survey*, 226.

[42]M.J.B. Molohan, *Detribalisation* (Dar es Salaam, 1957), 41.

[43]*Ibid.*, 42.

[44]*Ibid.*, 55.

seclusion was the norm and the closely approximated "ideal" for Muslim girls from the time of puberty through the period of their first marriages, divorce was common, and women frequently exercised substantially more independence in successive marriages. In addition, there were at least some opportunities for securing an independent income, including the possibility of acquiring a house and rental income through purchase or inheritance. Lack of education was not a barrier to wealth in an urban environment where the "first owners of the land" were relatively rich and not necessarily literate men and women, who continued to exercise substantial political and social influence in their communities in the 1950s.[45]

While there was substantial economic differentiation and obvious class formation, with a cult of domestic dependency growing among women of the newly educated, Christianized African "elite," this group was as yet too small and insufficiently well-established to effectively challenge or replace the so-called traditional community. I say "so-called," because in important respects, the views of the educated elite, though characterized as "modern" and "progressive," were conservative relative to those of the vast majority of Dar es Salaam's population. They were conservative precisely because the Western sex-role ideology which informed the conception of women's place in the emergent bourgeois class of which they were a part was an ideology which conceptualized women as inherently domestic and dependent.[46]

Consider, for example, the life and attitudes of the following "representative" professional woman from the Mission Quarter: A teacher, married to a teacher, she rises at 5 a.m. to clean, heat water, sweep, and make tea. She wakes her husband at 6:40 and while he washes, she cleans the bedroom, then washes and dresses. They eat breakfast together and go to work. In the afternoon, she washes and irons clothes, does some gardening, makes the meal, and gets the water from a standpipe. She accepts a division of labor which finds her at work both before her husband has awakened and after he has completed his job. She also accepts the new confinement appropriate to their "modern" status: "When my husband is out I have no permission to go out anywhere except to the Guides or the Police, or if I am called away urgently, I must leave my husband a note to show where I have gone and why . . . ."[47] Deeply committed to a "proper marriage," she also believes in the proper expenditure of any leisure time she might have. For example, she prefers traditional *ngomas* to dances because

> they are traditional and are danced by people of the same
> tribe, not just anyone. And as they are traditional anybody

---

[45] Leslie, *Survey*, 65-67; Iliffe, *History*, 384-395. For the history of Dar es Salaam before World War II, see David Henry Anthony III, "Culture and Society in a Town in Transition: A People's History of Dar es Salaam, 1863-1939" (Ph.D. thesis, University of Wisconsin-Madison, 1983).

[46] For a discussion of the effects on the small emerging petty bourgeoisie of the ideology of modernization and the growing dualism which led to distinctions between "modern" (good, Western) and "traditional" (bad, backward, indigenous) see Coulson, *Tanzania*, 92-93. The "domestication of women" ideology is the female version of modernization.

[47] Leslie, *Survey*, 91.

who is an outsider will be unable to create a disturbance; the elders are there too, to see that everything is done properly. I prefer this because people then dance in an orderly and organized manner.[48]

Not surprisingly, Dar es Salaam's early TANU activists emerged not from this self-consciously separatist minority, but from among those women who sold *pombe* and fish and *mandazi,* and who feared neither each other's "habits" nor the ethnic and class diversity common to urban life. These are perhaps the most obvious conclusions to be drawn from the life histories of twenty such activists, recorded during a five-month period in 1984.[49] Although this group spanned Leslie's 16-45 age group in 1955 and conformed to many of its characteristics, most of these women had been born between World War I and the early 1930s, and were in their mid-20s to late 30s at the time of nationalist mobilization. The oldest among them, Asha Ali and Binti Kipara, had been born before the Maji Maji Rebellion (1905-1907), and Asha Ali's father had fought in that war. The youngest, Hadija Kamba, was only 17 when she joined TANU.

Only four of the women had been born in or near (Ubungo) Dar es Salaam, and with the exception of Hadija Kamba, who had come to the capital from Tabora in the early 1950s, those born elsewhere had accompanied husbands to the city in the 1940s.[50] Although the fathers of two had been employed by the colonial government (one, a railway technician, the other, a water engineer) the other had been farmers, launderers, and hotel workers. Binti Kipara remembers her father's experience of forced labor vividly; Salima Ferouz's father sold ivory with the Arabs near Kilwa when she was young. The mothers of these women were "housewives" and in most cases, farmers. Tatu Mzee's mother sold *vitumbua*

---

[48]*Ibid.,* 92.

[49]The women interviewed were identified in a variety of ways. The names of several were listed in histories of TANU, and inquiries in Dar es Salaam yielded their whereabouts. Others were suggested by Mrs. Agnes Kasembe of the Dar es Salaam UWT Headquarters, herself a longtime activist. Still others were mentioned during the course of interviews as very important in the early days. All women were interviewed in their own homes, and all interviews referred to in this essay were conducted in Swahili, taped, transcribed and translated into English. Mr. M.W. Kanyama Chiume, himself a leader of the Malawian nationalist cause in the 1950s and a friend and colleague of many TANU leaders of the period, helped to arrange numerous interviews, and frequently accompanied and assisted me during interview sessions. In addition, he worked on the transcription and translation of many of the interview tapes. His assistance, enthusiasm, writing and translating skills (he has lived in exile in Tanzania as a journalist, publisher, writer of fiction and nonfiction) and knowledge of Dar es Salaam and the period were invaluable to me. I also received assistance with transcription and translation from Ms. Judica King'on, Mrs. Leah Semguruka and Mr. Steven Maloda. Research Assistant funds were provided by the SSRC and the University of Minnesota Graduate School.

[50]Prior to 1950, the vast majority of women migrants to Dar es Salaam accompanied or followed husbands seeking urban employment. Between 1950 and 1970, however, the proportion of unmarried women migrants rose from 13 to 33 percent. See Deborah Fahy Bryceson, "The Proletarianization of Women in Tanzania," *Review of African Political Economy,* 17 (January-April 1980), 4-27, 19-20; Nwanganga Shields, *Women in the Urban Labor Markets of Africa: The Case of Tanzania,* World Bank Staff Paper No. 380 (April 1980), 17-27; R.H. Sabot, *Economic Development and Urban Migration* (London, 1979), 89-97.

(rice flour fritters) after separating from her father, and later became a farmer in Rufiji.

Like 90 percent of Dar es Salaam's female population, all of the activists interviewed were Muslim. Two women, Titi Mohamed and Hadija Swedi, had attended colonial primary school for four and six years respectively; and a third, Halima Khamisi, was literate in Swahili and a teacher in a Koranic school in 1955. But the others had received little or no formal education (some mentioned a brief period of "reading Koran" as young girls) and, like the vast majority of the city's female population described above, were illiterate. Two women were in their 30s when they got their first taste of formal education in the late 1950s attending adult classes at Arnautoglu Community Center in Dar es Salaam.

All but one of the women had experienced a first arranged marriage at or near the age of puberty, having been confined prior to marriage for periods ranging from two years at one extreme to a brief seven days at the other. Binti Kipara was married for three years before she attained reproductive maturity. While most had been secluded by first husbands much older than they, subsequent divorces and remarriages as well as necessity brought varying degrees of relaxation to this coastal Islamic ideal. By 1955, all but one of the women had been married at least twice, and in several cases, three times, suggesting that Leslie might have found a much higher percentage of multiple marriages among Dar es Salaam's adult female population had his starting age been 20 rather than 16.

Those informants who earned money in the 1950s worked at jobs that were characteristic of the gendered urban colonial economy described earlier. Asha Ali sold *togwa* (beer), *vitumbua*, bread and firewood; Binti Kipara sold fish, and with other women sellers of various foodstuffs and beer, participated in a rotating fund which allowed each member periodic access to the total contribution of all participants. Futmua Abdallah sold firewood. Several farmed.

All of the women interviewed lived in "Swahili" houses. And all but one participated in a women's dance/musical organization. To the colonial administrators of the mid-1950s as to most African observers, popular women's dance/musical groups were nothing more than an innocuous if sometimes extravagent entertainment and activity of "common" women, earlier bannings of such organizations elsewhere (in 1936 and in 1946, in Bagamoyo)[51] notwithstanding. Surely there was nothing about the activities of "Roho Mgeni," "Safina," "Good Luck," "Submarine," or "British Empire" to arouse much interest, even less suspicion, on the part of colonial authorities. Three such groups, the musical clubs "Egyptian," "Alwatan," and "Lelemama," enjoyed the legitimacy of providing regular entertainment at the newly established Arnautoglu Community Center, where, according to financial reports from the years 1952-1958, proceeds from dances were second only to bar rental in providing income for the center.[52]

But women's dance groups embodied important values beyond entertainment and socializing. As a European social worker who sought to

---

[51] Salatiel R. Shemhilu, "The Economic History of Bagamoyo, 1885-1950" (M.A. thesis, University of Dar es Salaam, 1976), 134.

[52] TNA 540 27/6.

establish urban women's clubs modeled on the "lines of the Women's Institute in the U.K." noted, dance group members expressed a sense of "common bond," and this was an essential prerequisite for the success of the clubs she envisioned:

> all members are accomplished dancers and they are drawn together because esteem is won by being a good dancer, and they consider their dancing worth preserving and developing. Before clubs of the Women's Institute type can develop in Dar es Salaam, the domestic skills must be invested with the values which attach to the tribal dancing of the dance club.[53]

In fact, and unlike most male-dominated organizations which continued to be based on the exclusionary principles of tribal, regional, or religious affiliation,[54] the women's *ngoma* groups already embodied nationalist principles. They were trans-tribal in composition; they accepted all women willing to dedicate themselves to the group and recognize the authority of its leaders; and they were fully aware of the critical unifying force of Swahili as a common language.

> Wanyamwezi and whoever and whoever. Even in our Rufiji organization - others joined it. You couldn't restrict. Anyone with interest could join, since we all speak Swahili. I don't know Kinyamwezi. Ah! But we speak the same language . . . . Now there is no difficulty. All the people are mixed up together. Just like this.[55]

In 1955, Bibi Titi Mohamed was a 30-year-old Dar es Salaam-born "housewife." As lead singer in the group "Bomba," she was already widely known as a musician when she purchased TANU card number sixteen from Sheneda Plantan, the brother of her third husband, and thus became TANU's first female member. Plantan, a prominent Dar es Salaam businessman and long-time member of TANU's predecessor the Tanganyikan African Association (TAA), had been among the contingent of Dar es Salaam community notables to be included in TANU's central committee, established in 1954.[56] Thus Titi Mohamed was, at the very least, politically well-connected through her brother-in-law. But she was also sufficiently moved by what Plantan had to say about TANU's nationalist goals to want to become actively involved, and since a "Women's Section" was specifically mentioned in the new association's constitution,[57] she was surprised and

---

[53]Unsigned Memo, "The Urban Way," n.d., TNA 540/A 14.

[54]TNA 3/32. An obvious and importance exception, of course, were workers' union. For the history of men's dance associations, see T.O. Ranger, *Dance and Society in Eastern Africa 1890-1970* (London, 1975).

[55]Interview, Bibi Titi Mohamed, 10 September 1984.

[56]For further background and information on Plantan and other Dar es Salaam community leaders active in TAA and then TANU, see Anthony, "Culture and Society," passim, and Iliffe, *History*, 408-412, 507-513.

[57]Iliffe, *History*, 531.

disappointed when her initial inquiries were deflected with evasive allusions to men's objections.[58]

Under these circumstances, it is difficult to know when or how Dar es Salaam women might have mobilized had it not been for John Hatch's June 1955 visit to Dar es Salaam. Hatch had been sent to Dar to gather information on TANU for the Fabian Colonial Bureau and to offer the Bureau's assistance; when he queried TANU Central Committee members about a "women's section," he was assured that it existed. And when he asked to meet its leader, the quick-witted Plantan thought of producing his sister-in-law for a meeting with Hatch planned for the next day.

> But the fact is, they didn't have a woman then! You understand? Everyone had locked their wives away [in the house]. No one wanted to take his wife and say "this is my wife, this is the one," or even to say "she is not my wife." Everybody refused [until] Sheneda said, "I will go and collect Titi." "Bwana, ha! Titi is married!" [they said]. "But her husband is my friend. I will talk to him and she will come."[59]

Titi agreed to meet with Hatch so long as her friend and relative, Tatu Mzee, could be persuaded to go too. Thus both women joined the ranks of the TANU leadership and began to create a women's section in fact - not just on paper. Acutely aware that her appointment as "leader of a women's section" by TANU Central Committee was an act of necessity on their part that had neither been supported nor confirmed by any of the women she might be expected to lead, Bibi Titi's initial concerns were twofold: she needed to gain women's approval of her leadership, and she needed to incorporate other women into the leadership structure. By insisting that Tatu Mzee be invited to meet with Hatch, she had already begun the latter process. Shortly thereafter, she persuaded another friend, Halima Khamisi, to become active. Khamisi's participation was especially important because she was literate in Swahili and had taught in a Koranic school, and the women needed someone who could act as a secretary when necessary.[60]

Bibi Titi also began mass mobilization immediately.

> To mobilize the women, I went to the Ngoma groups. First of all, I went to their leaders. The leaders got together in a meeting,and after I spoke to them, they agreed to call all their people so I could come and talk to them about TANU .... For example, I talked to Mama Swaleh Kubunju, leader of the "Tongakusema," and she called together all of the "Tongakusema" women. I met them at Livingstone Street at the corner of Kariokoo Street where Mama Kibunju stayed.

---

[58]Interview, Bibi Titi Mohamed, 10 September 1984. Cf. Barongo, *Mkiki wa Siasa*, 93-94.

[59]Interview, Bibi Titi Mohamed, 10 September 1984.

[60]Interview, Halima Khamisi, 23 October 1984.

She said "Titi is calling you, and I have called you for the sake
of Titi. Here she is and she will tell you what she wants." . . . .
Then I went to Mama bint Makabuli, the leader of "Rumba."
She lives in Narumg'ombe Street near Lumumba Street. She is
still alive, but very old. She called the "warumba." And that's
how I went to "British Empire" and to "Ratu Sudan," and to
the "Sahina" group - I went to all of these groups.[61]

In this process, at least three dance leaders, Kibuyu bint Saleh, Binti Fundi
Mkono, and Rehema bint Seleman (all deceased in 1984) became instrumental
political mobilizers in their own right.

Although some dance club members, including women whose life
experiences dated back to German colonial rule, were hesitant to believe that it
was possible to get rid of colonialism, a vivid consciousness of colonial
exploitation more frequently found expression in enthusiastic support for TANU.
This consciousness was clearly expressed by my informants, when I asked why
they had joined TANU and had urged others to do so:

When I hear this talk, "We have too much trouble now; better
colonial rule," I see such a person as my enemy . . . . When I
remember how we suffered . . . . We were ruled by chiefs but
they had no say in government. They were only given orders.[62]

Under colonialism, we were sick at heart. People used to be
beaten like drums and taken away . . . . We parents would tie
our stomachs crying "My poor son!" When I got money I paid
for my [arrested] son's release and when he came back I
mopped his head with hot water. With conditions like this we
felt it was better to fight for our independence, whether we
were killed or not.[63]

When my clothes were stolen and I took my case to the police,
an African [policeman] told me to stop complaining or I
would be taken to the white man. I asked, "What's the big deal
about a white man?" He got furious and said, "Don't ever say
that again. You can go to jail or anything can be done to you."
I told him a white man was just a human being . . . . Those
fellows of mine all saw the white man as more important than
themselves who did all the work under the whites. But this
was not Africans' fault; it was the fault of colonialism. It is the
colonialist kind of thinking so they couldn't see that they had

---

[61]Interview, Bibi Titi Mohamed, 10 September 1984. Cf. Barongo's chapter on Bibi Titi Mohamed,
where it is stated that dance club leaders and members initially expressed the view that they should be paid
for registering TANU members, and refused to do so unless they were. *Mkiki wa Siasa*, 93.

[62]Interview, Asha Ngoma, 17 October 1984.

[63]Interview, Fatuma Abdallah, 26 September 1984.

more right to their country than those who were from outside.[64]

While the above statements are clear expressions of anti-colonial sentiment, they also suggest the extent to which women's consciousness reflected their gendered position in colonial Tanganyika. Far from being detrimental to their strength as nationalist mobilizers, women's relative lack of direct and daily contact with the colonial regime through wage labor relations, as well as their lack of experience with direct control, contributed to their ability to accurately perceive and analyze colonial conditions. Subjugation, they perceived, could lead to a "colonial mentality," but this was not evidence of African inferiority vis-a-vis Europeans; rather, it was proof that colonialism was harmful and distorting.

In other respects, both gender and religion shaped the women's direct experience of colonial oppression and therefore, their positive response to nationalist objectives as expressed through TANU. The colonial education system, explicitly in the case of mission schools and implicitly in government schools, demanded if not conversion to one brand or another of Christianity, at least the masking of one's faith and practices. The danger of this system to the Muslim community as a whole, in conjunction with negative attitudes toward girls' education, produced doubly discriminatory consequences for Muslim women. The nationalist movement, with its rejection of distinctions based on religion or sex, struck a responsive chord in women who sought for their children, and especially their daughters, an education which they themselves has been denied.[65]

As suggested above, the life histories of Dar es Salaam activists share features in common that, when considered in the context of urban cultural norms, clarify the responsiveness of a particular group of women to TANU moblization. As divorced, "middle-aged" women, they were no longer as constrained, socially or economically, as either younger Muslim women or the small urban minority of Christianized "elite" women. As members of a pan-ethnic urban community, they had already rejected many aspects of tribal exclusivity and had fostered in place of ethnic identification an ever-expanding sense of broad "sisterhood" through their dance associations in particular. While there is no reason to assume that Christian women would have been unwelcome, available evidence suggests that Christian women did not consider the dance groups appropriate places for them to be.[66] In addition to religious differences, Muslim women's lack of education no doubt created conditions under which

---

[64]Interview, Hadija Swedi, 7 September 1984.

[65]This view was expressed by nearly all of the women interviewed, and was referred to as well in response to questions about whether or not the lives of Tanzanian girls and women in 1984 were very different from those of girls and women in 1955.

[66]In contrast, ex-slave mission converts of Christianity participated in *Ngoma* in Mombasa, sharing ties with prominent Swahili families or sharing Swahili culture, particularly the slave components of it, through girls' initiation rites, etc. While the reference here is to Mombasa during an earlier period (early twentieth century), the difference is noteworthy. Personal communication from Margaret Strobel, 17 April 1986.

difference might be directly translated by both groups into terms of "inferiority" and "superiority."

Freed from some of the direct constraints attached to their position as women, my informants nevertheless clearly distinguished between colonial oppression and gender oppression, and saw in TANU a chance for further escape from the latter. This can be surmised from repeated references to the significance of TANU as a movement that stressed not only equality for all people, but the need for men and women to work "side-by-side" - an experience which all embraced wholeheartedly and for the first time as TANU activists. Respect and dignity were the concepts most frequently mentioned along with self-rule, when asked what they thought independence might bring to Tanganyikans. And these concepts were also central to their assessment of women's particular condition and the need for radical change in the structure of gender arrangements.

TANU's promises of equality, dignity and respect stood in sharp contrast to informants' characterizations of the daily oppression women experienced as women:

> The women had no say. We had nothing to say, and whatever we might have wanted to say, we had to follow . . . . We had no freedom at all. We were considered useless people. A woman was regarded as a useless person because she was a woman. That's why we put in more effort, after learning the saying "all people are equal," we understood well what that was supposed to mean and we said "we shall see if all people are equal; we must cooperate if this saying is to become true."[67]

> [A woman] was like a donkey. She had to do all the work, to cook, wash clothes, to cultivate, to pound grain, to look after children. All this time men were out drinking.[68]

> We were put inside. Let's say you were married. You stay inside . . . . What is going on outside, you don't know. You don't know what is happening in the world. So we thought that if we didn't get it [independence] ourselves, our children would get it. But we would work to get out of slavery.[69]

> To speak the truth, during colonial rule it was not easy to see a woman chairing a meeting. We had to follow what our husbands told or commanded us to do. And if he says you

---

[67]Interview, Mwasaburi Ali, 10 September 1984.

[68]Interview, Asha Ali, 26 September 1984.

[69]Interview, Salima Ferouz, 26 September 1984.

have to stay inside, you had to do so. You won't go to market.
You have to obey. We didn't know each other . . . .[70]

I remember how we suffered. A person was not respected as a
human being, especially we women. When a woman passed in
front of people she had to cover herself. A woman wasn't
considered a human being . . . . A woman was a woman. Her
work was in the kitchen - to cook, to give birth, to cultivate.
There was nothing else.[71]

The experience of working as TANU activists clearly brought Dar es
Salaam women to a consciousness of the personal as political.[72] Bibi Titi
Mohamed's words and leadership directly stimulated and provided a voice for
this process.[73] Her public exhortations to women, as well as to women and men,
reflected the sense of opportunity felt, and the need to seize the moment:

I told you [women] that we want independence. And we can't
get independence if you don't want to join the party. We have
given birth to all these men. Women are the power in this
world. We are the ones who give birth to the world![74]

We shouldn't feel inferior because of our womanhood! God
has planted a seed in the women. It has been in us. It has
grown. Ehee! We have given birth. All the men have fallen
down. Those you see with their coats and caps, they are from
here [pointing to herself]. They didn't come direct from their
fathers by way of our backs. Yalaa! God has given us this

---

[70]Interview, Mwamvita Mnyamani, 26 October 1984.

[71]Interview, Asha Ngoma, 17 October 1984.

[72]The process through which women engaged in political movements come to recognize and challenge aspects of their subordinate position previously accepted as "natural" within a particular cultural ideology has been a critical phenomenon within movements and cultures as diverse as the Chinese communist revolution (peasant women's "speak bitterness" sessions) and the second-wave American women's movement "consciousness-raising" groups which emerged among women participants in the U.S. civil rights movement and new left politics of the 1960s. For the African context see Pepe Roberts, "Feminism in Africa: Feminism and Africa," *Review of African Political Economy*, 27/28 (1983), 175-184.

[73]Bibi Titi herself was terrified in anticipation of her first large public address at Arnautoglu Community Center, and spent the entire night before trying unsuccessfully to memorize a speech prepared for her by other TANU officials. When she did rise to speak she felt as if she was "in shock." She recalls, "I stood up, as if God had caused me to rise. I didn't look at the people. I looked up so that I wouldn't feel ashamed. It was the first day, my historic day" (Interview, Bibi Titi Mohamed, 10 September 1984).

[74]*Ibid.*, recalling her speech to the women called together on her behalf by dance club leader, Mama Swaleh Kibunju.

power. He didn't do a silly thing . . . . Without our cooperation we won't achieve our country's freedom.[75]

Encouraging women to feel a higher degree of self-respect was a critical step in this consciousness-raising process, and one which Bibi Titi addressed directly, particularly in relation to women's shared sense of inferiority because of lack of education. It was true that many women lacked education, she said, and after independence, women would have an equal chance to go as far as they could in school. But lack of education didn't mean that a person was worthless, and women needed to understand that. They had a vital part to play in the struggle for freedom, and they had to take that responsibility.[76]

All of the women interviewed shared the widely held popular as well as official (TANU) view that initially, women's support for TANU in Dar es Salaam was stronger than men's, however this was measured. "Men were afraid and we were not," was the most frequently offered explanation. Women bought and hid TANU cards for men, and judging from my informants, thoroughly relished the "protector role" they assumed during the mobilization process. But they also accepted as the reason for their own greater courage, as evidenced in their greater numbers and more active public support for TANU, another widely held view. In this view, both women's greater participation and men's reluctance stem from men's fears that joining TANU meant losing their jobs, a view which in turn can be traced to government legislation prohibiting civil servants from joining political parties.[77] This ruling clearly affected government employees and private sector employers may have used it to discourage salaried workers. But this would hardly account for the behavior of the vast majority of Dar es Salaam's male population, since most workers were neither permanently employed nor working in the state sector. Rather, like many women, most men subsisted through petty commodity production and trade.[78] Under the circumstances, it seems reasonable to suggest that "fear of job loss" served as code for the more direct and coercive control which the colonial state exerted over the male population, and men's more extensive daily experience of oppression in this sense.[79]

---

[75]*Ibid.*, recalling her first public address at Arnautoglu Community Center.

[76]*Ibid.*, recalling various speeches.

[77]See Daniel R. Smith, "The Influence of the Fabian Colonial Bureau on the Independence Movement in Tanganyika," Ohio University, Monographs in International Studies Africa Series, No. 44 (1985), 27-33.

[78]Marjorie Mbilinyi, "'City' and 'Countryside,'" 89.

[79]Of course, where women acted as own-account workers - and this was far more common in urban than in rural areas - they could expect, and indeed did engage in direct confrontations with state attempts to exercise control. This was, not surprisingly, especially true in the case of prostitutes (TNA 3/14 Vol. VIII). See Luise White, "A Colonial State," in Cooper, ed., *Struggle*, 167-194. But it was also true of women engaged in beer brewing in Dar es Salaam (see Mbilinyi, "'City' and 'Countryside,'" 91-93), and of women wage laborers (see Jeanne Penvenne, "Here Everyone Walked with Fear: The Mozambican Labor System and the Workers of Lourenco Marques, 1945-1962," in Cooper, ed., *Struggle*, 148-153.

But the explanation above is only partial and inhibits full appreciation of women's actions and efforts, which in turn provides us with some insight into the process through which women's experience and consciousness is rendered historically less important and ultimately invisible except as indirectly related to men's situation. The logical if unstated conclusion from such an analysis - that women "spontaneously" filled a space left vacant by men who had more to lose - would be wrong. The women of Dar es Salaam did indeed seize a moment, but they did so with a consciousness of both colonial and gender oppression, and in response to TANU directives and objectives that offered freedom from both. The material conditions of the urban proletariat which the majority of women shared with each other and with their men, far from constituting grounds for alienation, had contributed to a new sense of multiethnic solidarity. A culturally approved place for the expression and further development of this solidarity among urban coastal women, including recent arrivals, had long been, and continued to be, the women's dance groups.[80] Islam and the Swahili language provided an inclusive and permeable framework. Through dance groups, as well as through networks of relations established among women beer brewers,[81] food sellers, and other women workers, Dar es Salaam's "ordinary" women possessed both an organizational capacity for reaching others that could be put to political use, and a social predisposition to TANU's goals of multiethnic unity and equality. This was especially true for Muslim women no longer subject to the firm cultural restrictions or expectations associated with young female adulthood - that period which lasted from the onset of puberty through a women's first marriage and most frequently entailed seclusion.

At the same time, it is clear that the relatively greater freedom experienced by "older" divorced and/or remarried women carried its own socio-cultural price tag. In rendering accounts of house-to-house recruitment, several women recalled being met with hostility and suspicion which took the form of accusations that they were after other women's husbands, and variations on this theme. Because they were engaging in political work within a cultural framework characterized by the absence of women in political roles, individual rather than social explanations were sometimes sought for their political activities. Thus, Bibi Titi was frequently charged with behaving with unseemly self-importance. "Ha! Do you expect to be queen?" demanded several of her suspicious critics.[82] In addition, the important role which women played in raising and collecting funds for all aspects of TANU work - for salaries, for Nyerere's trips abroad and legal fees, for example - led as well to charges of self-aggrandizement. Women endured these criticisms and frequently overcame them because the TANU leadership supported the women and affirmed the validity, honesty, and morality of their political activities.[83]

---

[80]The most comprehensive analysis of women's *ngoma* or dance organizations to date is Strobel's 1979 study focused on women in Mombasa. See Strobel, *Muslim Women.*

[81]See Mbilinyi, "'City' and 'Countryside,'" 91-93.

[82]Interview, Bibi Titi Mohamed, 10 September 1984.

[83]Both the charges and the importance of TANU support were mentioned in several interviews.

Women's political work throughout Dar es Salaam was invariably done on foot. This arduous task required contact in each of the city's many sub-areas, central as well as "suburban." Democratic delegation of leadership responsibilities to as many women as possible was therefore both practical, in terms of efficiency, and politically appropriate as a response to nationalist sentiments. Many of the women who became area leaders in Dar es Salaam were deceased by 1984; nevertheless, most of the women I interviewed had also been responsible for some aspect of the area-based organization of the TANU women's section in the city.

Although a discussion of women's participation in TANU throughout the country lies beyond the scope of this essay, a similar pattern of intense involvement and activity on the part of Muslim women in particular is evident, and bears further investigation.[84] Meanwhile, it is clear that TANU's male leadership found it fruitful to support and encourage women's political activism, even in the face of irate husbands.[85] They did so both because women's participation proved to be crucial to political mobilization and in order to substantiate nationalist rhetoric of "men/women, side-by-side." Women's nationalist activism therefore became at the same time an important move against gender oppression.

In Dar es Salaam, the focus of TANU's initial mobilizing efforts, women proved themselves to be critically important in many ways. While their crucial role in joining the party and recruiting other members is well known, they are also to be credited with the formation of active and effective branches of the "Women's Section" throughout the numerous districts and "suburbs" of Dar es Salaam. In so doing, they stimulated and facilitated the emergence of a grassroots leadership and democratized the process of TANU organizing while at the same time providing TANU's central leadership with a readily activated network for the transmission of information throughout the city. Whether the news was of an upcoming rally, a march or demonstration, or the need to support a strike, women were organized to respond.

Not surprisingly, given their experience within the socially sanctioned medium of dance groups, women were particularly adept at infusing marches, demonstrations, and rallies with the high spirit of their songs and energetic movement. Again, however, the more obvious and better known of their talents was combined with equally crucial and less well known activities. Women not only raised money through the active solicitation of membership fees and gifts to

---

[84]The preponderance of Muslim names among women listed as members of various TANU committees in the 1950s is striking. See Kandoro, *Mwito wa Uhuru*, passim; Ulotu, *Historia ya TANU*, passim. See also TNA 16, TNA A 6/8. I am grateful to John Iliffe for generously sharing his references to women in TANU from files available during his research, which also suggest that Muslim women were particularly active. Partial explanations would have to include the concentration of Muslims generally in the interior towns from which most of these records and lists are drawn (Dodoma, Tabora, Kibondo, Kondoa, Kigoma, and Musoma) and the significant role of Bibi Titi Mohamed herself in attracting other Muslim women in particular to active participation.

[85]Several women interviewed discussed difficulties with husbands and divorces which they attributed to their TANU activities. See also M. Anta, c/o PWD Korogwe, 1 December 1956, to D.C., Handeni, complaining of his wife's TANU activities (TNA 16); Barongo, *Mkiki*, 92.

meet that party's financial needs, they frequently contributed from their own typically modest resources. Selling or pawning jewelry - frequently the only personal possessions of value a woman owned - was common, as was the contribution of earnings from the sale of foods and other products.[86]

It is not necessary to discredit TANU's enthusiasm for women's participation during the 1950s to note that independence in 1961 brought with it an understanding of the requirements of "good government" that precluded direct involvement for all but a few of the many women who had assumed responsible positions of leadership in TANU and its Women's Section in the 1955-1961 period. Many scholars have traced the demise of both popular organizations (such as workers associations and unions, local cooperative unions) and indirect rule-inspired organizations (such as chiefs or local councils) during the first few years of TANU rule. They have either argued that such moves were inevitable given conditions within and pressures on the new state, or have seen these developments as the inevitable creation of a bourgeois, authoritarian state.[87]

To incorporate an understanding of a shift with respect to the placement of women within the structures of the independent government and party is to return to matters both obvious and ambiguous. An obvious factor in this shift involves assumptions regarding the need for literacy within government and parliament - an assumption which might account for the "disappearance" of most women leaders who emerged in and through TANU in the 1950s so long as there is evidence available to demonstrate a similar decline in participation on the part of non-literate males. Bibi Titi Mohamed, who survived the transition to independence, became a Legislative Council member and junior minister after taking a crash course in English through the British Council "at British expense."[88] She also became head of the women's organization formed to replace the women's section of TANU following independence. Tatu Mzee became a member of the National Executive Council of the party, and both Asha Ngoma and Hadija Swedi held a variety of party positions following independence.[89]

For others, the opportunities were of a different order. Binti Kipara accepted a job as a sweeper. Mwamvita Mnyamani took a job in a clothing

---

[86]Various interviews.

[87]The range of interpretation has been very great with respect to increasing state/party domination in Tanzania, and has, of course, changed markedly over the last twenty years. A recent collection of essays edited by Issa G. Shivji and authored primarily by Tanzanians focuses on aspects of this issue from a standpoint which argues that all previous assessments, from liberal to radical have been informed by "developmentalism." See Issa G. Shivji, ed., *The State and the Working People in Tanzania* (Dakar, 1985). For examples of the range, see Bismark U. Mwansasu and Cranford Pratt, eds., *Toward Socialism in Tanzania* (Toronto, 1979); Susanne D. Mueller, "The Historical Origins of Tanzania's Ruling Class," Working Papers in African Studies No. 35, Boston University African Studies Center (1980); John Lonsdale, "The Tanzanian Experiment," *African Affairs*, 67 (October 1968), 330-344; John Saul, "The Nature of Tanzania's Political System: Issues Raised by the 1965 and 1970 Elections," *Journal of Commonwealth Studies*, 10 (July 1982), 113-129; 10 (November 1972), 198-221.

[88]Listowel, *Making of Tanzania*, 269.

[89]Interviews, Tatu Mzee, 18 October 1984; Asha Ngoma, 17 October 1984; Hadija Swedi, 7 September 1984.

factory, and then worked as a cleaner at Radio Tanzania. As women did not constitute a power base that either represented or could be conceived of as constituting a threat to stability in the country and TANU's control,[90] they warranted no serious attention in that sense. Nevertheless, issues related to gender equality which resulted in legislation designed to enhance and improve women's position (the Affiliation Act, the Marriage Act, 1971, and the Maternity Leave Act) prompted vociferous debate in a Legislative Council not noted for its active role in government.[91]

Most telling of all perhaps was the independent government's determination of positions appropriate for women and which women ought to occupy them. That women's situation was best described in terms of and addressed through the ministries of Social Welfare and Community Development returns us to the familiar "domestication of women" trend which came not out of popular political mobilization but out of Western middle class understandings of "women's place" in society. These understandings complemented the normative gendered views of women equally operative in African society and served to calm any fears that male domination might in any way be challenged. Positions of leadership in these ministries and in related organizations devoted to "women's concerns" required, of course, the appropriate education. They were offered, therefore, not to those women whose efforts had constituted the backbone of nationalist mobilization. Rather, they went to that handful of women whose training in Western domestic science, nursing, cookery, sewing and child/maternal health had established them, from at least the mid-1950s as a minority class above and apart. Educated women were now called upon to offer their "less fortunate" sisters sewing lessons in place of politics, and domestic science and adult literacy in place of personal consciousness-raising.

With this shift, "ordinary" women were no longer seen as having leadership skills relevant to nation-building. Rather, they were viewed as the logical target population for services rendered - and rendered with diligence and commitment - by educated women. The cognitive shift required of activists was that they become consumers of skills and knowledge appropriate within the framework of domestic gender ideology. In general terms, what happened to and with this population had obvious parallels throughout post-independence Tanzania, where the perceived need to expand centralized control and establish development priorities frequently obliterated local dynamism, popular initiative and grassroots leadership.[92]

For Tanzanian women, the legacy has been particularly contradictory in its expression. I have dealt with the problems of Umoja wa Wanawake wa Tanzania (the national women's organization - an affiliate first of TANU, and

---

[90]For example, trade unions, the army, marketing cooperatives.

[91]See J.P.W.B. McAuslan and Yash. P. Ghai, "Constitutional Innovation and Political Stability in Tanzania: A Preliminary Assessment," in Lionel Cliffe and John S. Saul, eds., *Socialism in Tanzania* (Dar es Salaam, 1972), I, 196-215, esp. 202-206. See also H.G. Mwakyembe, "The Parliament and the Electoral Process," in Shivji, ed., *The State*, 16-56.

[92]Several chapters in Shivji, ed., *The State*, address aspects of this process.

then of the reformed Chama Cha Mapunduzi) elsewhere;[93] and others have addressed aspects of its functioning in both local and more general terms.[94] Thirty years - a full generation - after Kambona declared a "revolution [in] the role of women in African society," there is scant evidence of, much less vigorous political commitment to, such a revolution in Tanzania. And although women did indeed address the problem of their emancipation during the period of nationalist struggle, and continue to do so today, this problem has by no stretch of the imagination been disposed of, even at this later date.

---

[93]Susan Geiger, "Umoja wa Wanawake wa Tanzania and the Needs of the Rural Poor," *African Studies Review*, XXV, 2-3 (June/September 1982), 45-65.

[94]See, for example, Marie Antoinette Oomen-Myin, "Involvement of Rural Women in Village Development in Tanzania: A Case Study in Morogoro District," Research Monograph, University of Dar es Salaam Department of Agricultural Education and Extension, Morogoro, 1981; Birgit Madsen, *Women's Mobilization and Integration in Development: A Village Case Study from Tanzania*, CDR Research Report No. 3 (Copenhagen, 1984).

AN EPISODE FROM THE INDEPENDENCE STRUGGLE IN ZAMBIA: A CASE STUDY FROM MWASE LUNDAZI

Jan Kees Van Donge

This article offers an account of the events leading up to independence in Mwase Lundazi, a chieftainship in the eastern province of Zambia, and shows some of the complexities of nationalism in Zambia.[1] The main nationalist party, the United National Independence party (UNIP), undoubtedly had mass support in the late 1950s and early 1960s in the country as a whole. The period is, however, not merely characterized by conflict between Europeans and Africans. There were numerous conflicts within African society as well. These internal conflicts were enmeshed with the resistance against colonialism, but it would be dangerous to confuse these struggles as manifestations of similar political divisions. The issues that divided African society in these years cannot be brought under one common denominator.

It is especially difficult to discern unambiguous and definite links between nationalism and a particular pattern of class formation, as some observers have. A review of the literature on the period indicates this and the case of Mwase Lundazi shows it in detail. It makes more sense to see the nationalist movement as a rapidly shifting set of alliances than as part of a pattern of class struggle. This has a wider significance for the interpretation of African politics generally. Political behaviour in independent Africa has increasingly been interpreted as resulting from the class basis of nationalism.[2] This is doubtful in the case of Zambia and a change of perspective that stresses the capacity of nationalism to absorb widely different groups can be more enlightening. This could explain how UNIP has retained power for more than 20 years after independence by continuing to accommodate different social strata.

The enigmatic nature of Zambian nationalism

The delineation of a nationalist movement in Zambia is not clear cut. First, there is the question of when to date the beginning of a nationalist

The author is lecturer in political science at the University of Dar Es Salaam. The research for this article was carried out while he was on the staff of the university of Zambia.
1. Mwase Lundazi is situated along the Malawian border, to the east of Lundazi district headquarters. The research for this paper was carried out in 1977–8. The oral sources for this paper are 19 interviews with politicians or people with a history in politics in the area.
2. This thesis has been advocated strongly in two influential articles: J. S. Saul, 'The state in post colonial societies: Tanzania' in *The Socialist Register 1974* (The Merlin Press, 1974) and M. von Freyholdt, 'The post colonial state and its Tanzanian version' in *Review of African Political Economy*, no. 8 (1977), pp. 75–90.

265

struggle.   Demands for independence in the immediate future were only made after UNIP was formed in 1958.   The tradition of resistance against colonialism is of course much older, but this was mostly directed against discriminatory aspects of colonialism rather than colonialism as such. The fight against segregation in butcheries is a good example.   The struggle against the federation of the Rhodesias and Nyassaland in the early 1950s did not necessarily imply a principled rejection of colonialism; 'Self government our ultimate goal' was then very much a radical slogan.[3]

Second, there is no one particular category in Zambian society that can be designated as the core of the nationalist parties.   Various authors have, nevertheless, identified nationalism with particular classes in Zambian society.   Van Binsbergen, for one, has argued that UNIP was a proletarian response to the colonial situation;[4] according to Szeftel, on the other hand, nationalism was a movement of the middle stratum of privileged Africans in colonial society.[5]   Yet others maintain that nationalism was based on the emergence of a privileged stratum of kulaks.[6]   Reading the literature, then, draws attention to contradictions and paradoxes in the support that nationalism generated.   This suggests that the movement attracted a diversity of peoples which may well have changed through time.   It also suggests a need for more detailed research in the history of nationalism and the relevance of cases like the one presented here of Mwase Lundazi.

It is especially puzzling that Zambian nationalism has been labelled as a proletarian movement, because conflicts between trade unions and the nationalist movement were recurrent during the independence struggle.[7] These conflicts were complicated further by an attempt to organise the upper echelons of the African workers separately in a Mines African Staff Association on the Copperbelt.[8]   In some cases the nationalist movement appears to have found its support particularly among skilled workers[9] but other observers state that nationalism was mainly supported by the least

---

3.   F. Macpherson, *Kenneth Kaunda of Zambia; the times and the man* (Oxford University Press, 1974), p. 120.
4.   W. M. J. van Binsbergen, *Religious Change in Zambia; exploratory studies* (Kegan Paul International, 1981).
5.   M. Szeftel, *Conflicts, Spoils and Class Formation in Zambia* (Unpublished PhD, thesis, University of Manchester, 1978).
6.   C. L. Baylies, 'The Emergence of Indigenous Capitalist Agriculture: the case of Southern Province Zambia' in *Rural Africana* 4–5 (1979); M. Bratton, 'The Social Context of Political Penetration: Village and Ward Development Committees in Kasama district' in W. Tordoff (ed.), *Administration in Zambia* (Manchester University Press, 1980); M. C. M. Bwalya, 'Rural Differentiation and Poverty Reproduction in Northern Zambia: the case of Mpika District' in University of Edinburgh, Centre of African Studies (ed.), *The Evolving Structure of Zambian society.* (Proceedings of a seminar held 30 and 31 May 1980).
7.   A. L. Epstein, *Politics in an Urban African Community* (Manchester University Press, 1958); A. D. Roberts, *A History of Zambia* (Heinemann, 1976), p. 219; D. C. Mulford, *Zambia: the politics of independence 1957–1964,* (Oxford University Press, 1967, pp. 170–4.
8.   Roberts, *A History of Zambia*, p. 219.
9.   B. Kapferer, *Strategy and Transactions in an African Factory: African labour and Indian management in an African town* (Manchester University Press, 1972), p. 111.

educated and that the rank and file of the party was highly egalitarian.[10] The educated, it is true, probably endangered their jobs if they joined nationalist parties, and they therefore joined the party later, at least openly. Once it appeared likely that independence would come, however, the newly educated men became prominent in nationalist politics.[11] The failure to take such a diachromic view permits some to see the nationalist movement simply as a career opportunity for the less educated.[12] Put simply, then, the evidence which the literature provides on UNIP's urban support is highly ambiguous.

Nationalism was a rural movement as well and, once again, a hetero-geneous one.   The *cha cha cha* rising in 1961 was a rural revolt; but this incident was the only one which approached a mass insurrection during the independence struggle.   It was in any case limited to the northern part of the country and, limiting its generality further, some areas there were more involved than others.   The rising may be characterized as a *jacquerie* during which all symbols of government attracted aggression: schools were burnt, dip tanks and bridges were destroyed and roads were blocked.[13]   In other areas, by contrast, nationalism attracted the elite and was based on specific grievances, rather than a generalized anti-colonialism.   A group of retired pastors and teachers from the Seventh Day Adventist mission formed a nationalist nucleus near Choma in the southern province; the decision of the colonial government to treat them on a par with other African farmers rather than with European farmers in agricultural pricing was their main grievance.[14]   In Barotseland, UNIP attracted two different sources of opposition against the Lozi ruling groups.   First, a particular lineage of the royal family monopolized the administrative positions and therefore aroused opposition on traditionalist grounds.   Second, there was also opposition among the educated Lozi.   Their opportunities were limited in an administrative structure which was modelled on the pre-colonial state.[15]

There is not enough evidence to suggest that nationalism was rooted among the kulaks.   This may of course have been the case in some areas, but there are contrasting pieces of evidence.   The nationalist movement was supported in Uyombe by the privileged, like the successful returned migrants and the relatively highly educated.[16]   A direct contrast can be

10.   P. Harries Jones, *Freedom and Labour* (Oxford University Press, 1975) p. 154.
11.   Mulford, *Zambia*, pp. 264–5.
12.   I. Scott, 'Party-bureaucratic Relations in Zambia' in Tordoff (ed.) *Administration in Zambia*.
13.   Mulford, *Zambia*, pp. 170–4.
14.   M. A. C. Dixon-Fyle, 'The Seventh Day Adventists CSDA in the Protest Politics of the Tonga plateau', *African Social Research*, 26 (1978), pp. 453–69.
15.   G. C. Caplan, *The Elites of Barotseland 1878–1969* (Hurst, 1970).
16.   G. C. Bond, *The Politics of Change in a Zambian community* (Chicago University Press, 1976), p. 89.

found in the Luapula village Kasumpa, where the nationalist party attracted the poorest. This village was cut off from the major source of wealth in the area because it did not lie on the river. It was, therefore, not a fishing village and politically aware Kasumpa villagers 'explained that other villagers tended to be "lazy politically" because they were "rich" and were too busy to do party work'.[17] Cash crop farming was most advanced in the southern province, yet this comparatively advanced and affluent area was a stronghold of the first nationalist party—the African National Congress (ANC). This party was much less militant than UNIP. They allied themselves with other opponents of UNIP when it was clear that political independence would come in 1962. Lawrence Katilungu, the trade union leader, and former supporters of the United Federal Party joined them. To complicate the picture further, the numerous Jehovah's Witnesses were apathetic to nationalist politics; in Serenje they were the most prominent cash crop farmers and most nearly 'kulaks'.[18] Perhaps the most dramatic conflict in the period was between the newly formed African government and the Lumpa church, where religion clearly overrode class as a causative force.[19] The nationalist movement, therefore, was not a solid organization that was rooted in a particular pattern of class formation. It was a fluid coalition of people with diverse origins. Nationalists were not only in confrontation with the colonial power, as is to be expected, but also with many groups in African society during the relatively short period of nationalist agitation. These characteristics can also be found at the local level in Mwase Lundazi.

Decolonization in Mwase Lundazi

Nationalism came late to Mwase Lundazi. A UNIP organization emerged only in 1960, two years after the formation of the party. There was only one known member of the ANC, the party from which UNIP split. He remained neutral in the events that are described here. The main protagonists in the confrontation that ensued after 1960 were the senior chief Mwase and F K Phiri. The latter was the undisputed leader of the independence struggle in Mwase Lundazi and he was still considered the chief's major opponent 15 years after independence. This conflict originated as a private affair and culminated in a major insurrection.

Phiri had been a treasury clerk in the Native Authority, the chief's administration. He was sacked and informants agreed that Phiri's dismissal was caused by a conflict concerning private affairs. Chief Mwase

17. R. H. Bates, *Rural Responses to Industrialisation: a study of a village in Zambia* (Yale University Press, 1976), p. 81.
18. N. Long, *Social Change and the Individual: a study of the social and religious responses to innovation* (Manchester University Press, 1968).
19. A. D. Roberts, 'The Lumpa church of Alice Lenshina', in R. I. Rotberg and A. A. Mazrui (eds.) *Protest and Power in Black Africa,* (Oxford University Press, 1970), pp. 513–68.

endorsed 'modern' values; he advocated new agricultural practices and was a monogamist with a small family of one son and one daughter.   He also represented moral strictness.   It was a blow for him when his daughter eloped with the brother of his Native Treasury Clerk while she was still at school.   The chief brought the case before a subordinate court under his jurisdiction.   This court levied a charge of thirty pounds compensation against the family of the wrongdoer.   The family objected for two reasons. First, a settlement out of court should have been accepted by the chief. Second, they claimed that the amount of compensation was much too high. Three pounds was normal in such cases.   They appealed to the district commissioner who did not think there were grounds for reviewing this decision.   On the one hand, it can be seen that conflict between Chief Mwase and Phiri originated from private grievances; on the other hand, Phiri's objections can be seen as a protest against the authoritarian character of colonial administration which combined many powers in few offices like chief or district commissioner.

The existence of UNIP could furnish political consequences to conflicts between people in authority and their subordinates.   In the words of a councillor of the local authority: 'I was a naughty boy, so they sent me from school.   Because they sent me from school, I became a politician'.[20] Short, the last district commissioner, characterized UNIP activists as 'those who had to depart [government service] through faults of character or conduct or both'.[21]   In UNIP's eyes, by contrast, these conflicts were a natural consequence of their political opinions.   As UNIP could provide a modest alternative career structure in its organization, it provided an alternative for social mobility outside the influence of the colonial government. This undermined the influence of people like chief Mwase who worked within the framework of colonialism.

The 'winds of change' blowing through Africa, however, remained distant from the perspective of Mwase Lundazi.   The *cha cha cha* uprising in the autumn of 1961 hardly affected Mwase Lundazi, but it did not pass it entirely by.   The signposts to the model peasant farming scheme were destroyed and the dip tank was set on fire and people from Mwase Lundazi were involved in the burning of a school in neighbouring Zumwanda chieftainship.   The senior chief Mwase responded by identifying more and more with the opponents of UNIP.   Kenneth Kaunda, his old classmate, passed through the area on the way to Nyasaland [Malawi] in 1961, but he was not allowed to leave his motorcar; there was a ban on political meetings.   When Mwase went on a course in the United Kingdom in 1962, however, there were several small incidents of defiance of authority

20. Mr Grasswell Phiri, councillor for Luneva ward.
21. R. Short, *African Sunset* (Johnson, 1973), p. 209.

while he was away.[22]   The change in the political climate at the national level was, however, most dramatic when he returned from Torquay in 1962.

Nationalists and the British government agreed on new elections and political activity was permitted again in the territory.   Chief Mwase sided with the ANC at this time, despite the fact that a couple of prominent and highly educated UNIP candidates—Arthur Wina and Mwanakatwe—came to persuade him to change sides.[23]   Chief Mwase was one of the few people who attended the meeting held by the ANC candidate—S Soko— and received his at his palace.[24]   During the same election campaign Kaunda spoke in Mwase to a huge crowd with great success.   UNIP won in the constituency to which Mwase belonged.[25]

The supporters of the federation of Rhodesia and Nyassaland and white rule were ousted from power.   ANC and UNIP formed a coalition government after the elections of 1962.   The central question now was which party would win the next election to be held through universal suffrage.   it was not clear who would get into power in independent Zambia. The beginning of 1963 was ominous for chief Mwase.

'When chief Mwase of Lundazi, who had shown uncommon co-operation with the government by the manner of his banning of UNIP, was elected to the House of Chiefs, an angry demonstration took place outside the Chamber in the Secretariat'.[26]

Mwase had gathered enough support among his colleagues to be elected to the House of Chiefs.   He was, however, attacked by UNIP supporters, but Kaunda apologized for the incident and wooed his support.   Immediately, as Minister of Local Government, Kenneth Kaunda wrote to the President of the House to express 'sincere regrets that this shameful incident ever took place at a critical time when all those striving to set the Government . . . on its proper footing should be seeking co-operation with our natural rulers . . . as we regard your institution to be above the rough and tumble of party politics'.[27]

Kaunda did not always support existing authorities that came into conflict with UNIP.   For instance, he recalled the district commissioner in Lundazi after difficulties arose in neighbouring Magodi and chief Magodi was sacked.   The political agitation was the result of a visit by D Banda,

22.   These are well documented in Short, *African Sunset.*
23.   Only chief Mwase claimed knowledge of this event among the informants.   It is, however, corroborated by Short in a personal communication, 21 November 1983.
24.   This story is denied by chief Mwase.   However, it was mentioned by widely divergent sources, eg by Henry Phiri, Nthembwe village (a supporter of colonial government at the time) and Goodwin Nkunika, Mzamu village (a UNIP activist at the time).
25.   The result was: UNIP–1655 votes; ANC–792 votes; a liberal candidate polled 31 votes. D. C. Mulford, *The Northern Rhodesia General Election* (Oxford University Press, 1964), p. 196.
26.   Macpherson, *Kenneth Kaunda,* p. 404.
27.   Macpherson, *Kenneth Kaunda,* p. 405.

head of UNIP's youth brigade.   He was one of the many urban politicians who were looking for a possible political base in their home areas in anticipation of the next elections.   The atmosphere became heady towards independence.   People remember vividly the great expectations.   Most had stopped observing agricultural regulations.   Party activists were ambitious and they were convinced that there would be no more chiefs after independence.   In Mwase Lundazi tension was building up which led to a violent clash on 6 and 7 May 1963.[28]

On the sixth, a UNIP meeting was announced in Nthembwe, the chief's headquarters.   Politicians from the regional office in Lundazi were to speak.   A group of people marched from neighbouring Loti village to attend the meeting under the leadership of the dismissed treasury clerk, Phiri.   They were chanting slogans and carried drums and spears.   Just before Nthembwe the road from Loti joins the main road from Lundazi boma.   There, the procession met an African district officer, James Mapoma, on his way to the Native Authority for routine inspection.   The procession was perfectly legal and there was no reason for a clash with authority.[29]

Nevertheless, a conflict arose.   Mapoma objected to the spears and drums in the procession.   A scuffle broke out between the procession and the messengers accompanying Mapoma, who was assaulted.   The civil servants escaped in the landrover and, after a visit to the senior chief to recover, they returned to Lundazi.   It was clear that this meant 'war' and arrests could be expected.   The speakers at the meeting exhorted the crowd to be 'firm and try to crush anybody who was coming to disturb'.   Their advice was not conducive to keeping the peace; 'if you see anybody coming to arrest you, try to beat him', they encouraged, and 'defend yourself'.   People did not go home after the meeting but stayed in neighbouring villages, most of them in Loti village where the procession had originated.   The police arrived in the middle of the night and did not attack until very early in the morning when a procession was leaving Loti for Nthembwe.   Fighting broke out in which both sides used violence; several people were shot.   The police then proceeded to Nthembwe and attacked twice with tear-gas, by which time people had gathered from all over Lundazi.   At around 10am on 7 May 1963, during the second tear-gas attack, a full-scale riot erupted.   A whistle was blown and Nthembwe, a model of development under colonialism, was set aflame.   Although the

28.   The account of the following events is based on interviews with chief Mwase; G. Nkunika, Mzamu village; T. Nyirenda (Njathi), Villambana village; F. K. Phiri (Chiwoko), Kamaphina village; S. Zgambo, Majobe Jere Village.
29.   This was the opinion among all informants in Mwase Lundazi.   Short disagrees: 'At this time political meetings were subject to a permit, and James Mapoma was quite right to try to stop a procession with drums and spears'.   Personal communication 21 November 1983.

village was built in burnt brick, all the houses and offices had thatched roofs which were highly inflammable.   The whole village was burnt and looted.

The only buildings left untouched were the chief's house and the administrative headquarters of the Native Authority in which the police, the civil servants and their families were entrenched.   The police shot at anybody threatening to come near the building.   Chief Mwase had not joined the people inside; he was at home and heard his people shout from half a mile away that they wanted to kill him.   From inside the building, the civil servants saw how their belongings were being stolen and ruined by the masses outside.   At 2pm, two civil servants came out of the building waving their party cards in an attempt to rescue some of their property. They were met by spears and one was seriously wounded.   The mobile brigade (the riot police) had great difficulty in reaching Nthembwe as UNIP had cut down trees to block the roads.   They did not arrive until 4pm, by which time the riot had petered out.   In the night, the party activists fled to Malawi (which was to become independent two months later).   At the same time, ironically, so did senior chief Mwase.

Two days later, authority reasserted itself and chief Mwase returned from Malawi.   The police arrested people systematically, about 60 people in all, of whom 51 were brought before the courts and 30 were convicted. The four most serious cases were sent to Lusaka.   UNIP sent its lawyers to defend the accused.   However, the four in Lusaka remained in jail until just before independence.   The last one was released on 23 October 1964, the day before Zambia became independent.   The politicians who had fled to Malawi quickly learnt that they would not be prosecuted unless it was proven that they had harmed persons or stolen property.   They soon returned, except for the leader of the procession, Phiri.   He was hunted down, arrested on the charge of attacking Mapoma and convicted.   His arrest came one year after the riot in May 1964 but he was not released until 9 January 1965, long after independence.   The man who had thrown a spear at those leaving the administrative building waving their UNIP cards was sought.   One suspect was arrested seven times for questioning, spent a total of eight weeks in jail, but was never convicted.

Chief Mwase bought a party card after he returned to Nthembwe.   His authority reasserted itself, especially during the Lumpa rising when Lundazi suffered badly.   People then came from far way to take refuge in the chief's headquarters.   In Mwase Lundazi only three villages were destroyed during these troubles and 15 people were killed.   The Residential Secretary, UNIP's political representative in Chipata, the provincial capital, came to Mwase Lundazi and found his people burying the dead. This politician, A. J. Soko, who had established a good working relationship with chief Mwase, was elected as member of parliament for the area in 1964.   This was a great disappointment for local activists as they thought the position belonged to one of them.   Representatives had, however, come from party headquarters to instruct the people to vote for Soko and to dissuade local people from contesting the elections.   Chief Mwase remained chief, but the chiefs lost virtually all their power in independent Zambia.   Phiri remained a local politician.

Analysis
Mwase Lundazi was a showpiece of development under colonial rule and therefore a serious confrontation with nationalism seems logical.   The image of the area is best illustrated in the following eulogy by Short, the last district commissioner of Lundazi district:

> New methods of agriculture, schools, wells, drains, childcare, cattle dipping and inoculations were all accepted.   Prosperous it was, though further away from the town and markets, and its spirit—or 'esprit de corps'—was second to none.   The petty irritations so common to Africa were absent; sloth, decay, laissez-aller, petty corruption.   All pro-ceeded like clockwork; houses were built, roads were made and steadily, year by year, prosperity increased.[30]

Matteyo Phiri, who became chief Mwase in 1940, was the leading force in bringing these innovations.   His extraordinary capabilities as an administrator are praised by everybody.

Chief Mwase was a successful man in the framework of colonial rule. He was promoted to senior chief.   Traditional arguments were used to legitimize his claim to that title; it was, however, a bureaucratic promotion. In 1954 he was offered a study tour of colonial developments in Northern Rhodesia and a trip to Basutoland.   He attended a course on local govern-ment in Torquay in 1961/62.   He was awarded a medal by King George VI in 1947 and an MBE in 1960.   He was very well off by the standards of colonial society.   In 1958 he bought his first motorcar, a Ford Zephyr. He also pursued a private career as a successful farmer.

He strongly denies, however, that he was a stooge of the colonial govern-ment.   He saw and sees it as his task to obtain benefits for his people from outside authorities, whatever that outside authority may be.   He denies that he made any political concessions with respect to the most contro-versial issue in colonial times—the federation of Rhodesia and Nyassaland. Most chiefs resisted federation, but not all.   Mwase testified against the amalgamation of the territories to the Bledisloe Commission in Chipata in 1938.   He demonstratively left a dinner in 1951 held in Lundazi Castle Hotel, because he was asked to support federation.   This was a dinner at

30.   Short, *African sunset,* pp. 204–5.

which Europeans and Africans sat together, which was a highly exceptional event in those days. His colleague, chief Magodi, attended the dinner. Mwase refused to go to Salisbury to meet the Queen Mother as a protest against federation, although he met her in nearby Chipata. The Litunga of Barotseland, probably the most prominent chief in the territory, accepted the invitation to Salisbury. Mwase maintains that he never advocated opinions to please the colonialists. 'The only reason they liked me was because of this agriculture'. He complains about the racism of colonial officers. An exception among the colonial civil servants was Fox-Pitt, who advised him at an early stage that his future lay with black politicians and not with colonialism.[31]

Chief Mwase entered into a bitter confrontation with nationalism, despite this advice. A factor that reinforced this conflict was resentment of his discipline. People in Lundazi still remembered songs mocking his enthusiasm for agricultural change and the concomitant legislation. A visiting civil servant noted perceptively in the early 1950s the tensions which Mwase's forceful administration could arouse:

The organization by the Native Authority of the unpaid labour is in advance of voluntary effort seen elsewhere. Mwase will probably know when he is asking too much from his people and each successful project will make it easier.[32]

The dismissal of Phiri also illustrates the power wielded by chief Mwase. It was unavoidable that chief Mwase would come into conflict with people who were burning such things as schools and dip tanks, because his life work was building these. These elements in the protest bore little relation to what Mwase considered nationalist concerns. A similar argument can be made with respect to agricultural measures like contour ridging and cattle dipping that aroused resistance. It is hard to see maintenance of soil fertility or the protection of animal health as specifically in the interests of Europeans, colonialism or the world capitalist system. Yet they were the *symbols* of the relationship against which many, like Phiri, were fighting.

Protest against privilege was a common theme in the conflicts during the period. *Cha cha cha* directed itself against improved farming and schools; the visible avenues of progress in the system. It is difficult now to establish the class background of the early UNIP activists. Early activism

---

31. Rotberg describes T. S. L. Fox-Pitt as 'a distinguished provincial commissioner on the verge of retirement' during the campaign against federation. He joined the ANC in 1951. R. I. Rotberg, *The Rise of Nationalism in Central Africa: the making of Malawi and Zambia 1873–1964* (Harvard University Press, 1965). He supported UNIP when he was retired in Britain. See: Macpherson, *Kenneth Kaunda*, pp. 231, 279.
32. *District Notebooks and Annual Reports, Lundazi District,* Zambia National Archives KST 1/3 and KST 1/4.

has become a powerful legitimization for contemporary office, so that present office holders and their friends claim membership from 'the beginning', but this is contradicted by others.   There are also many claims of secret membership because people feared losing their jobs.   Interviews with people involved in politics produced 50 names of early activists.   However, only eight were mentioned more than five times.   The occupations of three of those eight prior to independence could not be established.   Four of the eight had been sacked from junior government positions and one had been expelled from secondary school.   This is at least suggestive.   The anarchic episode that befell Mwase Lundazi was, according to Short, a conflict between generations.   There was envy of the older generation's wealth, he claimed, particularly among those whose educational ambitions had been frustrated.[33]   Large farmers sided with chief Mwase and none of the 'model' peasant farmers were among the UNIP activists.   UNIP, however, did attract some people among the African elite in Mwase; many people mentioned that the civil servants working in the Native Authority were UNIP supporters, although none were mentioned as early activists. Perhaps they felt the burden of discrimination most acutely.

The destruction of Nthembwe highlights the aggression towards the privileged who were working for the Native Authority.   But it is difficult to place this as a strictly nationalist confrontation.   There was no aggression against Europeans, the obvious target of those claiming self-determination, and nationalists could be found on both sides.   Some civil servants inside the administration building were card carrying members of UNIP.   This did not, however, provide immunity when they attempted to break the siege.   The crowd was aggressive against nationalists in this case.   The hard core of UNIP activists were in the crowd, but those who were arrested and convicted had no previous record of party activism. Phiri was the exception.   And so was that same Mapoma who was attacked by the UNIP procession; he had good nationalist credentials for he had been sacked as a civil servant in Luapula in 1953 because he was one of the few who observed a national day of prayer in protest against federation. And it should be remembered that Chief Mwase in 1963 was on good terms with Mapoma.[34]

From the perspective of chief Mwase, the independence struggle appears as two separate sequences of events.   On the one hand, there was a continuing broadening of support at the grass roots for a general struggle against the privileged in colonial society.   On the other hand there was a nationalist movement among the elite, in which some of those privileged

33.   In 1977–8 it was also extremely difficult to establish oneself as an independent household for a young male in Mwase Lundazi.   See: J. K. van Donge, 'Rural-urban migration and the rural alternative: some insights from Mwase Lundazi, Eastern Province, Zambia' in *African Studies Review* 27 (1984).
34.   C. Baylies, *Luapula Province* (mimeo, n.d.) note 71; p. 73.

people were rapidly co-opted into the party. The demonstration against Mwase when he was elected to the House of Chiefs and Kaunda's subsequent apology shows the interaction of these two processes. The visit of Wina and Mwanakatwe is another illustration of the last process. Mwanakatwe had also moved from a position within the colonial structure to become a nationalist leader. He had been a representative of the Northern Rhodesia Office in London. Soko, who came to campaign for the ANC, changed sides after the 1962 elections. Mwanakatwe, Soko and Mapoma became prominent politicians after independence, and all reached cabinet rank.

In Mwase Lundazi we find that much of the action in the terminal phase of colonization for the largest part was a series of conflicts within African society rather than a confrontation with European power. The nationalist movement was attracting a variety of people. The poorest as well as the most privileged were part of the movement. The fluidity of the lines of conflict is especially illustrated in the events in Nthembwe in May 1963. At the same time as UNIP was co-opting members from the African elite in colonial society, it developed in Mwase Lundazi a mass base which attacked all symbols of privilege in Nthembwe in one outburst.

Conclusion

Nationalism is, by its nature, an ideological orientation that bridges class differences and it often plays a role in many internal, latent class conflicts. The Marxist doctrine of the autonomy of the state maintains that the nationalist state is seemingly representing the interests of those who are deprived of controls over the means of production in order to dampen class conflict. Marx's analysis of the Bonapartist state is often quoted as the supreme analysis of this phenomenon.[35]

The destruction of Nthembwe—which in Mwase Lundazi was the main manifestation of the rise of UNIP—can be protrayed as a nationalist struggle transformed into a class struggle. According to such a perspective. UNIP was at that time being taken over by a nascent bourgeoise, which was about to abandon the radical demands of the oppressed classes. The end result of the independence struggle, therefore, is the maintenance of a bourgeois hegemony or capitalism as a system.

Such an interpretation which stresses class analysis, in my view, is forced to construct a reification of events. There was class formation in Mwase, of course, but that does not *explain* nationalism. First, the large farmers in Mwase Lundazi sided with the chief. An important group that would normally be labelled as part of any nascent bourgeoisie was outside UNIP.

35. K. Marx 'The Civil War in France', in R. C. Tucker (ed.) *The Marx-Engels Reader* (Norton, 1972). The most imaginative application of this doctrine to Africa is in C. Leys, *Underdevelopment in Kenya* (Heinemann, 1975).

Second, many people who were active in 1963 had not been involved in nationalism previously. Indeed, the Nthembwe rising coincided with the coming of independence, but there is little reason to call it nationalist. The vacuum in authority released pent up aggression, possibly in a similar manner to the Lumpa rising.

UNIP was a party with constantly shifting support into which various groups were drawn at different times at the national level as well as in Mwase Lundazi. This perspective on the party can explain two striking features of the Zambian political system. First, it helps to explain the endurance of the party through time by suggesting that its particular capacity to co-opt may be a mechanism behind this. Second, Zambian politics is characterized by a host of contradictory policy initiatives in which the apparently irreconcilable is sometimes reconciled. With fragmented classes and a party whose strength lay in a loose nationalist coalition across classes, Zambia has been able to provide a broad accommodation between various groups.[36] Scholars' disagreement over the class basis of the nationalist movement before 1964 bears witness to its lack of cohesion and the example of Mwase Lundazi reminds us that local detail is often essential for any accurate interpretation of the measuring of political action in the last years of colonial rule . . . and afterwards, no doubt.

36. For a more elaborate description of these elements in Zambian political culture, see Jan Kees van Donge, 'Nadine Gordimer's "A Guest of Honour": a failure to understand Zambian society', *Journal of Southern African Studies* 9 (1982), pp. 74–93.

The Journal of Modern African Studies, 8, 4 (1970), pp. 563–84

Separatist Agitations in Nigeria since 1914

by TEKENA N. TAMUNO*

DURING the 1960s, Nigeria's stability was so severely threatened by such factors as reckless politics, military *coups d'état*, refugee problems, and secessionist movements that foreign observers predicted the failure of a hitherto glorified model of a newly independent, democratic, multi-national state in West Africa. In February 1966 pessimism about Nigeria's political future was so great that some observers inside and outside Nigeria believed that such a British-created federation as Nigeria's could not survive after the failure of the similarly launched Central African Federation, the West Indian Federation, and Malaysia (after Singapore's separation).[1]

Subsequent events, particularly after the collapse of the 'Biafra' movement in January 1970, however, belied such predictions, at least in the short run, and tended to give Nigeria a new lease of life. It would be tempting to examine why the earlier comparison of Nigeria with the abortive British-inspired federations in the Commonwealth proved false. It would be no less interesting to compare Nigeria, for her success in ensuring national survival, with the United States and Switzerland— the two most successful federal states today—in that each through victory in a civil war demonstrated her power, ability, and will to protect her sovereignty and territorial integrity.[2] There is no room here to go into the details of these other federal experiments and attempts at nation-building, although it may be conceded that each was unique in its historical development. It is therefore more pertinent to focus attention here on Nigeria's rather surprising durability since the 1914 Amalgamation; the reasons why it is surprising will be seen later.

In this article due emphasis is given to the stresses and strains encountered by a sizeable West African state in its attempts at national integration during the critical years of the transition from a colonial set-up to independence. The origins of the centrifugal and centripetal

* Senior Lecturer in History, University of Ibadan.
[1] *West Africa* (London), 12 February 1966, p. 171.
[2] The American civil war of 1861–5 and the Swiss war of the *Sonderbund* in 1847.

tendencies in Nigerian history, and some of the conflicts between them during this century, provide the central theme of this article. Historically, it was easier to establish the Nigerian state than to nourish the Nigerian nation. Though the former was to a large extent achieved through the 1914 Amalgamation, the latter eluded both British officials and Nigerians for several decades thereafter.

This article further helps to explain why a common national identity in Nigeria was a plant of slow growth. Attempts to cultivate it have met with serious obstacles from separatist agitations in Nigerian history, which go back as far as 1914; several of them are studied here. Although sometimes connected with demands for creating new Regions (later, States), most of them were of the nature of secessionist movements, and some constituted serious threats to the stability and territorial integrity of Nigeria, illustrating the failure, or limited success, of the efforts made to achieve national integration up to 1970.

OBSTACLES TO NATIONAL INTEGRATION

On 30 May 1967 secession became an overt act in Nigeria; before then it had been an idea. In July 1967 secession was backed by military force; previously, it had been no more than a verbal threat.

In Nigeria, secessionist threats, or separatist agitations, have been attributable to a number of factors—the country's heterogeneous ethnic composition, cultural diversity, vast size, difficulties of transport and communications, varied administrative practices, and controversial political and constitutional arrangements, besides all the problems connected with the introduction of federalism, personality clashes between Nigerian leaders before and after independence, and the absence of a strong ideological magnet.

None of the above factors, if taken singly, would have constituted an impregnable obstacle to the evolution of a strong national consciousness. Taken in combination, however, they paved the way for several serious separatist agitations in Nigeria.

Among the major obstacles to the rapid development of Nigerian unity has been the cultural diversity of a country of more than 250 ethnic groups. Though some of these had, for centuries, experienced various degrees of intermingling through commercial contacts along the waterways and caravan trade routes, through intermarriages, wars of conquest and the like, strong ethnic loyalties survived. Phenomenal progress in the fields of transport and communications, which Nigeria experienced from the beginning of the present century, came when ethnicity had already gained a strong foothold in a country which is vast by African standards.

Another important factor was the diversity of colonial political institutions in different sections of the country. In this, as in other matters, the first steps did count. In spite of Nigeria's common colonial experience, the record also emphasised the local differences in administrative practices, if not in policies, going right back to the early years of this century. Up to May 1906, the British authorities had totally different administrative structures to the east, west, and north of the Niger.[1] But the 1914 Amalgamation, which tried to remedy these defects, created problems of its own.

AN EARLY THREAT OF SECESSION

It would appear from Ahmadu Bello's autobiography that the first secessionist threat in Nigeria's colonial history came with Lugard's Amalgamation of 1914. To the late Sardauna of Sokoto, Ahmadu Bello, that Amalgamation was no less than 'the mistake of 1914'. In his recent autobiography, Ahmadu Bello observed:

Lord Lugard and his Amalgamation were far from popular amongst us at that time. There were agitations in favour of secession; we should set up on our own; we should cease to have anything more to do with the Southern people, we should take our own way.[2]

What the late Sardauna meant by 'we' and 'us' in the preceding quotation is not clear. Perhaps he referred merely to the chiefly class, because at that time the common people—the *talakawa*—had little or no freedom of expression in such matters of high policy. Thus appraised, the Northern threat of secession in 1914 was not necessarily a popular movement.

Whether the Emirs wanted secession *because* they considered the 1914 Amalgamation a 'mistake' is far from clear. Even if the late Sardauna—who in 1914 was only four years old—reported correctly the feeling of the Northern political class at the time, there remains the problem of ascertaining the source of the 'mistake' at the material time of the Amalgamation.

A single Governor-General for the Northern and Southern Provinces

---

[1] This is a rough demarcation. The internal boundaries of the three British administrations in Nigeria were much more complicated than that. Erroneously, these boundaries later gave rise to ideas of 'natural' internal demarcations, particularly during the period of the 'Biafra' agitation.

[2] Ahmadu Bello, *My Life* (Cambridge, 1962), pp. 133 and 135.

from 1 January 1914 constituted an important feature of Lugard's Amalgamation scheme, which resulted in the political fusion of North and South without compelling immediate or subsequent administrative unification.[1] Until April 1939, each of the two groups of Provinces had its own Lieutenant-Governor and other staff. From that date, a Chief Commissioner assumed responsibility to the Governor for the administration of each of three groups of Provinces: Eastern, Western, and Northern. The amalgamation of such key central departments as customs, railways, education, police, and prisons proceeded gradually from 1912 through the 1930s. Separate secretariats existed in the Northern and Southern Provinces until the 1920s. Moreover, until the Richards Constitution came into effect in 1947, the Northern Provinces had no representation in the Nigerian Legislative Council, which had been set up in 1914, except through British officials and the European members of the Chamber of Mines and the Kano Chamber of Commerce. If, then, a 'mistake' is to be attributed to British officials, it was the political fusion which began under Lugard's Amalgamation of 1914.

It would appear from Ahmadu Bello's account that the chiefly class in the North would have preferred a separate political future. Yet, after examining this prospect, he rejected it on economic grounds, since the North required an outlet to the sea for much of its external trade. There lay 'the rub', he said.[2] To the historian, this admission is significant as marking the completion of a revolution in trade routes. Till the nineteenth century, trans-Saharan trade had provided the main outlet for Northern Nigeria. With railway construction and extension, north and south of the Niger, since 1896, and the improvement of inland waterways, including the harbour works at Lagos and Port Harcourt, the northern dependence on southern outlets increased. But how far could the silken threads of economic interdependence be stretched in North–South relations?

There were moments of hope as well as moments of despair, over the years of precarious collaboration. Although frequently the Chief Commissioner of the Northern Provinces, his officials, and the Emirs, tried to encourage a separate development of the Northern Provinces vis-à-vis the Eastern and Western Provinces, officials in Lagos and the Colonial Office sought to discourage such tendencies.[3] Governor

[1] See S. Phillipson and J. R. Hicks, *Report of the Commission on Revenue Allocation* (Lagos, 1951), p. 11.
[2] Bello, op. cit. p. 136.
[3] Lord Hailey, *Report on Nigeria, 1940–41, with a minute by His Excellency the Governor, January 1942* (London, 1942), pp. 19–20.

Bernard Bourdillon (1935–43) agreed with Lord Hailey, who visited Nigeria officially between 1940 and 1941, that 'no encouragement should be given to the manifestation of separate tendencies in any part of the territory'.[1] Hailey added that Nigeria's future 'must lie in political unity'.[2]

SEPARATISM IN THE EARLY 1950S

New constitutional arrangements and party political rivalries during the 1950s, however, sparked off further separatist agitations in several parts of Nigeria. Their incidence constituted a patent source of embarrassment to the advocates of decolonisation and national unity. It was once fashionable in Nigeria and elsewhere to regard these recurrent flashes of sectionalism as the immediate or delayed consequences of a divide-and-rule policy adopted in the colonial era.

With reference to the general problem of the 'breakdown of adjustment' in societies subject to British colonialism, J. W. Burton has made a pertinent comment:

The British are given credit for being masters of 'divide and rule'. . . [but] they did not need to be master of this art, or deliberately divide and rule, for foreign rule itself was sufficient to cause divisions and conflict. There being no possibility of directing hostility towards the powerful foreign oppressor, it is transferred to a scapegoat within the environment. The scapegoat is not any object, it is a relevant one in terms of interactions within the community, and likely to be related to a religious, racial or political faction.[3]

Burton, of course, admits that his scapegoat theory cannot fully explain 'continuing conflicts' within societies. In the particular Nigerian environment, the scapegoat hypothesis lost much force after 1950, when Britain showed a willingness to share power and responsibility with Nigerian ministers. Dyarchy under such circumstances, however, threatened nationalist aspirations, in that the former common enemy posed as a friend even before independence and national unity were fully within grasp. These factors help to explain why, particularly during the 1950s, Nigerian leaders failed to heal their sectional wounds.

In 1950 Nigerians demonstrated their sectional interests, and conflicts between the North and the South were intensified, when their delegates met at Ibadan to review the Richards Constitution. Concerning one of the most controversial subjects then discussed—the ratio of representation in the Central Legislature—the Conference had at the

---

[1] Memorandum by Bourdillon of 27 January 1942, filed with Hailey's *Report*.
[2] Hailey, op. cit. para. 95.
[3] J. W. Burton, *Systems, States, Diplomacy and Rules* (Cambridge, 1966), p. 124.

committee stage recommended quotas of 45:33:33 for the Northern, Eastern, and Western Provinces respectively. In rejecting these proposed quotas, the Emir of Zaria, a member of the Northern delegation at that conference, made it clear 'that unless the Northern Region was allotted 50 per cent of the seats in the Central Legislature, it would ask for separation from the rest of Nigeria on the arrangements existing before 1914'.[1] The Emir of Katsina, another Northern delegate, supported this threat. Under the 1951 Constitution, the British Government conceded the Northern demand for parity of representation in the Nigerian Legislative Council on the basis of the existing population figures for the North and the South.[2] This arrangement, however, failed to remove the shadow of secession permanently from the Nigerian horizon.

The 'self-government' debate in the House of Representatives in April 1953 led to a chain of events which again put Northern leaders in a mood for secession. In place of the Action-Group-sponsored motion seeking self-government for Nigeria in 1956, the Northern Members of Parliament demanded self-government 'as soon as practicable'.[3] For their stand in this debate, the Northern M.P.s alleged, they suffered abuse from Lagos mobs. Thereafter, the relations between North and South deteriorated so fast that by the middle of May 1953 a riot between Northerners and Southerners broke out in the suburbs of Kano, following the arrival in that city of an Action Group delegation, led by S. L. Akintola, on a political tour of the North.

At this tense moment, the members of the Northern House of Assembly and the Northern House of Chiefs, in an emergency joint session in May 1953, endorsed an eight-point programme, which, among other things, provided for virtually independent Regional Governments. Under this scheme, there was to be a non-partisan, executive, Central Agency, responsible for such common services as defence, external affairs, customs, and West African research institutions. According to Ahmadu Bello, the arrangements represented 'our compromise on the suggestion of secession from Nigeria, as it then was'.[4] At this stage, Nigeria's solidarity demonstrably suffered a serious setback.

However, before matters reached the point of no return, the British

[1] *Proceedings of the General Conference on Review of the Constitution, January 1950* (Lagos, 1950), p. 218.

[2] The 136 elective seats of the House of Representatives were allocated thus: Northern Region, 68; Western Region, 34; and Eastern Region, 34. There were provisions for special and official members.

[3] Bello, op. cit. p. 118.   [4] Ibid. p. 144.

Secretary of State for the Colonies asked Nigerian delegates to visit London to discuss a revision of the existing constitution. During this conference, which took place between July and August 1953, the delegates agreed on a federation consisting of autonomous Regions.

At the same 1953 conference, Nigerian delegates again became painfully aware of the serious political differences which tended to mar the evolution of harmony between various sections. The controversy over Lagos, Nigeria's capital and leading commercial centre, caused more bitterness in 1953 than it had in 1950. During the 1950 and 1953 conferences which discussed this issue, delegates from the Eastern Region made it clear that they regarded Lagos as a 'no-man's land'.

The Western delegates, however, regarded Lagos as a Yoruba town which they wanted to administer on their own terms. During the 1950 General Conference, the Northern delegates, who held the balance, had also agreed that Lagos Municipality and the Colony districts should be merged with the Western Region for administrative purposes. During the 1953 Conference, however, the Northern delegates re-examined their stand, as they and the other delegates had recommended greater regional autonomy under a federal constitution. The Northern leaders in 1953 feared that whoever administered Lagos would control, and per-haps deny them, their key outlet at Apapa, then considered more important than Port Harcourt.[1]

During the 1953 Conference, the Action Group delegation led by Obafemi Awolowo emphasised the historical connexions between Lagos and Yorubaland. Awolowo expressed willingness to allow the Western Region to contribute towards the cost of building a new capital else-where, provided that Lagos and the Colony districts would continue to be administered by his Region.[2]

Oliver Lyttelton, the Secretary of State at the time, in consideration of the over-all interests of Nigeria, decided, when approached by the Nigerian delegates, that Lagos should be the federal capital of Nigeria, and that the municipal area of Lagos should be regarded as 'Federal Territory'. He thought that, though his decision would be disagreeable to the Action Group, it would 'make for a United Nigeria'.[3]

In October 1953 the Action Group (A.G.) and its supporters, including the *Egbe Omo Oduduwa* (a cultural-*cum*-political organisation named after Oduduwa, the mythical ancestor of the Yorubas), reacted sharply by reopening the question of Lagos. At about the same time,

[1] Ibid. p. 146.
[2] *Report by the Conference on the Nigerian Constitution, 1953* (London, 1953), Cmd. 8934, p. 20.
[3] Ibid. pp. 21–2.

Obafemi Awolowo, the Premier of the Western Region, sent the Secretary of State a strongly worded cable concerning this subject. In this communication, Awolowo claimed, among other things, the freedom of the Western Region 'to decide whether or not they will remain in the proposed Nigerian Federation'. Since Awolowo's cable was published, so was the Secretary of State's reply, as follows: 'The Secretary of State has directed that you should be informed that any attempt to secure alteration of that decision by force will be resisted, and in this context, I am to observe that any attempt to secure the secession of the Western Region from the Federation would be regarded as the use of force.' The National Council of Nigeria and the Cameroons (N.C.N.C.), then led by Nnamdi Azikiwe and others, gleefully observed that the Secretary of State had addressed the A.G. in the only language that the latter could understand.[1]

CONFLICTING PRINCIPLES IN FEDERALISM

The ghost of secession, not laid to rest in 1953, haunted the Resumed Conference on the Nigerian Constitution held in Lagos between January and February 1954. This conference included in its discussions the question whether any Region should have the right to secede from the Federation.

During these deliberations, the A.G. delegation demanded the recognition in the constitution of the 'right' of secession.[2] In support of that demand, the A.G. argued that any form of unity imposed from without would invariably lack enduring cohesion. It predicted that the 'dream' of a united Nigeria would fail unless the principle of freedom of association—implying freedom to dissociate—were conceded. The A.G. further pleaded that, whenever the terms of the association displeased any of the federating units, the constitution should allow that territory the right of 'contracting out' of the Federation. In making the above demands, the A.G. strongly upheld the principle of basing federalism on the consent of the people.

Dedicated to giving Nigeria a unitary constitution before it compromised on federalism, the N.C.N.C. delegation during the 1954 Resumed Conference in Lagos rejected the A.G. plea for the 'right' of secession. The N.C.N.C. then maintained that the Nigerian federation differed from a league of nations, which could allow its members to contract out whenever they so desired. But, so far as the N.C.N.C. was

---

[1] Kalu Ezera, *Constitutional Developments in Nigeria* (Cambridge, 1964 edn.), pp. 186–8.
[2] Because of existing regulations, my source cannot at present be disclosed.

concerned, states rarely provided, in their constitutions, for their termination. Though the N.C.N.C. recognised that Article 17 of the U.S.S.R. Constitution, inserted in 1936, conceded the right of secession, it compared the Nigerian Constitution to an 'organic law' which should not be broken by conceding the 'right' of secession.

At the end of that conference, the various delegates agreed that 'no secession clause should be written into the amended Constitution'.[1] The N.C.N.C., however, later repeated in public some of the arguments it had raised against the A.G. demands for the 'right' of secession.

After the 1954 conference, Premier Nnamdi Azikiwe, whose N.C.N.C. controlled the Government of the Eastern Region, made an important public statement on this issue. He was impressed, he said, by the views expressed by Chief Justice Salmon P. Chase in 1869 concerning the 'indissoluble union' formed by the people of the United States under their federal system of government. He also agreed with Professor K. C. Wheare's dictum that 'no right of secession rested with any state acting alone'. He went further, to justify the rejection by the N.C.N.C. delegation of a right of secession written into the Nigerian Constitution. Azikiwe's views, as expressed in January 1954, were that:

(1) Secession from a federation is incompatible with federalism.
(2) Secession from a federation is an illegal act.
(3) Secession from a federation is an invitation to anarchy.
(4) Secession from the Nigerian Federation between now and 1956 would be suicidal.

Clearly, three of the four reasons given above by Azikiwe against granting the right of unilateral secession in Nigeria were timeless. His concept of federalism, as emphatically expressed in January 1954, was of a perpetual arrangement, not to be broken except with the consent of the federating units.[2]

Other factors which help to explain Nigeria's difficulties in ensuring stability during the crucial transition from colonialism to independence can now be considered. The constitutional factor rightly occupied a central place. The principle of federalism, formally adopted in Nigeria from October 1954, partly solved some of the perennial problems relating to the lack of harmony and unity, while adding others. To understand some of the serious strains which developed under Nigeria's federal constitutions after 1954, it is pertinent to examine some of the conflicting principles inherent in federalism.

[1] *Report by the Resumed Conference on the Nigerian Constitution held in Lagos in January and February 1954* (London, 1954), Cmd. 9059, p. 12.

[2] Nnamdi Azikiwe, *Zik, a selection from the speeches of Nnamdi Azikiwe* (Cambridge, 1961), pp. 126–7.

Since 1954, Nigerians have combined the desire to be united for certain common purposes—expressed in the specific powers granted to the Federal Government—with the no less important desire to be separate or autonomous in other matters—expressed in the residual powers left with the Regions (later States). There were in addition concurrent powers shared by the Federal and Regional Governments. Aware of the danger of conflicts, the Constitutions of 1960 and 1963 explicitly provided that, where a law passed by the Federal Parliament conflicted with one made by any regional legislature, the federal law should prevail while the regional law should be void to the extent of the inconsistency.[1]

Since federalism thus provided a compromise between people who thought in nationalist terms and others who emphasised regional or sectional interests, it was a very delicate political arrangement to operate or sustain. In these circumstances, the degree of regional thinking was of crucial importance. Moreover, at both national and regional levels, consummate skill and statesmanship were required to avert a serious conflict between the component units of a federation such as Nigeria's.

It is arguable that, despite the existence of strong centrifugal factors in a country such as Nigeria, able and enlightened leadership could have lessened the effects of sectionalism or particularism. In this respect, the odds against Nigeria were considerable. Nigeria's dominant political leaders, before and immediately after the attainment of independence, were so eager to control and monopolise the machinery of the central (later Federal) Government that they encouraged rivalries which had the effect of playing off one ethnic group against another. Moreover, in their bid to assume or retain power, these same leaders winked at corruption, recklessness, victimisation, and other malpractices, which embittered their opponents to the extent of threatening revenge or secession. Such trends were becoming quite obvious in the 1950s, as Britain allowed representative as well as reponsible government in Nigeria. They assumed serious proportions after independence in 1960, when the Nigerian state—but not the nation—was internationally recognised.

---

[1] The Exclusive Legislative list of specific powers included such items as aviation, currency, customs and excise, defence, exchange control, external affairs, immigration, maritime shipping and navigation, mines and minerals, naval, military and air forces, passports and visas, railways, and trunk roads. The Concurrent Legislative list covered such matters as antiquities, arms and ammunition, census, higher education, industrial development, labour, and traffic on federal trunk roads.

For regional legislation inconsistent with federal legislation, see: *The Nigeria (Constitution) Order in Council, 1960* (Lagos, 1960), sec. 64(4), p. 42; *The Constitution of the Federal Republic of Nigeria* (Lagos, 1963), sec. 69(4), p. 37; and T. O. Elias, *Nigeria: the development of its laws and constitution* (London, 1967), p. 37.

In post-independence Nigeria, as elsewhere in Africa, the charismatic leadership of the advocates of decolonisation failed to ensure the stability of the newly emergent state. Moreover, till the end of 1965, the legitimacy of the post-independence governments in Nigeria suffered from low levels of popular participation in political decision-making through federal and regional elections, which were in most cases 'rigged'.[1] More seriously, the governments established after such controversial elections failed the other decisive test, of performance, in meeting such widely felt needs as stability, security, and welfare.

Apart from poor leadership, the absence of an ideology which could evoke and sustain mass appeal further encouraged separatist agitations. For a relatively brief period, though, decolonisation and the desire for political independence provided themes of such great mass appeal that separatist agitations, even when they occurred, did not have widespread support. Thereafter, neither the new message of economic independence through planned development nor the vague promises of the welfare state provided an effective catch-all for the masses, who were called upon to make burdensome sacrifices for the attainment of less clear goals.

POST-INDEPENDENCE CRISES

In this environment, the conflicts which could have been resolved by able statesmanship and timely concessions assumed such proportions as to threaten Nigeria's integrity continuously between 1960 and early 1970. The resultant divisive trends aroused more fears, if not open threats, of secession.

For example, the A.G. crisis in the Western Region in 1962 led the Federal Government to declare a state of emergency, during which an Administrator was appointed to govern the Region. But the man appointed, though well-meaning, failed to receive majority backing from the Yorubas. Even though the Administrator was later withdrawn by the Federal Government, public dissatisfaction in the Western Region nevertheless increased as the rift widened between the former Premier, S. L. Akintola, and Obafemi Awolowo, then the A.G. leader and leader of the Opposition in the Federal House of Representatives; matters became complicated by the imprisonment of the latter following protracted treason trials. These developments in the Western Region increased the antagonism of many Yoruba supporters of the A.G. towards the Federal Government, then controlled by an N.C.N.C.–

---

[1] In particular, the federal election of 1964 and the West Region election of 1965 fell into this category.

N.P.C. coalition. There were, however, no open threats of secession in the Region.

While the restlessness in the Western Region continued unabated, another major factor of irritation—the 1963 census—threatened the basis of Nigerian unity. The N.C.N.C.—whose principal support came from the Eastern Region—blamed its principal rival, the Northern People's Congress (N.P.C.), for inflating the Northern Region's figures. The N.P.C. and A.G. made similar charges against the N.C.N.C. leaders in the Eastern Region. Despite such charges and counter-charges, it was generally believed that Nigeria's 1963 census figure of 55·6 million was an over-count. Though bitterness over this issue was nationwide, no one Region was above reproach in the counting of 'ghosts' during the 1963 census exercise. Nevertheless, none of the major aggrieved political parties went to the extreme of proceeding with secession over this controversial issue.

Yet the immediate post-independence era of bitter party feelings, worsened by the A.G. crisis of 1962 and the 1963 census controversy, had not come to an end before more explosive issues arose to threaten the prospects of Nigerian unity. The political atmosphere during the federal election of December 1964 and the Western Region election of October 1965 was so tense that secessionist threats reappeared. Even before the December 1964 election took place, the N.C.N.C., then led by M. I. Okpara, the Premier of the Eastern Region, openly threatened secession. During an interview on 24 December 1964 with Nnamdi Azikiwe, the President of the Federal Republic of Nigeria, Okpara expressed the desire of the Eastern Region to secede from the Federation.[1] Earlier, on 10 December 1964, President Azikiwe had in a dawn broadcast to the nation warned of the dangers of disintegration arising from the allegations made about the conduct of the 1964 federal election. In the course of his nation-wide address, Azikiwe observed:

I make this suggestion because it is better for us and for our admirers abroad that we should disintegrate in peace and not in pieces. Should the politicians fail to heed this warning, then I will venture the prediction that the experience of the democratic [sic] Republic of the Congo will be child's play if it ever comes to our turn to play such a tragic role.[2]

Reacting the same day to Azikiwe's address, the Premier of the Northern Region, Ahmadu Bello, emphasised that the 1963 Constitution of the Federal Republic of Nigeria had 'no provision for secession or disintegration'.[3]

[1] *Daily Times* (Lagos), 13 January 1965, 'State House Diary of Events'.
[2] *West Africa*, 19 December 1964, p. 1419.   [3] Ibid.

The published *State House Diary of Events* before and after the 1964 federal election makes it clear that Azikiwe regarded the 'secession idea' as Okpara's.[1] In fact, another N.C.N.C. leader, Dennis Osadebay, then Premier of the Mid-West Region, did not appear to be in favour of secession. In a public statement on 19 December 1964, Osadebay regretted the talk of 'secession' and called upon Nigerians to affirm 'that Nigeria is one and indivisible'.[2]

It is not yet clear whether Okpara and other N.C.N.C. leaders in the Eastern Region actually altered their views on the question of secession after the 1964 federal election. If they did, it was perhaps the controversial, 'rigged' elections in the Western Region in October 1965 that reopened old grievances and made them realise that N.C.N.C. members and supporters were thereby prevented from controlling events in that vital part of the federation—vital in a North–South confrontation. At this stage, N. A. Frank Opigo, then an N.C.N.C. parliamentarian in the Federal House of Representatives, called for the secession of the Eastern Region from the Federation 'without any further delay'.[3] But the N.C.N.C., wisely, refused to carry out Opigo's proposal in 1965.

Meanwhile, another secessionist threat appeared in the Middle-Belt section of the Northern Region. The grievances of the Tiv people and the desire of a small section of them to secede in 1965, though connected with political considerations, were not directly related to the election controversies of 1964 and 1965. The major Tiv grievances arose mainly from deeply felt frustration with the maladministration of the Tiv area from colonial times to independence.

Briefly, the earlier British attempts to practise a system of indirect administration through big chiefs encountered serious difficulties among the Tiv. Not only was the village basis of the pre-colonial administrative system of the Tiv people unsuitable for government through a big chief, but the system of indirect administration, when attempted from the 1930s, was further discredited by the malpractices of corrupt, inefficient, and high-handed local officials.

Tiv difficulties became more complex from the 1950s because of political conflicts between the leaders of the United Middle Belt Congress (U.M.B.C.) and the N.P.C., the ruling party in the former Northern Region. The demands made by the U.M.B.C. for the creation of more states were stoutly opposed by N.P.C. leaders till 1965.

---

[1] Ibid. 16 January 1965, p. 53.   [2] Ibid. 2 January 1965, p. 3.

[3] *Nigerian Outlook* (Enugu), 15 November 1965. This newspaper reflected the views of the Government of the Eastern Region.

Disaffection in the Tiv area was compounded by a series of disturbances covering nearly four decades. During disturbances which took place in 1929, 1939, 1945, 1948, 1960, and 1964 and were put down by government police and military forces, many Tiv people lost their lives and property.

Among the aggrieved Tiv people, there arose a few leaders who advocated extreme measures for redress. One of these was Isaac Sha'ahu, the U.M.B.C. member for Shangev-Tiev (Tiv Division) in the Northern House of Assembly. During the debate in February 1965 on the Governor's address, which referred to the perennial Tiv disturbances, Sha'ahu stated:

Because the Northern Peoples Congress does not want peace in that Division [Tiv] and the only course we can take now since we are not wanted in the North, is to pull out of the North and the Federation as a whole. We shall be a sovereign State. We shall be joining nobody. We are 1,200,000 in population bigger than Gambia and Muritania [sic] and we have the manpower and every other thing.[1]

But another Tiv leader and parliamentarian showed no enthusiasm for secession. Vincent Orjime, the N.P.C. member for Iharev Nongov (Tiv Division) in the Northern House of Assembly and Parliamentary Secretary to the North Regional Ministry of Water Resources and Community Development, disagreed with Sha'ahu and asked the Tiv people in his Division to disregard the latter's 'stupid and impossible demand' for secession.[2]

Sha'ahu's secessionist threat met with further opposition from the non-Tiv leaders of the N.P.C.; Muhammadu Suleiman, Parliamentary Secretary to the Northern Regional Ministry of Establishments and Training, considered the threat 'reckless and dangerous'. Suleiman cited the 1963 Constitution of the Federal Republic of Nigeria and its 'safeguards' against 'any part of Nigeria seceding'.[3] But what those 'safeguards' were, Suleiman did not elaborate. Nevertheless, it is conceivable that he referred to the fact that the 1963 Constitution did not provide for secession and to the existence of the armed forces, whose oath included safeguarding Nigeria's territorial integrity.

The moment for testing the efficacy of such 'safeguards', on a small scale, came shortly after the military *coup d'état* of January 1966. After this coup, Major-General Aguiyi-Ironsi, an Ibo, became Head of State until his death during the second military *coup d'état* of July 1966.

[1] *Northern House of Assembly Debates* (Kaduna), 26 February 1965, col. 68.
[2] *Daily Times*, 2 March 1965. This newspaper usually adopted a neutral position.
[3] *Northern House of Assembly Debates*, 26 February 1965, col. 71.

Between these two military disturbances arose what was later described as 'a sort of secession'.[1]

The opportunity for a little secessionist bid came in February 1966. Its principal leaders—Isaac Boro, Sam Owonaro, and Nottingham Dick —were some of the frustrated advocates of creating a Rivers State out of the former Eastern Region. They feared that the establishment of the Ironsi régime, strongly supported by Ibos, prejudiced the long-standing demand for the creation of a Rivers State, an agitation which had begun seriously in the late 1940s. In their ill-fated gamble, these three leaders declared an illegal 'Delta Peoples Republic' and sought to defend it militarily.[2] Though members of the Nigeria Police Force stationed in the Eastern Region ran into disaster in the difficult terrain of the lower Niger Delta in their attempts to round up the leaders of the 'Delta Peoples Republic', units of the Nigerian Army had better luck. After a protracted legal trial, with an appeal reaching the Federal Supreme Court, Boro, Owonaro, and Dick were condemned to death for treason. But in response to repeated public pleas for clemency, before and after the creation of 12 States in May 1967, General Yakubu Gowon eventually exercised in their favour the prerogative of mercy. Before long, Boro, Owonaro, and Dick volunteered for military service in order to liberate the newly created Rivers State and safeguard Nigeria's territorial integrity. After them came more determined leaders of another secessionist bid, in the former Eastern Region.

THE 'BIAFRA' MOVEMENT

In view of the limitations imposed by the lack of access to classified documentary sources, it is not convenient at present to discuss fully the merits and demerits of the bigger secessionist attempt made by dis-affected Ibos following the military *coup d'état* of 29 July 1966 and the subsequent killing of their kinsmen in parts of the Federation. These were sad events, which then encouraged Ibos to think that they were unwanted persons whose security was in peril. It is sufficient here to emphasise that these Ibo casualties and fears resurrected in the most serious form the old spectre of secession.

Shorn of their emotional excesses, the arguments for and against

[1] *New Nigerian* (Kaduna), 14 May 1969. The phrase was that of Lt Sam Owonaro, the surviving member of the group which had attempted secession in February 1966. The other two leaders—Isaac Boro and Nottingham Dick—died in 1968 as military officers fighting on the federal side to suppress a bigger secessionist movement.

[2] Ibid. Interview by the correspondent 'Candido' with Lt Owonaro.

'Biafra' centred around controversial basic issues. These included: the 'right' of poorly protected and deeply aggrieved people to secede from their former state; the legality or illegality of any unilateral declaration of secession in Nigeria; the fate of ethnic minorities in the Nigerian federation; the control of the federal machinery of government; the honour, dignity, sovereignty, and territorial integrity of an independent African state; the obligation of the Organisation of African Unity to safeguard the territorial integrity of member states; and the special interests of foreign states and organisations, which sought, through intervention in the Nigerian conflict, to influence the political decision-making processes in the Federal-controlled and former secessionist territories.

All through the successive phases of the Nigerian crisis, 1966–9, the decisive issue was not necessarily which side was right or wrong. The fundamental issue was whether or not secession by any part of the Federation was the answer to Nigeria's perennial problem of ensuring the principle of unity in diversity.

Occasionally, the *dramatis personae* examined this central problem dispassionately; sometimes they advocated measures which seriously threatened Nigeria's solidarity and territorial integrity. Changing circumstances could explain changing viewpoints. Lt-Col (later General) Yakubu Gowon, who became Nigeria's Head of State after the military *coup d'état* of 29 July 1966, Lt-Col (later General) C. Odumegwu Ojukwu, the Military Governor of the former Eastern Region between January 1966 and 29 May 1967 and 'Head of State' of 'Biafra' from 30 May 1967 to 11 January 1970, and other leaders occasionally made conflicting or misleading statements on the basis of Nigerian unity. For example, in his first nationwide broadcast on 1 August 1966, Gowon declared:

Suffice to say that putting all considerations to test, political, economic as well as social, the base for unity is not there, or is so badly rocked not only once but several times. I therefore feel that we should review the issue of our national standing and see if we can help stop the country from drifting away into utter destruction.[1]

To remove any misunderstanding, Gowon made another statement, broadcast on 8 August 1966, emphasising that the above comment, made soon after the military *coup d'état* of 29 July 1966—which in certain respects had represented Northern Nigeria's reaction to the earlier coup of 15 January 1966 and the Unification Decree of 24 May 1966—referred only to his fears of dictatorship under the newly established unitary constitution.[2]

---

[1] Federal Ministry of Information, *Nigeria 1966* (Lagos, 1967), p. 33.   [2] Ibid. p. 35.

On 31 August 1966 the Gowon-led military Government passed a new Decree, which abolished the Unification Decree and brought the country back to the federal path. In his address to the *Ad Hoc* Conference on the Nigerian Constitution on 12 September 1966, Gowon again advised the delegates to rule out not only 'a complete break-up' but also 'a unitary form of government'.[1]

Though initially not clear about detailed solutions, Gowon, during his first week in office, correctly assessed one of the fundamental aspects of Nigeria's recent crisis. In his address to the world press in Lagos on 4 August, he pointed out that Nigeria was struggling, 'against great odds of history, geography, ethnography and the evil effects of imperialism', to build a nation in less than one-fiftieth of the time it had taken European states.[2] Gowon did not believe that secession provided the answer to the Nigerian problem. In a special contribution to the Africa Supplement of the *New York Times* in 1968, Gowon stressed:

There is no alternative to a Federation of Nigeria. The only possible alternative is the emergence of several armed groups in the country...Nigerians are, therefore, fighting to ensure that, long after the present ugly events shall have passed into history, there shall remain one strong forward-looking and prosperous Nigeria. A Nigeria in which no state and no ethnic group will be able to try to dominate the others. A Nigeria which will then be assured of the stability necessary for economic development to uplift the dignity of man in this part of the world.

In the same article, Gowon emphasised that the secession of 1967 was not the work of every Ibo man or woman. He observed:

The experience of Federal troops in the East-Central State so far shows that the ordinary Ibo man will have no guilty conscience after this war, because he was not responsible in any way for planning secession and its equally tragic aftermath. Secession and rebellion were planned and executed by the elite comprising some ex-politicians, university intellectuals, senior civil servants and, I regret to say, military officers. Once these people who abuse the power which knowledge brought them agree to lead their people to work for national reconciliation, the ordinary Ibo man will find a ready place in the heart of other Nigerians in all parts of the Federation.[3]

Whoever turned the scales in favour of a bid for secession in the former Eastern Region, the available evidence suggests that till June 1966 Ojukwu publicly stood for a united Nigeria. In his address during the banquet in honour of the installation of the Emir of Kano as Chancellor of the University of Nigeria, Nsukka, in June 1966, Ojukwu,

---

[1] Ibid pp. 14 and 40.

[2] *Nigerian Outlook*, 5 August 1966.

[3] Federal Ministry of Information, *Soldier of Honour* (Lagos, 1968), pp. 27 and 22–3.

then Military Governor of Eastern Nigeria, emphasised Nigeria's desire for unity and solidarity. He revealed that China, the U.S.S.R., and the U.S.A. inspired him as countries which had usefully deployed their large, diverse populations for nation building. Compared with these nations, Nigeria's record did not impress Ojukwu.

For years this country has striven for unity. In this they have met and passed many hurdles. All the danger points of disintegration have been passed. The common generality of the people of this country have come to regard one another as brothers and sisters. The conscious and unconscious apostles of disunity are not the common men and women of this country. They are the few with vested interests, selfish and inordinate ambition for power and wealth, men who fear losing their positions and privileges, who care more for self than for the nation and the common good. These men have tried to exploit our differences to the detriment of this country, when they should be expected to work for the removal of those differences. They have tried to make unhealthy capital of our diversity, when a healthy perception of our diversity could be turned to our national advantage as a source of strength— diversity of culture, of background, of outlook, of experience, of our education, of our upbringings.[1]

However, a new set of events—the severe loss of lives and property in parts of the Federation in September 1966, growing refugee problems, serious misunderstandings over the implementation of the Aburi 'decisions' between January and March 1967, and the creation by decree of 12 States on 27 May 1967—provided an atmosphere which did not promote timely and well-meaning concessions in order to avert the imminent threat of secession and civil war. After the *Ad Hoc* Constitutional Conference in Lagos from mid-September to mid-November 1966, it became increasingly clear that the secessionist threat could not be easily subdued.

During that conference, the delegates from the Eastern Region, the Western Region, and Lagos proposed that each component unit of the federation, confederation, or commonwealth which they advocated should be allowed to secede unilaterally whenever it so desired. The Northern Region delegates, who at first made similar proposals, later withdrew them. Only the delegates from the Mid-West, itself a collection of several ethnic minorities, resolutely opposed the insertion of a secession clause in the Nigerian Constitution. Convinced that 'Nigeria must continue as one political entity', the Mid-West delegates feared that unilateral secession, or the forcible breaking up of the country, would cause as much bloodshed as had previously occurred in such conflict-torn territories as Ireland, Palestine (Israel), India, Pakistan,

[1] Eastern Region Ministry of Information, *Nigerian Crisis, 1966* (Enugu, 1966), p. 18.

and Togo.[1] Congo-Kinshasa and the U.S.A. provided other close parallels.

Subsequent amendments to the Nigerian Constitution between mid-March and the end of May 1967, however, empowered the Federal Military Government to take steps against any unilateral declaration of secession in any part of the Federation.[2] Thereafter, attempts to resolve the serious conflicts in Nigeria without resort to secession and civil war completely failed in the atmosphere of intense bitterness and deep distrust among federalists and advocates of sectionalism. In these circumstances, the former Eastern Region, as 'Biafra', seceded from the Federation on 30 May 1967 and valiantly, but unsuccessfully, fought to defend its own rights, including that of self-determination.

After the declaration of secession, Ojukwu and his lieutenants justified their conduct and attempted to rationalise a rebellion which they called a 'revolution'. In a 'Voice of Biafra' broadcast in November 1967, the secessionist régime contended: 'An Irishman today is an Irishman forever. A Biafran today is a Biafran forever. An Ethiopian today is an Ethiopian forever.'[3] Significantly, that logic was not extended to Nigerians. Moreover, the secessionist leaders ignored the fact that, even if Nigeria could be regarded as a British creation, so was 'Biafra', which included Ibos, Efik, Ibibio, Ijo, and Ekoi, who before the advent of British rule had had different political destinies. The non-Ibos of the former Eastern Region had not only been among the strongest advocates of the creation of new states, but after May 1967 they also provided the greatest impediment, after food shortages, to the solidarity of 'Biafra', since the loyalty of most of the 5 million in these minority groups was pledged to the Federal Military Government.

Advocates of 'Biafra' also advanced moral arguments to buttress their claim for secession. In another 'Voice of Biafra' broadcast in November 1967, spokesmen of the secessionist régime argued:

The essence of government is for the good of the governed. As long as the government fulfils its duties it can lay claim to the loyalty of the governed. But when the government forsakes its duties, it also forfeits its claim to the people's loyalty. Biafrans have established a new government which they have empowered to protect them against all aggressors.[4]

[1] Ibid. vol. 4, *The Ad Hoc Conference on the Nigerian Constitution*, pp. 4, 17, 26, and 33–4. See also *An Address by His Excellency, Lt-Col Odumegwu Ojukwu to the Joint Meeting of the Advisory Committee of Chiefs, Elders and the Consultative Assembly, Enugu, 30 November 1966* (Enugu, 1966), p. 4.

[2] See the 'Aburi' Decree or The Constitution (Suspension and Modification) Decree (no. 8 of 1967); and The Constitution (Repeal and Restoration) Decree (no. 13 of 1967).

[3] *Biafra Newsletter* (Enugu), 1, 3, 24 November 1967, p. 6.

[4] Ibid.

The demand for freedom of association, the principle of basing government on the will or consent of the people, the 'artificiality' of the Nigerian state, and the claim to the 'right' of secession, it will be recalled, had been arguments advanced earlier in Nigeria's political history, particularly between 1953 and 1954. Neither in 1953–4 nor in 1967–9 did the majority of Nigerians, unequivocally, accept such arguments. Undaunted, Ojukwu in *The Ahiara Declaration* of 1 June 1969 asserted:

The Federation of Nigeria is today as corrupt, as unprogressive and as oppressive and irreformable as the Ottoman Empire was in Europe over a century ago. And in contrast, the Nigerian Federation in the form it was constituted by the British cannot by any stretch of imagination be considered an African necessity. Yet we are being forced to sacrifice our very existence as a people to the integrity of that ramshackle creation that has no justification either in history or in the freely expressed wishes of the people.[1]

Whatever the merits and demerits of the 'Biafra' movement, the issues of secession and territorial integrity in Nigeria were settled not through plebiscites but on the battlefield. With the collapse of the 'Biafra' agitation in January 1970, and subject to the further success of redoubled efforts in post-war reconstruction, rehabilitation, and reconciliation, the stage has been set for winning the peace and consolidating the Nigerian state and nation. In crushing the 'Biafra' agitation, the Federal Military Government in Nigeria has amply demonstrated that, in the final analysis, national boundaries are maintained, if not also established, by force. But nationalism, which basically is an attitude of mind, needs more than the use of force to nourish and consolidate it.

The historical sketch presented in this study indicates that, during the crucial period beginning from Lugard's Amalgamation of 1914, the threat of secession had come from all parts of the country except the Mid-West, which became a distinct Region (later State) only in 1963. That threat was in some cases a result of unwelcome aspects of political and constitutional arrangements: for example, the opposition of northern Emirs to the 1914 Amalgamation; the A.G. disapproval of the status of the federal territory of Lagos; the N.P.C. reaction to the 'self-government-in-1956' motion; and the resultant Kano riot and the creation of new States in May 1967. The N.C.N.C. leaders who

---

[1] C. Odumegwu Ojukwu, *The Ahiara Declaration* (Geneva, 1969), pp. 18–19.

threatened secession had other grievances, which arose from the controversial elections of 1964 and 1965. The disaffected Tiv, for whom Sha'ahu demanded secession in 1965, felt that they were unwanted and unprotected persons in the former Northern Region. The proclamation of the abortive 'Delta Peoples Republic' in February 1966 was intended to allay long-standing ethnic minority fears and grievances among the Rivers people before the creation of more States. The Ibo-inspired and largely Ibo-led 'Biafra' movement between 30 May 1967 and 11 January 1970 provided yet another crucial test for the solidarity of a culturally heterogeneous, newly emergent African state.

Though in this brief analysis separatist agitations in Nigeria have been emphasised, factors making for unity cannot be ignored. The latter include a common political history, particularly after 1914, age-old commercial and other links between the various ethnic groups, the complex cultural map which prevents the demarcation of mutually satisfactory boundaries for states attempting to secede unilaterally, the bloody consequences of unilateral declarations of secession based on ethnic and religious differences, and an undeniable economic interdependence.

Significantly, the late Ahmadu Bello saw clearly some of these aspects of the need for Nigerian unity shortly before the country adopted the Republican Constitution of 1963, and declared that it was no longer possible to 'imagine a Nigeria that is composed of anything less than its present territory'. He stressed the following reasons for his assertion:

I count the rivers of the Niger and Benue, the road, railway, and communications system, our openings to the outside world, the ports of Lagos and Apapa, and Kano airport. Each part of the country depends on the others for one service or another, and for one type of produce or another. Even the number of years we have been formally together have produced a great and wonderful unifying effect.[1]

Ahmadu Bello's views in 1963 acquire particular significance in contrast to his earlier denunciation of the 1914 Amalgamation as 'a mistake'; they may also be compared with the N.P.C. reactions in 1953 to the 'self-government-in-1956' motion which led to the Kano riot. Above all, this positive affirmation of Nigerian unity may stand alongside the ultimate fate of the several separatist agitations examined in this study, to indicate that the balance of advantage in the long run lies not with the centrifugal but with the centripetal factors. To put this

[1] *West Africa*, 28 September 1963, p. 1089.

differently, it is possible to relate the various secession threats and movements in Nigeria to the factors of push and pull usually associated with waves of migration, immigration, or emigration. The fate of the series of secession threats and movements examined in this article suggests that historically the 'pull' towards a united Nigeria has been of greater moment than the 'push' towards secession.

Journal of African History, **31** (1990), pp. 281-293
Printed in Great Britain

281

THE 'IGBO SCARE' IN THE BRITISH CAMEROONS, c. 1945-61

BY VICTOR BONG AMAAZEE

Ecole Normale Supérieure, Bambili, Mezam, Cameroun

ON 11 February 1961, the southern part of the British mandate in the Cameroons voted, by a large majority, to leave the newly independent federation of Nigeria and join instead the Republic of Cameroun, successor-state to the French mandate. A major factor in this plebiscite was fear of Igbo domination in trade, education, public and private sector employment, politics and social life. Igbo had begun to move into the Cameroons in the 1920s, and by 1955 there were nearly 10,000 Nigerians in the two southern-most divisions of British Cameroons, most of them Igbo or Ibibio. This immigration had been facilitated by the fact that, ever since the League of Nations had assigned mandates over the former German colony, Britain had administered the divisions of Victoria, Kumba, Mamfe and Bamenda as part of south-eastern Nigeria.[1] With the approach of independence, local resentment against the immigrants strengthened demands for an end to the Nigerian connection.[2]

There were indeed some grounds for this resentment, but politicians actively exploited ethnic stereotypes. The nature of these is illuminated by the novelist Chinua Achebe, himself an Igbo. He points out that Igbo culture was receptive to change, individualistic and highly competitive. This gave the Igbo an unquestioned advantage in securing the credentials for advancement in colonial Nigeria. The Igbo were bound neither by a conservative religion (as were the Hausa), nor by a conservative tradition (as were the Yoruba), and were correspondingly quick to make use of the opportunities created by the white man's civilization. Unfortunately, the Igbo's success bred in them pride and indifference to the feelings of others. Added to this was showiness, noisy exhibitionism, and disregard for humility and quietness. All this aroused envy and hatred.[3] Another writer has associated Igbo openness to new ideas with the adoption of new standards, an eagerness to be in the mainstream of progress, and an ambition to be noticed. A recurrent feature of Igbo life is a spirit of open rivalry. The man to be admired is he who has wives and children, bestirs himself, and makes money. The humble gentleman is not respected. A further aspect of the Igbo stereotype is 'aggressiveness'; this has been attributed to a combination of high population densities and an absence of large-scale social or political organizations. Characteristic of the Igbo is an egalitarian belief that there are no social and class barriers to self-advancement.[4]

---

[1] Until 1949 they constituted Cameroons Province (which up to 1939 was one of Nigeria's Southern Provinces and thereafter one of its Eastern Provinces). In 1949 Bamenda Division became a Province.

[2] T. Eyongetah and R. Brain, *A History of the Cameroon* (Harlow, 1974), 141-2.

[3] Chinua Achebe, *The Trouble with Nigeria* (Enugu, 1983), 46-7.

[4] Kalu Ezera, *Constitutional Developments in Nigeria* (Cambridge, 1964), 10.

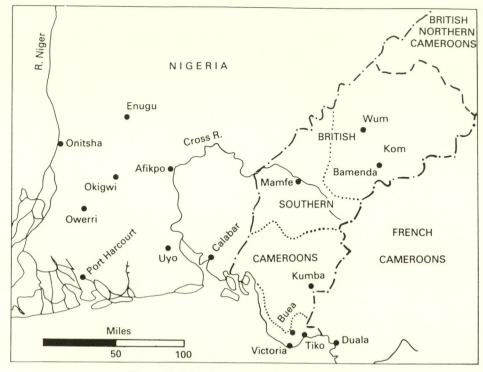

Fig. 1. British Southern Cameroons (1938).

Increasing contact between Igbo and other cultural groups tended to generate unfavourable stereotypes of Igbo behaviour. What the Igbo took to be virtues were liable to be regarded by others as weaknesses. In the light of values characteristic of many Cameroonians, the Igbo seemed self-centred, obsessed with wealth and lacking in respect for traditional authority. These supposed failings were in no way compensated by Igbo readiness to work hard; if anything, this only tended to exacerbate ill-feeling towards them. It was all too easy to arouse anti-Igbo sentiment where they seemed most threatening, especially in the towns of Victoria, Tiko, Buea, Kumba, Mamfe and Bamenda.[5]

The Igbo came into the Southern Cameroons in various ways. The first were government employees who had to accept whatever posting they were given. Others left home to work for expatriate firms. Some came to work on the Nigeria–Cameroons road; of these, some died on the job while others returned home, repelled by their working conditions. But the most resilient persevered; they followed the road into the Cameroons and settled in road-building camps. In the course of time, they brought their families and began to farm the land around the camps. Eventually, the road-builders diversified

---

[5] B. O. Nwabueze, *Constitutionalism in the Emergent States* (London, 1973), 84; K. W. J. Post and M. Vickers, *Structure and Conflict in Nigeria, 1960–1965* (London, 1973), 30.

into trade, at first part-time and then full-time. The original owners of the
land began to resent such Igbo.[6] Igbo also came to work on plantations: by
1932 these employed nearly a thousand Nigerians, most of whom were in
Kumba division, where they comprised a quarter of the plantation workforce.
By 1937 – when the total workforce on Kumba plantations had risen to over
4,000 – Nigerians still accounted for 15 per cent.[7] Many such migrants were
brought by canoe by Efik (Ibibio) from Calabar, who were paid by their
passengers once they had found employment. In 1955 there were 5,732 Igbo
and Ibibio on Victoria estates, and 1,540 on those in Kumba belonging to the
Cameroons Development Corporation (which had taken over the property of
German planters). Most of the Igbo came from the Owerri and Okigwi
divisions of Owerri Province, which included some of the highest population
densities in Eastern Nigeria; most of the rest came from around Afikpo. The
Ibibio mostly came from a densely populated area in Uyo division. Accustomed to a cash economy, quick to react to labour markets and undeterred
by distance, Igbo were generally predisposed to become migrant workers.
But by the same token they were on the alert for other ways to make money.
Cameroonian workers often complained that things left lying around
vanished when Igbo were in the camps, and claimed that Igbo had
introduced the practice of bribing headmen and overseers; they further
accused Igbo of arrogance, disrespect towards older men, causing trouble at
work and seducing the wives of local workers. The Igbo did not help matters
by regarding Cameroonians as unsophisticated and backward.[8]

What really mattered, though, was the way in which the Igbo turned to
advantage the economic backwardness of the Southern Cameroons. Even
after World War II there was a marked contrast between them and the local
population in terms of access to education as well as commercial aptitude and
experience. Igbo made the most of this, and consolidated their position in
trade and government in face of mounting hostility.[9]

The backwardness of the Southern Cameroons was largely due to the very
fact of the British Mandate. While the French administered their mandate as
if they would never leave, the British considered theirs a liability – a mere
appendage to Nigeria. In 1944 the Colonial Secretary admitted to the House
of Commons that the British Cameroons had been neglected, and attributed
the lack of public or private investment to the uncertain political future of the
territory. The British had scarcely improved the German system of roads
and communications, and the second departure of German planters, in 1939,
was a major setback to economic growth. By 1946 the territory had become
a 'lost world', isolated from the French mandate, yet deriving no material
advantage from its administrative incorporation in Nigeria. On the contrary,
the efforts of indigenous merchants were frustrated by the near-monopoly
of trade by foreign combines such as John Holt or the United Africa
Company. The backwardness of the Southern Cameroons was not due to any

---

[6] E. Isichei, *A History of the Igbo People* (London, 1976), 209.

[7] R. R. Kuczynski, *The Cameroons and Togoland: a Demographic Study* (London,
1939), 278. This tabulates labourers from territories other than the British or French
Cameroons; the basis for such statistics is discussed in *ibid.* 280–1.

[8] Edwin Ardener, Shirley Ardener and W. A. Warmington, *Plantation and Village in
the Cameroons* (London, 1960), 198–9, 105–6.

[9] *Ibid.* 199.

inherent economic deficiencies, and there was no substance in the argument that the territory necessarily depended on aid from Nigeria.[10]

The effects of the Nigerian connexion were especially evident in education and government employment. When the British replaced the Germans, they restored the five government primary schools, at Victoria, Buea, Kumba, Mamfe and Bamenda, to the standard six level. Apart from these five schools, and the teacher-training centre at Kumba, all other schools in the territory were run either by Native Administrations or by missions. There were no institutions for secondary education until 1939, when the Roman Catholic Mill Hill Fathers opened St Joseph's College at Sasse, in Victoria division. Thus it was extremely hard for Cameroonians to pursue higher learning and catch up with their contemporaries in Nigeria. They were liable instead to be relegated to the meanest and dirtiest jobs, whether in the plantations, in Government offices or in business firms, while the more lucrative and respectable jobs tended to be held by Nigerians, particularly Igbo.[11]

Up to the outbreak of World War II, very few Cameroonians found their way to Nigeria in search of secondary or higher education. Those who did acquired a grasp of English education and culture which enabled them to associate fully with Nigerians and to appreciate their strengths and weaknesses – especially those of the Igbo. Such Cameroonians were liable to find that even with a good education they were at a disadvantage: their path into the public service was blocked by Nigerians who had entrenched themselves in the days when there were no qualified Cameroonians. This point was only reinforced as Cameroonians after the war began to emerge from St Joseph's College: their difficulties in obtaining appointments in public service were attributed to obstruction and corrupt demands by senior Igbo clerks in government offices.[12]

To support this view, the principal of St Joseph's compiled in 1948 a list of those who had left the college in 1946–7 and were finding it hard to get a government job in the Cameroons. S. Ndely, from Bojongo (Victoria division), was an excellent shorthand typist with a grade II school certificate, yet despite many applications supported by references from the principal, he could not get a job locally and remained unemployed for ten months: in the end, he was taken on by the Secretariat in Enugu. S. Nyenti, with a grade III school certificate, had to wait nine months before finding work as a stenographer in Lagos. This was the irony: Cameroonians found it easier to get work outside the Cameroons than within it. This lent credence to their claim that the local administration was controlled by Igbo. D. Tiku, a Bayangi with a grade II school certificate, had his application to the Forestry Office turned down by the Igbo clerk in charge during the absence of his white superior. The post required the applicant to have either a grade I school certificate or an exemption from London matriculation. The clerk insisted on the first condition because he knew that Tiku satisfied only the second. Tiku eventually went to Ibadan for training in forestry, but after

---

[10] Cameroons Federal Union, *Memorandum submitted to the Visiting Mission of the Trusteeship Council of the United Nations Organization, November 1949* (Lagos, 1949), 1, 10, 28.

[11] *Ibid.* 17–18.

[12] Senior District Officer, Victoria Division, to Resident, Cameroons Province, Buea, n.d. (1948). Cameroon Archives, Buea (CAB), PC/h(1948)1, 'Conditions of Settlement'.

eleven months of unemployment. The principal also enquired at the hospital about openings, but they could only offer the job of nurse, which any primary school-leaver could get. As for the United Africa Company, they said that they got all their employees from Nigeria, despite advice to the contrary from headquarters.[13]

Injustice of this kind was so glaring that the senior British administrator, the Resident, expressed sympathy with the Cameroonian cause. In 1948 he commented thus on the charge that attempts by Cameroonians to control Igbo immigration amounted to racial discrimination:

... It depends on what is meant by discrimination. It might be called discrimination if we in England were to impose an immigration law forbidding the entry of all Irishmen, but it would surely be understandable if the Irishmen were capturing all our trade, filling a very large proportion of our public offices, and to cap all, we had to go to Ireland to get all the training necessary for a job in the public service. It might be said that the shoe was on the other foot and that it was the Cameroons people who have been discriminated against in that they have only to go to Nigeria to get the education, or enter the jobs, but apart from any other considerations, how were they to get there? Communications between this Province and Nigeria have been ludicrously inadequate for years, and still are.

I would emphasise that the Cameroons people are not generally against strangers as such, and it is very much in their own, and our, interest that they should not be. But they do wish to have the power to stop undesirables entering, persons who recognise no local native authority and behave as if they were a law unto themselves. It is essential that they should have this power if they are to feel free of the danger of being swamped.[14]

There could have been no better summary of the relationship between the Cameroons and Nigeria.

Meanwhile, in order to ensure that the natives of the Cameroons were given every opportunity of obtaining employment in Government service, the Governor of the Eastern Provinces of Nigeria had directed that the Eastern Provinces school-leavers Registry (which functioned under the aegis of the selection committee) should register the names of all those passing out of St Joseph's College. The Governor further recognized that the poverty of communications with the Cameroons made it difficult for a selection committee located at Enugu to interview candidates from the Cameroons. He therefore proposed, with the concurrence of the selection committee, that a sub-committee be set up at Buea, which would both register applications from Cameroonians for appointment and also, after interviewing them, forward the applications, together with the sub-committee's views as to their suitability for appointment, to the selection committee at Enugu.[15]

This was obviously a weakness in the Administration's positive measures because the new arrangements still meant that the final decision had to be taken at Enugu and not in Buea. The preference for Igbo to Cameroonians in employment would continue in an atmosphere dominated by Igbo. Worse still, the selection committee in the Cameroons dealt only with

[13] Principal, St Joseph's College, Sasse, to Fowler, 4 March 1948. CAB. *ibid.*
[14] Resident, Cameroons Province, Buea, to Secretary, Eastern Provinces, Enugu, 29 June 1948. CAB, *ibid.*
[15] Secretary, Eastern Provinces, to Resident, Cameroons Province, 13 May 1948, CAB, *ibid.*

appointments to the standard clerical and technical grades of Government service. The committee was not concerned with appointments to vacancies in commercial firms or in the unestablished grades of Government services, such as those of messengers and headmen. The Governor left it to the Resident of the Cameroons Province to make local arrangements to urge Provincial Departmental Officers to engage natives of the Province in the unestablished grades of Government Service. This could be affected similarly in the case of commercial firms. In any case, the Governor favoured a gradual adjustment and not a wholesale movement.[16]

The Government's inability to ensure equal opportunities for Cameroonians in Eastern Nigeria made the Cameroonians so desperate that they felt that their only hope of salvation lay in political separation from, at least, Eastern Nigeria. The need for separation was increased by the fact that even in the commonest posts like those of messengers and headmen, the Cameroonians had to go through Departmental Heads who were Igbo, and these Igbo preferred their countrymen to Cameroonians. Salvation would only come with an autonomous Cameroons region. While the Europeans wanted to reduce tensions in the larger interests of the territory, Cameroonian businessmen and politicians usually exploited all misunderstandings in their own private interests. They claimed that isolated cases of Igbo misbehaviour, real or merely alleged, were typical of Igbo in general. Cameroonians were all too ready to see malice, rather than mere accident, in cases such as that of an Igbo nurse in Victoria who in 1948 administered carbolic acid into the eye of S. A. Atabong, a Cameroonian.[17] Then the hand of a man missing from the Bambuko area was found with a party of Igbo traders. There were references to mysterious disappearances in Bakweri country, which could not all have been the fault of Igbo.

In early January 1948, a Court Messenger from Muea bought fish from an Igbo at Tiko. He and all who ate any of the fish were taken ill enough to need attention from the dispensary. The Court Messenger in question was produced before the District Officer, and the former seemed none the worse. The D.O. explained, as best as he could, the nature of food poisoning, but he did not make a good impression on the Bakweri Native Authority.[18] In the same year, quite unproven accusations were made that Igbo stole church bells in order to make counterfeit coin; they introduced corruption into public offices; they assaulted local women and made them sterile; in the medical department, they deliberately mistreated local patients; they desired to get the Cameroons into their control; they were violent people who conspired together to cause injury to local people; they sold poisoned food; they conspired together to assist each other to obtain public appointments; they profiteered and charged excessive prices to Cameroonians; they sold drugs, such as aspirin, quinine and M & B in adulterated form.[19] In 1951, a wild rumour had it that an Igbo man had killed and eaten a girl at Missellele. Police investigations proved the rumour false, but tracing such a rumour to its source was practically impossible.[20] The police advised the Igbo that

[16]   *Ibid.*   [17] *Ibid.* 'Ibo Tribal Mania, 1948'.
[18] D.O., Buea, to Resident, Cameroons Province, 22 Jan. 1948. CAB, *ibid.*
[19] D.O., Victoria, to Resident, Cameroons Province, n.d. (March, 1948). CAB, *ibid.*
[20] Ibo Tribal Union, Buea, to Superintendent of Police, Buea, 25 Aug. 1951. CAB, S1 (1948), 'Ibo Union petitions'.

rumours of that kind, implying ritual murder, had been known to occur in many parts of the world where trade and business had been taken over by a race or tribe not indigenous to the locality. The Jews, in particular, had suffered for centuries from such a calumny. All the same, the police advised the Igbo to resist provocation and refrain from being themselves provocative.[21]

Anti-Igbo propaganda was so effective that passionate outbursts by speakers carried the day at meetings and made rational discussion difficult. The government urged responsible people to cease introducing unsubstantiated generalizations into discussions. But the underlying causes of such propaganda were not easily disposed of: according to one British official they included resentment of the *imperium in imperio* affected by the Igbo Tribal Union; lack of Igbo respect for local institutions; vague apprehension regarding Igbo motives in the Cameroons; jealousy of Igbo success; a feeling of inferiority aroused by the Igbo through their proud speech and ways.[22] Thus rumours of 'atrocities', real or imaginary, usually spread like wildfire over the country, and Igbo everywhere were victims of verbal or physical attacks by frustrated Cameroonians.

The spread of anti-Igbo rumours in and after 1948 was partly due to the influx of Igbo plantation workers, traders and artisans which had followed the creation of the Cameroons Development Corporation in 1947. In January 1948 the Buea Native Authority attacked the character and behaviour of local Igbos and demanded their expulsion; it further charged that the government had deliberately encouraged Igbo recruitment for plantations. This the D.O., Buea, categorically denied. He felt that the people of Buea were constantly seeking reasons other than the true ones for the Igbo presence, which lay simply in their nature and economic circumstance.[23] The D.O., Bakweri, decided to bring that Native Authority under control by publishing a notice on 16 February 1948 in which he stressed that the administration had not, and would not, issue any order discriminating against Igbo or any other section of the community. He stressed that it was the duty of members and officers of the Native Authority and Native Courts to uphold the law, and he warned that if they did not do so they might be deprived of their officers.[24] The D.O. was reacting to the fact that early in February the Bakweri Native Authority had passed the following rules to control relations between natives and Igbo:

(1) Nobody is allowed to sell his or her house to an Ibo, neither must anybody give his or her house for rentage to an Ibo.

(2) No farm land must be sold to an Ibo or rented to an Ibo.

(3) Nobody must allow an Ibo to enter any native farm or forest for purpose of finding sticks for building or for any other purposes.

(4) Houses or farms already sold to any Ibo man shall be purchased by Native Authority who will afterwards resell same to some suitable person.

(5) Nobody shall trade with Ibos for anything of value or not.

(6) All landlords must ask their Ibo tenants to quit before 15 March 1948.

[21] Superintendent of Police, Buea, to Ibo Tribal Union, Buea, 29 Aug. 1951. CAB, *ibid.*

[22] D.O., Victoria, to Resident, Cameroons Province, n.d. (March 1948). CAB, PC/h (1948)1, 'Conditions of settlement'.

[23] D.O., Buea, to Resident, Cameroons Province, 22 Jan. 1948. CAB, *ibid.*

[24] Notice by D.O. in charge of Bakweri District, Buea, 6 Feb. 1948. CAB, *ibid.*

(7) No Cameroon woman is allowed to communicate with the Ibos in any form.

(8) Anybody disobeying these rules shall be liable to a fine of £5 or five months I.H.L.

(9) Any Ibo native disobeying Rule (3) above will be liable to prosecution in the Native Court.

(10) All Ibo Government Officials are exempted from Rule (5) above.[25]

The Government believed that the anti-Igbo sentiment had been organized and encouraged in its early stages by two local politicians, Chief Manga Williams and Dr E. M. L. Endeley. Williams tried to restrain excesses and correct the more extravagant statements, but he found this difficult. Endeley, for his part, protested his helplessness in the situation, but the Senior D.O. for Victoria thought him not averse to allowing the growth of anti-Igbo feeling; the same official revealed in March that such feeling in Buea gathered new strength soon after the district had been visited by P. M. Kale, a local politician.[26] In Victoria, the chief cause of anti-Igbo tension was criticism in the Nigerian press of Manga Williams, who was a member of the Eastern House of Assembly. Since several newspapers were owned by Azikiwe's Associated Press, Williams was prejudiced against the Igbo in general.[27]

A further cause of trouble in Victoria was the attempt by the Bakweri people to prevent the Igbo from entering the fishing trade. On 9 February 1948, a body calling itself the Cameroon Union asked the fishing heads of Mboko, Kongo, Mbome and Iseme to stop selling fish to any Igbo fish traders. The circular further directed the fishing heads to cease passing the Igbo through to any other near ports. In case the Igbo owned canoes of their own, the port ruler could arrange to obstruct the track in any way possible and suitable. Directives were given that anybody contravening the above instructions would be liable to a fine of £5. The quarrel over canoes and fishing ports was nothing but a trade war in which Cameroonians wanted to maintain a monopoly in the fishing industry. As usual, politicians like the members of the Cameroon Union always exploited such sentiments and urged the people into action.[28]

In Tiko, the tension over housing, farm land, fishing, trade and women[29] was directly instigated by Manga Williams, and the Tiko people did not hide it when they told the Igbo:

There was no enemy between Bakweri people and Ibo people here in Tiko. The matter concerning the fish and the other woe, woe, troubles to the Ibo people in Tiko, we Bakweri people in Tiko are innocent of the matter. We are here in Tiko as watch boys for the solid law and instructions given to us. To make peace with you Ibo people in Tiko could waste us no minutes but, if we make peace with you here in Tiko, what about all Ibo people in all Cameroons branches? Therefore we do not want to hide you anything. That this law and instructions were given to all

---

[25] Bakweri, N. A., Buea, to Senior D.O., Victoria, 21 Feb. 1948. CAB, *ibid.*

[26] Senior D.O., Victoria Division, to Resident, Cameroons Province, n.d. (March 1948). CAB, *ibid.*

[27] Ibo Union, Buea, to Commissioner for the Cameroons, 25 Aug. 1953. CAB, S1 (1941)1, 'Ibo Tribal Union'.

[28] Cameroon Union, Victoria, to fishing heads of Mboko, Kongo Mbome and Iseme, 9 Feb. 1948. CAB, *ibid.*

[29] Notice by N.A., Tiko, 8 Feb. 1948. CAB, PC/h (1948)1, 'Conditions of settlement'.

Bakweri people by chief Manga Williams and chief Ndele. So therefore, if you Ibo people want to make peace, you better meet chief Manga at Victoria and therefore, he will give us permission to cancel the matter. When you meet him, if he says that he knows nothing in the matter, let him give you hand-writing note and then you come to us and we make peace easily.[30]

Manga Williams' instructions were championed in Tiko not by the local Bakweri but by Bamenda grasslanders and French Cameroonians who were themselves immigrants in Tiko. They were jealous of Igbo commercial prosperity and thought that if the Igbo were out of the way they, the non-Bakwerian Cameroonians would be the new commercial masters of Tiko.[31]

In Mamfe division, the communal tensions were over rights to collect firewood,[32] house-building permits,[33] and a fight between Dr J. E. C. Iwenofu, an Igbo, and a Cameroonian palm-wine seller.[34] The D.O. blamed S. A. George, a local politician and 'number one agitator' who seized any opportunity to stir up the Banyangs against the Igbo and was 'long overdue for punitive measures'.[35]

The 'Igbo scare' became the main topic in party politics in the Southern Cameroons during and after the Eastern Nigerian crisis of 1953-4. Cameroonian members of the Eastern Provinces House of Assembly decided to break off their connection with Nigeria because they believed that, as a minority group within the assembly, they were unable to make their wishes respected, while the crisis was adversely affecting the Southern Cameroons. On 22-24 May 1953 a conference was held in Mamfe by the Assemblymen, Native Authorities, tribal organizations and chiefs. They addressed a petition to the Colonial Secretary which demanded a separate and autonomous legislature for the Trust Territory; this was taken to London by Dr Endeley, leader of the Cameroons bloc in the regional assembly. No immediate reply was received, but already things were moving very fast, politically, to the advantage of the Cameroons.

Hitherto, the Southern Cameroons had had no formal political party: such associations as existed were only pressure groups. But in June 1953 the Cameroons National Federation and the Kamerun United National Congress agreed to merge into one political party, the Kamerun National Congress (K.N.C.) led by Dr Endeley. The new party expelled N. N. Mbile because of his stand against the Cameroons bloc in the regional assembly; Mbile and his splinter group formed the Kamerun People's Party (K.P.P.).

The long-term result of the Eastern crisis was the Conference on Nigeria in Lancaster House, London, August 1953, at which the Southern Cameroons was represented by Endeley, Rev. J. C. Kangsen and S. A. George. Mbile went as a delegate of the N.C.N.C. while Mallam Abba Habib represented the Northern Cameroons. Endeley demanded regional auton-

[30] Jonah Dike, Tiko, to Ibo Federal Union, Victoria, 17 Feb. 1948. CAB, S1 (1941) 'Ibo Tribal Union'.

[31] President, Federated Council, Victoria, to Senior D.O., Victoria, 6 April 1948. CAB, ibid.

[32] Mamfe Ibo Union to Resident, Cameroons Province, 25 Jan. 1952. CAB, S1 (1948), 'Ibo Union petitions'.

[33] D.O., Mamfe, to Senior Resident, Cameroons Province, 9 March 1952. CAB, ibid.

[34] D.O., Mamfe, to Senior Resident, Cameroons Province, 10 Dec. 1950. CAB, Pdg (1950), 'Disturbances in Mamfe town'.   [53] Ibid.

omy or a separate legislature for the Southern Cameroons, while the Northern Cameroons preferred to remain within Northern Nigeria. As far as the Southern Cameroons was concerned, the Secretary of State made a categorical statement that if Endeley's K.N.C. won the elections, which were then pending as a result of the dissolution of the Eastern Nigerian House of Assembly, the creation of a Southern Cameroons legislature would be a foregone conclusion.[36]

This statement stimulated a vigorous campaign in the Southern Cameroons when the elections were called. The K.N.C. opened the campaign by turning a misfortune into a political asset. A section of the crowd had stoned them at Kano airport on their way to London. Back home, Endeley and his team filled a landrover with stones and displayed them all over the country as the stones with which they had been attacked in Nigeria. In a country where Nigeria was synonymous with Igboland, it was said that the Igbos had stoned Dr Endeley. Everywhere, the cry of the crowds was 'we want a Cameroons House'.[37] Fearing an attack by way of reprisal, Igbo in Bamenda Province asked the Resident for protection.[38] No such attack took place, but the K.N.C. in Bamenda tried more subtle tactics. On 23 September the assistant branch secretary, J. N. Foncha, challenged the Igbo's use of a brass gong in making music. He claimed that the gong was a symbol of traditional authority, *kwifor*, in Bamenda; its use by the Igbo was an infringement of Bamenda laws and customs.[39] The Igbo were surprised to hear this because, before the K.N.C. was formed, they had used gongs without offence to anybody; they saw the K.N.C. protest not as a defence of tradition and custom but simply as a political manoeuvre.[40] Before things could get out of hand, the Resident intervened on the side of the K.N.C., advising the Igbo that as strangers they should not only respect native law and custom but avoid action which might be interpreted by local inhabitants as an attack on custom or a breach of the peace. He trusted that the Igbo Union would appreciate the situation and co-operate.[41]

The Igbo did not help matters by using their jobs in the service of their political views. The Mamfe community intended to welcome the return from London of the Cameroons delegates with demonstrations, but these could not be arranged as telegrams announcing their arrival were delayed for some days by the Postmaster, Mr Okeke, an Igbo. Letters which S. A. George wrote from London, of political significance to the Cameroons people in Mamfe, were not delivered until a few days before George's arrival in Mamfe.[42]

Such behaviour only added fuel to the anti-Igbo gospel, which specially appealed to people who were every day coming face-to-face with the realities

---

[36] P. M. Kale, *Political Evolution in the Cameroons* (Buea, 1967), 42–3.

[37] *Nigerian Daily Times*, 19 July 1953.

[38] Ibo Union, Bamenda, to Resident, Bamenda Province, 7 Sept. 1953; Ibo Union, Buea, to Commissioner for Cameroons, 25 Aug. 1953. CAB, S1 (1941), 1, 'Ibo Tribal Union'.

[39] Foncha to Ibo Union, Bamenda, 23 Sept. 1953. CAB, *ibid.*

[40] Ibo State Union, Bamenda, to Asst. Secretary, K.N.C., Bamenda, 20 Oct. 1953. CAB, *ibid.*

[41] Resident, Bamenda, to Ibo Union, Bamenda, 14 April 1954. CAB, *ibid.*

[42] S. A. George to Divisional Surveyor, Posts and Telegraphs Dept., Enugu, 7 Oct. 1953. CAB, S1 (1948), 'Ibo Union petitions'.

of Igbo political, social, economic and administrative domination. The result was that when the elections were held, the anti-Nigerian K.N.C. won twelve seats while the pro-Nigerian K.P.P. won the only other one.[43] In his opening address to the Southern Cameroons House of Assembly on 26 October 1954, the Commissioner for the Cameroons bore in mind the prevailing anti-Igbo tone of the election. The K.N.C. victory had greatly alarmed the Igbo settlers, and the Commissioner sought to reassure them as to their future in the now autonomous Southern Cameroons. The territory, he said, could not afford any internal dissensions, jealousies and hostilities between one tribe and another or between 'persons settled here and persons born here'.[44]

Having achieved a quasi-regional status for the Southern Cameroons, the K.N.C. enjoyed the confidence of a cross-section of the population, including traditional rulers. The rival party, the K.P.P., suffered tremendous setbacks because it was misinterpreted as being in favour of the Cameroons remaining 'enslaved' to Eastern Nigeria. This was aggravated by the fact that the K.P.P. was the ally of the N.C.N.C. which was labelled as an Igbo-inspired party, just when the Igbo were very unpopular with the Southern Cameroonians.[45] However, the K.N.C. did not enjoy its popularity for long because, in early 1955, this party concluded an alliance with the Action Group of Western Nigeria. Endeley justified this in terms of political strategy within the central legislature in Lagos, even though he had recently defeated the K.P.P. precisely because it was in alliance with the N.C.N.C. One of his senior colleagues, J. N. Foncha, held to the view that the solution to the Cameroons' problems in Nigeria lay not in alliances of any sort but in complete withdrawal. Thus in March 1955 Foncha went into opposition, forming the Kamerun National Democratic Party (K.N.D.P.).[46]

In the 1957 elections to the Southern Cameroons House of Assembly, when the K.N.C. had switched to supporting the Nigeria connection, the K.N.D.P. exploited the 'Igbo scare' on the level of fantasy. Illiterate masses were made to believe that the Igbo were the only ethnic group that Cameroonians would meet in Nigeria, and that the crimes attributed to the Igbo would increase if the Cameroons remained part of Nigeria. Out of thirteen contested seats, the K.N.D.P. won five, the K.N.C. won six, and the K.P.P. won two.[47] As might be expected, these results reflected a variety of personal, regional and ethnic rivalries. It is, for example, striking that the K.N.D.P. won four of its five seats in the Grasslands, where it played heavily on the belief that the K.N.C. government represented the interests of the Bakweri and the more developed coastal areas.[48] Nonetheless, it was also clear that any party which deviated from an anti-Igbo stance was bound to lose votes.

Fresh elections were held on 24 January 1959. This time the K.N.D.P. won 14 out of 26 seats and so took control of government.[49] Again, one must

[43] *Nigerian Daily Times*, 11 Nov. 1955.
[44] 'Address by Brigadier E. J. Gibbons, C.B.E., Commissioner of the Cameroons, as President of the Southern Cameroons House of Assembly at its inaugural meeting in Buea, 26 Oct. 1954', 3–4. CAB, S1 (1941), 'Ibo Tribal Union'.
[45] Kale, *Political Evolution*, 43.
[46] United Nations Visiting Mission to Trust Territories in West Africa, 1958, *Report on the Trust Territory of the Cameroons under British Administration* (T/1426/Add.1), 14.
[47] *Ibid.* 38.   [48] *West Africa*, 4 May 1957, 411.   [49] U.N., *Report*, 6.

be careful not to exaggerate the role of anti-Igbo feeling. The failure of the K.N.C. was certainly due in part to other factors. For one thing, it lacked grassroots support, since it was essentially a congress of tribal and improvement unions: when K.N.C. leaders – such as S. T. Muna in Bamenda West – defected from the party, so did their local followings.[50] Besides, there was no electoral pact between the K.N.C. and the K.P.P.: they lost Tiko to the K.D.N.P. by putting up two candidates against it, while in Wum North the K.N.C. vote was split between the official candidate and an independent.[51] Yet the K.N.D.P. undoubtedly exploited anti-Igbo feeling to the full, as in the Grasslands area of Kom. Here the K.N.C. government had sought to enforce contour farming, in the interests of soil conservation, and the women of Kom revolted against this in 1958–9. The K.N.D.P. persuaded them that the government had sold the land to Igbo, who had in turn demanded that contour farming be practised as a prelude to their taking over the land.[52]

In 1960, the French mandate gained independence as the Republic of Cameroun, and the United Nations was anxious to end the British mandate as soon as possible. It did not consider that the 1959 elections had been conclusive in regard to the future of the Southern Cameroons, but hoped that a general agreement might be reached within the House of Assembly. Since such agreement was not forthcoming, the U.N. decided that early in 1961 a plebiscite should be held to resolve the question. The electorate in both parts of the British Cameroons was to be asked to choose between two paths to independence, either by joining the Federation of Nigeria, or by joining the Republic of Cameroun.[53] By this time, the K.N.C. and K.P.P. had been reunited, forming the Cameroon People's National Convention, under Endeley. This campaigned to preserve links with Nigeria, on a basis of regional autonomy, and stressed the value of the cultural heritage from Britain. The K.N.D.P. advertised the importance of escaping from eternal subordination to Nigeria and establishing instead a Cameroonian national identity by joining the Republic. This aim was certainly not based on much knowledge of the French territory, let alone French history: there was a naive belief that customs and institutions derived from the British could persist, which quite ignored the French preference for centralization and cultural assimilation. But 'far off hills look green', and most Cameroonians were easily persuaded that the new devil – the French Cameroons – could only be better than the old – Nigeria. Besides, Foncha's K.N.D.P. made the most of its time in office to influence voting through political patronage and arm-twisting. In the event, the Nigerian option attracted 97,741 votes in the Southern Cameroons; the Cameroun option won 233,571 votes. Thus throughout the period of party politics most Southern Cameroonians consistently stood out against any relationship with Nigeria, and as a result the Southern Cameroons became part of the Federal Republic of Cameroun on 1 October 1961.[54] In this story, the 'Igbo scare' can be seen as a river

[50] Kale, *Political Evolution*, 42–3; *West Africa*, 4 May 1947, 411; U.N., *Report*, 6.
[51] *Ibid.*
[52] The Fon of Kom to Commissioner, Southern Cameroons (Premier's copy), n.d. (1958). CAB, PC/C 1958/1, Mme disturbances, Wum District.
[53] *Southern Cameroons Gazette*, Buea, 27 Jan. 1961 (vol. 7, no. 4), 3–5.
[54] *Ibid.* 18 March 1961 (vol. 7, no. 14), 88.

reinforced by many tributaries whose waters were stained by the colour of the local mud.

SOMMAIRE

La peur de la domination de la tribu Ibo constitua l'une des raisons majeures pour la décision du Sud-Cameroun Britannique à voter en 1961 pour quitter le Nigéria complètement et de s'unir avec la République du Cameroun. Dès les années 1920, après que la Grande-Bretagne avait obtenu un mandat international sur un part de l'ancienne colonie allemande, elle le gouvernait comme apanage du Nigéria, et le développement, que ce soit économique ou culturel, était très tardif. Les indigènes faisaient concurrence à grande peine aux immigrants du Nigéria, surtout les Ibos, dont la résilience et l'ingéniosité dans le commerce, alliés à leur manque de modestie dans le succès, provoquaient l'envie. Les politiciens camerounais contribuaient aux stéréotypes ethniques en incitant des rumeurs fantasques. Certes, des autres rivalités importaient aussi, mais dans les élections de 1954, 1957 et 1959 le mécontentement avec les liaisons au Nigéria fut clairement associé aux sentiments anti-Ibo.

Journal of African History, 31 (1990), pp. 263-279
Printed in Great Britain   263

THE YOUNGMEN AND THE PORCUPINE:
CLASS, NATIONALISM AND ASANTE'S STRUGGLE FOR
SELF-DETERMINATION, 1954-57

BY JEAN MARIE ALLMAN

University of Missouri

At one period Ashanti national sentiment undoubtedly looked
forward to the evolution of the country into a separate political
unit, in which the Confederacy Council would be the recognized
organ of the legislative and administrative authority. But the
political integration of Ashanti with the Gold Coast Colony
effected by the constitution of 1946 has for the time being
diminished the general interest in this aspiration, nor does there
in fact appear to be any substantial grounds for its revival.

W. M. Hailey, 1951

When on a day in September this year a group of Ashanti youth
gathered at the heart of Kumasi up the Subin River and swore by
the Golden Stool and reinforced their Oath with the pouring of
libation to the Great Gods of the Ashanti nation and the
slaughtering of a lamb, an act of faith, of great national significance was undertaken.... And so Ashantis, backed by their
chiefs and Elders, their sons and daughters, and taking guidance
by the shadow of the Golden Stool, are now determined to live
and die a Nation.

Pioneer, 27 November 1954

ON 19 September 1954, the National Liberation Movement was inaugurated
in Kumase, the historic capital of Asante, before a crowd of over 40,000.[1]
Many who gathered at the sacred Subin River that day were dressed in
funeral cloth and chanted the Asante war cry, '*Asante Kotoko, woyaa, woyaa
yie*'! At precisely midday, the leaders of the new movement unfurled its flag.
The flag's green symbolized Asante's rich forests, its gold the rich mineral
deposits which lay beneath the earth, and its black the stools of Asante's
cherished ancestors. In the centre of the flag stood a large cocoa tree; beneath
the tree were a cocoa pod and a porcupine. The graphic was powerful and its
symbolism misinterpreted by none. The cocoa pod represented the major
source of wealth in Asante and the porcupine (*kotoko*) stood as the age-old

[1] This article, a version of which was presented at the 1988 meeting of the African
Studies Association in Chicago, is based on research carried out in Ghana and Great
Britain under the auspices of a 1983-4 Fulbright-Hays Dissertation Year Fellowship and
a 1988 Grant-in-Aid from the American Council of Learned Societies. I would like to
thank Ivor Wilks, Basil Davidson, Tom McCaskie, John Rowe, Ibrahim Abu-Lughod
and David Roediger for their suggestions and comments on my broader and more lengthy
examination of the NLM. See J. Allman, 'The National Liberation Movement and the
Asante struggle for self-determination, 1954-1957' (Ph.D. thesis, Northwestern
University, 1987).

symbol of the Asante war machine. Like the quills of the porcupine, '*wokum apem a, apem be ba*' – 'if you kill a thousand, a thousand more will come'.[2]

Over the next two and a half years, the National Liberation Movement (NLM) asserted Asante's right to self-determination in the face of Kwame Nkrumah's blueprint for a unitary government in an independent Ghana: a blueprint co-authored and supported by the British colonial government. NLM leaders alternated demands for Asante autonomy within a federated Gold Coast with calls for Asante's complete secession. Violence plagued the major cities of the region as colonial officials watched their model colony teeter on the brink of civil war. For nearly three years most Asante supporters of Nkrumah's Convention People's Party (CPP) lived in exile in Accra. Indeed, Nkrumah, out of fear for his safety, did not cross the Pra River, the boundary between Asante and the Colony, until well after independence in 1957. In short, the NLM not only posed a serious threat to the stability of Nkrumah's pre-independence government, but it destroyed the illusion, present since 1951 and reflected in Hailey's comment at the beginning of this article, that the Gold Coast's transition to full self-rule would proceed with rapidity and order.

Most scholars who have examined these turbulent years in Ghana's history, drawn by the dynamism and historic destiny of Nkrumah's CPP, have focused their attention on the party which was to lead Ghana to independence. As a result, the NLM has been cast into the murky shadows of historical inquiry and branded as a tribalist, regionalist, parochialist ghost of the past – a fleeting aberration in the Gold Coast-wide struggle against colonial rule.[3] Meanwhile, those who have devoted their careers to under-standing the specific dynamics of Asante history have seldom ventured beyond the beginning of the twentieth century.[4] This article is aimed at

[2] For detailed descriptions of the inauguration, see *Pioneer*, 20 September 1954 and *Daily Graphic*, 20 September 1954.

[3] See, for example, B. Amamoo, *The New Ghana* (London, 1958); D. Apter, *Ghana in Transition* (Princeton, 1972); D. Austin, *Politics in Ghana, 1946–1960* (London, 1964); G. Bing, *Reap the Whirlwind: An Account of Kwame Nkrumah's Ghana from 1950–1966* (London, 1968); F. M. Bourret, *Ghana: The Road to Independence, 1919–1957* (London, 1960); H. Bretton, *The Rise and Fall of Kwame Nkrumah* (New York, 1966).

[4] While it would be impossible to offer a full listing of works on pre-colonial Asante, a representative sampling might include: K. Arhin, 'Rank and wealth among the Akan', *Africa*, LIII, i (1983), 2–22; *idem.*, 'Peasants in nineteenth-century Asante', *Current Anthropology*, XXIV, iv (1983), 471–80; R. Dumett, 'The rubber trade of the Gold Coast and Asante in the nineteenth century: African innovation and market responsiveness', *J. Afr. Hist.*, XII, i (1971), 79–101; T. Lewin, *Asante Before the British: The Prempean Years, 1875–1900* (Lawrence, Kansas, 1978); T. C. McCaskie, 'Accumulation, wealth and belief in Asante history (to the close of the nineteenth century)', *Africa*, LIII, i (1983), 23–42; *idem.*, 'Accumulation, wealth and belief in Asante history (the twentieth century)', *Africa*, LVI, i (1986), 3–23 and *idem.*, 'Ahyiamu – "A Place of Meeting": an essay on process and event in the history of the Asante State', *J. Afr. Hist.*, XXV, ii (1984), 169–88; R. S. Rattray, *Ashanti Law and Constitution* (New York, 1969; 1st edition, London, 1911); E. Schildkrout (ed.), *The Golden Stool: Studies of the Asante Center and Periphery*, LXV, i of the *Anthropological Papers of the American Museum of Natural History* (New York, 1987); W. Tordoff, *Ashanti Under the Prempehs, 1888–1935* (London, 1965); I. Wilks, *Asante in the Nineteenth Century: The Structure and Evolution of a Political Order* (Cambridge, 1975); *idem.*, 'Dissidence in Asante politics: two tracts from the late nineteenth century', in I. Abu-Lughod (ed.), *African Themes: Northwestern University*

narrowing that historiographical gap. Its purpose is to extend the oft-debated history of the Asante kingdom into the twentieth century through an examination of the National Liberation Movement. It seeks to understand the NLM on its own terms, as part and parcel of Asante history, not as a brief aberration in the national history of Ghana. Though it is a story of continuity and of Asante tenacity, it is by no means the story of a nation united on an historic march to reclaim its right to self-determination. Indeed, to grapple with the twentieth-century tenacity of Asante nationalism – as manifested in the NLM – is to grapple with the historically-rooted contradictions of that nationalism and to confront many of the social and economic conflicts which pervaded Asante history for at least a century before the NLM's inauguration.

Although many in Accra – CPP members and colonial officials alike – reacted with surprise, if not disbelief, at the news of the NLM's founding, there had been indications as early as November, 1953 that some Asantes were beginning to question the government's blueprint for independence. The first murmurs of discontent arose during the debate over the distribution of seats for the new Legislative Assembly – the body envisioned as leading the Gold Coast to independence. A government report provided for the allocation of seats based on the population of the regions, allotting Kumase two seats and the Region nineteen.[5] In a legislative body which was to contain 104 seats, roughly 20 per cent would represent Asante. This allocation reflected a decline from Asante's 25 per cent share of seats in the 1951 Council. As far as the Asante representatives were concerned, the report reflected a total insensitivity to the historic, economic and political importance of Asante to the Gold Coast. Asante, they argued, should be entitled to no fewer than thirty seats. B. F. Kusi, who had resigned from the CPP a year earlier and who would become a staunch supporter of the NLM a year later, told the Council:

All Ashantis express the sentiment that Ashanti is a nation and that fact has been accepted. We are not a region at all; we should be considered as a nation.... Population alone does not make a country.[6]

But despite the burning nationalist pleas of many Asante representatives, the government's report was adopted. Many in Asante decried what they considered to be the government's total insensitivity to Asante's special position in the Gold Coast. Their bitterness was not to subside quickly.

A few months later, Asante discontent with the CPP surfaced within the offices of the CPP itself. As the June 1954 election approached – the election heralded as the last before independence – CPP candidates had to be chosen to stand for the 21 seats in Asante. In many cases, local constituencies disapproved of the candidates selected by Nkrumah and the CPP's Central

---

Studies in Honor of Gwendolyn Carter (Evanston, 1975), 47–63 and *idem.*, 'The Golden Stool and the Elephant Tail: an essay on wealth in Asante', in G. Dalton (ed.), *Research in Economic Anthropology*, II (1970), 1–36. See, also, I. Wilks and T. McCaskie (eds.), *Asantesem: Bulletin of the Asante Collective Biography Project*, I–XI (1975–9).

[5] Gold Coast, *Report of the Commission of Enquiry into Representational and Electoral Reform* [Chairman: Van Lare] (Accra, 1953).

[6] See Gold Coast, Legislative Assembly, *Debates*, 4–17 November 1953, *passim*.

Committee and submitted their own candidates for registration, defying the party's central authority.[7] As the election drew near some members agreed to accept party directives and removed their names from the ballot, but 32 in Asante chose to stand as independent candidates. Nine days before the election these Asante candidates were among the 81 'rebels', as Nkrumah termed them, publicly expelled from the CPP at a mass rally held in the Subin River valley in Kumase.[8] But the Subin valley had not seen the last of the Asante rebels.

On 13 August, the government passed an amendment to the Cocoa Duty and Development Funds Bill which fixed the price of cocoa at 72 shillings per 60 lb. load – a price which represented only one-third of the average prevailing world market price.[9] The Asante rebels were among those who galvanized opposition in Asante to this government ruling; in the process they transformed the campaign for a higher cocoa price into a political struggle. A leaflet circulating in early September, authored by one of the rebels, made the political connections explicit:

Ashantis produce more cocoa than the colony. IS THERE ANY COCOA IN THE NORTHERN TERITORRIES [sic]? NO! Why should Government tax cocoa farmers to develop the country in which Ashantis suffer most?...Ashantis! Save Your Nation and let others know that we are no FOOLS BUT WISE, kind and also we have the Worrior [sic] Spirit of Our Great Ancestors Within Us.[10]

It was abundantly clear that cocoa and *Kotoko* would stand at the heart of the struggle. Within a few weeks, Asante opposition to the cocoa price mushroomed into a broad-based Asante struggle against the CPP, its economic policies and its blueprint for self-government. The *Ashanti Pioneer*, a local paper whose owner, John Tsiboe, had opposed the CPP from its inception, published an editorial which proclaimed:

Great events...from little causes spring. Like an innocent match flame, the strange attitude of the all African CPP Government to the simple demand of farmers for a higher local price of cocoa has gone a long way to threaten to set ablaze the petrol dump of Ashanti nationalism.[11]

On 19 September, in the Subin River valley, that 'petrol dump' was officially ignited as tens of thousands participated in the inauguration of the Asante National Liberation Movement.

[7] Austin, *Politics*, 201. See also, *Pioneer*, 8 May 1954 for an account of local CPP officers' discontent over Nkrumah's appointing of candidates.

[8] As Nkrumah wrote, 'I called these people "rebels". Firm action had to be taken. It was vital that the Party should not be allowed to become disorganised or to be weakened by the split that this would ultimately bring about': K. Nkrumah, *Ghana: The Autobiography of Kwame Nkrumah* (London, 1957), 208.

[9] For the debates surrounding the passage of the Cocoa Duty and Development Funds (Amendment) Bill, see Gold Coast, Legislative Assembly, *Debates*, 12–13 August 1954. In 1953–54, the producer price per ton of cocoa stood at £134.40, while the average selling price obtained on the world market was £358.70. See B. Beckman, 'Government policy and the distribution of cocoa income in Ghana, 1951–56', Cocoa Economic and Research Conference, *Proceedings* (Legon, 1973), 285.

[10] E. Y. Baffoe, 'Cocoa price agitation' (Kumase, 1954). Copies of this leaflet and others were given to the author by Osei Assibey Mensah. They have been placed on deposit in the Melville J. Herskovits Memorial Library, Northwestern University.

[11] *Pioneer*, 4 September 1954.

Who was behind this massive resurgence of Asante nationalism? Who in Asante was capable of mobilizing a broad-based popular front of resistance against the government? Who welded the issue of cocoa to the spirit and grievances of *Asante Kotoko*? Scholars primarily concerned with the early years of Ghana national history have offered a variety of answers to these questions. Some, influenced by Clifford Geertz and the notion of 'national integration', saw the NLM as an almost inevitable response to the all-encompassing sovereign civil state – an expression of the primordial attachments of Asantes on the eve of independence.[12] Others, writing after the overthrow of Nkrumah in 1966, assumed the same Ghana-wide historical perspective as did the 'integrationists'. However, they argued in more materialist terms that the NLM was the product of large-scale cocoa farmers, powerful chiefs and businessmen, who exploited tribal attachments to gain the support of Asante workers and peasants in a class struggle against Nkrumah and his party.[13]

Only Richard Rathbone's work, based on extensive research in Asante, has revealed the theoretical limitations of attempts to understand the dynamics of the NLM solely within the context of Ghana national history. Rathbone recognized that the driving force behind the formation of the NLM was not the 'big men' of Asante and that the NLM could not be dismissed as simply the enigmatic expression of primordial attachments. Those responsible for the resurgence of Asante nationalism, for the forging of an Asante popular front of resistance against the CPP were, as Rathbone correctly argued, Asante's youngmen – those very same men who had spearheaded the CPP drive into Asante in 1949–51.[14]

Rathbone made a significant analytical leap in singling out the CPP rebels and their comrades in the Asante Youth Association (AYA) as the catalyst to the political upheaval of the mid-1950's. However, by focusing his concern on the wider contemporary struggle between the youngmen and the CPP during the transfer of power, he did not explore the historical dimension of his ground-breaking analysis. He saw the youngmen as a post-World War II phenomenon: Asante's version of the post-secondary school-leavers, the first mass-politicized generation. While this analysis goes a long way toward

[12] For a summary of national integration theory, see C. Geertz, ''The integrative revolution: primordial sentiments and civil politics in the new states', in Geertz (ed.), *Old Societies and New States* (New York, 1963), 109–30. See also, Apter, *Ghana*; *idem.*, 'Ghana', in J. S. Coleman and C. Rosberg (eds.), *Political Parties and National Integration* (Berkeley, 1965), 259–315; *idem.*, 'The role of traditionalism in the political modernization of Ghana and Uganda', *World Politics*, XIII (1960), 45–68; *idem.*, 'Some reflections on the role of a political opposition in new nations', *Comparative, Studies in Society and Hist.*, IV (1961), 154–68; Austin, *Politics*; *idem.*, 'Opposition in Ghana: 1947–1967', *Government and Opposition*, II, iv (1967), 539–55.

[13] See, especially, B. Fitch and M. Oppenheimer, *Ghana: End of an Illusion* (New York, 1966), 59–60.

[14] See R. Rathbone, 'Businessmen and politics: party struggle in Ghana, 1949–1957', *J. Development Studies*, IX, iii (1973), 390–401. See also Rathbone, 'Opposition in Ghana: the National Liberation Movement', *Political Opposition in the New African States* (University of London, Institute of Commonwealth Studies, Collected Seminar Paper Series, No. IV), 29–53; *idem.*, 'Politics and factionalism in Ghana', *Current History*, LX, ccclv (March, 1971), 164–7; *idem.*, 'The transfer of power in Ghana, 1945–1957' (Ph.D. thesis, University of London, 1968).

explaining the immediate thrust behind the resurgence of Asante nationalism, it cannot account for the conflicts and contradictions inherent in that
nationalism; for the events of 1954–7 did not simply represent the struggle
of Asante's youngmen against the government of the CPP. Those events also
reflected the historically rooted struggle within Asante (and within the
NLM) between the aspiring youngmen and the established powers of
Asante. It was the outcome of this long struggle, not the lone and immediate
aspirations of the youngmen, which would determine the course of Asante's
quest for autonomy.

The youngmen of Asante had been a potent and active political force since
at least the mid-nineteenth century when they were known as the *nkwankwaa*,
a term which has been consistently rendered in English as 'youngmen'. The
sense of the term was not that the *nkwankwaa* were literally 'young', but that
they existed in often uneasy subordination to elder or chiefly authority.[15] As
Wilks writes of the nineteenth-century *nkwankwaa*, they were men who
'belonged to old and well-established families but whose personal expectations of succeeding to office or even of acquiring wealth were low'.[16]
Channels for political advancement were obstructed by the traditional
requirements of office; channels for economic advancement were obstructed
by both the state and its monopoly on trade and what could be termed the
rising bourgeoisie or *asikafo* (literally, 'men of gold' or 'rich men').[17]
Perhaps best described as an emerging petite bourgeoisie, with an economic
base in trading and rubber production and economic interests directed at the
establishment of free and unencumbered trade with the coast, the *nkwankwaa*, according to Wilks, probably acquired 'their first experience of
political action in the anti-war and anti-conscription movements' of the late
1860s and early 1870s.[18] It was in the 1880s, however, that the *nkwankwaa*
made their first serious bid for political power in Asante. It was the Kumase
nkwankwaa who, angered when *Asantehene* Mensa Bonsu raised taxes and
imposed heavy fines for petty offenses, took a leading role in the movement
which eventually overthrew the *Asantehene* in 1883.[19] Capable of mobilizing
the support of the *ahiafo* (the 'poor' or 'under-privileged'), and in alliance
with the *asikafo*, whose economic standing was also threatened by Mensa
Bonsu's austerity measures and his state trading system, the *nkwankwaa*

[15] The etymology of the term '*nkwankwaa*' is somewhat murky. Its root is undoubtedly
'*nkoa*' which can be translated as 'subject' or 'commoner'. But as Busia noted,
nkwankwaa was often used synonymously with *mmerante* (literally, 'young men').
Clearly, *nkwankwaa* has come to have a very specific meaning – much more limited than
'commoner', and transcending, in many cases, the chronological or generational desig-
nation of *mmerante*. (During the 1950s, the youngmen active in the NLM ranged in age
from twenty to fifty.) See Tordoff, *Ashanti*, 374 ff. and K. A. Busia, *The Position of the
Chief in the Modern Political System of Ashanti* (London, 1951), 10 ff. In reference to the
nineteenth century, Wilks defines *nkwankwaa* as 'literally "youngmen" and sometimes
translated as "commoner"'. Wilks, *Asante*, 728.
[16] Wilks, *Asante*, 535.   [17] *Ibid.* 535–9 and 710–11.
[18] *Ibid.* 535. Unfortunately, more precise data on the early *nkwankwaa* are not
available. As Wilks points out, 'The leaders...in the early 1880's, as is appropriate to a
movement which although popular and mass-based had necessarily to be organized in
secrecy, are not identified in contemporary reports' (p. 535). Thus, it is difficult not only
to pinpoint the *nkwankwaa's* origins in time but to examine their specific social and
economic grievances.   [19] *Ibid.* 530.

were able to carry out a successful coup against the *Asantehene*; and since they were 'unconvinced of the virtues of a monarchical system', they were able to bring Kumase under a 'republican form of government' or a 'Council of commoners and chiefs', albeit for only a brief period.[20]

Though the *nkwankwaa* had made a serious bid for political power in the 1880s, their long-term goals differed markedly from those of the *asikafo* and *ahiafo*. In the last years of Asante sovereignty, the *nkwankwaa* were unable to forge a lasting political alliance capable of effecting a dramatic change in Asante politics.[21] By 1901, Asante was under the complete control of the British and the *nkwankwaa* faced an entirely new political and economic landscape. In the first three-and-a-half decades of the century, before the consolidation of indirect rule in Asante, the *nkwankwaa*, according to a 1924 colonial report, enjoyed a 'feeling of independence and safety which gives vent to criticism of their elders, and a desire when dissatisfied to take the law into their own hands'.[22] Their relationship with Asante's traditional authorities remained uneasy at best. Throughout the 1920s, the *nkwankwaa's* involvement in destoolment cases against numerous *amanhene* ('paramount chiefs') alarmed government officials and traditional authorities alike.[23] With their social and economic position bolstered by the growth in trade and the spread of education, the *nkwankwaa* became more resentful of the powers exercised by the chiefs, namely their ability to levy taxes and impose communal labor requirements. In 1930, the *nkwankwaa* were particularly outraged by news that the *Kumasihene*, Nana Prempe I, and his chiefs were considering a law which would require that a percentage of a deceased person's property be given to the *Kumasihene* and his chiefs. In a letter to the Chief Commissioner, they warned that it was a similar measure which led to the overthrow of Mensa Bonsu in 1883. After discussions with the Chief Commissioner, Nana Prempe I dropped the issue.[24]

That the *nkwankwaa* have origins dating back nearly a century before the founding of the NLM clearly has implications for our understanding of the events of 1954–7. Specifically, these pre-colonial origins allow for an historical (though admittedly tentative) class analysis of the youngmen – an analysis which repeatedly points to the *nkwankwaa's* reliance upon strategic alliances or popular fronts which they have forged with other groups in Asante society to further their own aims, be it an end to conscription, the abolition of communal labour, a lessening in taxes, or the opening up of free trade with the Coast. The *nkwankwaa* have been artful initiators of these alliances, capable of winning the support of the *asikafo* and *ahiafo*. Historically, they have also turned to the chiefs (or certain elements within the ruling elite) to gain the support and legitimacy necessary to further their causes.

That the *nkwankwaa* have had to turn to others, particularly to the chiefs, points to their weakness as a class. It also goes some distance toward explaining their pivotal and dynamic role in the turbulence of Asante politics

---

[20] For a brief description of the Council or *kwasafohyiamu*, see Wilks, *Asante*, 540. For additional interpretations of the tumultuous events of 1880–4, see Lewin, *Asante*, 69–76 and 115–16, and McCaskie, '*Ahyiamu*', 169–89.

[21] Wilks, *Asante*, 710.

[22] Great Britain, *Colonial Reports*, Ashanti, 1923–4, cited in Tordoff, *Ashanti*, 204.

[23] Tordoff, *Ashanti*, 375–82.   [24] *Ibid.* 268.

over the past century. The *nkwankwaa* have displayed an historical ability to take advantage of the fluid nature of Asante politics since the 1880s – galvanizing support in frequently opposing camps around common, though perhaps fleeting, issues, playing power against power. They accomplished this in 1883; and in 1934, in alliance with most of the Asante chiefs, they staged an important, though unsuccessful, hold-up of cocoa in response to the low price being paid for the crop by European merchants. In the following year, partly in response to the growing challenge the *nkwankwaa* posed to traditional authority, the British government decided to centralize that authority by restoring the Asante Confederacy Council, with the *Asantehene* at its helm. Some of the youngmen of Kumase, perhaps in an effort to tear apart the recently restored Confederacy, then collaborated with the *Dadeasoabahene*, *Bantamahene*, *Akyempemhene* and *Adumhene* in a plot to remove the *Asantehene*, Prempe II, from the Golden Stool.[25] The conspiracy was quickly uncovered, but the fact that 'irresponsible agitators' could win the support of such prominent chiefs required drastic action. Less than a year later, during 1936, the Council took matters into its own hands: in response to the *nkwankwaa's* vocal opposition to the colonial government's reconstitution of the Confederacy, their reluctance to perform various communal services and their role in the destoolments of so many paramount chiefs, including the attempt to destool the *Asantehene*, the Asante Confederacy Council abolished the office of *Nkwankwaahene* ('leader of the youngmen') and all *nkwankwaa* organizations.[26] The traditional position of *Nkwankwaahene* was not hereditary, nor did it confer membership in any council (whether local or divisional), but it did provide a recognized channel through which the youngmen could collectively criticize the government.[27] It was that channel the Confederacy Council sought to destroy. But the *nkwankwaa's* dissatisfaction could not be eradicated so easily. The Confederacy Council could not simply legislate away the historically entrenched *nkwankwaa* who were intent on attaining political power commensurate with their newly acquired Western education, their growing economic power via the expanding cocoa economy and their widening roles as the clerks, teachers and accountants of the new colonial bureaucracy.

In many ways, the Asante Youth Association, founded in 1947, came to assume the role and functions of the abolished *nkwankwaa* organizations, as its members shared common characteristics, as well as common grievances, with their counterparts of the late nineteenth and early twentieth centuries.[28] Most AYA members came from well-established families, but had no prospects of succeeding to traditional office. Their economic and social base remained petit bourgeois, but there had been many important changes over

· [25] Tordoff, *Ashanti*, 365–9.

[26] Asante Confederacy Council, *Minutes of the Second Session*, 23 January 1936.

[27] For discussions of the role of the *Nkwankwaahene*, see Busia, *Position*, 10 and Tordoff, *Ashanti*, 373–4 and 383.

[28] Two years before the AYA was founded, Fortes was in Asante completing his 'Ashanti Social Survey'. He observed that, despite the formal prohibition of the *nkwankwaa* ten years earlier, youngmen's associations and self-help groups (modeled on the *nkwankwaa* organizations) continued to give expression to the 'opinions of commoners'. See M. Fortes, 'The Ashanti Social Survey: a preliminary report', *The Rhodes-Livingstone Journal*, VI (1948), 26–8 and esp. 26 ff.

the last fifty years. No longer rooted primarily in petty trade and small scale rubber production, the youngmen of the post-World War II period were an economically diverse lot. Most had attained some degree of education which led them into such burgeoning occupations as journalism, teaching, accounting and clerking.[29] Some were shopkeepers and small-scale traders and some, were involved in cocoa production (if only in a small way). They were not chiefs (though many were related to chiefs) and they had no realizable aspirations to chiefly office. They can also be distinguished from the old guard intelligentsia – the relatively sparse, though politically significant, group of Asante professionals like K. A. Busia and I. B. Asafu-Adjaye – who had been trained to inherit the government upon the departure of the British, but who had been left out after the dynamic rise of the CPP. They were not the indigent or *ahiafo*, nor were they the *asikafo* whose wealth was based in a powerful combination of land ownership, large-scale cocoa and timber production, trading, transport and construction.[30] They were, quite simply, the youngmen, the *nkwankwaa*, or, for lack of a less cumbersome class definition, the petite bourgeoisie.

Perhaps what most distinguished the youngmen of the post-World War II era from the *nkwankwaa* of the previous decades was that they participated in (and, in some cases, helped to initiate) the mass nationalist movement. Many, including Kusi Ampofu, Osei Assibey-Mensah and Sam Boateng, played key roles in the founding of the CPP in 1949. For them, Nkrumah's party was the organization of the 'common man', the vanguard in a struggle against colonial rule and against the power and privilege of chiefly authority. Thus, the youngmen spearheaded the CPP drive into Asante and, in the process, they mastered the arts of mass mobilization, organization and propaganda. Only a few years later, these skills would be put to the test when the youngmen broke with the CPP and prepared to 'fight fire with fire'.

In 1954, though the political and economic landscape of Asante had changed dramatically since the 1880s, the goals of the Asante *nkwankwaa* were not so different from those of their predecessors. The youngmen continued to seek political power, and through it, economic power. However, instead of confronting the Asante state, the *nkwankwaa* were now confronting

[29] It is interesting to note that the four AYA members who played the most pivotal roles in the founding of the NLM – Kusi Ampofu, Sam Boateng, K. A. M. Gyimah and Osei Assibey-Mensah – were all journalists by trade.

[30] This is not to suggest that in the Asante of the 1950s there were four neatly packaged social classes or groups – the chiefs, the *asikafo*, the *nkwankwaa* and the *ahiafo*. The categories were not mutually exclusive, particularly with reference to the chiefs and the 'big men' or *asikafo*. Many chiefs, particularly the Kumase Divisional Chiefs (*nsafohene*), were wealthy landowners with an economic base in cocoa, transport and trading. At the same time, many of the *asikafo* aspired to traditional office and much of their wealth and power depended on maintaining a close relationship with, and courting the favours of, the traditional ruling powers. In an article dealing with wealth and political power in the nineteenth century, but with applicability to the twentieth century, Wilks notes that 'the analytically distinct categories of the office holders (*amansohwefo*) and the wealthy (*asikafo*) are, in terms of actual membership, largely overlapping ones; that is, office holders became wealthy through the exercise of their office, and persons of wealth acquired office through the use of their money'. Wilks, 'The Golden Stool', 17 and *passim*.

the CPP – a party which they had helped to found and build, a party through which they had sought to reach the political kingdom and all else that would follow.[31] Their break with the CPP, though precipitated by the freezing of the cocoa price, was based primarily on a growing perception that the CPP was no longer providing a means toward political and economic advancement; it was no longer offering the political kingdom to the majority of Asante's youngmen. The government's allocation of seats in the Legislative Assembly and the CPP's selection of candidates for the 1954 election were cited as *prima facie* evidence that the CPP did not and could not represent the youngmen of Asante. The freezing of the cocoa price and a development policy that was based on the expropriation of wealth from Asante cocoa farmers only served to reinforce the youngmen's growing alarm that the CPP was seeking to build its kingdom on the backs of Asantes *without* giving the youngmen of Asante a voice in that kingdom or allowing them to reap its rewards.

And just as the *nkwankwaa* of the 1880s had turned to *Akyempemhene* Owusu Koko in their bid to depose Mensa Bonsu, the youngmen of the 1950s turned to the paramount chiefs of Asante in an effort to legitimize their movement, culturally and politically, against Nkrumah. They believed that the support of the chiefs was an ideological necessity: the chiefs would bring with them the support of the spirits and ancestors of the entire nation and the struggle against Nkrumah would become the struggle of the Asante nation against political slavery, economic slavery and 'black imperialism'.[32]

It was recognized in September, 1954 that winning the support of the chiefs would take time and would require tactical manoeuvering, because the chiefs, not without cause, viewed the youngmen of the AYA as traitors. Only months before the NLM's inauguration, the *nkwankwaa* had been adamant supporters of the CPP and were directly associated with the CPP's oft-quoted policy of 'making the chiefs run away and leave their sandals behind'. At the same time, however, the chiefs could ill afford to turn away from any movement which held out the promise of effectively challenging Nkrumah and his attempts to curtail chiefly power. Thus, in an effort at reconciliation with the chiefs, the youngmen coupled their demands for a higher cocoa price and Asante autonomy within a federated Gold Coast with a call for the preservation of chieftancy and posited themselves as the defenders of that 'sacred institution'. As one editorial remarked,

...the youth of Ashanti have made it supremely clear that they would NEVER see the sandals removed from the Ahemfie [palace] to the Arena, the Subin Valley, or even the National museum. They would rather them still [be] kept in the Ahemfie so that the Chiefs could come out of their hide-outs and wear them again.[33]

In another strategic move to enlist the chiefs' support, the youngmen

---

[31] This is a paraphrasing of Nkrumah's famous statement, 'Seek ye first the political kingdom, and all things will be added unto you'. *Pioneer*, 5 March 1949. See also Fitch and Oppenheimer, *Ghana*, 25.

[32] As Dennis Austin so perceptively argued twenty-five years ago, 'those who saw the conflict that was arising between the farmers and the government as one affecting the rights and interests of Ashanti, were also ready to see the chiefs as still the most potent symbol of Ashanti unity'. See Austin, *Politics*, 259.

[33] *Pioneer*, 6 September 1954.

persuaded Bafuor Osei Akoto, one of the *Asantehene*'s senior linguists or *akyeame*, to serve as the new Movement's chairman. Akoto was, as *West Africa* reported, '*persona grata* to Otumfuo himself as well as to most Ashanti Paramount and Divisional Chiefs'.[34] He could provide the youngmen with a direct mouthpiece to the most important traditional rulers in Asante. Moreover, as a former apprentice engineer and fitter and as a major cocoa producer in his own right, Akoto virtually personified the popular front the youngmen were attempting to build. He was a man capable of bridging the gap between chiefs and commoners, cocoa farmers and urban wage earners. Bolstered by Akoto's presence, it was not long before the youngmen made headway with Asante's chiefs. On 11 October, the Kumase State Council voted openly to support the NLM and sealed their vow of support with the swearing of the Great Oath of Asante and with the decision to withdraw 20,000 pounds from the *Asantehene*'s New Palace Building Fund for the support of the Movement.[35] Ten days later, the Asanteman Council gave the NLM its full endorsement.[36] Thus, step by step in the days surrounding the inauguration, the youngmen began to forge a popular front of resistance against Nkrumah and the CPP. The links of that front, which bound cocoa farmer to chief to youngman, were forged with the fire of Asante nationalism.

This nationalism was, from the very onset, the justifying ideology of the Movement. It was not, however, its *raison d'être*. The youngmen did not spearhead the formation of the NLM because, as one of their leaflets proclaimed, 'Asante has history'. Their reaction was far from being a primordial, tribal or traditional response thrown up in the face of a new all-encompassing sovereign civil state. Rather, the youngmen's invocation of Asante nationalism represented the very modern use and construction of an ideology to justify opposition to the CPP, to rationalize and legitimize that opposition and, most importantly, to mobilize support and forge the links of a popular front of resistance under their control and direction. That Asante had existed as an independent historic kingdom, though useful, was of secondary importance to the creation of the NLM's unifying ideology, its myth of tradition. Of primary importance were the social, political and class dynamics which shaped the construction of that ideology.

Asante in the 1950s provided fertile ground for the nationalist message of the youngmen. It was a message which appealed to the large class of peasant producers of cocoa who had been unable to mobilize effectively against the price freeze. It appealed to the chiefs who had feared that any vocal opposition to Nkrumah on their part would lead to a further erosion in power.[37] It appealed to the old guard intelligentsia who had lost the political

---

[34] *West Africa*, 11 December 1954, 1161. This article contains a brief biography of Bafuor Akoto.

[35] Kumase State Council, *Minutes*, 11 October 1954.

[36] See *Daily Graphic*, 30 October 1954 and 6 November 1954. See also Public Record Office, Colonial Office [hereafter, PRO, CO.] 554/804: 'A Resolution by the Asanteman Council Praying for a Federal Constitution for the Gold Coast', dd. Kumase, 21 October 1954.

[37] Having experienced considerable power under the indirect rule system of the 1930s and 1940s, the chiefs foresaw their authority and their power being increasingly undermined by the centralization strategies of the CPP, the creation of local councils to assume the duties and functions of the old Native Authorities and the refusal of the CPP

moment to Nkrumah and had shown themselves incapable of mobilizing mass support.[38] Only the *nkwankwaa*, with their long history of forging alliances and their recent experience, via the CPP, of mass mobilization techniques and propaganda, were in the position and had the tools necessary to fertilize and cultivate the grounds of opposition in Asante. They were the political catalyst, just as they had been in the 1880s. They were the only class capable of articulating their *specific* aspirations for political and economic advancement – aspirations which had been historically thwarted by the pre-colonial Asante state, by the structure of indirect rule and now by the bureaucratization and centralization of the CPP – as general Asante aspirations. In short, the youngmen were able to hold together an all-embracing ideology which could articulate the varied and often conflicting aspirations of Asantes. Standing on the platform at the Subin River they presented themselves as 'the people' – the new ideologues of Asante nationalism. They fanned the fires of discontent by pointing to the failures, limitations and corruption of the reigning nationalist movement. They raised the issue of cocoa and resurrected *Asante Kotoko*.

For several months after the inauguration of the NLM, Asante's youngmen appeared to rule the day. Their burning nationalist rhetoric, their threats of secession and their ability to mobilize broad masses of the population in Asante engendered fear in the hearts of many a colonial official who watched as Britain's model colony disintegrated before their eyes. One official in London described his apprehension

that there might be organized in Ashanti a strong-arm group using firearms who would be prepared, if the need arose, to take to the forest. The country is such that it would not be difficult for 200/300 young men suitably armed to stage a Mau Mau of their own.[39]

Meanwhile, Governor Arden-Clark lamented in a letter home to his wife that the Asantes 'are nearly as difficult and unruly as the Scots once were [and] have suddenly decided that they don't like the present Government, want Home Rule for Ashanti, and are vociferously demanding a Federal Constitution'.[40] By the end of 1954, the colonial government had begun to draw up security schemes and emergency evacuation measures in the event of an all-out civil war.[41]

---

to incorporate a second, Upper House into the independence-bound parliament. As Arhin writes, 'they regarded Nkrumah and his party as parvenus, usurpers of power from the legitimate heirs to the British'. See K. Arhin, 'Chieftancy under Kwame Nkrumah', paper presented at the Symposium on the Life and Work of Kwame Nkrumah, Institute of African Studies, University of Ghana (Legon, 27 May–1 June, 1985), 5.

[38] As Richard Wright so eloquently observed of J. B. Danquah – the personification of the old guard: 'He was of the old school. One did not speak *for* the masses; one told them what to do'. See R. Wright, *Black Power* (New York, 1954), 221.

[39] PRO, CO. 554/1276: File Minute, dd. 17 May 1955.

[40] Cited in D. Rooney, *Sir Charles Arden-Clarke* (London, 1982), 159.

[41] The 'Ashanti Zone Internal Security Schemes' were authored by the Chief Regional Officer in Asante. All copies of the 'Schemes' were to be destroyed by fire immediately after they were read and digested by district officers and members of the Ashanti Zone Intelligence Committee consisting of representatives of the colonial administration in Asante, the Police and the Army. Fortunately, one of the 'Schemes' survived – No. IV, dated February, 1957. That 'Scheme' suggests that the first concerted security plans were

Perhaps these emergency plans were not entirely unwarranted. For a period of several months, Asante appeared to have seceded in fact, if not in name. When the Governor visited Kumase in March, 1955, he was forced to lie flat on the seat of his car to escape the barrage of stones hurled at him.[42] The irreverence shown by the people in Kumase that day for the highest ranking British official in the Gold Coast was unlike any seen since 1948. It was topped off during the minutes that Arden-Clarke spent greeting the *Asantehene*. During that time, 'one of the NLM boys,' recalled K. A. M. Gyimah, '...went and sat in his [Arden-Clarke's] car, and he said that the car belonged to us!'[43] The symbolism of the youngman's actions was clear to all: the colonial Governor, by siding with Nkrumah on the nature of the post-independence state, had thrown in his lot with the CPP. Thus, neither he nor his vehicle were sacrosanct. The youngman's occupation of the car stood as a popular declaration of Asante's right to confiscate or reclaim that very symbol of colonial officialdom, the Governor's limousine.

Among the NLM's rank-and-file, a popular culture of resistance emerged which was a strange tapestry of old and new, unmistakably Asante, undeniably contemporary. It combined the palanquin and the propaganda van, the gong-gong and the megaphone, the war dance and the rally. Women wore cloth bearing faces of Asante nationalist heros. There were NLM drumming and dance troupes. And there were, finally, the NLM Action Groupers – that self-styled vigilante group aimed at ridding the region of CPP supporters.[44] A *New Republic* journalist, after attending an NLM rally, was both amused and confused by the Movement's Groupers:

...they dressed in the movie version of American cowboy costumes, black satin with white fringe, and they wore high-heeled black, Texas boots brilliantly studded with the letters NLM and the words 'King Force'. They were called to the platform...and sang a song. I was told that their throwing arms were not impeded by their tight clothing, and that most of the bomb damage in Kumase, rightly or wrongly, was attributed to them.[45]

developed in 1954, then updated in 1955 and 1956, to deal with the threat posed to security by the NLM. The 'Schemes' included detailed information on intelligence gathering and on evacuation plans, noting that in the event of 'civil war or guerrilla war' the scheme would be superseded by a central plan devised in Accra. See National Archives of Ghana, Kumase, Regional Office Administration/2842: 'Ashanti Zone Internal Security Scheme', dd. Kumase, February, 1957.

[42] *Pioneer*, 23 March 1955; *West Africa*, 26 March 1955, 279.

[43] J. Allman, Field Notes: interview with K. A. M. Gyimah (FN/9/1), dd. Manhyia, Kumase, 20 July 1984, 73.

[44] The Action Groupers were formed in October, 1954, shortly after the murder of the Movement's Propaganda Secretary, E. Y. Baffoe, by a member of the CPP. Three youngmen – Sam Boateng, Frank Tawiah, and Kwaku Danso (a.k.a. 'Burning Spear') – were instrumental in organizing the group. It was first led by Fred Sarpong, a journalist, but after he became involved in publishing the NLM's newspaper, the *Liberator*, the Groupers were taken over by Alex Osei. See Allman, Field Notes: interview with Sam Boateng (FN/6/1), dd. Adum, Kumase, 3 July 1984, 39–40 and interview with Alex Osei (FN/3/1), dd. Asante New Town, Kumase, 26 June 1984, 11–14.

[45] A. Kendrick, 'Growing up to be a Nation', *New Republic*, 23 April 1956, 15–16. Cited in Yaw Manu, 'Conflict and consensus in Ghanaian politics: the case of the 1950's', *Conch*, VI, i–ii (1975), 103.

One can only hypothesize on the symbolism of the Groupers' attire. To a Western journalist it may have appeared incongruous, gaudy, perhaps even ridiculous. But the brilliant outfits of the Action Groupers were part and parcel of the new popular resistance in Asante, a marriage of old and new. The attire befitted the modern-day Asante warrior.

For several months, the youngmen seemed to preside over this popular culture of resistance, this resurrection of *Asante Kotoko*. Their potency as catalysts, nationalist ideologues and, at times, rabble-rousers, appeared unchallenged and unchallengeable as every Asante's political and economic grievance seemed to be brought under the nationalist rubric. Yet the historical conflicts and contradictions in Asante society could not be negated by or even subsumed within the NLM. In resurrecting *Asante Kotoko*, in enlisting the support of the chiefs, the *asikafo* and the old guard intelligentsia, the youngmen had turned to those very powers who had historically thwarted their bid for political power within Asante. The youngmen thus found themselves pitted against Asante's ruling class in a modern-day struggle over the very definition of Asante self-determination. It was a struggle the youngmen were bound to lose.

By the Movement's first anniversary, it was clear that the youngmen's power within the NLM was rapidly eroding, that control of the Movement was slipping irretrievably from their grasp. Though the youngmen continued to play very visible roles at Movement rallies and as writers for the NLM paper, the *Liberator*, their positions as leaders and decision-makers were gradually usurped by the long-established powers in Asante: the chiefs, the intelligentsia and the *Asantehene*. As one youngman recently recalled, '...those who were paying the money for the organization were the people who were actually dictating'.[46] When push came to shove, the energy and zeal of the youngmen were no match for the power and money of the chiefs backed by the political savvy and experience of the intelligentsia. The NLM's Finance Committee, which, according to one youngman, kept its affairs a closely guarded secret, was chaired by the *Kronkohene*, Nana Kwabena Amoo.[47] As early as February, 1954, at the insistence of the *Asantehene*, Kusi Ampofu – a leader of the AYA – was replaced by R. R. Amponsah as the Movement's General Secretary. Amponsah, a member of the royal family of Mampon, left the CPP only days before he assumed this top position in the NLM.[48] Shortly thereafter, Victor Owusu (a member of the Agona royal family who abandoned the CPP the same week as did Amponsah and Joe Appiah) became an ex-officio member of the Asanteman Council. Slowly, and perhaps imperceptibly at first, the NLM's seat of

---

[16] Allman, Field Notes: interview with N. B. Abubekr (FN/16/1), dd. Akowuasaw, Kumase, 28 July 1984, 127.

[17] N. B. Abubekr recently remarked that if anyone needed money, 'they simply went to Bafuor Akoto and he gave them money... Our knowledge of our accounts was limited only to that... We didn't know how much we had and we were not told what expenditures there were and all that'. See Allman, Field Notes: interview with N. B. Abubekr (FN/16/2), dd. Akowuasaw, Kumase, 10 October 1984, 189.

[48] For Kusi Ampofu's reactions to Amponsah's appointment, see Allman, Field Notes: interview with Kusi Ampofu (FN/24/1), dd. Asante New Town, Kumase, 15 October 1984, 198. For the reactions of other youngmen, see Allman, interview with N. B. Abubekr (FN/16/1), dd. Akowuasaw, Kumase, 28 July 1984, 127.

power was moved from the organization headquarters to the *Asantehene's* Palace at Manhyia.

While ex-CPP stalwarts like Amponsah and Owusu and old guard intellectuals from the United Gold Coast Convention (UGCC) like K. A. Busia and I. B. Asafu-Adjaye, not to mention Asante's chiefs, had been at political odds for years, their differences quickly faded in the context of the NLM. A process of consolidation occurred within Asante's ruling ranks, in which the *Asantehene* was instrumental. Nana Osei Agyeman Prempe II was the caretaker of the Golden Stool, the symbol of traditional political authority and the symbolic link between Asante's pre-colonial and colonial past and its present. He was the inspiration for and focus of Asante nationalism. Whoever received his recognition as the legitimate leadership of the NLM would become the Movement's indisputable leadership. In bestowing that recognition the *Asantehene* turned to those who shared his ideological and material interests, those who sought to preserve their own economic and social privilege. He turned to Asante's chiefs, its political intelligentsia, and its *asikafo* because he feared the youngmen and the rabble they could so easily rouse. Perhaps he perceived a threat that if the young-men retained control of the Movement, they would define Asante self-determination on their own terms or, worse yet, on the terms of those rank-and-file supporters who had stoned the Governor's limousine.[49] In short, the *Asantehene* turned to Asante's fragmented ruling class, including ex-CPP and ex-UGCC political intellectuals, *asikafo* and chiefs, united them and empowered them.

What could the *nkwankwaa* do in response to the consolidation of Asante's ruling class and its usurpation of the NLM? Nothing: the youngmen's potency as catalysts, ideologues and rabble-rousers was inextricably bound up with their impotence as a class. The very ideology they had constructed – Asante nationalism – denied their existence as a class and undermined the legitimacy of their own particular economic and political aspirations. The only way the *nkwankwaa* could have challenged Asante's ruling class and its usurpation of the Movement would have been to win the support of the dispossessed in a direct assault on the hegemony of the *Asantehene*. To do so would have meant challenging the very basis of their own nationalist ideology, and here lay the nub of their predicament. They were incapable of acting as a class; their fate was sealed. Never an officer corps, they were destined to remain the true and loyal foot soldiers of *Asante Kotoko*.

By 1956 Asante's political intelligentsia, backed by the *Asantehene* and the

---

[49] Despite the *Asantehene's* support for the Movement, he frequently let it be known that he distrusted the youngmen. On the occasion of the Asanteman Council's endorse-ment of the Movement, he rebuked the youngmen for the 'vilification, abuses and insults levelled against him...when the Self-Government wave started'. He was outraged that the youngmen felt they could force him to come out with a statement in support of the Movement. This, he declared, 'showed disrespect. It was an insult, disgrace and shame'. See *Pioneer*, 22 October 1954. A year later, disturbed by what appeared to be a reign of the rabble on the streets of Kumase, he denounced those youngmen who had broken the law. He claimed that 'he felt sorry for those few Ashantis who would not understand the issues at stake...for [whom] the ideas of good and right had no meaning. He decided that no ex-convict should have the privilege of shaking hands with him'. See Asanteman Council, *Minutes*, 28 October 1955.

chiefs of the Asanteman Council and the Kumase State Council, had successfully transformed the NLM from an extra-parliamentary movement – a popular front of resistance which embodied the diverse and often conflicting grievances of Asantes – into a proper parliamentary party. This party negotiated at length with the Colonial Office in London and competed in the 1956 general election, winning a majority of seats in Asante. However, it failed in its national electoral battle with the CPP, Nkrumah's party taking 71 of the 104 contested seats.

In August, 1956, not one *nkwankwaa* from among the group which launched the NLM took a seat in the parliament which led Ghana to independence. In that parliament, with the *Asantehene's* trustworthy supporters present, a compromise solution was worked out between the NLM and the CPP which entrenched the position of the chiefs in the constitution and gave some regional autonomy to Asante. The compromise may not have appeared as much of a victory for Asante in the battle with the CPP, but within Asante it marked a decisive victory for Asante's ruling class. Led by the *Asantehene*, they had succeeded, through constitutional means, in retaining their position – a position rooted in pre-colonial Asante and maintained through British colonial rule. It was a victory of continuity, tenacity and enduring hegemony.

The noted American historian, C. Vann Woodward, has remarked that counterfactual history 'liberates us from the tyranny of what actually did happen'.[50] It is useful here to explore one critical counterfactual question. What if Nkrumah had agreed to the earliest demands of Asante's youngmen for virtual autonomy for Asante? Clearly the terrain of struggle within Asante would have been much different. The fundamental social and economic contradictions between Asante's youngmen, the chiefs and the intelligentsia would have been brought into sharp relief as each group vied for control of an autonomous Asante. Indeed, by agreeing to the youngmen's demands, Nkrumah could have forced into the open the contest in Asante over the definition and control of that nation's self-determination – a contest heretofore distorted and overshadowed by the broader struggle against the CPP. In such a contest, the victory of Asante's ruling class was not inevitable. The formal demand for self-determination having been addressed, it could no longer shape the terrain of political struggle in Asante. Nkrumah would have unleashed upon Asante's ruling class those very youngmen and that very rabble who had transformed the Gold Coast's political struggle in 1948. Indeed, if Nkrumah had conceived of national liberation in terms broad enough to accommodate the demands of the NLM, perhaps the CPP would have found an effective 'ideological insert' into Asante, as Roger Murray describes it, and could have linked itself 'explicitly and concretely with poor farmers, floating agricultural proletariat and zongo dwellers *against* old and new privilege'.[51] In such a scenario, perhaps Asante's *nkwankwaa* would have escaped their fate as loyal foot soldiers of the Golden Stool.

[50] C. V. Woodward, 'Comments on the panel, *The Strange Career of Jim Crow Revisited*', American Historical Association Annual Meeting, Chicago, IL (December 1986).

[51] R. Murray, 'The Ghanaian road', *New Left Review*, XXXII (July/August 1963), 70.

But Nkrumah's conception of national liberation, though broad enough to encompass the entire African continent, was not broad enough to encompass the demand, within his own country, for self-determination in Asante. Thus, the social conflict within Asante has continued to take a back seat to Asante's broader struggle with the central government. The definition of Asante self-determination remains the definition offered by Asante's ruling class on the eve of independence and Asante nationalism remains the province of a ruling class which has consistently used it to foster its own privilege. Asante's youngmen, those who were the catalyst behind the 1954 resurrection of *Asante Kotoko*, remain locked in an historical limbo, prisoners of a nationalism so defined as to render them incapable of effectively challenging Asante's ruling class. Social and economic hegemony continues to be the preserve of those chiefs and political intellectuals who, since gaining control of the NLM, have held securely the reins of power in Asante. Those nameless, faceless men and women – the small-scale cocoa farmers, the *abusa* labourers and the urban workers whose militance and mass support made the NLM an imposing force – stand in foreboding stillness. They have not, as some predicted, been integrated into the modern civil state. They have been, quite simply, disarmed and silenced.

SUMMARY

This article examines the origins, background, composition and policies of the National Liberation Movement, a mass political organization founded in Asante in September, 1954. The central aim of the NLM was to advance Asante claims for self-determination and to oppose the CPP in their advocacy of a constitutional settlement with the British colonial government – a settlement that would bring about a unitary government in an independent Gold Coast [Ghana]. The analysis developed here places the 'youngmen' of Asante, the *nkwankwaa*, at the centre of these events. It is argued that this somewhat enigmatic group was the catalyst behind the formation of the NLM and the resurrection of Asante nationalism that it represented. The *nkwankwaa* forged a dynamic popular front of resistance in Asante to what they termed the 'black imperialism' of Nkrumah and the CPP. In exploring the pivotal role of the *nkwankwaa* in the rebirth and reconstruction of Asante nationalism, the discussion addresses the legacies of indirect rule in Asante, the importance of cocoa, the development of class, and the ambiguous role of Asante's political intelligentsia. Most crucially, it is suggested that the political development of the NLM turned upon the struggle within Asante between the *nkwankwaa* and the *Asantehene* (backed by the chiefs and Asante's political intelligentsia) over the very definition of 'nation' and of 'self-determination'. Thus, the article highlights the historical conflicts and contradictions within Asante society – contradictions which were softened by but not subsumed within Asante nationalism, and conflicts which were distorted, but not overshadowed, by the resilience of *Asante Kotoko* in the face of the centralized state. The reasons for the tenacity of Asante nationalism lay not in the struggle between Asante and what was to become the Ghanaian state, but in the unresolved struggles within Asante society.

Journal of African History, XI, 3 (1970), pp. 419–434
Printed in Great Britain

PATRIOTISM AND NEO-TRADITIONALISM IN BUGANDA: THE KABAKA YEKKA ('THE KING ALONE') MOVEMENT, 1961–1962[1]

BY I. R. HANCOCK

ON Saturday, 10 June 1961, a demonstration was held in the suburbs of Kampala in the British Protectorate of Uganda. According to the *Uganda Argus*, 'thousands' of people were involved.[2] But this was no ordinary nationalist demonstration. The principal enemy was not an alien colonial power but an indigenous African government, the object was not to promote national independence but to assert tribal solidarity, the popular cry was not 'Uhuru' but 'Kabaka Yekka'. The demonstrators were Baganda protesting against the election in March of a Democratic Party government led by Benedicto Kiwanuka. Kiwanuka's sins were threefold. He was a Catholic who had opposed the Protestant establishment in the Kingdom of Buganda, he had fought the election despite the boycott declared by the Kabaka's government, he was a Muganda and a commoner who had dared to set himself above his Kabaka. To the demonstrators these were the actions of a rebel, of an enemy of the throne and an enemy of Buganda. They declared they would not recognize his government and insisted that no one should precede the Kabaka on the soil of his kingdom. For a week the demonstrations continued, marking the beginning of concerted popular agitation against Kiwanuka's government in Buganda. Their weapon, publicly launched on 10 June, was a new loyalist movement under the name of Kabaka Yekka.

Kabaka Yekka quickly spread through many parts of Buganda. The 'gospel' was preached in the villages, branches were formed, funds collected, pamphlets distributed. By the end of 1961, when the movement had been officially endorsed by the Kabaka's government, it had become the rallying point for the opposition to the Democratic Party within Buganda. Kabaka Yekka had also become one of the most remarkable movements in modern African politics. For one thing, it was a mass movement organized to defend a neo-traditionalist and tribal cause. For another, it was apparently success-

---

[1] This article represents a modified version of seminar papers presented at Makerere University College and at Oxford University in 1969, and the writer is very grateful for the advice and criticism received. The article draws on research conducted in Uganda in 1965 and in 1969 and is based on press reports, interviews and the Kabaka Yekka files once owned by S. K. Masembe-Kabali, former secretary-general of the movement, and now deposited in the Library at Makerere University College. Unfortunately these files are only in rough order and at times the material can only be identified by referring to the folder number. The most relevant folders for the history of Kabaka Yekka have been catalogued by the Library as follows: numbers 65–71 (i), (ii), (iii), (iv), (v), (vi), (vii).

[2] *Uganda Argus*, 12 June 1961; *Uganda Empya*, 12 June 1961.

ful. The Democratic Party was routed in elections for the Buganda Lukiko (Parliament) in February 1962, and in the following April, Kabaka Yekka representatives joined a national coalition headed by Milton Obote, the leader of the Uganda People's Congress. Uganda's independence constitution, which came into force in October 1962, gave Buganda and her institutions a special protected position within Uganda. Buganda, it seemed, was safe from the iconoclasts of the African revolution. In the event this security proved to be an illusion. The federal status was weakened through centralist political and financial pressure and, in 1966, effectively destroyed by military force. Ultimately, then, Kabaka Yekka failed. Perhaps the only achievement had been to win a temporary respite.

Even on these terms there is a good case for investigating the early history of Kabaka Yekka. For there are two questions which need to be answered: (1) How and why did Kabaka Yekka succeed within Buganda? (2) Did the very fact or nature of this victory contribute to Buganda's subsequent eclipse? The first presents few problems. After all, one would expect that an appeal to neo-traditional loyalties would win support in a neo-traditionalist society. Yet there is some advantage in pursuing this question because the answer bears on the second. For Kabaka Yekka's victory in the Lukiko elections was really a victory for the *status quo* within Buganda. It further entrenched the power of the existing political and administrative leadership. Kabaka Yekka had aroused patriotism in defence of a neo-traditionalist cause, patriots who assumed that Buganda was a separate nation, neo-traditionalists who saw in separate nationhood a barrier against social change. So in this sense Kabaka Yekka became 'a movement of Buganda against the world'[3], and it was this rejection of the world, seen to be non-Ganda and anti-traditionalist, which increased Buganda's isolation from Uganda and invited intervention from the central government. This stand was not a new one. But in 1961 and early 1962 Kabaka Yekka helped to clarify and to consolidate it.

The background to the formation of Kabaka Yekka has been described by many writers.[4] For the purposes of this analysis there were two main developments in the period after the Kabaka's return from exile in 1955: the rise of a neo-traditionalist group which effectively controlled politics and administration and, coinciding with this, Buganda's growing isolation from the rest of the Protectorate. These developments highlighted a division within Buganda between, on the one hand, friends and supporters of Michael Kintu, the Katikiro (prime minister), who wanted to preserve the *status quo* protected by Buganda's separation from national politics and, on the other hand, a number of educated progressive politicians who formed parties to press for independence for Uganda and for reforms inside Buganda. In Ganda terms, the progressives were making revolutionary

---

[3] Audrey Richards in L. Fallers (ed.), *The King's Men* (London, 1964), 384.
[4] See, in particular: D. Apter, *The Political Kingdom in Uganda* (Princeton, 1961); D. A. Low, *Political Parties in Uganda, 1949–1962* (London, 1962).

demands: direct elections to the Lukiko, the removal of the twenty saza (county) chiefs who sat as *ex officio* members of the Lukiko, the abolition of privileged private use of official land. In opposing these demands, and the whole idea of modern nationalist parties operating from and within Buganda, the neo-traditionalists secured allies among the peasants and traders. It was a loose alliance based on a common attachment to throne, country (Buganda) and to some extent, the local Church. One effect of this combination was to isolate the progressives by equating their limited radicalism with disloyalty and so depriving them of popular support. Another effect was a suspicion of all political parties, even of those whose loyalty was never in question. Behind the alliance lay a determination to protect the Ganda identity from foreign constitutions and economic enterprise, a determination evident in the boycott of non-African trade organized by the Uganda National Movement, in the stubborn resistance to the concept of 'One Uganda', and in the increasing demand for the return of 'our things' through a new agreement replacing those of 1900 and 1955 and restoring the independence of Buganda's institutions.

Yet this kind of unity proved no barrier to the progress planned by the Colonial Office and demanded by Uganda nationalists. For both had agreed that Uganda, to include Buganda, should be granted self-govern-ment as soon as possible. The 1961 election was meant to be a big step in this direction but, fearing that anti-traditionalism would dominate the outlook of elected nationalist politicians, the Kabaka's government refused to participate without prior guarantees for Buganda's special position. To press the point, a number of neo-traditionalists led by Amos Sempa, the Omuwanika (treasurer), pushed a secession motion through the Lukiko. The election was not postponed and the Kabaka's government declared the boycott. Ninety-seven per cent of the Baganda observed the boycott; the remaining 3 per cent enabled the Democratic Party to win 20 out of the 21 Buganda national seats and to form Uganda's first African government. So within a few months two attempts had been made to protect Buganda's position. Both had failed. By mid-1961 the majority of Baganda, frustrated and demoralized, could well feel that they had nowhere to go.

In these circumstances Sepiriya Kisawuzi Masembe-Kabali formed the Kabaka Yekka movement.[5] Masembe was born in 1912; his father had once been Omuwanika in the Kabaka's government; four generations of his family had already served the royal court. Masembe went to King's College, Budo, which was an obvious choice for the Anglican son of a notable family. Later he went to Makerere and, after working for several years in the Protectorate prison service, retired in 1960, a comparatively

---

[5] There are various accounts of the origins of Kabaka Yekka. See, in particular: Richards, *The King's Men*, 381–3; C. Gertzel, 'How Kabaka Yekka came to be', *Africa Report*, IX, no. 9 (1964), 9–12; Willy Mukasa, 'KY not a political party', *Uganda Argus*, 25 November 1964; F. B. Welbourn, *Religion and Politics in Uganda, 1952–62* (Nairobi, 1965), 26–7. As will be seen, this account varies from the others mainly in giving a central place to Masembe-Kabali and to the lesser known figures from the Kampala suburbs.

wealthy man, to farm the family estates near Kampala. Clearly he had a stake in the existing structure of Ganda society. Certainly he was a conservative. In early 1961, in his first real intervention into politics, he drafted a programme for a Conservative party.[6] The party was to be open to all who were 'fighting for the Kabakaship', and it was to unite all Baganda in the common cause. The 'rebels', those who had taken part in the national elections, were to be excluded. So, too, were the professional politicians whose preoccupation with 'leadership scrambles' had promoted disunity and exposed the throne to danger. The two central objects were

2. ...[to] see that political changes do not destroy the good customs and traditions, do not destroy the kingdom, the clans and our way of life, all of which are valuable for our society.
4. The party will not allow anybody to be above the Kabaka.

The programme also included a general commitment to economic development, social welfare, religious freedom, racial equality and the rights of property—a commitment which neither defined nor imposed obligations. To Masembe these proposals were peripheral. His mind was fixed on the central issues which recur in all his writings and foreshadowed many of the themes of Kabaka Yekka: the emphasis on preserving 'traditional' Buganda, the link between 'traditional' Buganda and the supremacy of the Kabakaship, the rejection of party politics in favour of popular unity, the uncompromising, even menacing, distinction between 'loyalty' and 'rebellion'.

Masembe was not alone in trying to launch a Ganda party in early 1961. A number of politicians, veterans of progressive politics in Buganda like J. W. Kiwanuka and E. M. K. Mulira, were also working to form new parties or new coalitions out of old factions. Basically they all had the same objective: to arouse and unify the Baganda to protect the kingdom's position within Uganda.[7] The professional politicians, however, and in particular the progressives, were at a double disadvantage; their own loyalty was in question, and they all wanted to be leaders rather than followers. Although Masembe was aware of both these drawbacks, he tried to base his Conservative party on a series of alliances between these leaders of the small political factions. He soon experienced what he had already foreseen: the various groups were incapable of establishing unity among themselves, let alone of inspiring it in the rest of Buganda. And without a popular base there was no chance of winning the support from Mengo[8] essential for political success in the kingdom. So, on the advice of

[6] The programme appears in two versions in 71 (ii). The following paragraph is based on the second revised plan.
[7] The details of the manoeuvres can be followed in the *Uganda Argus* and in the vernacular press in early May. One of the moves involved the formation of the Federal party led by Mulira and financed by Masembe. The party held a general meeting at Kampala, but only thirty-five people attended. Interviews: Masembe-Kabali, 2 and 9 May 1965; Mulira, 3 June 1965.   [8] Mengo was the seat of the Kabaka's government.

Antoni Tamale, a close friend from the prison service days, Masembe decided to begin again—this time to unite 'the rich and the poor' in a popular movement and to by-pass the well-known politicians.[9]

Masembe turned first to those of his own kind, men who were substantial landowners from respected and prominent families. One obvious source for recruits was the Kakamega club.[10] This was a social club which had evolved out of friendships established when the young Kabaka was at Budo in the early 1940s. Masembe himself joined Kakamega after meeting some of the Kabaka's ex-school friends in the prison service. The club was exclusive; it was expensive, almost entirely Anglican, and the large majority of its thirty members came from notable families. The Kabaka was patron and principal host, his friends gathering around him for all-night drinking parties, outdoor sport, musical evenings and other amusements. A number of them, like John Bakka, Latimer Mpagi and James Lutaya, became leading neo-traditionalists in the later 1950s. They were all Kabaka's men, by conviction and through personal acquaintance. It was natural, therefore, for Masembe to turn to these people when it became a question of 'helping our friend'. The Kabaka thought so too. When in mid-May Masembe suggested the idea of a public demonstration of loyalty, the Kabaka approved the plan, urging him to 'consult our friends in Kakamega'.[11]

Five members of Kakamega, including Bakka, Mpagi and Tamale, joined Masembe to form Kabaka Yekka. These Kakamega members, however, constituted only one group within the movement. Other Kabaka Yekka founders came from an existing loyalist society base in Bulemezi county and from another group known as the 'chief's children'.[12] Together the three groups helped to foster the image of Kabaka Yekka as a collection of well-born and substantial landowners and business men, men who were independent of the Kabaka's government or not at the very centre of power, men anxious to safeguard a privileged position in Ganda society. The image was largely true of the intentions and characteristics of these people, but only partly true of Kabaka Yekka itself. For Tamale, through his contacts in the newspaper business, had introduced Masembe to a number of small traders, transporters and political activists who lived and worked near Kampala and who came into the movement as founder members. Indeed, more than half of the members on the 'official' list of thirty-seven founders, drafted on 24 May, were men of this type from the Kampala

[9] Delegates' Conference, *Minutes*, 4 March 1962, 71 (v).

[10] The Kakamega folder is listed as no. 67 in the library at Makerere University College.

[11] Interview: Masembe-Kabali, 9 May 1965. Mpagi, Bakka and Tamale informed the writer that they were given similar advice.

[12] See Mukasa, 'KY not a political party'. Mukasa's account attaches prime importance to these two groups in the formation of Kabaka Yekka. Although the present writer would argue that in point of time Masembe first approached those who can be identified as members of the Kakamega club, the precise location of the original source for recruits is less important than establishing the fact there there was a considerable overlap in the membership of the three groups.

area.[13] Some of them, like Sam Kalule, a hairdresser from Wandegeya, had been involved in the Uganda National Movement;[14] others like Ali Kitandwe, also a Uganda National Movement activist, had formed their own loyalist groups, combining a certain economic radicalism with some preaching and rowdyism on behalf of the Kintu government[15] in the Kampala suburbs of Natete and Katwe. Kabaka Yekka founders, then, were drawn from two areas and two levels of Ganda society: from the Kampala area and from the nearer counties, from the small-time 'malcontents'[16] of the towns, and from the friends and backbone of the establishment in the counties.

Very broadly, the founders had three things in common. First, they were all non-Catholics, and because of this it is tempting to see Kabaka Yekka in this early stage as an Anglican–Muslim combination against an alleged Catholic–Democratic Party threat to seize power in Buganda. Yet, if only for tactical reasons, the founders recognized that it was important to disguise this apparent religious orientation. After all, the object was to unite the Baganda, half of whom were Catholics.

Secondly, the founders were united in their devotion to throne and country and chose the name 'Kabaka Yekka' to express their stand. This did not mean that they shared a common view about the existing arrangements of Ganda society. Members of the Natete group and several of the minor 'preachers' who joined the movement belonged to the populist tradition of Ganda politics. Many of them had agitated for social and economic reform from as far back as the 1940s. For them Kabaka Yekka represented another means to advance their cause against the chiefly hierarchy. If there was an apparent contradiction in working both for the Kintu government and for the removal of the powers and privileges of the neo-traditionalist chiefs, it did not seem to occur to them. In any case the presence of this radical strain greatly worried Mpagi and Bakka, and explains why the latter opposed a later idea to establish a Kabaka Yekka office in Katwe.[17] Nevertheless, the different traditions could work together because of a further assumption that the Kabaka represented each and all of the sectional interests in Ganda society. This assumption was brought to the surface in the first Kabaka Yekka pamphlet published in

[13] 71 (ii). Unfortunately, one list, dated 24 May 1961 and shown to the writer in 1965, does not appear to be in the files. The figure of thirty-seven has been taken from this list. The folder includes several other lists, however, which match the one Masembe described as the 'official' list except that there are some important omissions and additions. Dr Lumu is cited in one place as a founder. In fact he stayed out. Interviews: Masembe-Kabali, 16 May 1965; Lumu, 30 June 1965. See note 30 below.

[14] See above, p. 421.   [15] See above, p. 420.

[16] The phrase 'political malcontents' was used by Professor R. C. Pratt in referring to this sort of people: quoted in D. A. Low, 'The advent of populism in Buganda', *Comparative Studies in Society and History*, vi (1963–4), 424. It is one of the assumptions of this article that the populist 'outburst' in 1959 carried over to 1961–2 in that the lesser known figures in the UNM played important roles off-stage in Kabaka Yekka.

[17] Interview: Bakka, 5 August 1965.

July, in which a letter signed by 'the people of Wankulukuku' claimed: 'We peasants in blood deeds and in nativity have a peasants' council in our hearts which prevents us from being weaned away from our Kabaka.'[18] It was to be one of Kabaka Yekka's outstanding achievements to bind interests of this kind to those represented by Mpagi and Bakka, to identify particular causes with the larger cause of throne and 'country'.

Yet Kabaka Yekka's early unity was more than an accident of its diversity. Whether they were neo-traditionalists or radicals, the founders were all patriots. They all believed that Buganda was a separate entity, distinctive above all because of its throne and institutions, the cornerstones of the Ganda identity.[19] A crucial development since 1955 had been the way in which these sentiments had been focused even more on the Kabakaship as the symbol and guardian of the 'national' interest. Simply, if the Kabaka were to be superseded in his kingdom, Buganda would cease to exist; 'without him there is no Muganda';[20] the traditions, the clans and the culture would be destroyed. The founders were certain of this. But they did not argue for outright secession. A statement of the kind which insisted that the Kabaka and the Lukiko alone represented Buganda's interests, a claim which applied equally against political parties within Buganda and to a government outside, was not pressed to the conclusion that Buganda should become a separate nation state. What the founders demanded was that the Kabaka and his Lukiko should be supreme in those things which mattered to the Baganda. Given these conditions, Buganda could take part in Uganda. Tamale made the point in the following way: 'There is no doubt that Buganda is the heart of Uganda. Buganda is the Engine of Uganda. Therefore after the Engine has been set up, the Buganda Kingdom should not be afraid to unite with the other parts of the United self-governing Uganda.'[21] The founders' stand presupposed Buganda's superior and central position within Uganda. It was an insular rather than a secessionist position, although the step from the one to the other was both short and logical.

The founders discovered that they had a third view in common. They wanted to present Kabaka Yekka as a popular movement and not as a political party. Masembe's experience led him to insist that Kabaka Yekka should not even have a formal structure, since he feared that the members would become absorbed in struggles for party office. Masembe in fact had come to believe that party machines were unable to reach the people. Mpagi saw the problem in the personalities who ran them. He insisted that the professional politicians, and in particular E. M. K. Mulira, be excluded

---

[18] First Kabaka Yekka letter, July 1961. The quotations which follow are based on two Kabaka Yekka letters or pamphlets edited by Masembe and published in July and August in 1961 and cited, for convenience, as First and Second.

[19] Cf. Welbourn, *Religion and Politics*, chap. XI.

[20] Sam Kalule, Second Kabaka Yekka Letter, August 1961.

[21] First Kabaka Yekka Letter, op. cit.

altogether.[22] Mpagi's view was that Mulira's past opposition to Mengo would discredit Kabaka Yekka, and that his present opportunism would divert its energies. Mpagi believed that the function of Kabaka Yekka was to protect the Kabaka and not to promote the careers of his subjects. He was convinced that the two objectives were fundamentally incompatible— and Kabaka Yekka's later history goes far to bear out this contention.

Although Kabaka Yekka soon expanded to include some Catholics and some professional politicans, most of the ideas to emerge from the founders' discussions at the end of May, the demonstration in June, and the pamphlets issued in July and August became the basis of Kabaka Yekka's propaganda. Not that the founders' invented an ideology—the material was already there, the ideas had all been aired before, and notably by the All-Buganda party.[23] The founders' contribution was to bring together a number of these ideas, to give focus and a name to a host of emotional attachments, to simplify Buganda's stand to one eternal proposition: 'That the Kabaka shall never be preceded by anybody else on the entire soil of Buganda. KABAKA YEKKA.'[24]

Masembe and his friends soon found that, while their message was popular, the peasants and traders in the country were reluctant to commit themselves until Mengo had signalled its approval. The problem was that Mengo was unlikely to take notice in the absence of an irresistible mass movement, and that such a movement itself was unlikely in the absence of Mengo's support. After the demonstration, therefore, with the Kabaka himself well in the background, the ministers, the chiefs and the political factions all remained aloof. Mengo alone could make something of Kabaka Yekka—and in November 1961 it was ready to do so.

The failure of secession and of the election boycott had forced the Kabaka's ministers to consider alternative schemes for securing Buganda's special position. On one side they were under pressure from the Lukiko to obtain the return of 'our things'. On the other side there was pressure from the governor to attend the Constitutional Conference in London in September, using promises of a continued withdrawal of financial grants at a time of a worsening budgetary position in Buganda. The breakthrough came following negotiations between leading Lukiko members and the leaders of the Uganda People's Congress. For while the Kabaka Yekka founders were spreading the 'gospel' in July and August, top level and

[22] Interview: Mpagi, 8 Aug. 1965. Mulira attended the demonstration and was photographed holding the manifesto of his Federal party. Mpagi used this as evidence that Mulira was really a self-seeker. Although formally excluded, Mulira continued an informal connexion with Kabaka Yekka through his friendship with Masembe. Interview: Mulira, 3 June and 23 July 1965.
[23] Formed in 1954, this party came to press for immediate independence for Buganda— with the other provinces and districts of Uganda to follow and join Buganda if they wanted to. See, for example, *Uganda Argus*, 26 Feb. 1957 and 25 Aug. 1959. At least six Kabaka Yekka founder members had belonged to this group and some, associated with the group, believe that Kabaka Yekka was simply the successor to the All-Buganda Party. Interview: Mrs Nkata, 23 Mar. 1969.   [24] First Kabaka Yekka Letter, op. cit., note 18.

secret discussions had been proceeding on the basis of the Munster recommendations for future constitutional relationships within Uganda.[25] The result was a compromise. In return for the Uganda People's Congress support for Buganda's claim to a special federal status, Buganda's representatives agreed to attend the London Conference. With the backing of the Uganda People's Congress, Buganda secured most of its demands at the Conference, including a provision in the new Buganda Agreement allowing the Lukiko to select Buganda's twenty-one representatives to the National Assembly. The Democratic Party leaders saw the dangers and protested. For although the Colonial Secretary had insisted that, apart from the twenty saza chiefs and the six Kabaka's nominees, the Lukiko itself should be directly elected, it was expected that candidates supported by Mengo would win most of the elected seats. In this way Mengo would control the selection of Buganda's representatives to the National Assembly and so preserve Mengo's authority within Buganda and destroy the Democratic Party's national majority. To ensure this, Amos Sempa negotiated a further agreement by which the Uganda People's Congress would stand aside from the Lukiko elections in favour of a Kabaka's party. In the event Mengo turned to Kabaka Yekka, a movement dedicated to limited and proper objects, and a movement which had popular appeal if not yet a popular following. Besides, there was no time to organize a substitute. The Lukiko elections were due in early 1962. On 10 November, therefore, the Kabaka's ministers agreed to join Kabaka Yekka.[26]

In November Kabaka Yekka became a mass movement and an election machine. Mengo's decision was the turning-point; anticipating it, most of the political factions dissolved themselves and joined Kabaka Yekka a few days earlier;[27] following it, the chiefly hierarchy was enlisted to become the principal agent in Kabaka Yekka's electoral campaign. The professional politicians were delighted. Here was the chance to prove their loyalty, exercise their talent and experience popular support. Above all, in the name of loyalty, they could use Kabaka Yekka as a lever for promotion and even as a base for operations against the establishment. The senior saza chiefs were less pleased. They could not free themselves of the suspicion that Kabaka Yekka was just another political party seeking to advance the

[25] The Munster Commission which began meeting after the 1961 elections advised that Buganda should be given a special federal status. The main negotiators were G. Ibingira and B. K. Kirya for the Uganda People's Congress and Dr Lumu and Amos Sempa for the Baganda. Later, Dr Obote intervened directly, and he made the necessary offers to the Ganda leaders and finally to the Kabaka himself.

[26] J. P. Musoke, the Omulamuzi (minister of justice), a Catholic, announced later that he had not joined Kabaka Yekka (*Uganda Argus*, 1 Feb. 1962).

[27] One group led by Augustine Kamya, a prominent figure around Katwe, refused to participate, despite Masembe's efforts. Kamya eventually formed his own organization ('Amabega gwa Namulondo'—'People behind the Throne') to fight the election. All his candidates lost their deposits. Kamya's complaint was that Kabaka Yekka leaders were self-seekers who would destroy the throne. The complaint against Kamya was that he always had to be leader.

ambitions of its members. Still the chiefs were constitutionally bound to follow the Kabaka's ministers, and the Baganda were bound to follow their chiefs. So Kabaka Yekka became the new bandwagon in Ganda politics, and once rolling, it was vital to be on board. Even Asian businessmen were affected—or at least those whose memories of the 1959 trade boycott were balanced by fears of further reprisals—and they provided most of the financial backing for Kabaka Yekka's campaign.[28] The important point is that while the ideas expounded by Masembe and his friends were readily acceptable, Mengo's commitment was essential if Kabaka Yekka itself was to become the acceptable means of expressing them. And, once given, Mengo's commitment turned Kabaka Yekka's opponents into heretics. Ultimately, then, the key to Kabaka Yekka's success lay in the hands of those closest to the Kabaka.

This transformation of Kabaka Yekka inevitably increased the number of interest groups which had to be contained within the movement. In a sense, the one common denominator had become opposition to the Democratic Party. Some of the progressives who joined Kabaka Yekka were primarily concerned to defeat the Democratic Party in Buganda as a step towards establishing national unity in Uganda. But the significant division lay between the neo-traditionalists and those reformers and ambitious younger men who were primarily interested in Buganda rather than Uganda politics. The clash between these groups, in the period from November 1961 to February 1962, came to matter almost as much as the election itself. For it was a clash over who should dominate Buganda after the Democratic Party had been eliminated.

The first stage in this internal conflict came with the election of a steering committee to lead Kabaka Yekka's campaign for the election.[29] In mid-November fifty branch representatives and former members of the political factions selected the twenty-one members of the steering committee. Only six of those elected, including Masembe, Bakka, Mpagi and Sam Kalule, were Kabaka Yekka founders; the Kabaka's ministers were not represented at all. Most members of the new committee may conveniently be divided into two groups. First, there were the former leaders of the political factions, and principally of the several surviving versions of the old Uganda National Congress, who felt compelled to join Kabaka Yekka as a means of pacifying the neo-traditionalists and so keeping Buganda within Uganda. Some, and in particular I. K. Musazi, a life-long opponent of Mengo, were frankly hostile to Mpagi's vision of Kabaka Yekka

[28] Unfortunately it has not been possible to determine how much Asian money was given to Kabaka Yekka. The funds were collected by individual Baganda. No accounts were kept and many charges of misuse of funds were made after the elections. All that the writer can say at the moment is that Kabaka Yekka was given several hundred thousand shillings. Masembe claimed that he spent his pension and 40,000 shillings of his own money on Kabaka Yekka. (General Meeting, *Minutes*, 19 May 1962, 71 (iv).)

[29] The committee was elected just before 15 Nov. 1961. The list of elected members will be found in 71 (ii).

as a buttress for neo-traditionalism, and did not share Masembe's emotional involvement with 'traditional' Buganda and the Kabakaship. On the whole, however, the Uganda National Congress group did not play much of an active role in Kabaka Yekka. The second group was more important. It included the educated younger men—Dr Lumu, Francis Walugembe, A. D. Lubowa[30]—whose popularity in the Lukiko had encouraged their ambition to displace the existing political leadership in Buganda. By now Masembe had come to share their objectives; his aversion to 'leadership scrambles' did not affect his own leadership ambitions.[31] These groups had two things in common: an essentially functional view of Kabaka Yekka and a desire for change in Buganda. But it was the second group, joined by Abu Mayanja, the extremely clever and ambitious Kabaka's minister for education, a group wanting to change the rulers rather than the system, who were determined to use Kabaka Yekka as an instrument for change.

The composition and form of the steering committee caused so much bitterness that the committee itself was almost disbanded.[32] Founder members complained that Kabaka Yekka had been taken over by its former opponents and by self-seekers. One, an activist from the days of the Uganda National Movement, objected to the preponderance of men from King's College, Budo, probably because populist leaders of his kind had come to distrust the reformist gestures of educated politicians who, once in office, quickly forgot about the 'common man'.[33] Other objections came from local loyalist groups who did not want any interference from Kampala. This difficulty arose partly from Masembe's own conception of Kabaka Yekka as a movement which would unite existing groups rather than superimpose an organization and a power structure. One such group which flatly asserted its independence of Kampala was Walugembe's own following in Masaka district. Walugembe himself was not disturbed by a possible conflict of loyalties. For in his view, Masaka district, rich in men and resources (and Catholics like himself), was the real centre of Buganda.[34]

[30] Lumu was a doctor, Walugembe a businessman, Lubowa a journalist. Lumu and Lubowa were then members of the Lukiko Constitutional Committee; Lubowa and Walugembe were Catholics; Walugembe had been a member of the Democratic Party and Lumu of the All-Buganda party; Walugembe and Lubowa were to become ministers in the Kabaka's government; after the Lukiko elections Lumu failed in his bid to replace Kintu, and became a minister in the Uganda government.

[31] Masembe has always denied that he was ambitious for office, but the evidence points increasingly to his attempts from late 1961 to obtain a ministerial post in the Kabaka's government. When Lumu challenged Kintu in March 1961, Masembe was on the steering committee 'ticket' for a place in the government.

[32] It was not until early January that it was finally decided to retain the steering committee. Delegates' Meeting, *Minutes*, 5 Jan. 1961, 71 (ii).

[33] Musa Bulwadda; see also the complaints by Katwe and Setimba (founder members), Steering Committee, *Minutes*, 15 Nov. 1961, 71 (ii). See also Steering Committee, *Minutes*, 20 Nov. 1961, 71 (v). One objection was that the Uganda National Congress group had not dissolved itself; see the press release by A. Kironde, 18 Nov. 1961, 71 (ii).

[34] Interview: Walugembe, 3 Aug. 1965.

The major problem, however, concerned the relationship between the steering committee and the chiefs. Nelson Sebugwawo, the saza chief of Kyandondo, did not approve of the idea of a steering committee in the first place.[35] He proposed that a committee of seven should look after affairs in Kampala, leaving the main work to organizations in the counties. His motive was plain enough. The great fear was that a central committee, through its command of branch activity, would create a power base to rob the chiefs of their local authority and reduce their influence at Mengo. It is this consideration which largely explains the chiefs' resistance to the Kampala politicians and to the campaigners sent out from the centre. The steering committee, on the other hand, lacked the means to combat this resistance. Kabaka Yekka had been built on enthusiasm rather than organization and, just as there was no clear chain of authority to bind Masaka to Kampala, there was no way of incorporating the chiefs in a structure which was not directly and formally controlled by the Kabaka's ministers. In any event, if Kabaka Yekka were to win the election, it would be the administration, headed by the ministers and worked by the chiefs, which would have to play the major role. At first the steering committee was happy about this. After all, the chiefs could virtually order a Kabaka Yekka victory at the polls. For this reason Masembe, who acted as secretary of the steering committee, instructed the campaigners to co-operate with the chiefs. He pointed out that, if there were no co-operation, the people would distrust Kabaka Yekka.[36] Masembe was well aware that the Baganda regarded the chiefs as spokesmen for the Kabaka, and that the Kabaka Yekka campaigners could do little more than remind the people to listen. The main trouble was that, by deferring to the chiefs, the steering committee abdicated control over the pre-selection of candidates, with the result that the new Lukiko was independent of the 'party machine'.

This was a problem for the future. What mattered in early 1962 was that Masembe's call for co-operation was often ignored by the chiefs themselves.[37] Kabaka Yekka candidates were selected by local committees over which a saza or gombolola (subcounty) chief would preside. Other local prominent figures—school-teachers, farmers and traders—would then assist the chief in choosing one of their number to stand for a particular constituency.[38] Although delegations sent out from Kampala sought to advise local committees on procedure, organization and tactics, and to adjudicate on pre-selection disputes, and although there are a number of examples of these delegations persuading local committees to choose

[35] Steering Committee, *Minutes*, 15 Nov. 1961, 71(ii).
[36] General Meeting, *Minutes*, 20 January 1961, 71(v). The Kabaka Yekka campaigners were young men from the Kampala suburbs who were organized by Masembe to go into the constituencies. After the election they proved a source of embarrassment by demanding funds, jobs and influence.
[37] Kintu did tell Masembe to give him the names of those chiefs who failed to co-operate. Interview: Masembe-Kabali, 16 May 1965.
[38] There is a very interesting and detailed account of the pre-selection process for the constituencies in Singo county in 71(v).

Catholics and Muslims as candidates, candidates favoured by the steering committee were usually rejected at pre-selection meetings.[39] This, of course, was not something peculiar to Buganda. Local–central conflicts occur in every political system. The significant point here is that this rejection of central interference was a deliberate attempt to affirm that politics in Buganda should be conducted through the proper channels. These channels led from the *miruka* (parish) chiefs through the hierarchy to the ministers, and finally to the Kabaka himself. So while Masembe was probably exaggerating in claiming that the chiefs obstructed Kabaka Yekka's activities in every constituency, he was right to suppose that the chiefs had an interest in obstruction. In any case, there is some evidence in the Kabaka Yekka files to support Masembe's claim.[40] Apart from those like the saza chief of Buyaga who supported the Democratic Party, there were a number of chiefs, Anglicans like Nelson Sebugwawo and the saza chief of Busiro, who flatly refused to tolerate the opening of Kabaka Yekka branches and who insisted on personally selecting Kabaka Yekka candidates.[41] All the non-Democratic Party chiefs, many of them avowed separatists, were urging the Baganda to vote for Kabaka Yekka, but their idea of Kabaka Yekka was a movement working through and sustaining the existing administrative and social structure. They did not like the Kabaka Yekka represented by the steering committee, and they worked successfully to curb its dominance. No doubt their view of the steering committee as a group of mischievous radicals was too pessimistic. But it was well to be sure.

The Kabaka Yekka which fought the Lukiko elections was not the same as the movement which had emerged out of the meetings at Masembe's house in May 1961. By February 1962 it had acquired mass support drawn from all levels of Ganda society. The simple objectives had become overlaid with personal ambitions and factionalism. Most important of all, Kabaka Yekka had become the instrument of official policy. Kabaka Yekka as directed by the steering committee was not the Kabaka Yekka which the Baganda had supported in the Lukiko elections. For the Kabaka Yekka which won these elections was a movement more obviously protecting a social structure and the ruling generation as well as the throne, the Lukiko, the clans, the customs and the traditions. The question is—why did this Kabaka Yekka win so decisively?

The victory was certainly impressive. On election day, 22 February, Kabaka Yekka candidates received 90 per cent of the votes cast and won

---

[39] One steering committee candidate who was accepted was L. Kalule-Settala, later minister of finance in the Uganda government, who was a member of the Uganda People's Congress standing in the name of Kabaka Yekka.

[40] It should be noted that the claim was made well after the election. Interview: 16 May 1965. See also General Meeting, *Minutes*, 19 May 1962, 71 (iv).

[41] See the reports of Kabaka Yekka delegations in 71 (i) and (vii). One of the difficulties in making this assessment is that the delegations would indiscriminately accuse all who opposed them of having Democratic Party sympathies.

65 of the 68 seats.[42] It is true that 10 per cent of the potential electorate of 900,000 did not register, that nearly 10 per cent of the registered electorate did not vote, and that nearly 10 per cent of the voters did not support Kabaka Yekka.[43] It is also true that Kabaka Yekka was helped by electoral arrangements which permitted a Kabaka's government official to draw up constituency boundaries in Kabaka Yekka's favour,[44] and whereby the chiefs, most of them already committed to Kabaka Yekka, were appointed to assist as registration agents and returning officers. Doubtless a number of Catholics in Masaka district were intimidated into supporting Kabaka Yekka or staying away from the polls. Yet when all the necessary qualifications are made, the fact remains that, as some Democratic Party leaders acknowledged,[45] Kabaka Yekka was the popular party in Buganda. It was partly a matter of crude intimidation, wild misrepresentation and clever electioneering.[46] It was largely, however, the effect of simplifying the issue into a choice between 'Ben' (Benedicto Kiwanuka) and the Kabaka.

In posing the choice in this way, Kabaka Yekka was presented as the defender of the faith, the party which was for Buganda and the throne. The Democratic Party had no counter to this sort of propaganda. Kiwanuka announced an increase in the price paid to coffee farmers, he promised to turn Buganda into a democracy, he denounced 'reactionaries' and 'tribalists', his followers swore loyalty to their Kabaka. The difficulty was that the chiefs and the campaigners were able to insist that to oppose Kabaka Yekka was to oppose the Kabaka. It was an argument which did not require elaboration and this was just as well. Kabaka Yekka had nothing else to say and nothing else could preserve its unity. Abu Mayanja did write a pamphlet promising strong, progressive, stable and impartial government. On his own admission the object was to impress the European and Asian voters.[47] The pamphlet which conveyed the real Kabaka Yekka message—*Kabaka atta Nabbe* ('The Kabaka kills the destroyer of the termite hill')—was written by a founder member and, despite being officially disowned by the steering committee, it was actively promoted as

[42] *Uganda National Assembly Elections, 1926*, appendix H. The three Democratic Party seats were in the 'Lost Counties'; in one the Kabaka Yekka candidate failed to submit his nomination papers on time. It is worth noting that one month before the election a Kabaka Yekka report on all constituencies expressed doubts about Kabaka Yekka's prospects in nearly half of them. See 24 Jan. 1962 in 71 (i).

[43] Cf. Low, *Political Parties in Uganda*, 55.

[44] The basic complaint was that the official (William Kalema—later a member of the Uganda People's Congress/Kabaka Yekka government and from mid-1963 a member of the Uganda People's Congress) subdivided Catholic strongholds to break up the Democratic Party vote. Kalema claimed that his object was to keep religion out of politics. Interview: 2 Aug. 1965.

[45] Interview: P. Semogerere, Publicity Secretary, Democratic Party, 27 July 1965; B. Bataringaya, in early 1962 a Democratic Party minister, later a leader of the Opposition in the National Assembly and then a Uganda People's Congress minister, 23 July 1965.

[46] The English and vernacular press are full of the enormities practised by both sides. For some good examples of misrepresentation see the Catholic paper, *Munno*, 11 Jan. 1962, and *Uganda Eyogera*, 15 Jan. 1962.

[47] Interview: 23 June 1965.

Kabaka Yekka 'policy'.[48] The booklet concentrated on only one issue: the question of who would exercise ultimate authority in independent Uganda. The writer claimed that the Democratic Party proposed to give this authority to the prime minister acting under the Head of State, who would be appointed by the Queen. Although the Kabaka had fought for years to regain his independence, 'the English want to hand over authority to a Scarecrow' (Kiwanuka). The writer's answer was to ask a devastating and fundamental question: 'What sort of Muganda are you who allows Benedicto Kiwanuka or any other person to sit over the Lion—His Highness the Kabaka of Buganda...?' In fact the question was so fundamental that it had become irrelevant whether the 'enemy' was the Democratic Party or some other party. It was a question which reminded a Catholic that he was first of all a Muganda, that the election was about identity and not about policy. Finally it was a question which reflected Kabaka Yekka's development into 'a movement of Buganda against the world', a movement represented by Masembe the patriot and conservative, rather than by Masembe the progressive who in 1962 had come to regard the chiefs as enemies of the people. So in asking this question Kabaka Yekka, the 'Kabaka's party', was bound to win the Lukiko elections.

The Lukiko elections marked the high point and last phase of the movement which was publicly launched on 10 June 1961. The 'enemy' had been defeated in Buganda, and in April, after national elections in the rest of Uganda, a Uganda People's Congress/Kabaka Yekka national government was formed. But the removal of the Democratic Party did not eliminate the problem which Kiwanuka had posed. No central government could permit the Kabaka to be the sovereign power in his kingdom. The Uganda People's Congress itself had invested too much emotional capital in the idea of national unity to tolerate the pretensions of 'tribalists' and 'feudalists'. Short of separation, therefore, Kabaka Yekka's objective, as understood by most of its followers, could never have been achieved. In early 1962 this did not present a serious problem; Dr Obote still needed the alliance, and Amos Sempa could still believe that it was a binding 'omukago' (blood brotherhood).[49] One fact, however, was inescapable. Kabaka Yekka had stirred and reflected emotions and interests which were frankly isolationist; it had formulated a case which pointed to separation. The movement had also aroused something which could survive its own disintegration into warring factions after the defeat of the Democratic Party. More important, Kabaka Yekka's very success in 1962 implied that any real accommodation between Buganda and Uganda was extremely unlikely. This is not to say that the confrontation of 1966 was inevitable. The argument is that when, in May 1966, the Lukiko ordered the Uganda government to leave the soil of Buganda, it did no more than press Kabaka Yekka's

[48] *Kabaka Atta Nabbe* (Kabaka Yekka, 1962).
[49] Interviews: Sempa, 31 May and 8 June 1965; Masembe-Kabali, 16 May 1965.

case to its logical conclusion. In the end secession became the only answer for those who posed the question asked in *Kabaka atta Nabbe*. For, by 1966, Dr Obote had become the 'other person'.

SUMMARY

In May 1961 a small group of men formed the Kabaka Yekka movement in the Kingdom of Buganda. Their simple objective was to unite the Baganda behind the throne, the symbol and guarantee of Buganda's separate identity. The great fear was that the election of a national Democratic Party government in the previous March had marked a decisive stage in the destruction of Buganda's special position within Uganda. Kabaka Yekka's appeal to Ganda loyalty was instantly successful, but it was not until the Kabaka's ministers agreed to accept membership of independent Uganda, and to support Kabaka Yekka in Buganda, that Kabaka Yekka could win popular support and deal effectively with the Democratic Party. But when Kabaka Yekka became an 'official' movement, its whole nature and function was changed. There had been differences at the beginning, but now the simple objective barely disguised the contradictions within the movement, while Kabaka Yekka became a means to personal promotion as well as the guardian of the 'national' interest. Above all, Kabaka Yekka now included the chiefs, who wanted to preserve the existing political and social arrangements within Buganda. So by February 1962 Kabaka Yekka had become the party for the Baganda and for the *status quo* within Buganda. It was a party which, because it was identified with the Kabakaship, was able to destroy the Democratic Party in elections for the Buganda Lukiko, and a party which, although in alliance with Dr Obote's Uganda People's Congress in national politics, had aroused sentiments and interests pointing ultimately, if not irrevocably, to Ganda separation.

The Journal of Modern African Studies, 7, 3 (1969), pp. 369-406

Ghana, The Congo, and The United Nations

by JITENDRA MOHAN*

The recurrent crisis in the (ex-Belgian) Congo, which first exploded soon after the country's independence on 30 June 1960, was the main event in the history both of the United Nations (U.N.) and of Africa during the 1960s. Its first phase (with which this paper largely deals) opened with the mutiny of the *Force publique* on 5 July, the intervention of Belgian troops on 10 July, and the proclamation of Katanga's independence on 11 July; it came to an end with the suppression of Katanga's secession, tentatively in December 1961 and conclusively in January 1963. The *Opération des Nations Unies au Congo* (O.N.U.C.) was authorised by the Security Council on 14 July, on the independent initiative of the U.N. Secretary-General, Dag Hammarskjöld, and in response to the Congo Government's appeals to the U.N. for technical and military assistance. The operation was the biggest and costliest by far in the life of the U.N.;[1] and its course was marked by political as well as financial ruin, from which the U.N. has never quite recovered. Evidence for this was furnished early. By the time the operation formally came to an end on 30 June 1964, the Congo was already in the thick of the second phase of the crisis; this phase, which began with the outbreak of rebellion in Kwilu in January 1964, was brought to an end of sorts by the Belgian–American military intervention in Stanleyville in November 1964, which produced few signs of activity by the U.N.

The Congo crisis also proved to be the turning-point in the recent political history of Africa. In the so-called Year of Africa it gave independent African states, whose number and self-consciousness were sharply on the increase, their first big opportunity to play a prominent international role, on an African issue, too; it gave them also their first and altogether disagreeable taste of foreign intervention and of the

---

* Lecturer in Political Science, University of Ghana, Legon.
[1] The so-called U.N. action in Korea, although far grander in scale, was essentially a war operation by western powers, conducted in the name of the U.N. but in fact under the command and control of the United States. In the light of the subsequent development of the U.N., it is hardly a relevant precedent.

cold war. It marked the first major break in the tidal wave of decolonisation, a recession in the triumphal march of nationalism in Africa. It materially affected the setting and progress of the movement of African unity,[1] immediately by crystallising the division of African states into 'conservatives' (Brazzaville, December 1960) and 'radicals' (Casablanca, January 1961), and in the long run by turning the course of the movement and de-radicalising it through its growing incapsulation in inter-governmental institutions and bureaucratic procedures. The over-all deflationary effect of the Congo crisis on Africa may be seen, first, in the epidemic of military *coups* on the continent and, secondly, in the impotence of African states—within the framework of the essentially conservative Organisation of African Unity (O.A.U.)—in the face of U.D.I. in Rhodesia and later of the civil war in Nigeria.

For Ghana, as for other African states, the crisis inaugurated an exercise in re-education and in the reorientation of policies. With particular regard to Ghana it was to give shape, substance, and direction to the keenly felt need among its leaders for radical change, which had yet found no definite or coherent ideological or institutional expression. During the year preceding the Congo's independence, the Convention People's Party (C.P.P.) Government, led by Kwame Nkrumah, began to look for and try new ideas and institutions, being increasingly conscious of the limitations of the rather primitive tactics of the anti-colonial struggle as the basis for a new strategy against the powerful and all-pervasive imperialism in which Ghana, a small, under-developed, as well as newly independent state found itself enmeshed at every step. By the time the Congo became independent, Nkrumah and the C.P.P. had a mixed bag of initiatives on their agenda, which were already meeting with obstruction and difficulties which the party leaders were predisposed to attribute to the 'manoeuvres and machinations' of imperialist interests, within Ghana and without. These difficulties Nkrumah (among others) called 'neo-colonialism'; the meanderings of the protracted Congo crisis were to help him expound them before Africa and the world at large.

In the overarching shadow of the crisis, too, the C.P.P. leaders sought to devise a new economic strategy for Ghana and a new political strategy for Africa. These strategies were, rather, the two prongs—one internal, the other external—of a single strategy, characteristic of

---

[1] For an illuminating analysis of the Congo crisis in relation to the movement of African unity, see Immanuel Wallerstein, *Africa: the politics of unity* (New York, 1967), ch. 4.

radical nationalism, which aimed at the total economic as well as political independence of Ghana-in-Africa.[1] The crisis was at the same time a critical lesson in the ambiguities of radical nationalism and in its limitations as an instrument of small-power revolutionary diplomacy.

BACKGROUND

Nkrumah's interest and Ghana's involvement in the Congo antedated the latter's independence and subsequent troubles. A handful of the politically minded among, perhaps, some 300 Ghanaian citizens in the Congo—the majority in Léopoldville and Stanleyville, mostly employed by commercial firms—sent occasional reports on the political situation in the Congo to George Padmore and others who, during 1958-9, administered Ghana's 'African policy'. When, some weeks after the Léopoldville riots of January 1959, Joseph Kasavubu and some other *Alliance des Bakongo* (Abako) leaders were flown to Belgium—to be imprisoned and tried there, it was presumed—Padmore was very active behind the scenes arranging legal representation for them. A Ghanaian official on the secretariat of the All-African People's Conference was specially flown out from Accra to Brussels via London to make the arrangements. (The arrangements turned out to be unnecessary, as Kasavubu and his colleagues were not put on trial.) But, while recognising and supporting the Abako as (at the time) an articulate and well-organised anti-colonial movement, the Ghanaians were already much bothered by the 'tribalism', separatism (subsequently modified in favour of a loose federation), and over-all conservatism of the Abako leaders. This in part accounted for the ambivalence in Nkrumah's attitude towards Kasavubu, which was to be a marked feature of Ghana's policies in the Congo.

With Patrice Lumumba, by contrast, Nkrumah felt a marked and mutual affinity. Lumumba had attended the Accra gathering of African nationalists in December 1958—for him a highly stimulating experience which quickly radicalised his outlook and gave his nationalism a pan-African perspective. In Lumumba Nkrumah saw an African nationalist very much of his own type and persuasion—an 'Nkrumaist' in the making, so to speak—and, given the size and importance of an independent Congo, a most valuable prospective ally. Lumumba, in his turn, was greatly impressed by Nkrumah and Ghana. He took Nkrumah

---

[1] I have analysed some aspects of Ghana's emerging foreign policy in 'Ghana Parliament and Foreign Policy, 1957–60', in *The Economic Bulletin of Ghana* (Legon), x, 4, 1966; and I have surveyed the general course of Ghanaian politics, with an accent on internal developments, in 'Nkrumah and Nkrumaism', in *The Socialist Register 1967* (London, 1967).

as the model for his own style of leadership and the C.P.P. as the model for his own *Mouvement national congolais* (M.N.C.); later he was to eye Ghana's (first) republican constitution as a possible model for the highly centralised, unitarist pattern of government which he thought necessary to consolidate the Congo's independence and unity. 'Like the CPP of Ghana,' as Nkrumah has himself noted, 'Lumumba's MNC was the first Congolese political organisation to recognise the need for a national leader and a national movement in accordance with the principles of Pan-Africanism.'[1] While giving its main support to Lumumba and the M.N.C., however, Ghana both before and after independence encouraged an Abako–M.N.C. alliance founded upon a Kasavubu–Lumumba partnership as the most expedient combination in the particular circumstances of the Congo. This combination, in spite of the Ghanaians' growing disenchantment with Kasavubu, was to remain a major fixture of Ghana's policy until Lumumba's death.

Nor were the similarities between the C.P.P. and the M.N.C., and particularly the affinity between their two leaders, lost upon Belgian authorities. At that time Ghana was seen by many in the west, and presumably also by the Belgians, as a fairly stable and successful experiment in African self-government, which had been kept on an even keel with a fair admixture of 'multi-racial co-operation' in several vital fields and which had, at least until the end of the 1950s, had no unduly injurious effect on western interests. The Belgians, who had at first encouraged the comparatively milder nationalism of Lumumba and the M.N.C. as a counterweight to the (then) much more strident anti-colonialism of Kasavubu and the Abako, now hoped to use the Ghanaians as a moderating and stabilising influence on Lumumba, as he began to emerge as the dominant figure and more and more a 'hothead' among Congolese politicians. In any event, the Belgian ambassador in Accra consulted the Ghana Government on the problems of establishing an African administration; and Ghana was allowed to set up an office in Léopoldville on 8 June 1960, with A. Y. K. Djin as special representative. (Djin, an important C.P.P. functionary, had earlier in the year twice visited Brussels on Ghana's behalf on 'Congo business'.) The Belgians at least hoped that the Ghanaians might help to bring the feuding Congolese leaders together.[2] This Djin did with considerable success, especially by persuading Lumumba of the need to

---

[1] Kwame Nkrumah, *Challenge of the Congo* (London, 1967), p. 16.

[2] See Catherine Hoskyns, *The Congo since Independence: January 1960–December 1961* (London, 1965), pp. 62 and 77. I have drawn heavily throughout on this excellent account.

recognise the strength of the Abako, particularly in and around Léopoldville, and to come to terms with Kasavubu.

There was more to the Ghanaian interest in the Congo, however, than either Nkrumah's growing friendship with Lumumba or Belgium's flattering approaches to Ghana. By the time trouble broke out in the Congo the C.P.P. leaders were well convinced of 'the high role' that 'destiny' had called upon 'the people of Ghana' to play in Africa.[1] This conviction was articulated by the basic similarity which they perceived to exist between the 'trends of national movements' in Ghana and other African territories. The struggle, for example, of the Ghanaian and Congolese national movements for independence 'was to some extent the struggle between nationalism and tribalism; more explicitly, between a unitary system of government and federation'. Thus Katanga was equated with Ashanti and the M.N.C. with the C.P.P., while the Abako and other parties ranged against the M.N.C. were equated with the cartel of 'tribalist' parties, all of them 'designed to destroy' the C.P.P., which had 'threatened Ghana's independence' during 1954–7. The tactics then adopted by the C.P.P. could now be applied in the Congo. 'As in Ghana, I was convinced that the Congo needed a strong unitary form of government.'[2] A two-day debate on the Congo situation in the Ghana parliament on 9–10 August 1960 turned out, in the main, to be an embittered rehash of the recent past, as well as a rehearsing of Ghana's current internal disputes.

This belief of the Ghanaian leaders in the fundamental similarity of African countries and African problems is an important key to the understanding of Ghana's official reflexes during the Congo crisis. Given Ghana's position as the pioneering 'pilot-state' in tropical Africa, such a belief seemed to them to justify the application of Ghanaian experiences and solutions to the rest of Africa; it seemed to them to indicate, even more, an active Ghanaian interest and involvement in African affairs. From the very beginning of the Congo crisis the Ghanaian spokesmen maintained not only that as an African country Ghana must go to the aid of another African country in distress, but also that Ghana's fate and future were interlinked with those of the Congo. 'If we allow the independence of the Congo to be compromised in any way by the imperialist and capitalist forces, we shall expose the sovereignty and independence of all Africa to grave risk. The struggle

---

[1] See Kwame Nkrumah, *I Speak of Freedom: a statement of African ideology* (New York, 1961), p. 179.

[2] Nkrumah, *Challenge of the Congo*, p. 17.

of the Congo is therefore our struggle.'[1] Their foremost task, Nkrumah declared, was to rid Africa of colonialism in all its forms. 'In this respect, I regard myself first and foremost as an African, and then only as a Ghanaian.'[2] It followed therefore that Ghana and other African states should play a leading part in ridding the Congo of 'Belgian aggression' and 'imperialist intervention'. From there it was but a short step to the position that the African states should have a *decisive* say in the shape and substance of the Congo's independence, which was 'more than a national [i.e. Congolese] affair...[but] was more particularly an African affair'.[3]

The C.P.P. leaders' perception of the 'one-ness' of Africa—their belief in the 'inseparability' of African countries—was to be reinforced in the course of the Congo crisis by the existential link which they postulated more and more between Ghana's own 'second revolution' and 'the African revolution'. All in all, it furnished the Ghanaian leaders with a new ideological map, which, as it was unrolled, produced the most unexpected and unorthodox departures in Ghana's African policies, not least during the Congo crisis.

PROTAGONISTS

Ghana's response to the 'call' of the Congo was swift and thorough. A high-powered Ghanaian delegation left Accra by air on 11 July 1960 to assess the political and military situation in the Congo. In its first public pronouncement on the crisis on 13 July, the Ghana Government offered 'all possible aid including, if it is desired by the Government of the Congo, military assistance', either directly and alone or through and in concert with the U.N.[4] Even though that very day Congolese deputy prime minister Antoine Gizenga asked for Ghanaian troops, the Ghana Government was nevertheless anxious to avoid *direct* military aid and wished to contribute Ghanaian troops only as part of a U.N. force. The same day Nkrumah spoke by telephone with Hammarskjöld to urge the need for a quick and favourable response to

[1] Nkrumah's address to the National Assembly, Ghana, *Parliamentary Debates* (Accra), 8 August 1960, col. 644.
[2] *African Unity: a speech by Osagyefo Dr Kwame Nkrumah...on opening Africa Unity House in London, 18th March, 1961* (n.d.), p. 3. Cf. Kasavubu's message to the President of the U.N. General Assembly of 13 October 1960: 'we are first and foremost Congolese and only secondarily Africans' (U.N. document A/4560).
[3] Nkrumah, *Challenge of the Congo*, p. 14.
[4] *Correspondence exchanged between Osagyefo Dr Kwame Nkrumah...and the Leaders of the Republic of the Congo on The Congo Situation* (Accra, n.d.), p. 4. This document is hereinafter referred to as 'W.P. No. 6/60'.

the Congolese request for military assistance and to offer Ghanaian troops for that purpose. A small advance group of officers and men of the Ghana Army, headed by the Chief of Defence Staff, Major-General H. T. Alexander, arrived in Léopoldville on 14 July. Regular contingents of Ghanaian troops began to arrive in the Congo on 15 July and were straightway deployed in the capital. By 25 July the Ghanaian troops, numbering 2,340, were the largest single national contingent in the U.N. force, which then totalled 8,396 officers and men.[1] Some 370 officers and men of the Ghana police presently followed. Senior Ghanaian ministers and officials visited and revisited the Congo in quick succession during the coming months.

Ghana keenly supported a U.N. intervention in the Congo for two obvious reasons. First, with its experience and resources the U.N. would help to secure a speedy withdrawal of Belgian troops. Secondly, by its prompt and effective intervention the U.N. should bar the way to all unilateral 'foreign intervention'. Ghana's main concern was to 'localise' or, rather, Africanise the crisis, by forestalling all *non-African*, and in particular imperialist and neo-colonial, intervention. This the Ghana Government sought to ensure not only by claiming for the U.N. a virtual monopoly of all outside intervention in the Congo, but even more by its demand that O.N.U.C. should predominantly be an African affair composed mainly of African troops and by its related emphasis that the independent African states, which bore a 'special responsibility' for developments within Africa, should maintain 'a positive solidarity' and a complete unity of outlook and policy over the Congo. This the Ghanaians appeared at first to believe should suffice to 'keep out' the cold war.

Once the U.N. was seized of the matter, the U.N. officials' main concern was to 'contain' the crisis and to 'neutralise' the Congo, by forestalling all *non-U.N.* intervention that could possibly 'internationalise' the crisis or draw the Congo into the orbit of the cold war. This they also believed would best be achieved by making and conducting O.N.U.C. primarily as an African operation. This initial coincidence of views disguised a subtle but significant distinction, which (reverting to the principals of this study) was to be the archetype and source of many a radical disagreement between Nkrumah and Hammarskjöld later. The boundaries of the intervention which Nkrumah wished

---

[1] See Hoskyns, op. cit. pp. 158–9; also *Parliamentary Debates* (Accra), 29 July 1960, cols. 339–40, for a statement by the Minister of Defence on Ghana troops in the Congo. See also two articles, 'Review of Ghana's Role in the Congo' and 'Ghana's Help to the Congo Reviewed', in *The Evening News* (Accra), 12 and 13 December 1960, for particulars of Ghana's considerable help in the medical and technical fields.

to exclude were *not* necessarily conterminous with those of that which Hammarskjöld wished to exclude. It was because the United States— the third principal in the U.N. Congo operation, as well as its main financial provider—for its own reasons supported the U.N. secretariat as against Ghana and other Afro-Asian states that O.N.U.C. developed its particular orientation and the Afro-Asians increasingly became estranged from the secretariat.

The respective views and policies of Nkrumah and Hammarskjöld were in fact based upon fundamentally dissimilar first principles in rela- tion to the Congo. Both viewed the external situation of that country in terms of its internal situation. Thus, Nkrumah's main aim was for the U.N. to strengthen the forces of 'genuine', i.e. radical, nationalism by protecting and upholding the Congo's political and popular institutions, in which those forces appeared to him to be embedded and dominant at the time of independence. That was the only way, he felt, in which the Congo could be freed from the shackles of imperialism and secured against the dangers of the cold war. By contrast, Hammarskjöld's main concern was for the U.N. to establish 'law and order' by restoring and strengthening the Congo's administrative and 'civil' institutions, shattered by the precipitate Belgian withdrawal, which restoration appeared to him to be constantly threatened by the petty political warfare among the Congolese. That was the only way, he believed, in which the Congo could be spared the horrors of anarchy, Africa the horrors of the cold war, and the world at large the horrors of destruc- tion.

The American objective, in Africa as elsewhere, was to fill the 'vacuum' being created by the erosion of, and indeed actively to dis- place, the European colonial presence. A collateral objective was to preclude 'Soviet Communist penetration' in order to promote stability and prevent revolution in a region protected and pacified no longer by European power. As the situation deteriorated and the outline of the crisis in the Congo became clearer, American commentators intoned the dangers of Communist penetration and a Soviet take-over there. Had that been a real or imminent danger, the United States, of course, had the means at hand to check it by a unilateral intervention, if it so chose. It did not so choose. It was later stated on authority that the United States had 'a national security interest in what happened in the Congo';[1] but American interests in the Congo and Africa did not, in

---

[1] [United States Assistant Secretary of State for International Organisation Affairs] Harlan Cleveland, 'The UN in the Congo: three questions' [February 1963], in Helen Kitchen (ed.), *Footnotes to the Congo Story* (New York, 1967), p. 71.

July 1960 at any rate, appear to the Eisenhower Administration to be in such danger of Soviet encroachment as to justify the considerable inconveniences and risks of a unilateral intervention. A U.N. intervention was then reckoned sufficient to take care of whatever risk there might exist of Soviet penetration: the United States is not really in the habit of entrusting big anti-Communist jobs to the U.N.[1]

U.N. intervention in the Congo was instrumental to the American 'national security interest' for a very different reason, however. The American objective in the Congo, as elsewhere in Africa, according to the under-secretary of state, George W. Ball, in a major policy address in December 1961, was 'a stable society under a stable and progressive government', a government that 'should be strong enough and determined enough to safeguard its real independence'; and it was 'important that it maintain with us, and with the European states that are contributing to its successful development, the kind of friendly and constructive relations that will serve our mutual purposes'. The 'extremist' Lumumba (or its 'successor' Gizenga) Government hardly fitted that description; and the United States early sought and promoted a 'moderate' substitute, 'a free, stable, non-Communist government for the Congo as a whole'. 'What is important is that behind the shield of United Nations troops and protected by the United Nations from massive great-power intervention, the basically moderate political leadership in Léopoldville began to pull itself together.'[2]

(In contradistinction to the familiar division of the new states into 'conservatives' and 'radicals', African 'moderates' were a happy discovery of American scholars and statesmen made in the wake of the Congo crisis. In fact, 'moderates' were merely a new variety of 'conservatives'; witness, for example, the smooth and easy transition from the Brazzaville to the Monrovia–Lagos group. There was indeed little *fundamental* difference between the two classes, unlike that which distinguished both from the radicals or 'extremists': except that in practice the 'moderates'—e.g. Ethiopia, Liberia, Nigeria, Tunisia, Somalia,

---

[1] Much, though, would be heard later from American sources to the effect that a U.N. intervention in the Congo was the *only* alternative to a 'big-power intervention' or 'Soviet–American confrontation' in the heart of Africa. This may be compared with the case of the present civil war in Nigeria, in which both marked Soviet activity and marked U.N. inactivity have evoked in Washington neither major protests at 'Soviet penetration' of Nigeria or West Africa, nor ominous warnings of a 'Soviet–American confrontation'; nor have there even been calls for U.N. intervention.

[2] *The Elements in Our Congo Policy* (Washington, 1961), pp. 2–3, 19–20, and 8–9. While attesting to Adoula's 'moderate' character, in the same address Ball referred to Gizenga as 'the Communist-chosen instrument' and 'the agent of Communist designs' in the Congo (pp. 11 and 15).

Sudan and the like—more closely followed United States policy, while the 'conservatives' more firmly adhered to the policy of the 'mother-country', i.e. Britain for Malawi, France for the Brazzaville group, or Belgium for 'independent' Katanga, as the case might be. This difference counts for little, except in case of a major conflict of interest or policy between the United States and its European allies, as for example over the issue of suppressing Katanga secession by force, in late 1961 and then late 1962, when American partiality for the 'moderates' took on a special significance. 'In the final analysis', however, as Ball noted, 'the interests of the Katanga and those of the moderate leadership in Léopoldville are parallel'[1]—presumably against the 'extremists'. It may be noted, too, that the Afro-Asian 'moderates' led by India and Nigeria, alongside the United States, more or less consistently supported O.N.U.C. right up to the end.)

An American summing-up of the Congo crisis observed that 'the U.N. presence on balance reinforced those elements inside and outside the Congo which sought to replace Lumumba and to frustrate Soviet ambitions in Central Africa'.[2] Lumumba's removal was probably more easily accomplished by a collective U.N. than by an exclusive U.S. intervention. Setting Soviet ambitions aside, Ghana's policy and initiatives throughout the crisis were by contrast riveted on Lumumba as the symbol of nationalism, democracy, and legality in the Congo, and in addition as the mainstay of Congolese unity and independence. In these circumstances, the Ghana Government became, as the operation progressed, increasingly embittered with O.N.U.C., which it saw as but the instrument, unwitting perhaps, unwilling even, of United States and/or western policy in the Congo. This is indeed the whole point of this fleeting overview of the question from the particular angle of American interest and policy in Africa. The radical divergence of outlook between the Ghana Government and U.N. officials was brought into focus, within a matter of days after the Congo operation began, by the issue of the U.N. troops' entry into Katanga.

[1] Ibid. pp. 18–19. For a first detailed classification of the new states into 'radicals' 'moderates', and 'conservatives', see Robert C. Good, 'The Congo Crisis: a study of post-colonial politics', in Laurence W. Martin (ed.), *Neutralism and Nonalignment: the new states in world affairs* (New York, 1962). Good was later Director of African Research in the State Department under Roger Hilsman, who in his book *To Move a Nation: the politics of foreign policy in the administration of John F. Kennedy* (New York, 1967), pp. 240–3, implicitly follows Good's classification.

[2] Ernest W. Lefever, *Crisis in the Congo: a United Nations force in action* (Washington, 1965), p. 176; altogether an eye-opening book.

As early as 16 July, while the U.N. operation was still being improvised, Moïse Tshombe, head of the secessionist régime in Katanga, declared his opposition to U.N. troops entering his domain and gave warning—which he was to repeat at regular intervals—of 'rioting and trouble everywhere in Katanga' if they came. By the end of the month the U.N. officials had made no attempt to send troops to Katanga, though U.N. troops had during several days past entered every other province in the Congo. A visit to Léopoldville beginning on 28 July gave Hammarskjöld an indication of the Congo Government's strong resentment at the U.N. failure to enter Katanga. A visit to Elisabethville by his special emissary Ralph Bunche on 4 August persuaded Hammarskjöld of the great danger of violence were the U.N. troops to try and enter Katanga in the teeth of the provincial administration's well-publicised and seemingly well-organised opposition.

Hammarskjöld applied to the Security Council for its guidance, making clear his own preference that the U.N. should negotiate rather than force its way into Katanga. In his background report to the Council on 6 August he stated that the dispute between the central Government and Katanga 'did not have its root in the Belgian attitude' and that the U.N. should refrain from any action 'which would prejudge the solution of the internal political problem'. Hammarskjöld returned to the Congo on 11 August, armed with the resolution adopted by the Council two days earlier, which had largely underscored his interpretation of the situation in Katanga and sanctioned his proposed course of action. Accompanied by a contingent of U.N. Swedish troops, he flew to Elisabethville on 12 August to settle with Tshombe the modalities of U.N. entry into Katanga, which formally began the next day.

While Hammarskjöld had been thus occupied, between 2 and 8 August Lumumba had been making a round of African capitals, where he found considerable sympathy for his resentment of Hammarskjöld's interpretations and methods. Thus Nkrumah on 6 August gave a press conference and also sent messages to the heads of independent African states; on 8 August he issued a joint declaration with Lumumba, and during 8–10 August sought and received the mandate of Ghana's Parliament: all to the effect that, if Belgium persisted in its 'aggression' by refusing U.N. troops entry into Katanga, Ghana would lend all armed assistance to the Congo Government—outside the U.N. framework, if necessary—'even though it meant that Ghana and Congo had to fight alone against Belgian troops and other forces maintained and supplied from Belgium'.[1] This was largely a gesture of solidarity, though Lumumba appeared to take these and similar strong words in other African capitals as firm promises of African troops for his Government's own use. The Ghana Government hastened to welcome the new Security Council resolution as a dispensation from any unilateral action against the Belgians. The Ghanaians were soon displeased with Hammarskjöld, however, as he followed up his success in the Council by negotiations with Tshombe, in the course of which he conceded most of the conditions laid down by the Katangans. Tshombe successfully sought guarantees, among others, that the U.N. would not include 'Communist' troops in its Katanga contingents, and for good measure made it clear that he included in that category troops from Ghana and Guinea.[2] Ghana reacted furiously to the whole transaction.[3] In Léopoldville Lumumba took an even stronger view of the matter, and an exchange of letters between him and Hammarskjöld on 15 August produced a complete rupture between the two. To indicate his grim view of the situation, next day Lumumba declared a state of emergency throughout the country.

The entry of U.N. troops into Katanga did not, of course, produce the collapse of the Tshombe régime. At this point in the crisis there was, among the onlookers, only a very incomplete idea of the extent and complexity of the Belgian military and political presence, which, as Belgian troops were withdrawn from other parts of the Congo, was increasingly concentrated and consolidated in Katanga. Lumumba was determined to crush Katanga (and since 9 August the new South Kasai) secession, and he set in motion plans for a military campaign against the 'rebellious' provinces. For that purpose he accepted in principle the Soviet offer of military transport. A military operation of sorts was launched against South Kasai on or about 25 August.

That very day representatives of African states met in Léopoldville for a conference which lasted until 30 August. At this conference, having already written off the U.N. as a possible source of sympathy and support, Lumumba turned for these to fellow-Africans. While naturally long on sympathy, the African states were short on support, as their lack of capability—with their meagre military resources already heavily committed to O.N.U.C.—only reinforced their reluctance, born of their profound attachment to the U.N., to act against or outside

---

[1] Nkrumah's press statement of 6 August, cited in his address to the National Assembly, *Parliamentary Debates*, 8 August 1960, cols. 641–2.

[2] See Hoskyns, op. cit. pp. 170–2.

[3] Ghana Government Note to the U.N. Secretary-General of 10 August 1960, W.P. No. 6/60, pp. 9–10.

O.N.U.C. on the side of the Lumumba Government's military campaign. The Africans refused to second Lumumba's anti-U.N. sentiments and advised him instead to mend his fences with Hammarskjöld. Kojo Botsio, leader of the Ghanaian delegation, for example, was reported as saying that Ghanaian troops would remain in the U.N. force (rather than being transferred to the Lumumba Government) and that Lumumba should settle his differences with the breakaway provinces by peaceful means.[1]

At a different level, the Ghanaians in Léopoldville warned Lumumba and his top military aides, Joseph Mobutu and Victor Lundula, that the operation against Kasai and Katanga could not possibly succeed and that the use of Soviet aircraft was bound to have serious repercussions.[2] The Soviets gave Lumumba 100 military trucks and some 15 planes—as well as, presumably, an indeterminate quantity of 'advice'—at the very end of August, which were presently employed to transport 'loyalist' troops from Stanleyville to Kasai. The campaign was already disintegrating in hopeless confusion, however, and whatever little progress it had made was at the expense of considerable pointless violence and adverse publicity. The Ghanaians very much feared that Lumumba had talked himself into a hazardous military enterprise with a patently inept army and an increasingly insecure political base.

For Ghana, from the very beginning, the secession in Katanga was the crux of the Congo crisis, and the Ghana Government was in no two minds that O.N.U.C. should give the central Government all possible aid to suppress it. It felt certain that any failure in this matter would cause the economic collapse of the Congo and the political collapse of nationalist forces in the country. The Ghanaians presented their case in several different lights. To them the Katanga secession was simply a case of neo-colonialism at work. The Belgian intervention had 'not been primarily directed at saving the lives of Belgian nationals [as Belgium claimed], but has had as its object the detachment of the Katanga Province from the rest of Congo'.[3] The secessionist movement had never appeared in Katanga 'until Belgium militarily occupied

---

[1] See Catherine Hoskyns, 'The Part Played by the Independent African States in the Congo Crisis July 1960–December 1961', in Dennis Austin and Hans N. Weiler (eds.), *Inter-State Relations in Africa* (Freiburg i. Br., 1965), p. 38. See also Alex Quaison-Sackey, *Africa Unbound: reflections of an African statesman* (New York, 1963), pp. 86–7. Djin was prepared to go to Elisabethville and plead with Tshombe himself to end Katanga's secession, but was not allowed to do so by Lumumba.

[2] See Hoskyns, *The Congo since Independence*, p. 190.

[3] Ghana Minister of Foreign Affairs, Note to the President of the U.N. Security Council of 1 August 1960, U.N. document S/4415.

the area'.[1] In so far as the secession was a creature or at least a consequence of Belgian aggression and was only kept going by large-scale Belgian assistance, its suppression was in the Ghanaian view an integral part of the 'duty' of the U.N. to secure the withdrawal of Belgian troops from the Congo. This duty was linked with the 'duty' of O.N.U.C., in terms of the original mandate handed down by the Security Council, to help the central Government by all means (including, if necessary, force) with 'the restoration of law and order' throughout the country (including, in particular, Katanga), and generally 'to see to it that the existing constitution of the Congo is respected' and to oversee its implementation and enforcement.[2]

Katanga secession, once again, was the pivot of the whole question of 'foreign intervention' as the Ghanaians saw it. If the Lumumba Government was not given help by O.N.U.C. to liquidate the secession, it would be unable, for the sake of its very survival, to resist the temptation to act on its own, and to do so, worse still, by accepting foreign aid, which under the circumstances could only be forthcoming from the Soviet bloc. As early as 20 July Nkrumah told Hammarskjöld that he had written to Kasavubu and Lumumba—who on 17 July had threatened to invite Soviet aid unless all Belgian troops were withdrawn from the Congo within 48 hours—urging 'moderation in the requests for outside military aid', as 'the intervention of any of the great Powers would be likely to provoke a most dangerous situation'. He added, however, that Lumumba 'is in the most difficult position and there is the gravest danger of outside Powers being involved unless the Belgians can be got out of Katanga in particular and Katanga is not detached from Congo by any means'.[3] The Ghanaian policy thus was to dissuade Lumumba from seeking or accepting 'outside' military aid, while pressing the U.N. hard, at the same time, to give his Government all possible aid to liquidate 'Tshombe's rebellion'.

An essential condition of this policy was that Lumumba should work with rather than against O.N.U.C.; and the Ghanaians, both in Léopoldville and New York, were active behind the scenes trying to promote better understanding and co-operation between him and Hammarskjöld. Throughout Lumumba's effective tenure as prime minister, and

---

[1] Nkrumah's press statement of 6 August 1960. There was in fact an abortive attempt to secede Katanga from the Congo just two days before the country's independence; and there had long been a 'secessionist movement' among Katangan whites which had latterly been 'Africanised'.

[2] Nkrumah's address to the National Assembly, *Parliamentary Debates*, 17 August 1960, col. 816.

[3] W.P. No. 6/60, p. 5.

particularly during the critical phase beginning mid-August, Nkrumah ceaselessly urged him to act with 'restraint' and 'moderation' towards the U.N. and Hammarskjöld personally, to check Congolese soldiers from attacking U.N. soldiers, and not to ask or push O.N.U.C. out of the Congo. Nkrumah warned Lumumba through Djin that 'African solidarity in relation to our fight is not sufficient unless it is backed by the United Nations' and that their common interests would be seriously impaired, and their objective in the Congo frustrated, by any attitude of hostility towards the U.N. or by the withdrawal or collapse of O.N.U.C.[1]

The Ghanaians were equally unrelenting in their pressure on Lumumba not to accept 'outside aid'. They were in no doubt, in particular, that the acceptance by the Lumumba Government of Soviet military aid would open the flood-gates of the cold war on to the Congo. Nkrumah dropped several hints to Lumumba to proceed with the utmost care and tact in the matter of 'outside' military aid and technicians, to do nothing that would involve the Congo 'in a cold war situation', and to 'take advice from the Ambassadors of the African States and not from others whose motives might be misinterpreted'.[2] All these, under the circumstances, were a warning to Lumumba to avoid a Soviet 'entanglement' at all costs.

There were several reasons for Ghana's attitude on this question. First, Soviet aid, no matter how little—and in the circumstances it could hardly be other than little—would furnish colonial and western powers with one more pretext to step up their own aid to Tshombe and other 'rebels'. It would also give Lumumba's inconstant partners in the shaky coalition which he headed the excuse to brand him a 'Communist', thereby further weakening his deteriorating position. Finally, it would be incompatible with Ghana's own prized principle of non-alignment, with its central principle of eschewing 'foreign', i.e. non-African, military links. (That is to say, the *theoretical* core, for in practice Ghana, like many another newly independent, under-developed country, depended heavily on *western* military officers, training, and equipment.) Thus, far from being an instrument or intermediary of 'Soviet penetration of Africa', as his detractors at home and abroad made him out to be, Nkrumah was all along firmly, if quietly, opposed to any Soviet intervention in the Congo, which, moreover, could not significantly advance Lumumba's objectives and indeed could not but

[1] Nkrumah's letter of instructions of 17 August 1960 to Djin, Ghana's ambassador in Léopoldville, W.P. No. 6/60, p. 12; also Nkrumah's letters to Lumumba dated 19 and 22 August and 12 September 1960, ibid.

[2] Ibid.; also Nkrumah's letter to Lumumba dated 'September, 1960', ibid. p. 21.

further undermine his position both internally and externally. Not surprisingly, Accra and Moscow on occasion made slight digs at each other.

Keeping out 'foreign intervention' from Africa was for Ghana, however, not merely a matter of excluding *Soviet* 'penetration'. The Soviet presence in Africa was both recent and tenuous, and to prevent its malignant growth—as distinct from its normal growth in the form of diplomatic and commercial activities, which the new emphasis in Ghana's policy of non-alignment not only tolerated but in fact encouraged—was a minor, essentially prophylactic, exercise which the Ghanaians believed was best performed by independent African states severally or jointly, without the benefit of outside 'help'. The Soviet-bloc diplomats were expelled from the Congo on 17 September; the Soviet aircraft which had been lent to Lumumba were flown out of the country by their crews at the same time. With this all Soviet activity within the Congo virtually ceased, though the Russians continued to give Lumumba their verbal if inconsequential support at the U.N. and elsewhere.

Soviet diplomats were only allowed back into the Congo some two years later and—a further illustration of their tenuous and transient presence—they were once again ordered out of the country in November 1963, *before* the Congo had fully entered the second phase of its crisis. Speaking more generally, the danger of a Soviet–American confrontation in the heart of Africa, which American spokesmen continually invoked, was of little real significance in terms of 'Soviet penetration' of an area at best of only marginal use or interest to the Soviet Union. The Russians moreover lacked the means and, above all, the inclination for a 'forward' policy in Africa, at a time when peaceful co-existence with the United States had already become the lodestar of Soviet foreign policy. (Soviet enthusiasm for 'world revolution' had long been a thing of the past.)

Keeping out 'foreign intervention' from Africa was for Ghana fundamentally a matter of expelling *western* 'penetration'. As the western presence in Africa was both long-established and all-pervasive, however, to remove its malignant forms would be a major surgical operation. This was in part because of the supposed legitimacy and apparent harmlessness, not least in the eyes of most African leaders themselves, of much western activity—missionary, educational, technical, even commercial, in short 'developmental'—in the erstwhile colonies. In the particular case of the Congo, the Ghana Government expected the U.N. to perform that operation, as the Congolese or

Africans presumably could not do it on their own. Thus, on the Katanga issue, the Ghanaians from the beginning asked O.N.U.C. to remove the Belgian incubus, by force if necessary. This included not only the withdrawal of Belgian regular troops but also the barring and expulsion of all types of Belgian 'irregular' presence—civilian and political as well as military, 'volunteers' as well as mercenaries—as evidence mounted of a massive Belgian build-up in Katanga over and beyond the 'regular' and 'legitimate' Belgian presence.

But the issue of Belgian intervention in Katanga was in a radical sense linked with the issue of western intervention in the Congo. In their international relationships, as Nkrumah frequently pointed out, colonial powers were an integral and organic part of the western bloc. The African quest for economic independence, as one aspect of 'genuine' independence, adversely affected and antagonised the colonial powers. The African quest for international independence, as another aspect— which in the particular situation of a newly independent state inevitably entailed behaviour increasingly different from and on many vital issues opposed to that of the west—adversely affected and antagonised the western powers.[1] The African quest for genuine (as distinct from 'formal' or 'fake') independence thus reinforced the natural alliance of colonial and western powers. 'Anti-communism' was the *leitmotif* of this alliance. Nkrumah's repeated warnings against introducing the cold war into Africa, in the context of his emphasis on banishing all forms of colonialism from the Congo, were a sanguine—and unsuccessful—attempt to deflect the full weight of this alliance from being brought to bear on the Congo crisis, an eventuality which, as Nkrumah saw, the Lumumba Government could not possibly survive. It was because Lumumba was trying to follow the path of genuine independence, Nkrumah felt, that he became the target, and was eventually to become the victim, of the combined stage-work of European colonial powers and the United States within a neo-colonial, cold-war, but ostensibly anti-communist setting. The 'conspiracy' against Lumumba and against the Congo, Nkrumah was later bitterly to complain, was 'carried on under the banner of anti-Communism'.[2]

The United States, without any substantial American economic presence in Katanga, had at first no definite interest in or policy on Tshombe's secession, in contrast to the growing sympathy for him of influential sections of the Belgian and British Governments. Lumumba's

---

[1] Perhaps the most succinct statement of this point is Nyerere's June 1966 memorandum on foreign policy: Julius K. Nyerere, *Principles and Development* (Dar es Salaam, 1967).

[2] See Nkrumah's letter to the U.N. Secretary-General of 16 December 1963, cited in his *Challenge of the Congo*, p. 238.

growing 'extremism' and hostility to the west and his acceptance of Soviet military aid, however, made him appear to the Americans as a threat to their twin objectives in the region: a 'moderate' régime in Léopoldville and keeping out 'Soviet penetration'. The United States was therefore easily persuaded that in Lumumba it had on its hands a 'Communist' and/or 'Soviet agent'—as Tshombe and his foreign sponsors and supporters had maintained all along—and that his elimination as a political factor was the first essential step towards a 'satisfactory' solution in the Congo.

Hammarskjöld's preoccupations were rather different from the Americans', and even more so from the Ghanaians', though his conclusions turned out to be remarkably parallel rather to the former than to the latter. In his view the primary assignment of the U.N. force was to replace Belgian troops in the Congo. O.N.U.C. had been given no mandate, let alone any responsibility, by the Security Council to 'liquidate' the abstract or ill-defined consequences of Belgian 'aggression' or to uproot the Belgian (or western) 'colonial' presence, in so far as these went beyond the physical presence of Belgian regular troops. Katanga as such had no particular part in Hammarskjöld's calculations; and he readily accepted its secession as 'an internal political problem' between Léopoldville and Elisabethville, with which the U.N. had no concern, the better to secure a quick withdrawal of Belgian troops from Katanga without U.N. troops having to force their way in. His much more legalistic approach and his obvious distaste for enforcement action were in sharp contrast to Nkrumah's much more political approach and his much more ready advocacy of force.

In any event, Hammarskjöld's negotiations with Tshombe as well as his interpretations—which were to be the basis of his actions, or inactions, on the Katanga issue until the Security Council revised its mandate in February 1961—gave the Tshombe régime a vital if minimal measure of international recognition and a valuable breathing space by which it was able to consolidate itself; the more so as not even an attempt was made by the U.N. to clamp down on Belgian military supplies to Katanga until after the necessary authorisation was given by resolution of an emergency session of the General Assembly on 20 September 1960. On the other hand, as Lumumba turned to the Soviet bloc for military aid, he appeared to Hammarskjöld and other U.N. officials—quite apart from their 'marked distaste and distrust for Lumumba', to which U.N. Swedish General Carl von Horn, for example, was later to own—to become a growing threat to *their* twin objectives: checking violence and bloodshed in the Congo and sealing the country against the cold war. Not unnaturally, the 'neutralisation' of Lumumba appealed to U.N. officials as the first necessary step towards 'neutralising' the Congo.

CONFLICTS

By early September President Kasavubu in Léopoldville had arrived at a somewhat similar conclusion. The withdrawal of Belgian combat troops from the Congo was virtually complete; this severed the only real link between Kasavubu and Lumumba, their shared hostility to the Belgian military incubus. In Kasai, Lumumba's military campaign was grinding to a halt; both his acceptance of Soviet aid and his methods in general increasingly alienated Kasavubu. The fragile Kasavubu–Lumumba alliance quickly broke down. On 5 September Kasavubu announced Lumumba's dismissal as Prime Minister; the next day Lumumba and his supporters reciprocated by 'dismissing' Kasavubu as President. Following Kasavubu's announcement and Lumumba's hostile reaction, Andrew Cordier, the top U.N. official in Léopoldville, decided that there was an imminent danger of a general breakdown of law and order, and particularly of civil war in the capital itself, which he considered it to be the overriding duty of O.N.U.C. to prevent. In the night of 5 September, therefore, he ordered the closure of major airfields throughout the Congo to all but U.N. traffic; the following day he ordered the sealing of the radio station in Léopoldville. Kasavubu had himself requested both these actions, though Cordier presumably took the decisions on his own. Hammarskjöld endorsed Cordier's actions in the Security Council on 9 September, and he hoped the Council would register the fact that Kasavubu's dismissal of his Prime Minister had been (so Hammarskjöld implied) according to the constitution. Kasavubu asked Joseph Ileo to form a Government, which was formed on 11 September but never confirmed by Parliament.

Both the bans imposed by U.N. officials turned out to Lumumba's serious disadvantage in his political struggle with Kasavubu, and were the occasion for Ghana's second major censure of the conduct of O.N.U.C. Nkrumah's first reaction when he heard of Lumumba's dismissal was to advise the latter to 'exercise restraint'.[1] On 7 September Nkrumah broadcast a general appeal for restraint and 'cool action' to 'the leaders, Government and people' of the Congo and warned against 'improper interference' from outside Africa. The Ghana Government

---

[1] Nkrumah's telegram to Lumumba of 6 September 1960, W.P. No. 6/60, p. 15.

considered, for example, that 'foreign intervention had much to do with the setting up of this illegal [Ileo] regime'.[1]

Immediately, however, it was the use of U.N. Ghanaian troops to deny Lumumba access to Radio Léopoldville which confronted the Ghana Government with a difficult situation. Lumumba was furious and treated Nkrumah to the unwonted taste of his heavy and bitter invective. Lumumba complained of 'the aggressive and hostile attitude' of Ghanaian soldiers, who, he alleged on 11 September, were 'in a state of war against our Republic'. Two days later he threatened to break off diplomatic relations with Ghana unless the Ghanaian troops were withdrawn from the radio station, and said: 'We are highly disappointed. We had hoped to find effective support from Ghana and its troops.'[2] Nkrumah wrote to mollify Lumumba. On 12 September he informed Hammarskjöld of the 'most embarrassing and invidious' position in which Ghana found itself vis-à-vis 'the legitimate Government of the Congo Republic in that at present Ghana's troops are used almost exclusively as [a] cat's paw against Lumumba, preventing him from using his own radio station'; particularly as at the same time Radio Brazzaville, 'which is controlled by France', and Radio Elisabethville, 'which is in effect under Belgian control', were 'allowed to indulge in the most violent propaganda against the legitimate Lumumba Government...Thus Ghana is used virtually to tie Lumumba's hands behind him while a permanent member of the Security Council [i.e. France] is allowed to whip him.' Nkrumah warned that if this situation continued Ghana would 'withdraw her troops forthwith from the United Nations command' and reserve the right to place them entirely at the disposal of the Lumumba Government.[3]

This may be an appropriate point at which to offer some comment on the role of Ghanaian troops of the U.N. in the Congo. At first the appearance in Léopoldville of Ghana's Major-General Alexander as well as other white officers in the Ghana contingent was a fertile source of Congolese misgivings about the Ghanaians. The Ghanaian ambassador, Djin, found the British officers to be a great liability in his endeavours to project a radical image of his own country. Alexander made himself particularly obnoxious to Congolese politicians and soldiers alike, soon after the Ghanaians first arrived, by his unilateral decision to disarm soldiers of the Force publique. Alexander's British nationality fed the suspicion of the Lumumba Government that his action was

[1] Ghana Government statement of 16 September 1960, Ghana Today (London), 28 September 1960.

[2] Nkrumah, Challenge, pp. 39 and 48.

[3] W.P. No. 6/60, p. 16.

perhaps a British, and indirectly a Belgian, manoeuvre to disarm the central authorities of their only likely means of crushing the Katanga rebellion, incredible though this may seem in the light of the past record and contemporary form of the *Force publique*. Alexander's disarming of Congolese soldiers was stopped by U.N. officials, following energetic representations by Lumumba and Gizenga. On 21 July in New York, Alexander personally presented a report urging the acceptance by the U.N. of his 'disarmament' proposal, which Hammarskjöld refused, and which Nkrumah later fully supported.[1] There was sufficient evidence of Congolese hostility towards Alexander for the Ghana defence minister, C. de Graft Dickson, to announce in Léopoldville, soon after Alexander left for New York, that he would *not* return to the Congo.[2]

This whole episode left among the Congolese a trail of suspicion and hostility, which was to dog the Ghanaians' footsteps wherever they moved in the Congo, and which rapidly resurfaced after the Radio Léopoldville episode. Djin's reports to Nkrumah from Léopoldville at this time are particularly revealing.[3] The Ghanaian and other pro-Lumumba African diplomats in the capital canvassed the possibility of using their countries' troops to crack the U.N. radio blockade of Lumumba, but their efforts came to nothing because of the refusal of their own army officers to comply with any 'political advice' which was contrary to O.N.U.C. instructions. If Lumumba expected Ghanaian troops to do his bidding, Djin expected Ghanaian officers in Léopold-ville to do his. In this Djin found the Ghanaian officers to be singularly disobliging. Brigadier S. J. A. Otu and Colonel J. A. Ankrah, the two most senior Ghanaian officers, held out in the face of Djin's constant pressure to make them act outside orders from their U.N. superiors. Djin complained of their failure to appreciate his own 'political point of view', just as he continually charged Alexander with 'intrigue and subversive action' and advised Nkrumah to dismiss him and recall all expatriate officers with the Ghana contingent, though all in vain.

Even had the 'Ghanaian'—i.e. African—officers been willing to do Nkrumah's or Djin's bidding, however, the command structure of the Ghana Army, including particularly the Ghana contingent in the Congo, was then so designed as to rule out the possibility of any effective 'political manipulation' from Accra. The Africanisation of the officer corps had made little progress since independence, with a bare handful

---

[1] For Alexander's proposals and Nkrumah's endorsement, see U.N. document S/4445 (19 August 1960). For General Alexander's version of the Congo story, see his *African Tightrope* (London, 1965), passim.

[2] See *The Evening News*, 27 July 1960.

[3] Cited in Nkrumah, *Challenge*, pp. 39–41 and 47–54.

of Ghanaian officers placed in the public view in comparatively senior command positions, while British officers continued to occupy the bulk of command positions at intermediate levels. It was they, rather than the few Ghanaians at the top, who commanded and controlled the large majority of Ghanaian soldiers in the Congo on routine operations. They were on the whole more pro-Belgian, just as the Ghanaian officers were on the whole more pro-Congolese; this as well as purely professional considerations produced some mutual suspicion and tension between Ghanaian and British officers.

None the less, sufficient *esprit de corps* existed among all 'Ghanaian' officers to ensure that Ghanaian soldiers were not 'improperly' used in any way except in strict accord with U.N. directives. The most complete proof of their fidelity to their U.N. commanders was furnished a little later by another incident involving, as it happened, the luckless Lumumba. Following Lumumba's arrest by Mobutu's soldiers on 1 December, the commanding officer of Ghanaian troops on duty in that part of Kasai requested permission to rescue and release him; this the top U.N. officials concerned firmly refused, and the Ghanaians dutifully made no attempt to act otherwise in a manner which would most probably have met with the approval of their own Government. The conduct of U.N. Ghanaian troops throughout belied accusations by Nkrumah's critics that they were doing his and not the U.N. bidding. Nkrumah himself indeed was not above pointing this out and claiming a sort of credit for it, though the conduct in particular of Ghanaian officers had to do more with their own 'colonial' notions of professional rectitude than with any direction or manipulation by their Government.

While Ghana was publicly criticising O.N.U.C. officials for their 'partisanship' against Lumumba over the use of Radio Léopoldville, Kasavubu's 'constitutional' coup was foundering on the rock of Lumumba's control of parliament. On 14 September Colonel Mobutu, chief of staff of the *Armée nationale congolaise* (A.N.C.), followed up with a military coup which purported to 'neutralise' all politicians—the President, the two 'rival' governments, i.e. Lumumba's and Ileo's, and parliament—until the end of the year, while the country was to be 'run by 'technicians'. Mobutu also ordered the Soviet-bloc diplomats out o the country within 48 hours, presumably in order to affirm his 'moderation' and 'independence'. On 16 September his soldiers cleared the parliament building of parliamentarians; on 20 September the administrative building housing government offices was cleared of 'politicians', i.e. members of the government. The same day Mobutu appointed a number of Congolese university graduates and students to form a College of Commissioners, with Justin Bomboko as president, who were pledged to protect the Congo 'from Communist colonialism and from Marxist-Leninist imperialism'.[1]

Although the commissioners were chosen only because of their technical ability and were therefore supposed to be 'politically neutral', their marked antipathy to politicians in general and to Lumumba in particular, as well as to 'politics' in the abstract, was immediately apparent. For Kasavubu by contrast they admitted to a respect which he returned; accordingly on 29 September at a ceremony at his residence Kasavubu 'officially installed' the College. By early next month Mobutu, who had been somewhat reluctant so quickly to 'de-neutralise' Kasavubu, was persuaded by his College of the need for them all to work under the umbrella of the President's constitutional authority.

The new alliance of Kasavubu, Mobutu, and the College was a rough-and-ready approximation to 'a free, stable, non-Communist government for the Congo as a whole', which, as the much-sought 'moderate' replacement for the Lumumba Government, the United States actively supported and promoted. Belgium, too, found it supportable, as the inexperienced commissioners surrounded by administrative chaos turned more and more to Belgian advisers, who from early October began to arrive back in Léopoldville in droves. The only trouble with this otherwise excellent arrangement was that it would not work. As time passed the alliance increasingly demonstrated its want of stability as a viable political entity, its want of effectiveness as a government, and its want of authority over the country as a whole. Its one sanction was the army, its one cohesive link anti-Lumumbism.

Mobutu's authority never ran any farther than the A.N.C. garrison in Léopoldville. Similarly, the College's authority ran no farther than the capital itself, both because the commissioners themselves lacked any political base and because by their neutralisation of politicians the College had deprived itself of the services of the only vital (if in the circumstances necessarily defective) network of political communications between the capital and the provinces. The well-documented report of the head of O.N.U.C., Rajeshwar Dayal, dated 2 November, virtually certified the utter worthlessness of the Kasavubu–Mobutu alliance as a basis for solving the Congo's problems; instead it indicated a return to representative government as the only possible hope for a solution. Smelling in this an opening for Lumumba's return to power, the United States publicly voiced its disagreement with the report.

Nkrumah enthusiastically welcomed the Dayal report, however, as

[1] See Alan P. Merriam, *Congo: background of conflict* (Evanston, 1961), p. 267.

but confirming the soundness of his own line of reasoning and policy over the past two months. In view of the ease and speed with which the Kasavubu–Mobutu alliance was forged, the Kasavubu and Mobutu *coups* were seen from Ghana as but two stages of a single 'imperialist-sponsored' *coup* against Lumumba and Lumumbists. This was a gross affront to the very principle of democracy in Africa, Nkrumah claimed. But what most enraged the Ghana Government against the western powers as well as Mobutu was the belief that Mobutu's *coup* was a 'desperate' manoeuvre by 'imperialist intrigue, stark and naked', to forestall the 'imminent' success of Ghanaian and other African efforts to reconcile Kasavubu and Lumumba.[1] These efforts had been the nearly unanimous reaction to the breach between the two leaders, whose alliance was regarded by most African diplomats in Léopoldville as essential to any satisfactory settlement in the Congo.

Ghana's determined support of Lumumba and persistent refusal to have any dealings with Mobutu and his commissioners, who were damned with a string of choice pejoratives, made Ghanaians—diplomats, soldiers, and politicians—increasingly unpopular and unwanted, as the Kasavubu–Mobutu alliance consolidated itself in Léopoldville. It was this growing mutual hostility, rather than any hard evidence of Ghanaian involvement in 'subversive activities of a serious nature', which led Kasavubu and Bomboko on 7 October to declare Djin, N. A. Welbeck, and Botsio *personae non gratae*, and to charge them with having 'mixed themselves up in the internal affairs of the Congo in an inadmissible way'. Specifically, the Ghanaians in Léopoldville were said to be using their diplomatic facilities to transmit abroad messages favouring Lumumba. Sensing the general mood, the U.N. commanders decided on an early transfer of the Ghana contingent from the capital; on 16 October an advance party of Ghanaian officers and men left for Kasai to prepare the way for the move.

The Ghana Government resisted both these developments. Nkrumah refused to acknowledge the legality even of Kasavubu's order against Ghanaian diplomats; he thought it 'imperative', in face of the 'imperialist' activity in the Congo, that 'Ghana and other African states should be effectively represented in Léopoldville'.[2] Similarly he opposed the planned transfer from the capital of Ghanaian troops (which in fact

[1] Nkrumah's address to the U.N. General Assembly on 23 September 1960, cited in *I Speak of Freedom*, p. 268. For Djin's report on the reconciliation attempts, see Nkrumah, *Challenge*, pp. 58–61; see also Hoskyns, *The Congo since Independence*, pp. 219–22.

[2] See Nkrumah's letter to Welbeck of 21 November 1960, in *Challenge*, pp. 86–7. For the Congolese note declaring Djin *et al. personae non gratae* and for the Ghanaian reply of 10 October, see W.P. No. 6/60, pp. 25–6.

Mobutu had demanded soon after he seized power), because of its likely adverse consequences for both law and order in general and Lumumba and Lumumbists in particular. The Ghanaian troops were moved out of Léopoldville by early November, however; and the Ghanaian diplomats were forced out of the country, following an attack on the Ghana embassy on 21 November by a detachment of Congolese soldiers.

The decision of Léopoldville authorities to expel the Ghanaian diplomats, while no doubt favoured by the transfer of the Ghana contingent, was precipitated by Ghana's dogged resistance to moves during the preceding fortnight to recognise and seat Kasavubu's nominees in the U.N. General Assembly as the Congolese 'official delegation'. The United States decided on a pre-emptive strike against the Dayal report in order to block a Lumumbist restoration. It hoped to be able to make this an 'African' operation in part, as it discovered among the new French-speaking African states latterly arrived at the U.N. several ready subscribers to its own partiality for Kasavubu. In the Assembly Ghana moved adjournment of the debate on credentials, with success on 9 November, without success on 18 and 22 November, in order to prevent any decision on the issue, whose outcome appeared more and more certain to favour Kasavubu's nominees against Lumumba's. The Ghanaians opposed this 'obvious manoeuvre' mainly because they saw it as an attempt by western powers to impose upon the Congo a 'solution' of their choice, whose limitations were daily becoming clearer and which simply would not work while the Lumumbists were excluded from it.[1] The removal of the Ghanaian diplomats and the seating of the Kasavubu delegation in the General Assembly, both on 22 November, were major factors in Lumumba's decision to leave Léopoldville and set off for Stanleyville. About a week later Nkrumah sought Kasavubu's consent to the appointment of a new Ghanaian ambassador to the Congo, which was virtually denied.

On 1 December Lumumba was caught by Mobutu's soldiers while on his way to Stanleyville. The news of his arrest and maltreatment produced a marked sharpening of temper and tone in Ghana. The Ghana Government laid the blame for the actions and excesses of Mobutu *et al.* squarely at the door of 'imperialist powers', i.e. Belgium and her allies. On 27 November, in a message ostensibly dealing with the insecure position of Ghanaians in Léopoldville, Nkrumah had apprised Hammarskjöld of 'the view held by impartial observers that colonialist powers are supporting Belgium in her attempts to regain control over the Congo', and furthermore that 'America, Britain and France are

[1] See Quaison-Sackey, op. cit. pp. 90–1.

aiding and abetting these attempts'.[1] On 4 December the Ghana Government broke off diplomatic relations with the Belgian Government and asked the Belgian ambassador to leave Ghana within 48 hours (which he did), because it considered the Belgian Government 'responsible for recent developments in the Congo, and for the breakdown in the administration of the legitimate Government and Parliament of the Congo of which Mr Patrice Lumumba is Prime Minister'.[2]

Nkrumah nevertheless continued to appeal to N.A.T.O. powers to persuade or compel their ally Belgium to release Lumumba from the clutches of 'a military dictatorship of a brutal and ineffectual type'. Soon after Kennedy's inauguration in January 1961 as U.S. President, Nkrumah in a characteristic message reminded him of American professions of democracy and anti-colonialism. He urged Kennedy personally to intervene on Lumumba's behalf and warned that 'the reputation of the United States could be irretrievably damaged in Africa if your powerful nation sits by and watches one of your close military allies—Belgium—which is after all dependent on the United States for its defence and to a considerable measure economic existence crumpling up democracy in Africa in flagrant disregard of the unanimous opinion and sentiment of all those African people who are free to express their views.'[3]

The Ghana Government, in spite of all its strong words, was in no position to make its influence felt either in western capitals or in Léopoldville. Its resentment at the turn of events instead found vent in bitter criticism of the U.N. On 7 December Nkrumah sent Hammarskjöld a long letter sharply criticising O.N.U.C.; on 15 December he made a radio broadcast even more categorical both in its denunciations and in its demands. During the second half of the month he gave several public addresses critical of the U.N. in the Congo. Throughout December these criticisms were enlarged upon by the C.P.P. newspapers, *The Ghanaian Times* and *The Evening News*, with an impassioned violence untempered by any niceties of diplomatic decorum. The Ghanaian official attitude towards Hammarskjöld himself was now markedly different from that of the previous September, when at the U.N. both Quaison-Sackey and Nkrumah had paid him fulsome tribute, while deploring the lapses of his subordinates in the Congo. If Hammarskjöld could not carry out the 'orders' of the U.N., challenged Nkrumah on 17 December, 'because he thinks he is more legalistic than the United

[1] *The Ghanaian Times* (Accra), 28 November 1960.
[2] Ibid. 5 December 1960.
[3] *Challenge*, p. 102. Lumumba was then already dead, but at the time of Nkrumah's letter to Kennedy this was not yet public knowledge.

Nations itself, then he must have the moral courage to resign from the General Secretaryship of the United Nations'.[1]

The substance of the Ghanaian indictment was that, in the shadow of its unevenly applied policy of non-intervention in the internal affairs of the Congo, O.N.U.C. had allowed the Belgians to 'reinfiltrate' the country on a large scale, just as it had allowed Mobutu and his 'band of adventurers' to suppress the country's political institutions. O.N.U.C. had thus reneged on its own 'duties' as well as jeopardised the Congo's independence. In its turn the Ghana Government proposed a vigorous U.N. initiative to activate the Congolese 'national institutions', while immediately it asked O.N.U.C. to subdue and disarm diverse A.N.C. 'factions', to set free all political prisoners (and particularly Lumumba and his colleagues), and to clear the Congo of 'Belgian *saboteurs* of Congolese independence'.[2]

To U.N. officials such proposals bore no touch with 'reality' as they saw it, nor with the Security Council mandates which guided and bound them in their conduct of O.N.U.C. They were now themselves, in fact, very much caught in the coils of their own contradictions. As the Congo operation moved, it had become increasingly clear to the large majority of Afro-Asian states with troops there that there could be no real solution of the acute disturbance in the country—a veritable hurricane, of which by mid-September Léopoldville appeared to be the eye—unless the Katanga issue was resolved. There could be no resolution of that issue, however, unless the Belgian military and para-military personnel were removed and barred from the province. The Afro-Asian consensus on this point was largely embodied in the resolution adopted by the General Assembly on 20 September, which called upon all states to refrain from providing assistance in arms and men for military purposes in the Congo except via the U.N. At the beginning of October Hammarskjöld tried to implement this directive by resuming his earlier correspondence on the subject with Belgian and Katangan authorities, who were thereby further embittered against the U.N., but without the U.N. securing any significant reduction of the Belgian military presence in Katanga in the absence of any necessary enforcement action. This was not authorised until February 1961 and not instituted until several months later.

Similar hesitations marked the course of U.N. policy towards the authorities in Léopoldville. After Dayal was firmly in the saddle as

---

[1] *Ghana Today*, 21 December 1960.

[2] See *The Congo Situation* (Accra, n.d.), containing the texts of Nkrumah's letter to Hammarskjöld of 7 December and of his radio broadcast of 15 December 1960.

officer-in-charge of O.N.U.C., it became U.N. policy to recognise only such institutions and actions as were in accordance with the *Loi fonda-mentale*. He refused to recognise the College of Commissioners, for example, or to arrest Lumumba as his enemies demanded. This infuriated both the Léopoldville authorities and their western friends. Dayal's report of 2 November set the coping-stone on their hostility to O.N.U.C. and to Dayal himself in particular. At the same time, the U.N. preoccupation with 'restoring law and order' led O.N.U.C. in diverse ways to 'collaborate' with and thereby to bolster the Léopold-ville authorities.

The main concern of the officers in charge of the U.N. military operation was to check fighting among different armed factions in the Congo and to restore some discipline among Congolese soldiers. Thus, in the wake of the breach between Kasavubu and Lumumba, U.N. officials gave Mobutu a substantial sum of money for the wages of the A.N.C. units in Léopoldville; for this payment, made on 10 September, he was allowed to claim credit in the eyes of his soldiers, whom he presently turned and used against the constitutional authorities. At least two further payments were made to Congolese soldiers out of U.N. funds, one some ten days later, the other early in October.[1] In each case the U.N. officials concerned acted with a view to restoring discipline among the forces, when the alternative presumably would have been looting and massacre of the local population by the unpaid soldiery; in each case the result was to strengthen Mobutu's authority among his troops (though in the last case, the garrison in Stanleyville, Mobutu's success was short-lived). 'In other words,' as Nkrumah put it in March 1961, 'instead of suppressing the mutiny of the *Force publique*, the United Nations actually paid for it.'[2]

Similarly, the main concern of the officials in charge of the U.N. civilian operation was to restore essential services and establish some semblance of administration in the Congo. Thus they co-operated with the College of Commissioners—which was, after all, the only available 'government' in the field—particularly in instituting a number of 'essential' monetary and financial reforms in conjunction unavoidably with the Belgians, in order to restore some order to the Congolese economy. The cumulative outcome of these various actions of the U.N. was in some degree to strengthen the hands of the Léopoldville authorities. But, while given arms, so to speak, these authorities were denied

---

[1] See Hoskyns, op. cit. pp. 213, 217, and 244.

[2] Nkrumah's address to the General Assembly on 7 March 1961, *Osagyefo at the United Nations: solution for the Congo* (Accra, n.d.), p. 10.

the formal recognition and full support of U.N. officials. The result, of course, was a virtual state of war declared by the Kasavubu–Mobutu alliance against O.N.U.C. The Dayal report indeed saw some of these contradictions; it became in fact the trigger which set off the western powers in their pursuit of some measure of international recognition for the 'moderates' in Léopoldville.

Lumumba's arrest was only the spark that lighted the fuse. The Afro-Asian radical states threatened to withdraw from O.N.U.C. altogether and instead to lend their troops to the Stanleyville régime. Even those less radical saw that something had very much gone awry with the whole operation, particularly those with troops in the Congo, who largely shared the substance if not the spirit or tone of Ghanaian criticisms of O.N.U.C. The Ghanaian solutions, both because of their longrange objectives and their short-term methods, aroused much less sympathy. In any case there was a general outcry from the Afro-Asians for a change of course by O.N.U.C. But Hammarskjöld by contrast saw no need for such a change. The General Assembly debates on the Congo on 16–17 and 19–20 December provided him with an opportunity to seek a new mandate, if he chose to ask for one. He did not. The Assembly was unable to decide on a new course, so O.N.U.C. continued on its old one.

In explaining and justifying their actions, both at the time and later, U.N. officials often spoke of the 'limitations' of their mandate. The real criticism of Hammarskjöld's policy, particularly in December 1960, is that, long after the Kasavubu–Mobutu alliance had proven its futility as the basis for a generally acceptable and durable political settlement, while violence mounted and a civil war loomed ahead, he did not speak out and stand up for a new and broader mandate hinging on the 'threat' and possibility of the use of force by the U.N. Perhaps, in the face of the western powers' stubborn support of the Kasavubu–Mobutu alliance and their growing hostility to Dayal's stewardship of O.N.U.C., Hammarskjöld did not think his 'parliamentary situation' at the U.N. sufficiently hopeful of success for a new mandate, which ideally speaking might have advanced the cause of pacification and political settlement in the Congo through a restitution of Lumumbist forces. Be that as it may, the whole tendency of O.N.U.C., if not its intent, had been to neutralise the nationalist forces in the country—a tendency which culminated in Lumumba's death. Unwittingly or not, the U.N. continually sided against Lumumba, in favour first of Tshombe, then of Kasavubu, and finally of Mobutu.

To the few states on Ghana's 'left',—notably Guinea, Mali, the U.A.R., and Indonesia—the U.N. failure to secure Lumumba's release, and in general the likelihood of O.N.U.C. continuing on its existing course, appeared to indicate their own withdrawal from O.N.U.C. as the only logical step, which they soon took and according-ly recalled their troops from the Congo. With this Ghana did not agree. In spite of its marked affinity and close association with the radical states, Ghana in fact ploughed a lonely furrow on several other major issues (e.g. the 'problems' of Israel and Mauritania) as well as on the Congo. At the Casablanca conference in January 1961 Nkrumah firmly stood his ground in the face of great pressure from his colleagues that they should all withdraw their troops from O.N.U.C.

When the radical states first threatened to withdraw their contingents from O.N.U.C., Nkrumah interceded with their leaders to dissuade them from their proposed course of action. If (as was probable) *only* the pro-Lumumba states were to withdraw their troops, but *not* other African states with large contingents in the Congo—so Nkrumah warned Sékou Touré—'we may be faced with a situation in which we will find some of the African troops still serving under the United Nations...and most probably collaborating with the imperialists in the Congo.'[1] A unilateral withdrawal of troops by the radical states would then simply give imperialists an opportunity for direct military intervention on the side of their *protégés*. There was, however, little pro-spect of any countervailing reinforcement of the position of the nationalists, whose African supporters were in no position to match, let alone to out-match, the formidable resources available to their enemies.[2] 'Withdrawal would only play into the hands of Lumumba's enemies', Nkrumah felt.[3]

Instead of a total pull-out from the Congo, Guinea and the U.A.R., for example, professed their intention to *transfer* their troops outright to Stanleyville's side. This latter should have presented itself as a more attractive policy alternative, around the turn of the year, when all across the Congo a marked resurgence and expansion of Lumumbist forces appeared to be in progress, rather than their decline and con-

---

[1] Nkrumah's message to Sékou Touré of 14 December 1960, in *Challenge*, p. 110.

[2] The limitations of the radical states were very real indeed. Thus by the end of July 1960 nearly half and by far the best part of the Ghana Army was fully engaged in the Congo. Between the financial years 1959–60 and 1960–1 Ghana's defence budget was nearly doubled, to some £10m.; in 1961–2 it was increased to some £14m. Source: *Economic Survey 1962* (Accra, 1963), p. 106. Elaborate plans were afoot to expand and reorganise the Ghana Army, in spite of a sceptical and reluctant General Alexander; in 1961 the Soviet Union was tapped as a fresh source of military equipment and training. Inevitably, there was a tendency for ambitions to run well ahead of resources. But, whatever their final outcome, these long-term plans could not be turned to any immediate advantage in a real situation like that in the Congo. What was true of Ghana was true also, *mutatis mutandis*, of other radical African states. The U.A.R., the one possible exception, already had too many irons in the fire, committing its resources to the full.   [3] *Challenge*, p. 111.

traction, as the Ghanaian argument presumed. Nkrumah was probably aware of this; but, perhaps in view of the general international and African situation as well as the radical states' own deficiencies of military organisation, supplies, and the rest, he felt that this particular alternative would fail of its objective, while further complicating the over-all situation in the Congo.

On the other hand, so long as their troops stayed on in the Congo as part of O.N.U.C., the radical states—so the Ghanaians felt—would have a *locus standi* and a legitimate opportunity of influencing developments in that country, by seeking to reorientate the whole operation and by giving the Lumumbists in Stanleyville whatever aid was possible 'on the side'. Thus Ghana continued to support O.N.U.C., in practice as well as in principle. Of the radical states it alone, for example, took part in the work of the U.N. Conciliation Commission for the Congo.[1]

CONCLUSIONS

The announcement of Lumumba's death on 13 February 1961 at last sprang the Security Council into action. On 18 February Nkrumah once again presented Hammarskjöld with a set of far-reaching proposals on the Congo operation. The foreign ministers of the Casablanca states (minus Guinea) met in Accra on 20 and 22 February and came up with detailed proposals as an addendum, so to speak, to Nkrumah's general guide-lines. On 7 March Nkrumah personally presented these proposals to the General Assembly, accompanied by a lengthy address, which contained an extended critical analysis of the workings until then of O.N.U.C. as well as suggestions for its drastic reorganisation.[2]

The sum and substance of Ghana's proposals was a complete 'Africanisation' of the U.N. military and civilian operations in the Congo. O.N.U.C. should be thoroughly Africanised, not so much in its personnel—although that was important—as in its 'spirit' and 'objectives', and completely freed from 'western control', whether in New York or Léopoldville. Until the Congo's national institutions were fully and effectively reactivated and a representative 'nationalist' (rather than a

---

[1] Alex Quaison-Sackey, Ghana's representative on the Conciliation Commission, refused, however, to sign its final report; for his reasons, see U.N. documents A/4711 and Addenda 1 and 2, Annex xx.

[2] For Nkrumah's proposals to Hammarskjöld and the Casablanca foreign ministers' proposals, see *Challenge*, pp. 134–8. For Nkrumah's address to the General Assembly, see *Osagyefo at the United Nations*. See also Nkrumah's note to Adlai Stevenson some days later, as an informal gloss on his own General Assembly address; *Challenge*, pp. 146–51. Guinea attended the Accra meeting, but did not endorse the final declaration.

mere 'national') government assembled, the completely transformed O.N.U.C. should meanwhile 'assume authority, as a temporary measure, for the internal affairs of the Congo'. O.N.U.C. must take full charge of and govern the country—including its internal and external security, its administration, and particularly its finances—as well as suppressing all secessionist activity. In a nutshell, the Ghana Government proposed a virtual, if temporary, 'U.N.' trusteeship over the Congo, actually to be administered by African 'independent' states with the help of Asian 'uncommitted' states—that is to say, by Afro-Asian states free from western control—in a sort of holding operation, while the colonial presence in the country was uprooted, the supporting western intervention eliminated, and the forces of genuine nationalism were allowed to recover, reorganise, and reassert themselves. Nkrumah in effect proposed for the Congo a veritable 'revolution from above', made by the radical nationalist states via the U.N.

Ghana's revolutionary manifesto evoked little interest or response, and the subsequent development of O.N.U.C. in no way fulfilled Nkrumah's expectations. The proposals were, however, of real significance as the ideological key to Ghana's African and international policies during the 1960s, right up to the Ghana coup in February 1966. Immediately, some of the proposals of the Casablanca group were incorporated in the resolution adopted by the Security Council on 21 February,which was to be reinforced by another and stronger resolution by the Council some nine months later (24 November). Nkrumah, among others, credited the new U.N. policy to the combined pressure of Afro-Asian states and the U.S.A. But, as the shift in U.S. policy—partly because of a new administration in Washington—was the one new element in the situation around the time Lumumba's death was announced, the credit for the new U.N. policy really belonged to the United States.

The mandate of O.N.U.C. was redefined and considerably broadened. On the political side, the U.N. helped to reassemble the rump Congolese parliament, which in August 1961 installed a 'government of national unity' under Cyrille Adoula. The U.N. also encouraged and assisted with plans for a new federal constitution for the Congo, culminating in the Thant plan for national reconciliation (August 1962), which had been largely prepared in Washington and packaged and presented by the U.N. Secretary-General.[1] On the military side, the U.N. lent the

---

[1] According to Arthur M. Schlesinger Jr, *A Thousand Days: John F. Kennedy in the White House* (London, 1965), p. 503: 'During the summer of 1962 British, Belgian and American officials worked together on a new unification plan [for the Congo] which U Thant put into final form and sponsored in September.' The plan 'was based on proposals submitted by the United States to the Secretary-General on August 9' and 'slightly modified' by him. It

reconstituted central Government armed assistance against secessionist activities in the country. U.N. troops were used in September 1961 in an attempt to exclude Belgian and other foreign military and para-military personnel and mercenaries from Katanga, in December 1961 to end Katanga secession (without success), in January 1962 to help suppress the secessionist régime in Stanleyville, and in December 1962 in Katanga yet again to suppress Tshombe's secession (this time with success).

In the midst of these operations the United States found itself moving into the centre of the Congo drama, while the Afro-Asians found them-selves pushed more and more into the wings. Inside the Congo the United States displaced Belgium as the leading international political factor. It vigorously supported the O.N.U.C. campaigns against Katanga, on the ground that it was necessary to block a Soviet penetra-tion and 'take-over' of the whole region, by way either of Stanleyville (in late 1961) or of Léopoldville itself (in late 1962). The dreaded Soviet presence was in fact as little in evidence in Léopoldville at the end of 1962 as it had proved to be a bogey in Stanleyville at the beginning of the year. The real point of United States policy on Katanga was primarily to help consolidate the 'moderates' in Léopoldville, who were more and more in a state of disarray and nearing total collapse.[1] It also, incidentally, offered an easy justification for smoking out the surviving 'extremist' elements from their few pockets of retreat and passive resistance in different parts of the Congo. The Adoula Government—with the U.N. and the United States as its godparents—was generously supplied with American economic and military aid. Much of the economic aid was channelled through and used by O.N.U.C. to restore the country's civil administration, while the Americans themselves, with the help of some of their allies (notably Belgium), took charge of the task of 'reconditioning' the A.N.C. as a suitable instrument for 'nation-

'reflected a growing convergence of American and Belgian views on the desirability of salvaging Tshombe for a positive role in a unified Congo'—thus Lefever, op. cit. pp. 102–3, who also states that the Soviet Union 'was in favour of the Plan without any reservation whatsoever'. See also Jules Gérard-Libois, *Katanga Secession* (Madison, 1966), pp. 254–5.

[1] A scrutiny of three 'inside' accounts of the Kennedy administration—two from inside the White House, one from inside the State Department—fails to disclose any hard evidence for the claim that the Soviets were about to make a big 'kill' in Central Africa. What it does disclose is that it was the State Department's mounting anxiety as to the chances of survival of the 'moderates' in Léopoldville which moved it to argue with vehemence for firm action against Tshombe. In view of the opposition from interested quarters to the proposed course of action, however, the State Department found it expedient to base its 'public' case, in Congressional and press 'backgroundings', on 'the imminent threat of a Soviet take-over' in the Congo. See Schlesinger, op. cit. pp. 503–4; Theodore C. Sorensen, *Kennedy* (London, 1966), pp. 704–5; and Hilsman, op. cit. pp. 264–8.

building' and 'modernisation' of the Congo. The Adoula Government was soon every bit as dependent on the United States as the Tshombe régime had been on Belgium.[1]

These developments were all a consequence, directly and indirectly, of the implementation by O.N.U.C. of its new mandate, which had been redefined in line apparently with general wishes and views, not least of the radical states themselves. Yet these developments—which together served further to undermine Congolese nationalist forces— sharply clashed with Nkrumah's conception of O.N.U.C. as an 'arm' of radical nationalism in the Congo and, on a longer perspective, of the U.N. as an instrument of 'the African revolution'. How did this come about?

The radical programme which Nkrumah proposed for the Congo was based on a number of unstated and untested assumptions about Congolese nationalism. These assumptions were themselves the result of a somewhat uncritical application of Ghana's own experiences to a colony of which the Ghanaians knew but little at first hand and whose socio-economic and political characteristics were in many respects very different from those of the Gold Coast.

The anti-colonial movement in the Congo moved abruptly, like an avalanche, in the latter part of 1958, and much of it flowed into political expression along the existing traditional or 'transitional' channels. The M.N.C., the first modern nationalist party, made its appearance only in October 1958; the other parties which in the following months mushroomed on all sides were, in the main, merely political labels stuck in a hurry to the already existing ethnic and local associations. The main handicap of the scattered elements of nationalism at that time was their utter lack of organisation, ideology, and experienced leadership, largely reflecting the country's economic and social discontinuities; there was no background of political work in the countryside nor cadres at hand to give shape and direction to manifestations of rural protest. During 1959, however, there was a marked intensification of political activity in the towns—particularly because of the coupling of the évolués, the urban petty bourgeoisie, with the urban proletariat— which redounded to the advantage of the nationalist elements.

The unexpected quickness of the Belgian decision to relinquish political control in the Congo produced a sharp turning away of Congolese nationalists from political to constitutional activities; during 1960 there was a marked decline of political activity all across the country.

[1] The present Mobutu régime in the Congo is in many respects the direct successor to the Adoula régime.

During the first half of the year the politicians were mainly occupied with constitution- and government-making, first in Brussels and then in Léopoldville. During the second half a breakdown of order and administration, caused by a colonial *gendarmerie*, the *Force publique*, on the rampage, produced in its turn a total fragmentation and dissipation of authority and leadership, all mixed up with and aggravated by widespread foreign intervention. These conditions were hardly conducive to any sustained political activity, which might have allowed the nationalist forces to organise, orientate, and consolidate themselves. The Lumumbist vanguard of the nationalist movement, which after Lumumba's arrest retired to Stanleyville, confused and demoralised, was after his death and throughout 1961 increasingly cut off from the 'grass-roots radicalism' which, not having found a definite form and firm direction, had subsided, to break out to the surface again in 1964. The Gizengists who made their peace with Léopoldville and joined the Adoula Government were a provincial coterie of politicians, rather than the representatives of a popular régime 'powered' by a mass movement.[1]

The consolidation and radicalisation of the nationalist forces, which was the crucial assumption behind Nkrumah's programme for the Congo, thus failed to materialise. As a result the benefits of the U.N. 'pacification' of the Congo—which Nkrumah and other radicals had expected to accrue to the Lumumbists—in fact accrued to the 'moderate' and 'federalist' elements in the country, which derived their support and force from the longer established and better founded ethnic and local particularisms, to the growing detriment of nationalist forces. If Nkrumah misjudged the general condition of Congolese nationalism and seriously misread its revolutionary potential, it was a misjudgment which was at least understandable; and of the very few strategies available to African states Ghana's was by no means the least worthy or the one least likely to succeed. Less excusable, however, was the other grievous misjudgment—a fertile source of the Ghanaians' frustrations and failures in the Congo—which made Ghana look upon the U.N. as an instrument or ally in the African anti-imperialist struggle.

[1] For the ups and downs of Gizenga's own party as a microcosm (as it were) of Congolese politics, see Herbert F. Weiss, *Political Protest in the Congo: the Parti Solidaire Africain during the independence struggle* (Princeton, 1967). The state of Congolese nationalist forces may be illustrated with one example. Leading factions within the *Conseil national de libération*—which had been established in October 1963 by ex-Lumumbists and ex-Gizengists to pave the way for 'revolution' in the Congo—were severally in negotiation with Tshombe early in 1964, presumably to enlist him on the side of 'revolution'. Tshombe did return to the Congo a few months later, but for purposes other than 'revolutionary'.

There was little warrant indeed for this view, in the light both of the history and of the structure and procedures of the U.N. The successes which are customarily claimed for the U.N. in the field of decolonisation are, on closer examination, seen to be the result of other, more fundamental causes. Nor has the U.N. had any significant success in the direction of restructuring international economic and political relationships in favour of the newly independent countries. The U.N. in fact was never meant or designed to do so: it is a profoundly conservative institution. It has had some success in shielding the new states against 'the cold war', but only against 'Soviet penetration' when this was a possibility. The U.N., however, has not shielded them against American penetration, nor freed them from the supposedly natural and legitimate colonial presence or from western intervention.

In the particular case of the Congo, the Security Council mandates which established and governed O.N.U.C., as well as the patterns of power and influence within the Council, the General Assembly, and the Secretariat, made the U.N. a very unlikely partner in the anti-imperialist struggle. Hammarskjöld's overriding anxiety was to keep out the cold war from the Congo, just as the main concern of the United States was ostensibly to avoid a direct confrontation with the Soviet Union in that region. As Lumumba became more and more intrepid in his demands and intemperate in his attacks on the U.N. as well as the United States, Hammarskjöld and O.N.U.C. officials came to see him as a very likely channel of Soviet penetration, as well as being the major obstacle to 'national reconciliation' and 'pacification' in the Congo. They were certainly not sorry to see him 'go'. Nkrumah, by contrast, looked upon Lumumba as the only hope of Congolese independence and thus the only real barrier to the cold war.

It was Hammarskjöld's view which prevailed, not Nkrumah's, largely because it coincided with the American reading of the situation. 'Soviet penetration of Africa' was hardly a danger. What *was* a real danger, from an American viewpoint, was the possibility of Congolese 'extremists' establishing themselves firmly in power. It was by misrepresenting the Lumumbist-Gizengists as black 'Marxist-Leninists' or 'Soviet agents', against the backdrop of the anxiety of Hammarskjöld and the large majority of Afro-Asians to keep out the cold war, that the United States succeeded in placing the 'moderates' in charge of the Congo, at least for the time being. It is nothing short of fantastic, in these circumstances, that Nkrumah should have expected to use the U.N. as an instrument of the 'African revolutionary cause'.

When the end of Katanga secession appeared in sight, following the fighting and the Kitona agreement of December 1961, the Adoula Government turned its attention to the 'secession' in Stanleyville. Gizenga's autonomist posture was quickly liquidated once Lundula, who headed the A.N.C. garrison in Stanleyville, transferred his allegiance to Léopoldville; the handful of soldiers still loyal to Gizenga were easily overcome in January 1962 by the main body of the garrison, with token assistance from U.N. Ethiopian troops. Gizenga himself was removed to Léopoldville and locked up. Nkrumah was presently busy appealing to all and sundry for Gizenga's release, but he was clearly hard put to it to justify and find much sympathy for a 'secessionist'. The wheel had, indeed, turned full circle. The Ghana Government perforce began to distinguish between 'different types' of secession, not an easy exercise for a government which had all along placed such a heavy emphasis on the 'sacred' principle of national unity and territorial integrity. Secession on behalf of African nationalism was in Nkrumah's eyes of a different order altogether from that on behalf of what he called neo-colonialism; for him the two were not comparable at all. For others they were; and Ghana was ceaselessly charged with duplicity and double-talk and with 'interfering in the internal affairs of the Congo'.

In point of fact, there was little that Ghana could do effectively to 'interfere' in the Congo. All along, its resources lagging far behind its sympathies, the Ghana Government had been able to offer the nationalist forces little more than comfort and the promise of some slight material aid. Even here, though, the political obstructions to the supply line between Accra and Stanleyville—owing to the refusal first of the Sudan, then (in 1964) of Kenya, to allow the passage across their territories of any aid outside the U.N. framework—meant that Ghana was actually able to fulfil few of its promises of material help.

On the diplomatic front, Ghana henceforth continually pressed the need for a just recognition of the 'claims' of Lumumbist forces in any political settlement in the Congo. In inter-African and U.N. councils, the Ghana Government was mainly concerned, in different ways, to keep the Congo issue alive, while waiting for the recovery and reorganisation of the nationalist forces and their renewed offensive against imperialism. Two examples of this policy may be given. Nkrumah attempted, in the first quarter of 1963, to have Tshombe arrested by the U.N. and arraigned for Lumumba's murder;[1] and later in the year Ghana proposed that an all-African force should replace the U.N. contingent in the Congo.[2]

On the wider international front, Ghana increasingly linked Africa's struggle against imperialism with similar struggles in other parts of the world. This link was inaugurated with the Bay of Pigs fiasco in April 1961, following which Nkrumah affirmed Ghana's 'solidarity' with Cuba for the latter's 'heroic resistance to colonialism, for we see the same danger threatening the peace and security of Africa today'.[3] During a comprehensive tour of the Soviet Union, Eastern Europe, and China, July–August 1961, Nkrumah extended this link and further revised his strategy of anti-imperialist struggle. This not only opened a new phase in Ghana's policy of non-alignment but also exposed it to bizarre charges of becoming 'the first Soviet satellite in Africa'.

On the African front, Ghana waged its battle against neo-colonialism with an increasingly revolutionary zeal: by a more active pursuit of the goal of 'African political union', by a dogged resistance to projects of regional co-operation in different parts of Africa (and particularly East Africa), and by its support and aid for radical nationalist forces in *other* African states—policies cohering together ideologically, more or less, but not necessarily compatible one with the other in the short run, and exposing Ghana to further charges of 'interference' and 'subversion'. The establishment of the O.A.U. in May 1963 appeared to broaden somewhat the options and means available to Ghana. But, to Nkrumah's obvious disappointment, the O.A.U. was to prove itself as inadequate to advance the African revolutionary cause, during the second phase of the Congo crisis in 1964, as the U.N. had been inadequate to defend the African nationalist cause during the first phase of the crisis in 1960–1.

[1] See Nkrumah's correspondence on this subject in January 1963 with the U.N. Secretary-General and Prime Minister Adoula, in *Challenge*, pp. 214–23. The Congolese Foreign Minister, Bomboko, dismissed the Ghanaian initiative as a 'flagrant interference in the internal affairs' of his country. In March Ghana dropped its demand for Tshombe's arrest as its contribution towards smoothing the way to the founding conference of the O.A.U. in May 1963.

[2] See *Challenge*, ch. 21. The Ghanaian proposal was opposed by the Congo Government. Nkrumah in a message on 2 October 1963 advised the Ghana Foreign Minister then in New York to 'insist that this question [of an all-African force] is particularly an African problem and not one for the Congolese people alone because none of us can escape the consequences of a stongly-entrenched neo-colonialist force in the Congo'. Ibid. pp. 231–2.

[3] *Ghana Today*, 26 April 1961. In the past, on issues such as Korea and Hungary which, like Cuba, bore directly on the interests of the super-powers, Ghana had been scrupulously 'correct', i.e. neutral.

The Journal of Modern African Studies, 14, 3 (1976), pp. 427-447

Nationalisation
and Indigenisation in Africa

by LESLIE L. ROOD*

IN the last decade the states of black Africa have taken over a score of large industries owned by multi-national corporations and thousands of small enterprises owned by non-African residents. The methods of take-over, the targets, and the stated justifications vary from country to country, and yet there is a pattern throughout it all. Africans want control in their own house. This article reviews the facts of the takings in black Africa, considers the changing international law of nationalisa-tion, and looks into the future of this confrontation between Africans and foreigners.

THE CAUSES

This tide of takeovers results from the conjunction of two unusual conditions – the foreign dominance of the modern sector of the black African economy, and the growing feasibility of nationalisation.

Though foreign ownership has been prominent in the commerce and industry of almost all of the world's developing countries, it has had complete dominance in black Africa. This was a logical development growing out of Africa's special situation. Unlike the Americas, where waves of immigrants joined with or displaced the indigenous people and later started industries, and unlike Asia where the inhabitants already had partially developed economies of their own, black Africa had little possibility of generating locally owned enterprises during the colonial years. Large foreign trading companies spread over much of the region in the early twentieth century to buy local products and to sell consumer goods; later these trading houses and the European settlers established small manufacturing plants to process local products and make simple articles. At the same time Indians, Pakistanis, Syrians, Lebanese, Greeks, and Portuguese (sometimes lumped together as Asians), usually keeping one foot in the homeland, entered into small trade and, occa-sionally, small manufacturing.

The large multi-national corporations during all of this century have been carving out plantations, digging mines and, most recently, drilling oil wells; coincident with their sprawl over the globe in the last

* Associate Professor of Law, Georgia State University, Atlanta.

two decades, which has put them in control of the bulk of the world's foreign investments, they have established manufacturing plants to serve the black African market of over 200 million people. Foreign banks, insurance companies, public utilities, and service companies have arrived at a steady pace. But relatively few Europeans have come to live permanently, the white settlers of East Africa being the nearest parallel to the immigrants who populated the United States and Australia. While this influx of foreign enterprise into an underdeveloped area was not in itself unusual, the failure of local enterprise to have a concomitant growth was.[1]

By the time of independence, during the early 1960s, the economy of a typical black African state consisted of three levels: Europeans and Americans at the top holding the large industries, Asians in the middle doing much of the wholesale and retail trading, and Africans at the bottom continuing in farming, market trading, and rudimentary services. This state of affairs should not be surprising. Most of the peoples of black Africa lived in primitive circumstances up to World War II. Even now the usual literacy rate is less than 20 per cent and the average income *per capita* is less than $200. Their own culture did not orient them towards industry, and by the time of independence there were few people prepared by training or experience to function in modern business enterprises. Rarely were Africans encouraged by colonial governments or foreign owners to progress further than the low rungs on the career ladder.

With the abrupt end in the 1960s of the political domination which had made possible this upside-down economic situation, the local people, so long colonial nonentities, woke up to find themselves in command – seemingly able to do as they wished with their economies. But the euphoria of independence passed, and they learned that the path out of underdevelopment was to be long and arduous. Somewhat frustrated, it was only natural that their attention turned to mines, oil fields, plantations, factories, and banks which prospered in their midst. Or perhaps it would be more accurate to say that they now found themselves in a position to do something about these rich foreign enterprises which they had long regarded with envy.

[1] Leslie L. Rood, 'Foreign Investment in African Manufacturing', in *The Journal of Modern African Studies* (Cambridge), XIII, 1, March 1975, p. 19; Dharam P. Ghai, 'Concepts and Strategies of Economic Independence', in ibid. XI, 1, March 1973, p. 21; Walter Chudson, 'Africa and the Multinational Enterprise', in H. R. Hahlo, J. Graham Smith, and Richard W. Wright (eds.), *Nationalism and the Multinational Enterprise* (Leiden, 1973), p. 136; Carl Widstrand (ed.), *Multinational Firms in Africa* (Uppsala, 1975); and Rita Cruise O'Brien, 'Lebanese Entrepreneurs in Senegal: economic integration and the politics of protection', in *Cahiers d'études africaine* (Paris), XV, 1, 1975, p. 95.

The second condition which has engendered the tide of takeovers in tropical Africa has been the increasing acceptance of nationalisation throughout the world. Prior to this century there were few takeovers because foreign investments were in colonial possessions or weak countries where unruly conduct could be curbed by outside investor forces, or they were located in mature countries where they were protected by deep respect for private property. In this century nationalisation has become common and, though the investors and their governments have continued to protest, the takeovers have stirred less and less interest.

As might be expected, the black African states, striving for an economic autonomy which would match their new political independence, turned to nationalisation as a solution. After all, it was being used by other underdeveloped countries with long experience; there were economic and political benefits to be had, seemingly at little cost; and the investor countries no longer had effective deterrents in diplomacy, warships, courts, or economic pressures. There was also an absence of legal inhibitions within the African cultures: the sanctity of contract, the law of the responsibility of states for their actions, and the whole system of international law which had grown up in the West were not a part of the African heritage.[1] They have been thinly grafted onto the African system, and without much thought or consent by the local people. Rather than holding these legal concepts sacred, as do westerners, Africans are more likely to regard them as the means by which the outsiders maintained injustice for centuries. More is said of this later.

A word might be said here about terminology. The terms nationalisation and expropriation are both used to describe the taking of property by a government. *Expropriation*, the original legal term, carries with it the image of the early takings of individual pieces of property. As used in the legal literature it often has the connotation of being a somehow wrongful act which can only be justified if it meets certain redeeming requirements, such as a public purpose and adequate compensation. *Nationalisation*, on the other hand, is a term which came into use in this century to describe broad-scale takings which are a part of a social and economic reform for the betterment of the people – for example, the takeover of steel in Britain or the means of production in Russia. While the terms have different connotations, and even dissimilar legal consequences in the view of some writers, these differences are often blurred

[1] See Max Gluckman, *The Ideas in Barotse Jurisprudence* (New Haven, 1965), p. 170.

in United Nations resolutions, national legislation, court decisions, and legal writings. The friendly word is nationalisation; the critical word is expropriation. If compensation is not provided, the taking is sometimes described as confiscation. This article will use the term usually employed by African governments – nationalisation.[1]

Indigenisation is the process by which a government limits participation in a particular industry to citizens of the country, thus forcing alien owners to sell. It is usually aimed at small- and medium-sized enterprises which many Africans believe they can manage successfully, and therefore hits hardest at the Asians who often control that level of business. Though it does not fall within the strict definition of nationalisation, because the government does not itself take the property, it shares with nationalisation the objective of recovering control of the economy and promoting local enterprise. Indigenisation often overlaps nationalisation – for example, in cases where the programme starts off to be a sale of property to local citizens but, because of haste or lack of ready buyers, ends up being a transfer to the government.

Africanisation, in this article's use of the term, is the process of replacing non-African employees by Africans, and is usually accomplished through a governmental requirement that an industry limit the employment of foreigners to a designated number. It is a transfer of jobs, rather than ownership. However, the term is sometimes used in a broad sense which covers indigenisation and even nationalisation.

There are some governmental actions which technically might have fallen within the scope of this article, but because they are considered usual rather than unusual, they have been omitted from this analysis. For example, governments have expelled tens of thousands of non-citizen Africans, have taken over public utilities, and have assumed minority positions in new foreign-owned ventures.

THE ACTS

Most of the takings of foreign property in Africa fall into one of three categories: the nationalisation of large extractive industries owned by multi-national corporations; the nationalisation of small branch enterprises of multi-national corporations, typically banking, insurance, and petroleum distribution; and the indigenisation of small- and medium-sized enterprises owned by alien residents. However, there are some takings which do not fall neatly into these categories: nationalisation in the socialist countries has included manufacturing, buildings, and

[1] See Ian Brownlie, *Principles of Public International Law* (Oxford, 1973), p. 517.

plantations; and indigenisation in the free enterprise countries has touched some fairly large European-owned companies. Each kind of taking can be blunt or sophisticated, compensated or uncompensated, voluntary or compulsory.

Table 1 gives a summary of the takeovers in black Africa in the years 1960–75. This information has been gathered from news reports, periodicals, and recent personal visits to nine of the countries, and to a minor extent from fragmentary official sources. All information about takeovers – whether it concerned a single enterprise or a class of enterprises – was recorded in the research, but the tabulations set forth here are drafted in terms of categories of industries. No attempt was made to calculate the number of instances or the value of property. Value is a slippery concept and, in any event, the data are not available. The number of instances can be misleading; for example, Shell-B.P.'s huge Nigerian operation and a village store each count as one unit. And should one count an amicable acquisition by the government of a minority share? and the thousands of instances of indigenisation?

The data are far from perfect. Government decrees designating industries for takeover are publicised, but the failures to implement them are not. Administration is halting and uneven. Official censuses of industries taken over have yet to be made. Even observers on the scene are imprecise as to which enterprises within an industry have been taken. What is clear is that the total of takeovers is massive, and that the movement is all one way – towards local ownership.

The magnitude of the movement in Africa is confirmed by a recent United Nations count of nationalisations and takeovers in the world.[1] In the 1960–74 period it found more instances in black Africa than in any other region: of 875 cases of nationalisation in 62 countries of the world, 340 (or 39 per cent) were in black Africa. The region led in all categories of industry except petroleum – that is, in instances of nationalisation of mining, agriculture, manufacturing, trade, public utilities, banking, and insurance. That some $4 billion of the property of U.S. nationals alone was nationalised world-wide in the period 1960–73 suggests the total values involved.[2]

Some obvious conclusions can be drawn from the data which have been assembled. There has been a takeover of some nature in almost every country with an attractive target, the Ivory Coast, Liberia, and

---

[1] U.N. Secretary General, *Permanent Sovereignty Over Natural Resources*, A/9716 (Supplement to E/5425), 20 September 1974.
[2] Ibid. Annex p. 1.

TABLE 1

Takings of Foreign Investments in Black Africa, 1960–75[a]

I. Four Leading States

NIGERIA   Stock of private foreign direct investments: 1967 – $1,109 million; 1973 – $2,400 million.[b] *Nationalisation*: massive but selective. Petroleum production (Shell-B.P., Phillips-Agip, Safrap, Mobil, Gulf) valued at $1,500 million–55%. Banking–40%. Insurance–49%. Some petroleum distribution (Shell) – 60%. *Indigenisation*: comprehensive. Wholly reserved to Nigerians: all enterprises in 22 categories (e.g. small retail, bakeries, newspapers, and garment manufacturing); all small enterprises (under ₦400,000 capital and ₦1,000,000 turnover) in 33 categories of more complex industries (e.g. brewing, construction, large retail, and cement). Nigerians must hold 40% share in large enterprises in the 33 categories. Guesstimates that ₦500 million involved.[c]

ZAÏRE $481/640m. *Nationalisation*: massive but selective. Copper (Union Minière) valued at $700 million – 100%. Diamonds(M.I.B.A.). Petroleum production – 15%. Plantations, petroleum distribution, transportation, many large manufacturing and commercial companies – 100%. *Indigenisation*: comprehensive. Retail, wholesale, and some other enterprises indigenised in 1973; large enterprises (turnover above Z1,000,000), including those indigenised in 1973, and much manufacturing taken by the Government in 1974 in preparation for later sale to public; in 1975 some former owners were offered 40% equity in their former enterprises. Net result is widespread, uneven takeover.[d]

GHANA $260/410m. *Nationalisation*: selective. Large (over ₵500,000 capital or ₵1,000,000 turnover) mineral enterprises: gold (Lonrho), diamonds (C.A.S.T.), bauxite (British Aluminium), and manganese (Union Carbide) – 55%. Large timber operations – 55%. Large enterprises producing basic necessities (e.g. sugar, fertilisers, and rubber products) – 55%. Petroleum refining – 100%. Authorised but not implemented: aluminium industry (Valco) – 30%; petroleum production – 20%. *Indigenisation*: comprehensive. Wholly reserved to Ghanaians: small retail and wholesale enterprises (under ₵500,000 capital and ₵1,000,000 turnover); all enterprises in 19 categories of simple industry (e.g. surface transportation, bakeries, and real estate). Required Ghanaian participation: large retail and wholesale, 46 categories of industry (e.g. petroleum distribution, auto assembly, pharmaceuticals, and plastics) – 40/50%;

[a] Sources systematically examined were: *Africa Research Bulletin. Economic, Financial and Technical Series* (Exeter), 1964–75; *West Africa* (London), 1970–75; *Africa* (London), 1971–75; *African Development* (London), 1970–75; *Keesings Contemporary Archives* (London), 1960–75; U.S. Department of Commerce, *Overseas Business Reports*, 1960–75; U.S. Department of Commerce, *Foreign Economic Trends*, 1970–75; U.S. Department of State, *Background Notes*, 1960–75; U.S. Library of Congress, *Expropriation of American-Owned Property by Foreign Governments in the Twentieth Century*, U.S. Congress, Committee on Foreign Affairs, 88th Congress, 1st session, 1963, reproduced in *International Legal Materials* (Washington), II, 6, November 1963, p. 1070; and U.S. Department of State, *Nationalisation, Expropriation, and Other Takings of United States and Certain Foreign Properties since 1960*, 30 November 1971, reproduced in part in *International Legal Materials*, XI, 1, January 1972, p. 84.

[b] O.E.C.D., *Stock of Private Direct Investments by D.A.C. Countries in Developing Countries – End 1967* (Paris, 1972); and *Stock of Private Investment by Member Countries of the Development Assistance Committee in Developing Countries – End 1973* (Paris, 1975). Since O.E.C.D. estimates are made with very conservative criteria, these figures may be only half the actual market values.

[c] *Nigerian Enterprises Promotion Decree, 1972*, reproduced in *Investment Laws of the World* (Dobbs Ferry, 1974), 17:2D, App. I; Alan Hutchison, 'Last Minute Rush to Nigerianise', in *African Development*, March 1974, p. N41; Paul Collins, 'The Political Economy of Indigenization: the case of the Nigerian Enterprises Promotion Decree', in *The African Review* (Dar es Salaam), IV, 4, 1974, p. 491; M. I. Jegede, 'The Nigerian Enterprises Promotion Decree No. 4 of 1972', in *Nigerian Law Journal* (Lagos), VII, 1973, p. 153; George P. Macdonald, 'Recent Legislation in Nigeria and Ghana Affecting Foreign Private Direct Investment', in *International Lawyer* (Chicago), VI, 3, July 1972, p. 555; Jerome F. Donovan, 'Nigeria After Indigenization: is there any room left for the American businessman?', in ibid. VIII, 3, July 1974, p. 600; and *West Africa*, 11 February 1974, p. 142, and 1 April 1974, p. 362.

[d] *Zaïre* (Kinshasa), 10 December 1973, p. 44; *African Development*, April 1974, p. 10, July 1974, p. 10; and *Africa*, January 1975, p. 16.

banking – 40%; small timber and mineral enterprises – 40%; small enterprises producing basic necessities – 50%.[e]

KENYA $172/280m. *Nationalisation*: minor. Banking – 60%. Petroleum refining – 50%. Electric power – 51%. Some farms for redistribution to Kenyans. *Indigenisation*: comprehensive. All enterprises outside of six cities; dealing in commodities mainly consumed by Africans (e.g. sugar, rough textiles); wholesale and retail; export-import, brokerage, manufacturers' representatives, and real estate. Implemented gradually but forcefully since 1967. Half of 140,000 Asians have departed.[f]

II. States which have Nationalised Minerals but done little else

MAURITANIA $101/170m. *Nationalisation*: iron (Miferma) – 100%; copper (Somima) – 100%.

SIERRA LEONE $68/80m. *Nationalisation*: diamonds (S.L.S.T.) – 51%.

SENEGAL $154/230m. *Nationalisation*: phosphates (Taiba) – 50%.

TOGO $42/70m. *Nationalisation*: phosphates (Benin) – 100%.

III. Socialist States

ZAMBIA $421/300m. *Nationalisation*: massive and comprehensive. Copper (Anglo-American, Roan Selection Trust) valued at over $600 million – 51%. Most manufacturing, transport, freehold land, banks, newspapers, and hotels. *Indigenisation*: comprehensive. Decree covers most wholesale and retail trade, and other categories of small business. Largely thwarted by loopholes.[g]

TANZANIA $60/80m. *Nationalisation*: comprehensive. Plantations, manufacturing, large buildings, hotels, banking, insurance, petroleum distribution, export-import, and wholesaling. *Indigenisation*: accomplished through nationalisation.[h]

UGANDA $48/19m. *Nationalisation*: comprehensive. Small copper mine, plantations, banking, insurance, export-import, petroleum distribution, wholesale and retail trade, and virtually all manufacturing. *Indigenisation*: comprehensive and abrupt. Expelled all 40,000 Asians in 90 days who owned wide range of trading and manufacturing enterprises. Government took temporary possession of property.[i]

ETHIOPIA $50/80m. *Nationalisation*: comprehensive. Essential industry (e.g. food, beverages, textiles, leather, chemicals, iron, and printing), petroleum distribution, banking, insurance, and plantations.

SOMALIA $13/17m. *Nationalisation*: selective. Banking, insurance, electric power, sugar mill, petroleum distribution, and shell fishing plant.

[e] *Ghanaian Enterprise Decree, 1968*; *Ghanaian Business (Promotion) Act, 1970*; *Investment Policy Decree, 1975*; *West Africa*, 12 May 1975, p. 533; W. Paatii Ofosu-Amaah, 'Restriction of Aliens in Business in Ghana and Kenya', in *International Lawyer*, VIII, 3, July 1974, p. 452; Macdonald, loc. cit. p. 548; and U.N. Economic Commission for Africa, *Investment Africa* (Addis Ababa), III, 2, September 1975, p. 8.

[f] *Trade Licensing Act of 1967*; Ofosu-Amaah, loc. cit. p. 452; *African Development*, May 1975, p. 49; *Africa Research Bulletin*, May 1975, p. 3492; V. O. Umozurike, 'Nationalisation of Foreign-Owned Property and Economic Self-Determination', in *East African Law Journal* (Nairobi), VI, 1, March 1970, p. 79; Charles G. Lubar, 'Government Protection of Foreign Investment in East Africa', in ibid. VII, 1, March 1971, p. 108; Swadesh S. Kalsi, 'Encouragement of Private Foreign Investment in the Developing Country: provisions in the laws of Kenya', in *International Lawyer*, VI, 3, July 1972, p. 576; and Donald Rothchild, *Racial Bargaining in Independent Kenya* (London, 1973), p. 266.

[g] Richard L. Sklar, *Corporate Power in an African State* (Berkeley, 1975); Umozurike, loc. cit. p. 93; Andrew A. Beveridge, 'Economic Independence, Indigenization, and the African Businessman: some effects of Zambia's economic reforms', in *African Studies Review* (Syracuse), XVII, 3, December 1974, p. 477; and *African Development*, October 1974, p. 249.

[h] *Africa Research Bulletin*, February 1970, p. 1592, and October 1971, p. 2159; Chanan Singh, 'Nationalisation of Private Property and Constitutional Clauses Relating to Expropriation and Compensation', in *East African Law Journal*, VII, 1, March 1971, p. 85; D. D. Nsereko, 'The Tanzania Nationalisation Laws', in *East Africa Law Review* (Dar es Salaam), III, 1970, p. 8; Peter Neerso, 'Tanzania's Policies on Private Foreign Investment', in *The African Review*, IV, 1, 1974, p. 61; Lubar, loc. cit. p. 119; and Umozurike, loc. cit. p. 92.

[i] Frank Wooldridge and Vishnu D. Sharma, 'International Law and the Expulsion of the Ugandan Asians', in *International Lawyer*, IX, 1, January 1975, p. 30; *African Development*, June 1974, p. 27; *Africa South of the Sahara* (London, 1975), p. 919; and Lubar, loc. cit. p. 124.

CONGO $90/110m. *Nationalisation*: selective. Timber operations, sugar mill, insurance, petroleum exploration, and distribution.

BENIN $18/30m. *Nationalisation*: selective. Most manufacturing, banking, insurance, petroleum distribution, telecommunications, and port facilities. But not large trading houses (e.g. S.C.O.A., John Holt).

MALAGASY REPUBLIC $72/140m. *Nationalisation*: selective. Banking, insurance, cinemas, large trading house (C.M.M.), and electric power.

GUINEA $93/180m. *Nationalisation*: selective. Large bauxite operation (Fria) – 49%. Most manufacturing and commerce. Petroleum distribution. Small disputed bauxite operation (Alcan) taken over in 1961. *Indigenisation*: foreign businessmen banned in 1968.

MALI $7/9m. *Nationalisation*: comprehensive – accomplished in early 1960s.

IV. States which have taken Minor or No Action

IVORY COAST $202/375m.

LIBERIA $300/440m.

GABON $265/425m. *Nationalisation*: projected iron mine (Bethlehem); cement plant; and some petroleum distribution.

CAMEROUN $150/240m. *Nationalisation*: electric power.

CENTRAL AFRICAN REPUBLIC $37/55m. *Nationalisation*: petroleum distribution; and shoe manufacturing (Bata).

MALAWI $30/70m. *Indigenisation*: Asian traders forced to leave rural areas.[j]

NIGER $23/35m.

UPPER VOLTA $16/20m.

CHAD $18/22m.

BURUNDI $14/20m.

RWANDA $15/20m.

GAMBIA $2/7m.

Gabon being notable exceptions to this generalisation. There have not been takings in some poor countries where there are no attractive targets. Large petroleum and mineral extraction industries have been nationalised in Nigeria, Zaïre, Zambia, and Mauritania; lesser mineral industries have been taken in Ghana, Senegal, Sierra Leone, and Togo. Extensive takings based on socialist ideology have been carried out in Tanzania, Zambia, Uganda, Ethiopia, Somalia, and Benin. There have been broad indigenisation programmes in Nigeria, Ghana, Zaïre, Kenya, Uganda, and Zambia.

The takeovers are not directed at any particular investor country; they hit whatever country has properties. The United Kingdom – the biggest investor in the region, the major holder in the Nigerian petroleum fields, and the ex-mother country of the leaders in indigenisation – has been hit hardest. France, the second largest investor, has been struck by nationalisation of extractive industries in several countries, but little touched by indigenisation. The United States, the third investor, has been affected primarily by nationalisation of large

[j] *Africa Research Bulletin*, April 1970, p. 1676, April 1975, p. 3459, and July 1975, p. 3553.

extractive industries. Belgium, the fourth, has suffered extensive take-overs, including that of copper in her former colony, Zaïre.

However, it helps to maintain perspective by taking note of what has not, as well as what has, been taken over. In the Ivory Coast, Liberia, Gabon, and Cameroun there have been no significant takings. In socialist Guinea the Halco and Fria bauxite operations continue to be privately controlled. In Ghana the Valco aluminum plant, despite the 1975 decree authorising a 30 per cent takeover, continues to be privately owned. Cameroun's aluminum plant, Alucam, is also privately controlled. In Zaïre, which has been zealous in takeovers, many large new manu-facturing plants, such as General Motors and Goodyear, are untouched. In Nigeria, despite the massive nationalisation of petroleum and the comprehensive indigenisation of lesser enterprises, there are scores of foreign-owned construction and manufacturing corporations which are doing a handsome business. These are only some notable examples of the continued flourishing of privately-owned enterprises.

Extractive industry

There were roughly two score sizeable petroleum and mineral extrac-tive projects in black African countries a few years ago. Well over half of them in number and value have now passed to government control through nationalisation. Some of the early takings, for example, in Zambia and Zaïre, caused bitter disputes and prolonged negotiations, but as the methods of the host governments became more sophisticated, and as the world attitude towards nationalisation softened, the takings began to resemble modern business deals where one of the parties had overwhelming strength. Some compensation has been agreed upon in most cases, customarily in the form of long-term payments out of future profits of the operation.

The petroleum, copper, iron, bauxite, phosphate, gold, and diamond operations are natural targets, not only because the pattern for their seizure has been established on other continents, but because they are highly visible, rich, and apparently profiting at the expense of the local inhabitants. The people are deeply disturbed that a foreign corporation is taking from the soil – their soil – a natural resource which can never be replaced.

The main justification in the takeovers has been that the national government must be in control of the exploitation of its own natural resources. The countries have discovered that, with a little outside help, they can operate the mines and wells. There is, in fact, no longer a great deal of time or rhetoric spent in justifying the takeovers or in arguing against them in principle; in contrast with the Mexicans of 1918 and the Iranians of 1951, whose expropriations were regarded as somehow akin to theft or to the dishonourable breaking of a sacred contract, Africans do not face a hostile world opinion.

Services

Petroleum distribution, branch banks, and insurance operations belonging to large foreign companies are common targets of nationalisation. It is not unusual for there to be three or four branch operations of each of these industries in each country. The justification is the usual one – the need to control what is essential. But these takings differ from those in extractive industry: since the assets involved in each taking are usually valued only in hundreds of thousands of dollars the corporations can suffer expulsion without strain and, looking to future business relations or being resigned, they offer less resistance.

In many countries there have been assumptions of ownership of public utilities, such as electric power, telecommunications, urban transit, port facilities, and civil aviation. Though these are nationalisations, they have excited little interest because such facilities are usually publicly owned in Europe.

Manufacturing

In selective nationalisations, contrasted with the complete takeovers in communist and socialist countries, manufacturing is rarely a target. This is true for Africa and the world. Manufacturing is free of most of the characteristics of mines, oil wells, banks, and insurance which attract takeovers. It is not an essential element of the economy, and rather than taking out an irreplaceable natural resource it brings in the useful articles that people want.

But more important, it is not considered feasible to take over manufacturing. A manufacturing plant in a developing country, unless it is one which merely processes a local raw material for export, is usually an integral part of a multi-national corporation's world-wide system. Usually in Africa it receives most of its components from abroad and assembles them for local marketing, as in the case of automobiles. It receives a continuing flow of know-how from the parent company which enables it to keep abreast of advances by competitor plants in other countries. Under these circumstances, a government which nationalises a manufacturing plant obtains only a building, some machinery, and the know-how of the past; the flow of materials, components, techniques, and relationships ceases, and the plant languishes.

It is this impracticality which is the greatest deterrent to nationalisation of manufacturing.

Indigenisation

Transfer of small- and medium-scale business from aliens to citizens in black African circumstances is natural and inevitable. Africans are on the move from village life to the modern world; they covet the many enterprises which are operated by foreigners in their midst, and believe they are capable of managing them. Dislike of the Asian community plays a part in all countries, but the forced sale of European enterprises, notably in Nigeria and Ghana where large companies are affected, demonstrates that indigenisation is a genuine effort to promote local enterprises and not just an anti-Asian movement.

Indigenisation assumes many forms. Nigeria's programme, which is one of the most comprehensive, bans all foreigners in 22 categories of enterprises, most of them fairly simple. In 33 other categories which may present greater complexity the decree requires that the small enterprises be owned exclusively by Nigerians, and that large enterprises have a 40 per cent Nigerian participation in ownership. Major enterprises, such as United Africa and Costain Construction, have sold shares to the public, and small owners, many of them Lebanese and Indians, have either departed or shifted to new businesses. Due to the bountiful financing provided by the oil boom, as well as to firm administration, the programme has moved ahead and has won wide approval. The only complaint of the Nigerians is that it does not go far enough; 40 per cent does not give much local control.

Ghana's programme resembles Nigeria's, but since inauguration in 1968 has been hampered by ministerial indecision and lack of funds. The Government renewed its efforts with a decree of 1975, and now large corporations, such as C.F.A.O. and Texaco, and the banks are selling the necessary 40 per cent interest to the public, and many small owners are selling out completely. However, the programme is so extensive and the costs are so great that implementation will probably be prolonged.

Zaïre is struggling with a vaguely stated, unevenly administered, and inadequately financed programme. An indigenisation decree of 1973 directed primarily against Portuguese, Greek, and Belgian retailers and wholesalers was thought by the Government to have merely replaced a foreign élite with a local élite. It was succeeded by a 1974 decree in which the state took over most large enterprises, foreign and domestic; but beneficial foreign enterprises – for example, the modern manufacturing plants which had come in under the 1969 investment code – were not touched. In a decree of 1975 the Government back-tracked by offering to restore 40 per cent ownership to some old owners if they would return and provide management. Thus, there is a curious mix of indigenisation and nationalisation.

Kenya, wishing to eliminate a large Asian business community without damaging her favourable investment climate, has administered a thorough programme with consideration for the evicted; by denying renewal of business licences she has gradually excluded aliens from certain categories of commerce and industry. Zambia has attempted to oust Asians from transportation, construction, and most retail and wholesale trade by denial of licences, but, as in other countries, the programme has been partially thwarted. Tanzania attained her ends by nationalising rather than indigenising. Uganda abruptly expelled her 40,000 Asians in a 90-day period; they were forced to transfer their property to designated agents, ostensibly for later sale, but no compensation has yet been arranged.

Implementation of indigenisation programmes has been imperfect and delayed in all countries. Their complexity has presented formidable administrative problems for inexperienced bureaucracies: aliens have sought evasion through ownership fronts, exceptions to the rules, and citizenship changes; local citizens have lacked the capital to buy out the aliens; and corruption has been common. Even the most humanely administered of these programmes is harsh: whether the deadline is three months or three years, a mandatory sale in a capital-scarce economy yields low compensation; in many instances nothing more is received than a government promise to pay in the distant future. Added to this is the human anguish of uprooting long-established families.

Compensation

Though details about the amounts of compensation in African nationalisations and indigenisations are lacking, it seems clear that the payments usually fall far short of what the foreign property holders regard as adequate. Funds to pay for the nationalised extractive industries are usually promised out of future earnings of the operations. While the measure of valuation and the method of payment may be unsatisfactory to the old owners, there are limits to their counteraction. The multi-national companies owning extractive industries have preferred to arrive at settlements, inadequate though they may be, and to maintain the relationships which assure them of a continuing supply of raw materials for their operations downstream.

The multi-national banks, insurance companies, and petroleum distributors, whose many small operations are affected, have often found it best to settle in order to maintain a business connection. The thousands of Asians and Europeans whose smaller properties have been indigenised have usually come off badly. Even in Nigeria, where the deadlines were liberal and the money problem was eased by the current oil prosperity, foreigners received patently low compensation.

THE LAW

By what standards of law are these many African takings of foreign property to be judged? By the law of the state where the property is located? Or by international law? and if so, by what version? The comfortable answer for westerners, familiar with legal systems which are protective of private property, is to place reliance upon classical international law which requires adequate compensation for the taking of an alien's property.[1] But we are faced with the difficulty that the new states of Latin America, Asia, and Africa, the location of most nationalised property, have not adopted the whole of classical international law;[2] though the rules of the game called for them to accept it on entry into the world community, they have instead been selective, accepting most of it, but rejecting those parts with which they disagree. They found much of it tailored to the needs of the great powers and not to their own situation.

[1] On expropriation and nationalisation in general, see Brownlie, op. cit. pp. 504–34; Max Sorensen, *Manual of Public International Law* (New York, 1968), pp. 485–9; D. P. O'Connell, *International Law* (London, 1965), pp. 836–67; Gillian White, *Nationalization of Foreign Property* (New York, 1961); B. A. Wortley, *Expropriation in Public International Law* (Cambridge, 1959); Konstantin Katzarov, *The Theory of Nationalization* (The Hague, 1964); Henry J. Steiner and Detlev F. Vagts, *Transnational Legal Problems* (Mineola, 1976), pp. 408–95; William W. Bishop, Jr., *International Law* (Boston, 1971), pp. 851–99; Abram Chayes, Thomas Ehrlich, and A. F. Lowenfeld, *International Legal Process* (Boston, 1969), p. 838; Marjorie M. Whiteman, *Digest of International Law*, Vol. 8 (Washington, 1967), pp. 1020–1185; and Ingrid Delupis, *Finance and Protection of Investments in Developing Countries* (New York, 1973).

[2] For authorities questioning the classical view on expropriation, see R. P. Anand, *New States and International Law* (Delhi, 1972), p. 62; S. Prakash Sinha, *New Nations and the Law of Nations* (Leiden, 1967), p. 11; F. C. Okoye, *International Law and the New African States* (London, 1972), p. 175; Jorge Castaneda, 'The Underdeveloped Nations and the Development of International Law', in *International Organization* (Madison), xv, 1961, p. 38; S. N. Guha Roy, 'Is the Law of Responsibility of States for Injuries to Aliens a Part of Universal International Law?', in *American Journal of International Law* (Washington), lv, 4, 1961, p. 863; and Padilla Nervo and R. B. Pal, *Yearbook of the International Law Commission, 1957*, Vol. 1 (New York, 1957), pp. 155–8.

Writers on Africa, aside from Okoye, op. cit. pp. 178–84, pay relatively little attention to the subject: see T. O. Elias, *Africa and the Development of International Law* (Dobbs Ferry, 1972); Romain Yakemtchouk, *L'Afrique en droit international* (Paris, 1971); E. L. Nwogugu, *The Legal Problems of Foreign Investment in Developing Countries* (Manchester, 1965); and Samuel Suckow, *Nigerian Law and Foreign Investment* (Paris, 1966).

International law, like domestic law, is largely a reflection of the norms of those elements in the community which have enough influence to make them prevail. It is not a neutral theory of justice arrived at through pure reason, or a set of rules delivered to mankind at the mountain top. There is, of course, more to international law than the dictates of the powerful, and justice and universal principles are not absent from it, but one must bear in mind that it has a relationship to the self-interest of the states who make it. And this does not apply only to the great powers. The new states are rejecting part of the established international law, not because of cultural differences with the old states, as is sometimes thought, but because they regard it as being contrary to their own self-interest.[1]

Development of the law of nationalisation

Until fairly recently the world was dominated by a handful of powers in Europe and North America, and their ideas about international law prevailed.[2] What they formulated on the expropriation of alien property was greatly influenced by their own domestic law that the taking of a citizen's property was permissible only if it was for the good of the country and if the citizen was compensated.[3] In the international cases which arose in the first two decades of this century – typically, a 'backward' country taking the property of a citizen of a 'civilised' power – this rule was usually applied.[4] International law paid some attention to the idea that the local law should govern but, usually finding such law inadequate, it devised an alternative called the international minimum standard of justice: if a state was deficient in legal safeguards, international law would impose upon it an international standard, in effect the minimum standard used in the investor countries.[5]

The first major attack on the existing international law of expropriation came in the Russian Revolution of 1917 in which all industries, farms, and businesses, including some alien property, were taken by the Government without compensation.[6] The second blow came in Mexico in the years 1915–40 when the Government took over many agricultural and oil properties. The United States, some of whose nationals were affected, conceded that a country had a right to take property for the social betterment of its people, but strongly argued that compensation –

[1] See Wolfgang Friedmann, *The Changing Structure of International Law* (New York, 1964), p. 317; and Anand, op. cit. pp. 48–66.

[2] J. L. Brierly, *The Law of Nations* (New York, 1963), p. 43.

[3] F. V. Garcia-Amador, *Yearbook of the International Law Commission, 1959*, Vol. II (New York, 1959), p. 18; and Anand, op. cit. p. 41.

[4] Castaneda, loc. cit. p. 39; and Nervo and Pal, op. cit. pp. 155 and 158.

[5] Brownlie, op. cit. pp. 509–11; and Anand, op. cit. p. 41; and Steiner and Vagts, op. cit. p. 357.

[6] Katzarov, op. cit. p. 323.

prompt, adequate, and effective – must be paid. Mexico replied that the social benefits of nationalisation in an impoverished country were justification for not paying compensation. Although compromise payments were made, the principle involved was not resolved.[1]

After World War II circumstances made nationalisation much more feasible: colonies and dependent countries became independent; socialism and nationalism prospered; the ideals of the United Nations and the inhibitions of the nuclear stalemate made it impractical for investor nations to resort to force. Iran, another poor country saddled with a lucrative concession, nationalised its oil in 1951; Egypt seized the Suez Canal in 1957; Indonesia took over its oil in 1958. In the negotiations and court cases which arose out of these takings it became ever plainer that there were several different views on the law of nationalisation; and in no instance was classic international law effective in obtaining satisfactory redress.

The pace of nationalisation quickened during the 1960s and 1970s, particularly in the takeover of natural resource industries in underdeveloped countries: Zaïre, Zambia, Chile, Peru, Algeria, Libya, and Saudi Arabia were notable examples. The legal situation became even more obscure; in the *Sabbatino* case of 1964 which concerned nationalisation in Cuba, the U.S. Supreme Court said: 'There are few if any issues in international law today on which opinion seems to be so divided as the limitations on a State's power to expropriate the property of aliens'.[2]

There are at least three views of the law. The position of the investor countries, based on the assumptions prevalent in liberal régimes of private property, is that the nationalisation of alien property is lawful, but only if it is for a public purpose, non-discriminatory, and accompanied by compensation which is prompt, adequate, and effective.[3] By far the most common challenge to nationalisation comes on the question of the adequacy of compensation.

The communists regard nationalisation as the unquestioned right of the state. Though they at one time argued in principle that compensation was unnecessary, they have more recently recognised a need for at least some to be paid.[4] However, no reasonable compensation has

[1] G. H. Hackworth, *International Law*, Vol. 3 (Washington, 1942), pp. 655–65; and White, op. cit. p. 232.   [2] *Banco Nacional de Cuba v. Sabbatino*, 376 U.S. 398, 428 (1964).
[3] Brownlie, op. cit. p. 518; and Statement of Policy by the President of the United States Concerning the International Minimum Standard, reproduced in N. E. Leech, C. T. Oliver, and J. M. Sweeney, *International Legal System* (Mineola, 1973), pp. 1070–2.
[4] Friedmann, op. cit. p. 321; Katzarov, op. cit. p. 339; and Chayes, op. cit. p. 843. Also Dale R. Weigel and Burns H. Weston, 'Valuation upon the Deprivation of Foreign Enterprise: a policy-oriented approach to the problem of compensation under international law',

been paid in the communist takeovers in the U.S.S.R., China, and Cuba, and the payments made have usually been dependent upon assets or trade benefits which the property owner's government held within its grasp and was willing to trade off to the communist state.[1]

The views of the underdeveloped countries are less categorical. There is no single position articulated by all of them, but rather a variety of practices which have arisen out of their takeovers. Though they almost never deny the obligation of compensation, they are unwilling to be held to the formula of 'prompt, adequate, and effective'. One facet of their position is that aliens are entitled only to the same treatment as the nationals of the host country. A Mexican judge on the International Court of Justice said recently: 'Investors who go abroad in search of profits take a risk and go there for better or for worse, not only for better. They should respect the institutions and abide by the national laws of the country where they chose to go.'[2]

A decade of effort by the developing countries culminated in 1962 in the U.N. General Assembly Declaration of Permanent Sovereignty over Natural Resources.[3] This goes a step towards establishing broad policy favourable to the nationalising states by such language as 'the inalienable right of all States freely to dispose of their natural wealth and resources in accordance with their national interests', and 'respect for the economic independence of states'; in the article on nationalisation there is a call for 'appropriate' compensation in accordance with local and international law. While the Declaration recognises the principle of compensation, its broad language is favourable to the aims of the nationalising countries, and its substitution of 'appropriate' for 'adequate' makes it very helpful to these governments.

Briefly, the underdeveloped nations contend that they have a right to control their own natural resources, that nationalisation is the only way to attain this right, and that they are unobligated and unable to make full and prompt payment.

Compensation

The fundamental problem in almost all nationalisations now comes down to the measure of compensation. The American judge on the International Court of Justice said in the *Barcelona* case in 1970:

in Richard B. Lillich (ed.), *The Valuation of Nationalized Property in International Law* (Charlottesville, 1972), p. 4.

[1] See Steiner and Vagts, op. cit. pp. 433–5; and Bishop, op. cit. pp. 864–5.

[2] *Barcelona Traction, Light and Power Co., Ltd.*, International Court of Justice Reports 1970, p. 250.

[3] U.N. General Assembly, Official Record, 17th Session, Supplement No. 17 (A/5217), p. 15.

In States having different types of economic and financial problems, international law has become increasingly permissive of actions involving nationalisations. In place of what used to be denounced as illegal expropriation, the issues now turn largely on the measure of compensation, since even the famous General Assembly Resolution on Permanent Sovereignty over Natural Resources provides that compensation is due.[1]

It must be recognised that there are sound arguments of principle for questioning the rule that a state must compensate an alien for the nationalisation of his property. Most states in the western world have sanctified the concept of private property and limited their own power of takeover. 'But', as put by John Fischer Williams almost half a century ago in arguing against a universal requirement of compensation, 'the duty of a government towards individuals in respect of their property varies with each successive stage of civilisation; it is not the same in the modern world as in ancient or medieval societies, nor is it the same in all countries today.'[2] He pointed out that a general dogma as to the inviolability of private property could no more be erected into an international duty than any other political or economic doctrine. The spread of communism and socialism to half the people of the earth has reinforced his reasoning. It is certainly arguable that a state wishing to institute socialist measures should no more be bound by private property rules than a free enterprise state should be bound by socialist rules.[3]

In truth, all states violate the sanctity of private property when it suits their needs. Western states do not crudely confiscate when they take property: 'they adopt a more elegant procedure'.[4] When national interest requires, they devalue currency, levy near-confiscatory taxes, reduce the value of distilleries by prohibiting alcohol, uproot citizens of enemy descent and seize enemy property in time of war, and take personal property though abolition of slavery, all without adequately compensating the owner of the private property.[5] Internationally, great states have been known to assume control of their continental shelves, or even of neighbouring countries, if vital interests required it. A poor country, fearful of its economic dependence upon a foreign-owned copper mine, may regard its national interests as being as imperative as does the great power.

---

[1] *Barcelona Traction...*, p. 167. See also Bishop, op. cit. p. 866.

[2] John Fischer Williams, 'International Law and the Property of Aliens', in *British Yearbook of International Law* (1928), p. 15.

[3] See also Brownlie, op. cit. p. 521; Brierly, op. cit. pp. 284–5; Wolfgang Friedmann, *Law in a Changing Society* (Baltimore, 1964), p. 345; and F. S. C. Northrop, *The Meeting of East and West* (New York, 1946), pp. 45–8. See White, op. cit. pp. 183–243, for an earlier, contrary view.   [4] Williams, loc. cit. p. 22.

[5] Ibid. p. 22: also Friedmann, *Law in a Changing Society*, p. 346.

When a natural resource or a major industry has been nationalised as a part of a programme of development – and this is the typical taking of the day – the nationalising state usually has the sincere belief that historical circumstances relieve it of the requirement of full compensation. It may argue as follows: the concession was obtained from a colonial government or an illiterate tribal chief who had no power to bind the people; the profits received by the company over the years far exceed the original investment; the company has concealed its true earnings; the operation has not promoted development of the local economy; and the people have been exploited. These arguments are used by governments to reduce the compensation to a fraction of that demanded or even to zero.[1]

In the confrontation which results, the developing country derives strength from its legitimate desire for local control, from a set of appealing arguments about the injustice of the concession, and from its empty pocket. The multi-national corporation, finding no tribunal capable of enforcing 'prompt, adequate, and effective' compensation, can only harass the country by industry boycotts, international financial pressures, and minor suits in foreign courts. And the corporation may find it politic to limit its offensive actions in a struggle it knows it cannot win. As has been said above, this standoff usually results in a settlement for what the corporation considers only partial compensation.

Indigenisation

What has been said above refers to the transfer of private property by the classical means of nationalisation or expropriation: the taking of property by the government for itself. Indigenisation – the governmentally forced transfer of property from alien owners to African citizens – has the same public purpose as nationalisation (recovery of control of the economy), and produces the same effect upon the alien owners (loss of their property), but the law does not easily term it expropriation. In Kenya and Nigeria, where the process was developed, indigenisation has been carried out with considerable attention to legal form and social justification. While the programmes have often resulted in severe economic losses and personal disruptions, they have been carefully planned and moderately implemented.

If these African countries were being judged by the due process standards of the developed world, their indigenisation practices might be considered improper; but they are being judged by their own

[1] James A. Rohwer, 'Nationalization', in *Harvard International Law Journal* (Cambridge, Mass.), XIV, 2, Spring 1973, p. 378.

constitutional standards. Their new constitutions, perhaps drafted with the present moves in mind, provide less protection against discriminatory treatment of aliens.[1] In any event, governments everywhere tend to interpret constitutions in the light of their contemporary conditions and needs, and African governments believe that they are burdened with outsiders who are exercising unreasonable economic domination. Hence, the domestic legal systems offer only a dim avenue of redress for the aliens affected. In international forums the prospects are not much brighter. International law does not guarantee to aliens the privilege of practising a trade or profession in another country, except in so far as that privilege may be given by a treaty, and African countries have refrained from entering into such treaties.[2]

It is, of course, arguable that indigenisation is a taking of property by government action and is therefore expropriation, but this argument encounters several difficulties. First, the government usually is not itself taking in the strict sense, but rather creating conditions forcing the owner to sell the property to someone else. And even if it is, in effect, a taking by the government, the reply is that the property owner has been given a reasonable time to sell and to obtain a fair price.

Whatever may be the legal position of the parties, there has apparently been no serious litigation about the problem. Nigerian and Ghanaian law professors say privately that a frontal attack in the courts is out of the question. The Governments are fully supported by public opinion and would tolerate no such attack. While there has been litigation on questions peripheral to indigenisation, no mention of a case on the basic issue has been found in the voluminous news reports and legal articles on the subject.[3]

In indigenisation, as in nationalisation, the law plays less than a commanding rôle. True, there is discussion by writers of the right of the evicted aliens to compensation, but the aliens are weak in practical legal remedies. Since they have little negotiating strength, they are dependent upon the evicting government's sense of fairness and sensitivity to world public opinion. Some governments have been fair and sensitive; others have not.

[1] Ibid. pp. 466–7; Wooldridge and Sharma, loc. cit. p. 69; and Delupis, op. cit. p. 67. For the opinion that the withdrawal of a license is not a taking of property under the Kenya Constitution, see Singh, loc. cit. pp. 103–4.

[2] Brownlie, op. cit. p. 505; and Ofosu-Amaah, loc. cit. pp. 474–6.

[3] See Singh, loc. cit. p. 103; and Wooldridge and Sharma, loc. cit. p. 62.

THE FUTURE

African governments have now assumed control of (*a*) most of the extractive industries, and (*b*) a large share of plantation agriculture, public utilities, petroleum distribution, banking, insurance, and wholesale trade, but (*c*) very little of modern manufacturing. African private citizens have acquired full or part ownership of a variety of smaller enterprises, particularly retail and wholesale trade. The situation varies greatly from country to country, but the trend is clearly towards the ownership patterns of the rest of the world.

As was to be expected, efficiency has declined. Inexperienced Africans cannot manage complicated mining operations as well as the departing Europeans; nor can they even run retail shops and wholesale distribution systems as well. But to pass judgement on economic grounds is to miss the point. Africans want control for reasons of self-respect, status, power, and nationalism – political reasons. Moreover, on the economic plane Africans may be correct that their earnings from industry – particularly the extractive – are higher under local ownership. And Africans are receiving experience in managing the businesses and industries – now.

What actions will various states take in the future? The pattern of takeovers during the last decade in black Africa, as well as that in the rest of the world, suggests very strongly that they will continue to nationalise and indigenise enterprises whenever they believe it will serve their own interests. The only limitations will be practical ones. First, there is the decreased number of attractive targets after the massive takeovers of recent years; second, many of the remaining targets are indigestible, notably the modern manufacturing plants. The Ivory Coast, Kenya, Gabon, and Cameroun will probably move towards the main stream of the movement. The mini-countries and the least developed will probably also follow the leaders, but only slowly because they have little to take over except trading and simple manufacturing. There is nothing very radical about these predictions. Even if they all were to take place the foreign control in Africa would still be far greater than that in the developed world.

What will foreign investors do? Their future is similarly indicated by the recent past. The small- and medium-scale foreign investors – Indians, Lebanese, French, and British who settled on a semi-permanent basis and started business – are on the downhill slope; they are gradually being restricted in all states. This leaves the field to the multi-national companies, complex entities motivated not only by profit but also by the corporate urges for expansion and raw materials. The oil companies continue to invest, although at a slower rate, even while Nigeria nation-alises them; auto and tyre companies complete plants in Zaïre while the President announces broad plans to takeover the economy; plans for new investments appear in the press each month along with news of further nationalisations. Despite the risk, or even the certainty, of eventual takeover the multi-nationals will go in, selectively of course, to obtain needed raw materials or to preserve markets.

Africa may be at the bottom of the priority list for world investors, but they will not wholly neglect it. The O.E.C.D. data in Table 1 show that private foreign direct investment increased in every black African country except two, Zambia and Uganda, in the period 1967–73.[1] Management contracts, turnkey deals, raw material buying relation-ships, joint ventures, and other arrangements which risk a minimum of the investor's capital, and yet bring to the host country the benefits of modern industrial knowledge, will play an increasingly important rôle in the future.

What will be the legal future? The law of nationalisation will con-tinue to be unsettled. The accretion of compromise settlements and United Nations resolutions is gradually making partial payment res-pectable, but the question whether the payment should be 5 or 75 per cent goes unanswered. Since each nation's view of the law is shaped by its own self-interest, it seems unlikely that a single view will be estab-lished until the interests of the contending nations converge. Meanwhile, the growing strength of the natural resource blocs such as O.P.E.C., the spread of socialism, and the increased acceptance of nationalisation vastly improve the bargaining position of the nationalising countries.

[1] The O.E.C.D. data take into account the disinvestments by nationalisation. The United States, Japan, and Germany, in particular, have continued to invest in extractive industries in the region. Letter from O.E.C.D. to the author, 10 October 1975.

TOWARD CULTURAL INDEPENDENCE IN AFRICA: SOME ILLUSTRATIONS FROM NIGERIA AND GHANA

Robert W. July

To a large extent the independence movement in Africa was a movement toward westernization. If political independence had any purpose beyond its own self, African political leaders stated that it was meant to bring the fruits of economic growth and modernization, long stinted under colonial controls. All this seemed appropriate enough. Had not the West made gigantic strides, particularly in science and technology, advances that had brought steadily rising living standards, better health, housing and schools, and greater leisure with which to enjoy the many new material advantages of life? During the colonial era and before, Europeans had unceasingly assured Africans that their own culture was barbaric and dated, that was best to emulate the European as quickly as possible, to get on with the business of joining the modern world. Africans seemed to agree. At independence governments moved forward at full pace to mechanize their agriculture, to establish modern industries, to introduce all the manifestations of high technology. Among the planners and the politicians there seemed to be little hesitation. All eyes were on the future and the model was the West.

Africa is no monolith, however. Africans may have glimpsed a new and better life in the image of a modernized, western-oriented society, but an age-old civilization still survived, still offered its people much that was satisfying and much that worked. There were Africans who recognized this fact, who were concerned that too rapid and unreflective an adoption of foreign ways might lead to complications, unforeseen and dangerous. They did not wish to turn their backs on the West but they did warn that African needs and conditions should always be given first priority.

The years directly after the Second World War were especially conducive to the revival of indigenous culture. Postwar nationalist movements preached political independence and economic modernization, but there was also the urge for a concurrent reaffirmation of Africa's own values as expressed in its arts, its literature, its philosophy, and its history. Political freedom would thrive best, it was said, when accompanied by a parallel autonomy of cultural expression. What follow are some examples chosen to illustrate the exertions by humanists on behalf of a cultural independence they felt to be an essential part of the decolonization process.[1]

325

HISTORY

It was to be expected that independence movements in Africa would be accompanied by an intensified interest in Africa's past. New nations sought legitimacy in a long-lived, and preferably illustrious, history. The postwar years were marked, therefore, by the establishment of university departments and research insitutes devoted to what was then regarded as the novel and experimental field of African history. The work of a number of individuals broke new ground, for example, the research of the Kenyan historian, Allan Ogot (1967), working in oral history; the innovative and provocative writings of the Senegalese, Cheikh Anta Diop (1955, 1959, 1960, 1967); and the efforts of the Nigerian scholar, J. F. A. Ajayi (1961, 1965), to give shape, direction, and purpose to a virgin field.

It was in Nigeria, in fact and more particularly at the national University of Ibadan, that there appeared at the time the single most active and illustrative growing point in the expansion of teaching and research in African history. This development was due in large measure to the energy and foresign of K. O. Dike, Ibadan's first African professor of history, who later went on to serve as principal and vice-chancellor of the University. Dike joined the Ibadan faculty in 1949 as a young lecturer under inauspicious circumstances. The department was then staffed with British expatriates teaching a syllabus that gave scant recognition to Africa except through the writings of such colonial preconsuls as Harry Johnston and Alan Burns. Dike was regarded as a person of "dangerous ideas;" his recommendations for greater attention to teaching and research on Africa were met by an effort to sidetrack him in favor of a British Africanist, presumably of more orthodox persuasion.

Change was in the air, however. As African colonies moved toward independence, African history slowly began to gain acceptance as a legitimate field of study. In 1956 Dike became department chairman and was able to begin recruiting a generation of Nigerian historians, choosing promising undergraduates for doctoral study and eventual return as members of the history faculty. Most of those selected were sent abroad for postgraduate training at major university centers, pursuing research topics that opened up new areas of the history of Nigeria and of Africa more generally. Dike arranged for their theses to appear in the Ibadan History Series of the London publishing house of Longman, an impressive collection of works that had swelled to some twelve or fifteen volumes by the 1970s, with new manuscripts arriving for consideration and other African universities paying Ibadan the compliment of imitation.[2] By 1959 a small number of Nigerians, including J. F. A. Ajayi, had returned as lecturers, forerunners of many others who soon converted the Ibadan department into one of the most innovative centers anywhere active in the study of African history.[3]

The new lecturers soon inaugurated a variety of courses on Africa. Some were general surveys, others concentrated on geographic regions or on subjects like Islam and economic history. Still others were limited to specialized topics that introduced students to the utilization of primary sources. At the same time the overweighted emphasis of the history syllabus on British and western European history was rectified through attention to other areas of the world such as the United States, Latin America, and eastern Europe. Further, there was a cautious beginning in postgraduate study, but withall, the main emphasis shifted unambiguously to Africa.

In all cases, research and the collection of documents brought forth new material. In this respect, the pre-university schools were not neglected. A conference and workshop was organized in 1963 for school teachers from the West African Commonwealth countries of Nigeria, Ghana, Sierra Leone, and Gambia. The workshop resulted in two survey volumes (Ajayi and Espie, 1965; Anene and Brown, 1966) covering, respectively, West Africa and Africa during the modern period. There followed shortly publication of a useful bibliography of journal articles dealing with African history (Webster, 1965), as well as the 1965 inauguration of *Tarikh*, a periodical providing short essays on various aspects of Africa's history, especially designed for school consumption. Library acquisitions of Africana were steadily expanded and featured a substantial microfilm collection of early West African newspapers and missionary materials.

Many of these curricular developments were the work of Ajayi and the others who had taken over direction of the history department when Dike moved on the become vice-chancellor in 1960. Before leaving the department, however, Dike had introduced several other innovations not directly related to the University but certainly important in the encouragement of the research and teaching of African history. The first of these had to do with the establishment of the Nigerian National Archives.

Dike had long argued for a positive program to retrieve, preserve, store, and classify Nigeria's public records. Official papers and private collections were in varying stages of neglect and decay, rotting, attacked by insects, ill-stored with many documents lost or discarded. Dike submitted a report in 1954 recommending the creation of a public record office for conservation and administration of state papers and other historical records. His blueprint formed the basis for the ultimate establishment of the National Archives with Dike serving as first director.

During the mid-fifties Dike also helped form the Historical Society of Nigeria. The Society soon became a forum for lively discussion on local history, both among academics and the public in general, stimulating research that found outlet in the pages of its journal and the sessions of the Society's scheduled meetings.[4] At the same time Dike was able to encourage activities of an interdisciplinary character through an Institute of African Studies that began life at the University in 1962, and a study of the ancient kingdom of Benin, a wide-ranging survey instituted in 1956 that attempted to coordinate research in such fields as history, anthropology, archeology, and linguistics. While both the Institute of African Studies and the Benin scheme encountered difficulties and generally fell short of initial expectations, they represented additional facets of an energetic and imaginative effort at Ibadan to mark African independence with an appreciation of Africa's past culture and history.[5]

HIGHER EDUCATION

Research and teaching in African history and culture was by no means the exclusive preserve of Ibadan University. Particularly in the new universities of the former British colonies, departments of history were quick to introduce courses on the African past while interdisciplinary institutes of African studies also appeared on a number of African campuses. One of the first and most successful of these establishments was the Institute of African Studies that was inaugurated at the University of Ghana in 1962. Its activities are particularly noteworthy because they were closely related to ideas on education then being argued by the Ghanaian head of state, Kwame Nkrumah.

In many ways Ghana and Nkrumah were the catalysts of African independence, offering inspiration and example to others who were to follow. As prime minister and president of Ghana, Nkrumah became quickly involved in many political problems; for Nkrumah politics was the engine that helped achieve other ends—a better material life for Africa's peoples, a clearer image of Africa's destiny in the contemporary world. Far from distracting Nkrumah's attention from cultural affairs, politics served to distill his thoughts and concentrate his concern for the creation of a new African society. He saw this new society as one retaining much of traditional African civilization, blended with imported, mainly Marxist, ideas of a better society. It is not surprising, therefore, that Nkrumah placed much importance on education and sought to develop a university in Ghana that subserved in training and research the objectives he had in mind.[6]

Development of an appropriate university, however, turned out to be no easy task. Nkrumah sought for Africa an intellectual decolonization, as he put it, to take its place alongside political independence. African universities therefore should have as a first order of business the training of individuals who could help construct the new African society. Nkrumah saw Ghana and Africa moving into an age where socialism shaped societies and Africans joined in a union of states that embraced the entire continent. To achieve this objective the African university would have to produce citizens whose thinking was consonant with these ideas, who were aware of Africa's destiny as Nkrumah then understood it.

The university that Nkrumah inherited from the colonial administration, however, was ill adapted to his needs. It had been created in faithful replica of British models with a rigid structure of degrees that emphasized western institutions and values to the virtual exclusion of Africa, its history and way of life. At independence the then University College of Ghana had a special relationship with the University of London which supervised curricula and conferred London degrees on Ghana graduates. The University College faculty consisted mainly of expatriates, with some few Ghanaians, most convinced that their academic freedom was threatened by Nkrumah and his associates in the government who sought an Africanized curriculum and a radically altered educational philosophy that stressed, in Nkrumah's words (1963b: 3), "the history, culture and institutions, languages and arts of Ghana and of Africa in new African centered ways, in entire freedom from he propostitions and pre-suppositions of the colonial epoch."

To a considerable extent, therefore, fears at the university were justified. Nkrumah's educational philosophy was basically political and, if put into action, would have dictated a sharply changed set of criteria for curriculum, degree structure, and entrance requirements. Nkrumah and his colleagues saw themselves footing the bill for a university bent on training a small privileged elite who thought like Europeans and who seemed determined to oppose efforts to create a new Ghana and a new Africa. Here was an insupportable situation calling for strong action that would set Ghana's national university on a new course.

Stymied by faculty opposition at the university and increasingly entangled with the complexities of leadership in Ghana and Africa, Nkrumah failed to take any decisive action, and, until his fall from power in 1966, the University of Ghana continued its activities without any fundamental changes in policy. At the same time, however, there was a growing awareness among some members of the faculty that academic fields, such as history or religious studies, stood in need of greater attention to African materials. Over a period of several years discussions took place that led ultimately to the establishment of an Institute of African Studies, a move hailed by Nkrumah but generally regarded with suspicion on the campus at Legon Hill.

The Institute was fortunate in having the British scholar, Thomas Hodgkin, as its first director, for Hodgkin was not only a thoughtful and well informed student of African affairs but one who was both sympathetic with Nkrumah's objectives and highly respected in university circles in and out of Africa. Hodgkin and those he brought to the Institute set about generating teaching and research on a broad range of subjects dealing with Africa, "to create a new kind of African," as he said, "in order to break away from . . . being cut off from one's own culture.[7]

Basically the Institute offered graduate instruction in a two-year Master's degree, but there was also a survey of African civilization required of all undergraduates. The curriculum comprised four categories—languages and linguistics, history, social and political philosophy, and the humanities. Each of these was further subdivided; history, to take one example, beginning with Ghana, then expanding outward to embrace much of the African continent, at the same time reaching back into prehistory and examining related fields such as geography, archeology, or historical methodology. With diversity there was also unity and coherence. Hodgkin understood the necessity of studying the institutions of Ghana in the context of a wider African and non-African world, of making the new states of modern Africa intelligible through a familiarity with their predecessor societies of the precolonial world.

What the Institute attempted and achieved in the humanities took on a special character largely due to the exertions of J. H. Nketia, a musician and musicologist who organized the Institute's School of Music and Drama as a center for teaching and research, chiefly in the performing arts. Nketia ultimately succeeded Hodgkin as director of the Institute and remained in that post for fifteen years, but his early association with the university was a good deal more modest. In 1952 Nketia was appointed to the position of research fellow in the department of sociology at the behest of Kofi Busia, who was then a member of the university staff. For several years Nketia had no teaching responsibilities since there was no place for his work in the syllabus. He therefore concerned himself with the transcription and organization of traditional musical materials collected in the field, while producing compositions of his own through which he sought to express traditional modes in new ways. In those days Nketia was a kind of one-man institute of African studies, largely isolated from the rest of the academic community, but it was an invaluable experience. His work was later translated into the curriculum and objectives of the School of Music and Drama.

Nketia's ideas matured over the years, converging with those of Nkrumah and Hodgkin. It was thus a natural move when he came to the Institute to head the performing arts school in 1962. To begin with, Nketia was determined to bring new life to African music, and through music, to dance, theater, and the arts more generally. For Nketia these were not primitive, picturesque exercises, as often represented by unsophisticated westerners, nor were they oddities worthy of study only in some esoteric branch of anthropology. These were artistic, social, religious, or ethical expressions of a vital culture, to be retrieved and given fresh expression in the modern world. What was called for, said Nketia, was collection and analysis, but not just the arid scholarship of one specialist talking to another.

Performance and new composition would follow research. There had to be points of dissemination to the public, reviving memories of the traditional arts, offering the opportunity of participation as performer and observer, providing new validity to ancient values.

Translated into the practicalities of a viable curriculum, there ideals emerged in a variety of forms, serving both academic and utilitarian needs. The music program dealt in the theory, composition, and performance of both western and African music, and offered training from elementary courses to advanced musicology, along with formal study for matriculated university students seeking credits toward the general university degree. The dance program presented modern dance techniques, dance notation, and stagecraft, with basic emphasis on African dance idioms. Drama could be studied at varying levels of complexity involving speech, acting, play analysis, and the technical aspects of production.

The purpose of the entire curriculum was to train teachers for the nation's schools as well as performers in musical ensembles and in dance and drama groups. Because the Institute of African Studies, though part of the university, was not bound by the undergraduate degree structure, it possessed the flexibility to offer certificates and diplomas that testified to proficiency at various levels. Undergirding such multidimensional instruction was basic research providing the materials that eventually found their way into the classroom. Field work in music recorded traditional forms and oral sources, including research into the popular "highlife" style. In dance, social background was studied along with choreography. The literary media of folk tales and minstrel poetry were explored along with modern writing forms. Drama students examined village ceremonies, festivals, and religious rites as a basis for development of modern dramatic writing.

Most staff members of the School of Music and Drama were seasoned performers; this made direct participation in community activities such as chiefly investiture or public festivals, and the organization of workshops and seminars for children or adults possible. This was no mere gesture, for Nketia felt strongly the obligation of the School to those citizens who had helped preserve and restore the ancient traditions of the country. The Institute of African Studies also maintained a library and archive and stood ready to advise individuals and communities on such diverse questions as how to tie a traditional cloth properly or to identify the appropriate forms for naming ceremonies. These were important activities, insisted Nketia. They developed community stability and pride. They evoked understanding among peoples seeking to give birth to new and viable nations.

THE AFRICAN PERSONALITY

Kwame Nkrumah was no closet philosopher. His concept, "African Personality,"[8] reflected no set philosophical system; if the term meant anything, it argued an African presence of unique culture in the world, determined to pursue African interests in the arena of international affairs. But did African Personality mean more than this? Was there indeed a special quality to the black man, something brought on by the African environment, something, perhaps, even genetic?

Many observers, European and African alike, had thought so. The whole Negritude movement was built upon the concept of African uniqueness, cultural and psychological as well as physical; it was no accident that Negritude made its strongest impact at the time of the independence movements, adding a cultural argument to demands for political freedom. The tenets of Negritude varied somewhat from person to person but the major characteristics were generally agreed upon—closeness to nature, sensitivity to religious and artistic impulses, a communal affinity, and, possibly above all, the idea that the black mind was intuitive rather than analytical. The Senegalese poet-statesman L. S. Senghor put forth these views most persuasively, but there were many others, especially in the years directly following the Second Worl War, who gave and enthusiastic testimony to the uniqueness of the black soul.[9]

Belief in the special character of the black man was on thing; however, it did not necessarily embrace all the concepts of Negritude. The West Indian psychiatrist Frantz Fanon for example, found initial solace in the affirmation of blackness contained in the doctrine of Negritude, but ultimately came to reject its message as a betrayal of black individuality, at least in the dialectical argument presented by the French existentialist Jean-Paul Sartre. According to Sartre the black man, having discovered his Negritude, was at once obliged to cast aside this newly-found racial pride and allow his special existence to lose itself, fusing its black anti-racist racism with white racism in a higher non-racial humanity.[10]

Self-denial at the moment of self-discovery made little sense to a seeker of black identity like Fanon, and there were others, equally convinced of the unique character of the African, who could not accept the special precepts of Negritude. An early doubter was the Nigerian playwright Wole Soyinka, whose oft-quoted comment about tigers and tigritude seemed to argue that the idea of Negritude was essentially redundant, but who, in fact, had more seriously reasoned doubts about the movement.

On first consideration, Soyinka's reservations concerning Negritude might seem surprising for, like Senghor and the apostles of Negritude, Soyinka was intent on establishing the identity of the black race. Yet there were differences in method if not objective. Negritude set out to identify an array of black values, to celebrate an African nature. To do this, says Soyinka, it sought its criteria not in Africa but in, of all places, the West. To Soyinka's astonishment Negritude ignored the metaphysical continuity of African psychic existence in favor of a European dialectical argument wedded to a western racist premise. The result was a syllogism, Soyinka points out, wherein European understanding was pictured as analytical, the African as intuitive. Logical analysis being the mark of advanced development—so the argument ran—European civilization occupied a high point of achievement. According to Soyinka, the secondary phase of the syllogism (what Sartre terms the "weak stage of the dialectic progression" [1963: 60]) implied that intuitive thought was of a lower order and the African therefore less highly developed. This would explain, says Soyinka, the consequences of slavery and colonialism. Nevertheless, the racist slur was avoided since both Sartre and Negritude decreed that intuitive thought was also the mark of development. The African was saved. He too could be regarded as advanced.

For Soyinka all this was patent nonsense, another example of Europe imposing its own standards and drawing its own conclusions concerning Africa. The primacy and western monopoly of analytical thought was never examined, Soyinka insists, nor was the nature of intellectual processes in Africa. What particularly outraged Soyinka, however, was the unquestioning acceptance of these Eurocentric axioms by the apostles of Negritude. If the end result was an affirmation of African civilization, it came not on its own merits but by sufferance, sustained through the charity of outsiders.

To those who know Soyinka as a poet and playwright, such an excursion into the nature of the African mentality may seem out of character, but in fact, Soyinka's writings are infused with reflections on the quality of African society, culture, and history.[11] He tells us he was initially drawn to the theater because of all the art forms, it communicated simultaneously to everyone. Crowded onto the microcosm of the stage was a whole universe involving man and his gods, a drama of ritual and epic—ritual that helps man find himself in a cosmic infinity, and epic that signals triumph of the human spirit over the forces that shackle and destroy.

For Soyinka this is a particularly African man in an African universe. Drawing from Yoruba cosmology, Soyinka cites a pantheon of gods more fallible, certainly more accountable, than those of the Greeks to whom they have sometimes been compared, more in need of man who provides them with the final element of their totality and who erases their transgressions through ritual. This interdependence of man and his gods is fundamental to the Yoruba world view, and characteristic of the African mind, says Soyinka, setting it off so clearly from the particularism of the West.

There are ulterior objectives to Soyinka's concern with the epic and ritual drama of man and his gods. First, it is through the drama of ritual that African societies search for harmony in their universe, and for the formulation of social standards and moral verities. Beyond this, Soyinka sees epic drama as the means through which the African returns to his sources, grasping the world of African metaphysics through myth and literature and thereby clarifying his self-apprehension and his understanding of the contemporary African social psyche. Self-apprehension is absolutely fundamental, Soyinka insists, for African civilization can be understood only in its own terms, through its own points of reference, never by way of another civilization superimposed from without. "The man," says Soyinka (1976: xi), "who . . . tries to sever my being from its self-apprehension is not merely culturally but politically hostile."

Thus African civilization is its own civilization, says Soyinka. The western mind, he points out, tends to compartmentalize emotions, phenomena, institutions, or scientific observations, and these in their diversity and mutual isolation lose their relationship to any comprehensive world view. For the African in his Yoruba mutation, the cosmos is a seamless whole. The gods are eternal, man but the mark of earthly transience. Past, present, and future are a continuum containing the ancestors, the living, and the yet unborn, all in contemporaneous existence.

Viewed from another perspective, Soyinka continues, the African world view is a striving for harmony. Man, the community, and nature are concentric circles, and their consonance defines a structure of moral order. A breakdown in one area must affect the others, and the consequent disharmony is potentially catastrophic. In this way the sickness of one individual is no isolated phenomenon, and may be seen as the sign of a general malady. Individual fertility cannot be separated from the regenerative promise of earth and sea:

> Because of visceral intertwining of each individual with the fate of the entire community, a rupture in his normal functioning not only endangers this shared reality but threatens existence itself (1976: 53).

What emerges is an idiomatic African world, age old and valid in its antiquity, but also fresh and forward looking, ready to face the future, to absorb what is new and useful. At bottom Soyinka's image of the African Personality seems little removed from Senghor's Negritude. Each seeks to restore the character of a race and to celebrate its qualities.

THE ARTS

This desire to restate in modern terms the verities of traditional African values is expressed in varied fashion. It is found in the novels of Chinua Achebe and Ayi Kewi Armah, in the choreography of A. M. Opoku and his Ghana Dance Ensemble, and in the art of such varied craftsmen as Ibrahim el Salahi and Twins Seven-Seven, and in the plays of Efua Sutherland or the poetry of Taban lo Liyong. Not the least important contribution of Frantz Fanon was his demonstration that mental illness could be correctly identified and treated only in terms of social context and custom. Others, notably the Ghanaian physician and sculptor Oku Ampofo, have made good use of the pharmacopoeia of traditional African medicine, even as Ampofo has utilized the colors and textures of indigenous woods to express the African world he sees.

One who began this process of rediscovery long before the independence years was the Gold Coast composer, Ephraim Amu. Amu's beliefs came hard for they were expressed at a time when such notions were not in fashion, when African culture was regarded as primitive or quaint, and when questioning the relevance of European institutions was thought to be eccentric, even impious. Indeed, for the courage of his convictions, Amu lost his first job as a teacher, an event that nevertheless launched him on a life-long career as a composer of new African music based upon the traditional modes of the land.

The event had comic as well as serious aspects. As catechist and sometime preacher at the local Presbyterian church in Akropong where he was working, Amu had noticed that the congregation remained silent during the period set aside for hymns, a situation that he correctly ascribed to unfamiliarity on the part of most parishioners with the western-style music and its accompanying English text. Determined to rectify the situation, Amu, who was a trained musician, wrote a hymn based upon airs drawn from the region, then secretly rehearsed his composition with a choir of students. When his chorus was prepared, Amu quietly arranged to have his music performed at Sunday service, compounding his heresy by conducting, not in the black broadcloth suit that was conventional attire on such occasions, but in the traditional cloth of his people. He stationed his podium near a side door, he tells us, since he was unsure what sort of reaction there might be; a handy escape exit was a prudent precaution. As it happened the whole affair went off without a hitch, and Amu was congratulated after the service by a leading cleric of the parish. This was in 1928, however, at the height of European colonialism, both cultural and political, far too early for such egregious behavior. Soon a reaction set in. Amu was reprimanded by the church fathers. When he remained unrepentent and unwilling to conform, he was relieved of his post at the local training college.

Hindsight marks this momentary loss as a major step forward, for it set Amu on a course devoted to the renascence and promotion of classical African culture, particularly through musical composition and the revival of traditional instruments, already half forgotten and falling out of use. The two pursuits necessarily went hand in hand, for the old instruments had a quality of tone appropriate to the old songs. There were, however, problems to be surmounted, both in composition and performance. To begin with, rhythm and drumming were the core of all African music while traditional songs had their own melodic line and harmony, governed by the speech rhythms in the texts of a tonal language. Amu reconciled the two by arranging his songs in parts, then assigning each part to a particular drum rhythm, the ensemble coming together in a polyphonic structure that maintained interest and tension without the intrusion of unacceptable dissonances.

For Amu the drum gave shape to his songs, but his interest in traditional African instruments focused in particular on the indigenous flutes of the region. He remembered as a child hearing a certain six-note bamboo flute, played transversely, but it was only after much searching that he was able to locate the instrument and one or two players. Other instruments gradually came to light, many that were difficult to play because of technical limitations in the design — the length of the column of air, for example, or the placement of stops. Amu set about redesigning several of these instruments, his considerations partly esthetic and partly practical. The bamboo flute called *atenteben* was difficult for many students to play transversely; consequently Amu converted it into an end-blown recorder, thus facilitating performance without losing the special character of its sound. Another woodwind, the cane flute *odurugya* had a lovely tone, but was limited to five notes because its great length inhibited additional fingering. Amu bent the flute at an angle, thereby facilitating reach which in turn made possible a full scale that extended through two and one-half octaves.

Ghana's tonal languages provided Amu wide latitude for experimentation in melody, while the flutes and "talking" drums could be made to produce sounds that had the literal meaning of speech. Amu's music was traditional and therefore recognizable, but it was also modern and experimental. The melodies were simple, the harmonies elementary, and the music accessible to all. The complexities lay in the performance that wedded the harmonies of tonal languages with African drum rhythms. Beyond this there was a genuine synthesis of indigenous materials from different regions. Amu wrote his songs in both the Ewe and Twi languages, and he found no problem of communication, even with students from Nigeria who seemed completely comfortable in a strange tongue.

Aside from reviving old music in new forms, Amu's work had the wider significance of drawing together Africans of diverse background, of helping not only to rekindle respect for the artistic merits of traditional culture but of contributing as well to national awareness and pan-Africn unity. Amu was born in the Ewe area of eastern Ghana, but his music has drawn inspiration from many other of the country's regions. On one occasion he was commissioned to compose a song for the opening of a school in Ashanti. When King Prempeh heard the song he was greatly moved (Anquandah, n.d.: 14). "Who wrote it?" he wanted to know. "It was Amu," was the reply. "Ah," said Prempeh proudly. "Our own Amu."

CONCLUSION: AN AFRICAN IDIOM AND AN AFRICAN VOICE

As yet the premise of independence in Africa has remained largely unfulfilled. New nations struggling with new problems have been sorely pressed to maintain political stability in the face of centrifugal forces within their societies. Concurrently, prospects have faded for the material advantages that freedom was expected to provide. The reasons are many and complex. They range from perennial drought and population increase to official inefficiency or regional antipathies, from inflation and global depression to the effects of economic nationalism practiced by the world's developed nations.

Part of Africa's difficulty has taken the form of policies of westernization too quickly pursued and too imperfectly understood. The humanists who called for a reaffirmation of Africa's traditional values and customs may have preached better than they knew. Dike's efforts to establish a continent's history as seen by the African himself, Nkrumah's desire to create a university curriculum that directed the wisdom of the past to the problems of the present, Soyinka's search for the verities of existence in the ancient cosmology of his people, Amu's renascence of the old music in modern form offered lessons that reached beyond their own arguments. Each was saying that the old ways were still virile, still persuasive. An ancient culture offered something of value to be enjoyed on its own merits, but it could also be directed to meet the demands of a modern world, a better design for living than foreign cultures ill-adapted to African need.

This point of view has been well stated by the Nigerian architect and designer, Demas Nwoko. There is no question of Africa's need for the best of high technology, Nwoko says. What is essential, however, is a technology expressly designed and adapted to African requirements. At independence African governments hastened to modernize, Nwoko points out, by importing, without reflection as to cost and utility, technology that had been created for other purposes and places. There are two things wrong with this tactic, Nwoko continues. In the first place, the technology cannot and will not work in a tropical setting for which it is poorly suited. Secondly, African leadership, particularly in government circles, has been too intent on catching up with the West through blind imitation, and Africa is no better adapted to many western ideas and institutions than western technology is adapted to African conditions. The result has been a disaster characterized by hopelessly crowded and unworkable cities, inefficient communication systems, deteriorating highways, chronic power failures, fuel shortages, and rusting unserviced machinery, to say nothing of the economic chaos brought on by, among other things, imperfect comprehension of the economies new governments were trying to build.

Nwoko suggests that Africans should clarify their own special needs and demand technology that meets these needs. Very often the solution is already available, both in local materials and in techniques that have been perfected by traditional African societies over long centuries before Africa's self image became blurred by European imports. In architecture, Nwoko points out, many newly constructed buildings are doomed to destruction by fire. Designed for other places, they are overloaded with needless electrical appliances, particularly air conditioning, that strain circuits and invite disaster. What Africa wants, Nwoko explains, are buildings planned for cooling by natural air currents. Such tried and workable designs exist in the centuries old traditional architecture. Inexpensively constructed, they utilized local materials in lieu of expensive imported steel and concrete.

The observations of Demas Nwoko on Africa's high technology carry the argument one step further. Africa's humanists make a plea for the renascence of traditional arts, history, philosophy, and literature, but the process goes beyond to comprise all human endeavor. A successful solution to Africa's problems must be idiomatic, a genuinely African solution, perhaps something old in a new form, perhaps an import but one tailored to local conditions. Then may African societies begin to realize the potential of their political independence, advancing toward goals long sought, and contributing an African voice to contemporary civilization.

NOTES

1. Much of this article is a brief synopsis of selected sections from the author's forthcoming book *An African Voice* which deals with the influences of the humanities on African independence movements.
2. Some others, in addition to Ajayi (1965), were: Adeleye (1971), Ayandele (1966), Cookey (1968), Ikime (1969), and Oloruntimehin (1972). Among those who followed the Ibadan-Longman example, the University of Ghana inaugurated its Legon series of monographs, also in collaboration with Longman. The University College, Nairobi, began its *People of East Africa* series, published by the East African Publishing House, with Ogot (1967) and Were (1967).
3. Dike's own doctoral thesis (1956) broke new ground in presenting African history as a field of serious study in its own right, rather than as an appendage of European colonial affairs.
4. See the *Journal of the Historical Society of Nigeria*. The special "Independence Issue" (V. 12, 1960) contained a particularly noteworthy collection of articles on Nigeria by such authorities as R. G. Armstrong (linguistics), Frank Willett (art), A. H. M. Kirk-Greene (history), and Thurston Shaw (archeology).
5. The Benin study produced much useful evidence, chiefly from documentary material, oral tradition, anthropological research on present-day Benin, and archeological remains. The interdisciplinary task of correlating these different types of material proved formidable and a coherent picture of a multi-dimensional past remained elusive despite the quantities of data gathered. Published results have been scanty but one major study (Ryder, 1969) should be noted.
6. Nkrumah's ideas on education and nation building in Africa appear throughout his writings. See, for example, 1961, 1963a, 1963b.
7. Personal interview with T. H. Hodgkin, September 27, 1980.
8. For an expanded version of this section, see July (1981).
9. Senghor's extensive writings contain many commentaries on aspects of Negritude (cf. 1956, 1964, 1977).
10. Sartre's analysis of Negritude appeared originally as an introduction to an anthology of black poetry published by Senghor in 1948. Sartre published an English translation in 1963.
11. See, for example, such diverse works as Soyinka 1963 and 1976.

REFERENCES

Adeleye, R. A. 1971. *Power and Diplomacy in Northern Nigeria, 1804–1906*. New York: Humanities Press.

Ajayi, J. F. A. 1961. "The Place of African History and Culture in the Process of Nation Building in Africa South of the Sahara." *Journal of Negro Education* 30/3: 206–13.

———. 1965. *Christian Missions in Nigeria, 1841–1891*. London: Longman.

Ajayi, J. F.A. and Espie, I. A. (eds.) 1965. *A Thousand Years of African History: A Handbook for Teachers and Students*. Ibadan and London: Ibadan University Press and Nelson.

Anene, J. C. and Brown, G. N. 1966. *Africa in the Nineteenth and Twentieth Centuries: A Handbook for Teachers and Students*. Ibadan and London: Ibadan University Press and Nelson.

Anquandah, James. n.d. "Men of Our Time: Dr. Ephraim Amu." Unpublished manuscript.

Ayandele, E. A. 1966. *The Missionary Impact on Modern Nigeria, 1842–1914*. London: Longman.

Cookey, S. J. S. 1968. *Britain and the Congo Question, 1885–1913*. London: Longman.
Dike, K. O. 1956. *Trade and Politics in the Niger Delta, 1830–1885*. Oxford: Clarendon.
Diop, C. A. 1955. *Nations Negres et Culture*. Paris: Présence africaine.
———. 1959. *L'Unité Culturele de l'Afrique Noire*. Paris: Présence africaine.
———. 1960. *L'Afrique Noire Pré-Coloniale*. Paris: Présence africaine.
———. 1967. *Antériorité des Civilisations Negres*. Paris: Présence africaine.
Fanon, Frantz. 1968. *The Wretched of the Earth*. New York: Grove Press.
Ikime, O. 1969. *Niger Delta Rivalry*. London: Longman.
Journal of the Historical Society of Nigeria. 1960. "Independence Issue." V. 12.
July, R. W. 1981. "The Artist's Credo: The Political Philosophy of Wole Soyinka." *The Journal of Modern African Studies* 9: 477–98.
Nkrumah, Kwame. 1961. *I Speak of Freedom*. London: Heinemann.
———. 1963a. *Africa Must Unite*. London: Heinemann.
———. 1963b. *The African Genius*. No publisher.
Ogot, B. A. 1967. *History of the Southern Luo*. Nairobi: East African Publishing House.
Oloruntimehin, B. O. 1972. *The Segu Tukulor Empire*. London: Longman.
Ryder, Alan. 1969. *Benin and the Europeans, 1485–1897*. London: Longman.
Sartre, J. P. 1963. *Black Orpheus*. Paris: Présence africaine.
Senghor, L. S. 1956. "African-Negro Aesthetics." *Diogenes* 56: 23–38.
———. 1964. *On African Socialism*. New York: Praeger.
———. 1977. *Liberté 3: Négritude et Civilisation de l'Universel*. Paris: Le Seuil.
Soyinka, Wole. 1963. *Dance of the Forests*. London: Oxford.
———. 1976. *Myth, Literature and the African World*. Cambridge: Cambridge University Press.
Tarikh. 1965–present. Ibadan: Historical Society of Nigeria and Longmans.
Webster, J. B. 1965. *Reading List on African History*. Ibadan: University Press.
Were, G. S. 1967. *A History of the Abaluyia of Western Kenya*. Nairobi: East African Publishing House.

WHOSE DREAM WAS IT ANYWAY?
TWENTY-FIVE YEARS OF AFRICAN
INDEPENDENCE*

MICHAEL CROWDER

WHEN THE UNION JACK was lowered at midnight and the green white and green flag of Nigeria raised in its place on October 1st 1960, there was considerable optimism in the British press about the future of that erstwhile British colony. The leaders of its three political parties were all by their own declarations committed to the practice of liberal democracy Westminster-style. The constitution that enshrined the ideals of Westminster had been patiently negotiated over a decade between the British and the leaders of the three main political parties. The former colonial masters left with the warm words of the new Prime Minister ringing in their ears: 'We are grateful to the British officers whom we have known, first as masters, and then as leaders, and finally as partners and always as friends'.[1] Many stayed on under the new Nigerian leadership, particularly those in commerce and industry, especially as Nigerians had only taken over the political infrastructure of the state from the British. The economic infrastructure remained largely intact in the hands of big British firms like UAC. The prospects for the country seemed rosy with its apparently sound agricultural base and the promise of additional foreign earnings from its proved oil reserves. An optimism about Nigeria pervaded most of the British press for the next five years. The riots that were taking place in Tivland at the very time the new flag of Nigeria was being raised were conveniently ignored by many pressmen intent on conveying an appropriate euphoria to their British readers. Indeed, the Prime Minister of the Federation, Sir Abubakar Tafawa Balewa, remarked wryly on the adulation of the world's press that 'even some of the big nations of the world are expecting us to perform miracles and solve their problems for them'.[2] That adulation had indeed been fairly universal but *West Africa* did note that one foreign visitor to the Independence Celebrations did not share the 'general satisfaction and optimism' and that was Mr. Sisnev, the correspondent of *Trud*, but it concluded 'even if

Michael Crowder is visiting Professor at the Institute of Commonwealth Studies, University of London.

*I am grateful to Lalage Bown and Roland and Irene Brown for helpful comments on a first draft of this paper which was originally presented in the series of lectures on Africa since Independence sponsored by the Yale University African Studies Program in Spring of 1986 under the title 'Things Fall Apart?'.

1. Sir Abubakar Tafawa Balewa, Speech made on Independence Day, 1 October 1960 in *"But always as Friends": Northern Nigeria and the Cameroons, 1921–1957*, (London, George Allen and Unwin, 1969), Frontispiece.
2. *West Africa* 19 November 1960.

7

Nigeria sounds too good to be true, the Nigerian story is one of the most remarkable and creditable in the modern world'.[3] *Time* talked of Nigeria's 'impressive demonstration of democracy's workability in Africa'.[4]

Despite the many internal strains which the country experienced in its first few years of independence, including the suspension of the constitution of one of its three constituent regions and the jailing of the leader of the opposition for treason, the British press appeared to share the belief that as one Nigerian newspaper put it: 'Nigerians seem to have perfected the art of walking to the brink of disaster without falling in.'[5] Indeed the British Prime Minister and his officials were apparently so ignorant of the real breakdown of law and order in the country that in January 1966 they flew to Lagos to attend the Commonwealth Prime Ministers Conference on the Rhodesian question.[6] A day after they flew back to London, the Prime Minister of Nigeria was assassinated and the first military regime was installed. In the twenty years that followed, Nigeria has suffered four more military coups, at least one failed coup, a three year long civil war, a brief return to an elective form of government that made a mockery of liberal democracy, and an oil boom that permitted lavish spending and corruption on a massive scale, followed by the near bankruptcy of the country, which today is economically on its knees. As a result, Nigerians of all classes have developed a deep cynicism about their leaders, both civilian and military, and certainly have little faith in the liberal democracy and mixed economy that were the legacy of their colonial rulers.

I have chosen Nigeria as an example of the disillusion that has attended the first twenty-five years of independence not only among the former colonial rulers who transferred power but also among those who inherited that power, because it contains a quarter of the population of the African continent. Its experience has unhappily not been atypical but rather the norm for the majority of African countries.

The same optimism that attended Nigeria's independence attended that of the Francophone countries, and the British territories in East, Central and Southern Africa. In each case, what was transferred was a constitution inspired by the metropolitan model. All these states committed themselves in their national anthems and the mottoes on their coats of arms to variations of freedom, justice and equality.

Of all these states only one has realised the pious hopes of those who transferred power: Botswana, which alone has suffered no *coup* or *coup manqué* and has maintained intact its liberal democratic constitution in

---

3. *ibid.*
4. *ibid.*
5. See Michael Crowder *The Story of Nigeria* (London, Faber, 1978), p. 259.
6. To be fair the usually well informed magazine *West Africa* raised no alarm in its columns either on the eve of the Conference nor during it, even though its own representative 'Griot' was touring the country at the time.

both spirit and practice.[7]   The story everywhere else has been the same.
Majority parties voted to establish one party states which western apologists
were quick to justify as reflecting true African democracy encouraging the
politics of consensus where two or multi-party democracy was divisive.[8]
In reality, such moves usually proved but a cloak for the establishment of
personal rule, as Jackson and Rosberg have put it.[9]   Even military regimes
that intervened were seen by optimists as mere correctives for temporary
aberrance in the practice of democracy by young nations.   Military coups
were invariably staged in the name of cleansing the state, after which the
soldiers would return to the barracks.   And this they did in Sudan, Ghana,
the former Upper Volta and Nigeria, only to fling wide the barrack gates
again as it became clear that the politicians had learnt nothing except how to
abuse power more successfully.   The excesses of the second Obote regime
in Uganda were reputedly greater than those of Amin himself.[10]

Coupled with the abuse of the inherited constitutions and the acquisition
of personal power through manipulation of the ballot box or the barrel of the
gun has been the expropriation of the resources of the state by the few and
the apparent progressive immiseration of the masses as a result.   The
famines that have caught the world's attention in the past few years have
increasingly been laid at the doors of the politicians and military leaders
rather than nature.   And yet, grasping at straws, westerners refused to see
their dreams shattered.   Nigeria's return to democracy in 1979 was seen as a
vindication by those who believed that Africans could and would adhere to
the ideals of Western liberal democracy.   Similar optimism attended the
return to civilian rule under Obote, with the British government even
helping to train the army he used to establish a worse record with Amnesty
International than Amin.[11]

But by 1985, a quarter of a century after the *annus mirabilis* of African
independence, the dream had been shattered and replaced by a profound
disillusion whereby Africa had become the world's basket case, a permanent
mezzogiorno for which there was little if any hope.   Ghana and Uganda, the
jewels in Britain's African colonial crown had, despite their extensive
educated elites, sunk in the former case into an economic slough of despond

---

7.   See Michael Crowder 'Botswana and the Survival of Liberal Democracy in Africa'
in Prosser Gifford and Wm.   Roger Louis eds.   *African Independence: the Origins and
Consequences of the Transfer of Power in Africa* (Newhaven: Yale University Press)
(forthcoming).
8.   See for example James S. Coleman and Carl G. Rosberg Jr. eds.   *Political Parties and
National Integration in Tropical Africa* (Berkeley and Los Angeles, University of California
Press, 1964), especially their 'Introduction'.
9.   Robert H. Jackson and Carl G. Rosberg *Personal Rule in Africa. Prince, Autocrat, Prophet,
Tyrant*.   (Berkeley, Los Angeles and London, University of California Press), 1982.
10.   The first indications that this might be the case came to public attention as a result of the
Namugongo massacre of May 1984, when both Baganda Muslims and Christians were
murdered, thus giving it a genocidal character.   I am grateful to Michael Twaddle for this
reference.
11.   See comments on the Amnesty International Report in *The Times* 28 June 1985.

and in the latter into anarchy.   In the chanceries of the West, officials
wished Africa would just go away and this has been reflected most dramatically in Britain, still the country with the largest investments in sub-Saharan
Africa, which has reduced its support for the study of Africa to a level lower
than it has been for the past twenty years.[12]

The universal wisdom has become that African independence has been
an abysmal failure.   Thus the conservative London *Daily Telegraph* in a
recent editorial wrote that Uganda 'the one-time pearl of Africa can fairly be
described as having become a symbol of everything that has gone wrong in
that continent over the past 20 years or so.   Since independence it has
experienced violence (with hundreds of thousands killed), poverty, misgovernment on an an enormous scale, and terrible suffering.   Steadily
the pillars of government, of law and even economic life have been
destroyed. . .'.[13]

But is this not to judge the past twenty five years in terms of a dream
manufactured in Europe not Africa, and a dream that took no cognisance
either of contemporary African realities, nor, more important and less
forgivable, of the legacy of colonial rule?

Was not this dream of a model Africa in which Africans would faithfully
adhere to the liberal democratic institutions transferred at independence and
uphold a mixed economy in which the interests of the ordinary people would
be served in reality a pipe dream in the context of a plethora of states that had
for the most part only been cobbled together fifty odd years before?   Will
not historians be kinder in their judgement of these sometimes unlikely
states created by the colonial rulers when they come to assess the post
independence period than the journalists and political scientists who wring
their hands in despair today?   Will they not judge the experience of independence in terms of the African experience of colonial rule, which has been
undergoing serious revision by historians as the true secrets of the colonial
rulers emerge from the archives?   Will they not compare favourably the
impressive economic transformations that even the most impoverished of
African states in question have undergone since independence with the little
that was done for them under colonial rule?   Given the little attention that
any of the European colonial powers gave to building national political and
economic structures during the period of their rule will not historians of the
future see the very survival of these states as something of an economic and
political miracle?

In this essay, therefore, I want to try and project myself forward and see
what sort of perspective historians may have on what so many see today as
'the African disaster'.

12.   See Michael Twaddle 'The State of African Studies' *African Affairs* 85, 340, July 1986
especially p. 444 and Richard Hodder-Williams, 'African studies: back to the future', *African
Affairs* 85, 341. October 1986 pp. 593–604, with their gloomy prognoses for the future.
13.   'Agony in East Africa'.   Editorial in *Daily Telegraph* 28 January 1986.

I suggest they will look at the developments of the past twenty five years as part of a continuum in which independence will not be seen as a historical dividing line. All that has happened in the past quarter of a century will be set much more firmly in the context of the colonial experience than is the custom for present-day political scientists and journalists to do. So I first want to examine how the colonial experience has affected the way Africa has developed over the past twenty-five years and I shall suggest that there are many more parallels to be found between the colonial state and the independent state than are usually conceded.

I believe that historians will consider that contemporary judgements about the so called failure of Africa are really judgements made in terms of a Eurocentric dream for an independent Arfrica in which liberal democracy would be the norm, a dream that was shared only by a few elitist politicians like the Danquahs,[14] who were pushed aside in the struggle for independence by politicians with mass following like Nkrumah. I shall suggest that most African politicians did not share this dream and at best thought as Nyerere did that liberal democracy would only be a slowly acquired habit,[15] and at worst like Nkrumah only paid lip service to it.[16]

Finally I believe that future historians will set against the obvious failures of independent African states the very real achievements they have made in comparison with the record of their colonial masters.

A: THE COLONIAL LEGACY

In considering continuities between the colonial period and independence, let us look at the sort of model the colonial state provided in terms of the *Daily Telegraph* editorial. The violence which the editorialist posited as characteristic of contemporary African states was no stranger to the colonial state. The many studies of resistance to colonial occupation have shown that for the most part the colonial state was conceived in violence rather than by negotiation. This violence was often quite out of proportion to the task in hand, with burnings of villages, destruction of crops, killing of women and children, and the execution of leaders.[17] Some military expeditions were

14. See L. H. Ofosu-Appiah *The Life and Times of Dr. J. B. Danquah*, (Accra, Waterville Publishing House, 1974), in particular Danquah's letter of protest against the Removal Order served on him, 12 March 1948, p. 61, in which he wrote that 'the people directly charged with the administration of Government should be directly responsible to the people, with power in the people to change the personnel of Government when they feel that the Government or Cabinet of the day had failed them, or served its time. This constitutional goal I am pledged to pursue without flinching. . .'
15. Julius K. Nyerere interviewed by William E. Smith in 'A Reporter at Large: Transition'. *New Yorker*, 3 March 1986.
16. On the very day of Independence Nkrumah was presenting himself as a committed democrat. See below page 13.
17. See H. L. Wesseling 'Colonial Wars and Armed Peace, 1870–1914' *Itinerario* V, 1981, 2, pp. 53–69.

so barbaric that they caused outrage in the metropolitan press, as did the Voulet and Chanoine expedition in Niger.[18]   The colonial state was not only conceived in violence, but it was maintained by the free use of it.   Any form of resistance was visited by punitive expeditions that were often quite unrestrained by any of the norms of warfare in Europe.   The bloody suppression of the Maji Maji and Herero uprisings in German East and South West Africa are well enough known.   The less known atrocities committed in the suppression of the Satiru revolt in Northern Nigeria by the Sultan of Sokoto's forces acting on commission for the British in 1906 were such that the missionary Walter Miller wrote that 'it would be worth Leopold of Belgium's while to pay ten thousand pounds to get hold of what we know of this'.[19]   As Edward Lugard, brother of the British High Commissioner in Northern Nigeria, wrote: 'they killed every living thing before them', Women's breasts had been cut off and the leader spitted on a stake.[20]

   Lest these be thought too distant events in the colonial record to have much bearing on the present, one must recall that a man aged eighteen at the time of Satiru, would only have been 72 at the time of Nigeria's independence.   Furthermore, the use of violence to suppress protest continued throughout the colonial period and into the period of decolonisation.   The bloody massacre of Tirailleurs Sénégalais protesting against delays in paying their benefits and effecting their demobilisation at Thiaroye in Dakar in 1944 sent shock waves throughout the French African empire,[21] as did the revelations about the brutal treatment of Mau Mau prisoners by the British at the Hola Camp in Kenya through the British African colonies.[22]   The colonial state, it must be remembered, maintained troops for internal security, not for defence against external agression.   These armies were of course used for this latter purpose when the occasion arose, most notably in the two world wars where African soldiers experienced violence on an unprecedented scale.[23]   So too did civilians when their territory became part of the theatre of war.   As Terence Ranger wrote of the impact of the First World War on East Africa 'it was the most awe-inspiring, destructive and capricious demonstration of European 'absolute power' that Eastern

18.   See Finn Fugelstad *A History of Niger 1850–1960* (Cambridge, Cambridge University Press, 1983), p. 61.
19.   Walter Miller to Sir Frederick Lugard, 24 September 1907 in Rhodes House Library, Oxford, Mss. Brit. Emp. s.62. 'Lugard Papers'.   Cited in Robert Shenton *The Development of Capitalism in Northern Nigeria* (London, James Currey, 1986), p. 27.
20.   *ibid.*   Edward Lugard to Sir Frederick Lugard.   21 May 1908.
21.   Myron Echenberg ' "Morts pour la France": the African Soldier in France during the Second World War' *Journal of African History*, 26, 4, 1958, p. 376.
22.   It also convinced Britain's new Colonial Secretary, Iain Macleod, that 'swift change was needed in Kenya'.   Quoted in Jeremy Murray-Brown *Kenyatta* (London, George Allen and Unwin, 1972), p. 299.   See also A. Marshall Macphee *Kenya* (London, Ernest Benn, 1968), pp. 151–3.
23.   See for example the special issues of the *Journal of African History* on the two world wars: 'World War I and Africa', 19, 1978 No 1; and 'World War II and Africa', 26, 1985, No 4. David Killingray and Richard Rathbone eds.   *Africa and the Second World War* (London, Macmillan, 1986).

Africa ever experienced'.[24]   It must be remembered too that the colonial rulers set the example of dealing with its opponents by jailing or exciling them, as not a few of those who eventually inherited power knew from personal experience.[25]   Indeed if the colonial state provided a model for its inheritors it was that government rested not on consent but force.   Indeed when Nyerere was once pressed on the subject of preventive detention in his country he was quick to point out that Tanzania had inherited the practice from British colonial times.[26]

If we take up the second theme of the *Telegraph* leader, that of poverty, this was certainly no stranger during the colonial period.   The colonial state was certainly not run for the benefit of its inhabitants.   The roots of rural poverty, as Palmer and Parsons' volume of essays of that name on Southern Africa demonstrate, lie deep in the policies of the colonial powers.[27]   In the white settler colonies the best land was appropriated from the African farmer who was crowded into less fertile reserves often with disastrous ecological results.[28]   Where the main agent of exploitation was the African farmer, he was forced to produce the crops that the colonial rulers required rather than those he needed.   Through taxation, compulsory crop cultivation, forced labour and requisition, and in the case of the Portuguese teritories physical coercion, the farmer produced the cash crops that the big companies overseas required even at the risk of impoverishment of the land and famine. For many Africans taxation of any kind was a complete innovation. Many others had only paid indirect taxes.   And where direct taxation was imposed, it was rarely, if ever, as high as that of colonial state, which at its most oppressive extracted taxes directly in the form of cash, labour and compulsory crop cultivation, and indirectly through duties on imported goods.[29]   Robert Shenton in his recent book on *The Development of Capitalism in Northern Nigeria* has shown how British taxation policies designed to increase cultivation of cotton and groundnuts in some cases took

24.   T. O. Ranger *Dance and Society in Eastern Africa 1890–1970: the Beni Ngoma* (London, Heinemann, 1975), p. 45.
25.   For instance Jomo Kenyatta of Kenya, Hastings Banda of Malawi, Kwame Nkrumah of Ghana, Sultan Mohammed V of Morocco, Seretse Khama of Botswana.
26.   William P. Smith 'A Reporter at Large'.
27.   Robin Palmer and Neil Parsons eds.   *The Roots of Rural Poverty in Central and Southern Africa* (London, Heinemann, 1977).
28.   For instance Robin Palmer *Land and Racial Domination in Rhodesia*, (London, Heinemann, 1977) but see also Paul Mosley *The Settler Economies: Studies in the Economic History of Kenya and Southern Rhodesia 1900–1963* Cambridge, (Cambridge University Press, 1983) where he expresses reservations about the conventional view of settler economies in Africa.
29.   While it is difficult to calculate the relative burden of taxation imposed on their subjects by those pre-colonial polities which raised revenue through direct taxes and that exacted by the colonial state, it is significant that many inhabitants of pre-colonial polities that did impose direct taxation in cash or kind, for example in Niger, French Soudan and Chad, were forced to migrate in order to earn enough to pay their taxes. See Elliott P. Skinner *The Mossi of the Upper Volta* (Stanford, Stanford University Press, 1964), pp. 156–8 for the early impact of taxation by the French on the Mossi, who were later to be one of the chief suppliers of migrant labour in West Africa.

up to 50% of a farmer's income from him and led to shortages of subsistence crops which in turn led to famines.   As he shows, the colonial rulers themselves were fully aware of the consequences of their policies.[30]   Similarly later colonial government marketing boards were used as a means of taxing further the potential earnings of the farmer.   Yet critics of the independent African regimes seem to suggest that this neglect and exploitation of the farmer was new rather than a major legacy of colonial rule.[31]

Urban poverty and the slums associated with it were not a function of independent Africa but were established features of colonial rule.   I recall arriving in Nigeria for the first time in 1953 and nearly retching as I crossed from the Mainland to Lagos Island by Carter Bridge, so rank was the stink from the slums beneath its piers.   The bidonvilles of Dakar were a colonial creation of which Senghor was so ashamed that after independence he built a high wall around them so that visitors to his country should not see them as they entered Dakar from the airport.

The third theme in the *Telegraph* editorial is the misgovernment that has characterised independent African governments.   Here again we must remind ourselves how little opportunity Africans had of participating in the machinery of government of the colonial state until a few years before its demise.   In British Africa only a few chiefs under British indirect rule were allowed any initiative in the administration before 1945.   Otherwise all Africans in the administration, whatever the colonial regime, fulfilled a purely subaltern role without executive initiative.   As to legislative functions, again these were limited to local government under the system of indirect rule, and to a handful of elected Africans in Nigeria, Senegal and the Gold Coast.   Generally in British and French Africa preparation for taking over the legislative, executive and administrative organs of the colonial state by Africans began only after the Second World War.   Even where some effort was made to prepare African administrative cadres, they were often treated as second class members of the administration.   In.the 1950s, newly appointed African administrative officers in Uganda were specifically barred from access to the confidential files, a point that led to much bitterness on their part.[32]   In many African countries not a few inhabitants exercised the right to vote for the first time at the elections that brought their independent governments to power.

The Congo perhaps provides the most notorious example of the lack of preparation for the transfer of the institutions of state, while Guinea provides a different kind of example, where the French actually tried to destroy

30.   See in particular Chapter 6 of Shenton *The Development of capitalism in Northern Nigeria*.
31.   See Robert H. Bates, Essays on the Political Economy of Rural Africa (Cambridge, Cambridge University Press, 1983), especially Part III, though he has trenchant criticisms of the effect of the colonial agricultural regime on the peasant.
32.   Personal Communication from Professor Lalage Bown based on direct observation in the Eastern Province of Uganda 1955–60.

the very fabric of that state before they departed. They even removed the books from the law library of the Ministry of Justice.[33] Yet the scuttling Belgians received surprisingly little blame in the press for the disasters of the Congo compared with the Congolese themselves. Surely historians of the future will be less preoccupied by the anarchy and savagery that flowed from independence than by the marvel of the survival of the Congo intact as the huge state of Zaire, however far the former corporal who is its current head of state may deviate from the standards of good government as conceived in Brussels, Paris or London.

If the Belgians only prescribed the medicine of democracy for their Congolese subjects on the eve of the transfer of power, we must recall that neither the Spaniards nor the Portuguese rulers of the day had any faith in this type of medication for their own peoples, let alone their African subjects. They had no qualms about their conviction that their states were based on force not consent.

No aspects of post-independence Africa has drawn more criticism by scholars and journalists of the West than the personal power exercised by its leaders. Again it is instructive to look at the colonial model. Colonial governors enjoyed very wide powers without brakes from below. Even in British Africa where some territories had legislative councils these were dominated by an official majority which could be relied on to vote as solidly for any new policy or programme introduced by the Governor as the legislators in today's one party states. In many territories the Colonial Governor ruled by decree or proclamation and even where he had an executive council his decision on policy was overriding since that council's members were all his officials. The Governor also enjoyed to the full the outward trappings of power, living in an imposing palace, driven in large limousines flying the flag, deferred to by all, and on ceremonial occasions dressed in cocked hat and plumes and a quasi-military uniform. In the British territories, he alone was allowed to use red ink to minute or sign official documents.

This again was a model not lost on the inheritors of the colonial state. The model for the successors was invariably derived from that of the colonial masters. Thus ex-Sergeant Jean Bedel Bokassa modelled his coronation as Emperor of Central Africa on that of a former French corporal. Americans will recall Washington Irving's allegorical version of the European folk-tale about Rip Van Winkle. In Irving's version he becomes a Catskill villager who slumbers through the American Revolution to awake to the many changes that have taken place in his village. Among these is the new sign on the Inn. Before he slept it was a crude picture of George III. The

33. Personal communication from Irene Brown. Most of the examples of what the French did on leaving Guinea are not published but fall into the category of 'on dit que'. See, however, Claude Rivière *Guinea: the Mobilisation of a People* (Ithaca, Cornell University Press, 1977), p. 83, where he says of the departing French that some destroyed equipment before they left, others carried away files, while one group of soldiers set fir to their barracks.

uniform has now been changed and the name transmogrified from King George to George Washington.[34]   For a more sinister comparison we might remember that the OGPU of the Russian revolutionary state had its direct antecedents in the Tsar's okhrana.

Another theme in the *Telegraph* leader is the destruction of the pillars of law in African societies.   Again we must look back at the colonial model.   In French Africa until 1946, all Africans but a few citizens were under a regime of administrative law whereby they were subject to summary justice with no right of appeal.   In 1914 Lugard specifically outlawed the representation of defendants by lawyers in the magistrate's courts of the South where a British model judiciary had been installed, albeit with massive problems and defects.   In The Congo and Portuguese territories, too, the Africans had no access to metropolitan style legal institutions. These existed only for the European inhabitants or in the case of the Portuguese territories the handful of *assimilados*.   They were made available to Africans only on the eve of independence or immediately afterwards.

Again, what is remarkable is that so much of the trappings and spirit of these hastily implanted systems have survived rather than broken down. I am sure all were moved that out of the misery and anarchy that has bedevilled Uganda for the past decade and a half the apparent end should be marked by a bewigged and scarlet robed Chief Justice swearing in the new Conqueror-President Museveni—and what is more that it should have been a white Ugandan in a post that in Uganda has held few promises of retirement benefits.

The final point made by the *Telegraph* leader was that economic life had been destroyed.   Of course in terms of exports and imports this has often been the case as countries like Nigeria have built up massive overseas debts, cannot afford imports and have neglected agricultural exports.   But as Pius Okigbo, former economic adviser to the Nigerian Government, so forcefully pointed out in a recent lecture, the real problem is that the health of African economies is judged by the outside world in terms of the size of their imports and exports.[35]   This too of course is a legacy of the colonial period when the colonial rulers were little concerned with measuring the African domestic economy but were principally interested in the size of its import-export economy.   Thus during the Depression of the 1930s there was crisis for the colonial rulers whose income was reduced, for the import-export firms whose crops fetched abysmal prices on the world market, and for those

34. Marcus Cunliffe 'The Cultural Patrimony of the United States' in Prosser Gifford ed.   *The Treaty of Paris (1793) in a Changing States System* (Lanham, Maryland, University Press of America and Washington D.C., Wilson Center, 1985), p. 177.
35. Pius Okigbo 'The Nigerian Economy in the next decade: possibilities of self-reliance.'   St. Antony's College Oxford, African Affairs Seminar, 13 March 1986. Discussion.

African farmers who were involved in the sector of the agricultural economy. But for the subsistence crop producer and the craftsmen there was something of a boom.[36] Similarly in many countries that are apparently suffering in terms of their import-export economy, there is today something of an internal boom. If African leaders have tended to judge the health of their economies in terms of imports and exports, they are only following a colonial precedent.[37]

The colonial rulers, furthermore, hardly set a good example of operating the economy in the best interests of their subjects: profits were expatriated not invested in local industries, providing a parallel with, though here not a model for, the present salting of ill-gotten gains by African leaders in the banks of Switzerland and other safe havens of the Western world. We must recall too the price rings, the lack of local industrial development and the lodging of the assets of marketing boards in metropolitan banks before we talk too much about mismanagement of the economy by African successor states. As Ralph Austen has recently emphasised, Patrick Manning has demonstrated that considerable economic damage was done to Dahomey by the French 'who used it to subsidise less profitable French possessions, to fulfil their own ambitions, or to respond to the pressures of local European economic interests.'[38] As Austen further emphasises: 'The economic and political malaise afflicting the African continent today with such breadth and severity. . . must have deep roots in a past about which so little is generally known'.[39]

A final point concerning the colonial legacy to Independent Africa concerns the state structures that were handed over at independence. The borders of these states, it may be tedious to remind ourselves, were erected without reference to African realities in the chanceries of Europe. But having created them, colonial powers did little to foster a sense of national unity within them. The French territory of Upper Volta for instance was not created until 1920, was dismembered in 1932 and divided up among its neighbours, only to be re-established in 1947, thirteen years before it became independent, German Kamerun and Togo were divided between the French and British after the First World War, while, although the

36. See S. M. Jacobs 'Report on Taxation and Economics of Nigeria', 1934 in Rhodes House Library Mss. Afr. t. 16 where he writes '. . . Nigeria in *all internal respects* has not suffered from an economic depression. Her production of yams, cassava, fish, corn, and her exchange of all her produce goes on as before'. Quoted in Shenton *The Development of Capitalism in Northern Nigeria* p. 101.
37. The health or otherwise of a colonial economy was measured almost exclusively in terms of imports and of agricultural and mineral exports since there was little attempt by the colonial authorities to assess the volume of production of food crops for local consumption or of locally manufactured goods, for example cloth, pots and iron work.
38. This point from Patrick Manning's *Slavery, Colonialism and economic Growth in Dahomey, 1640–1960* (Cambridge, Cambridge University Press, 1982), (see especially Chapter 10) is made by Ralph Austen in 'African Economies in Historical Perspective' *Business History Review*, Spring 1985, p. 103.
39. Austen in *ibid* p. 101.

separate Protectorates of Northern and Southern Nigeria were amalgamated by Lugard in 1914, it was a token amalgamation which did not truly bring them into a meaningful relationship with each other.[40]   The two French federations of Equatorial and West Africa were broken up by the French against the wishes of the majority of the constituent colonies on the eve of independence.   Furthermore it has been argued, convincingly, that the system of indirect rule, employed by the British, was a divisive one in that it emphasised the integrity of the pre-colonial political unit as against the new colonial state.   And up until the mid-forties there were still powerful advocates in the Colonial Office who saw the native authorities as the building blocks of independence.[41]

This has been a deliberately selective view of the colonial past but, I hope, a corrective one that the Cassandras of contemporary Africa would be adviced to take into account.

B: WHOSE DREAM WAS IT ANYWAY?

We come now to my second theme: how far did Africans share the dream of the colonial rulers for Africa? In the first place, it has to be remembered that the liberal democratic ideal was espoused only by the British and French for their African colonies.   Though at home the Belgians shared these ideals, they only very belatedly suggested that they might be appropriately transferred to their colonial subjects.[42]   In both Spain and Portugal liberal democracy had succumbed many years since to Fascist regimes, so for their overseas subjects there was not even a metropolitan model of democracy to aspire to.   In the case of the Portuguese their African colonies were considered integral parts of the metropolis and, far from instruments of power being transferred to African subjects, control of the state was seized by them by force of arms.   There was thus no obligation placed on the victors to maintain any particular form of government.[43]

In all the French Black African states, with the exception of Guinea, and in all the British African states, including Zimbabwe, the transfer of power was negotiated and made conditional on the acceptance of a liberal demo-

40.   See Michael Crowder 'Lugard and Colonial Nigeria: Towards an Identity' *History Today* 36, February 1986, pp. 23–29.
41.   R. D. Pearce *The Turning Point in Africa: British Colonial Policy 1938–1948* (London, Frank Cass), 1982, especially Chapter 3.
42.   Crawford Young *Politics in the Congo: Decolonisation and Independence* (Princeton, New Jersey, Princeton University Press, 1965), Chapters 3 and 4.
43.   In Guinea-Bissau, for instance, the PAIGC carried out a General Election in the liberated zones in 1972 two years before the Portuguese recognised the independence of its former colony, an independence which the Guinea-Bissau leaders had anyway effectively proclaimed in September 1973.   See Basil Davidson 'Portuguese-speaking Africa' in *Cambridge History of Africa* 8 (Cambridge, Cambridge University Press, 1984), p. 788–9.   Another example would be the Algerian Revolution though here there was a deliberate move to revalidate many of the institutions and much of the legislation of the erstwhile colonial regime because the FLN had failed to build political institutions of its own during the long and bitter struggle with the French.   See Clement Henry Moore 'The Maghrib' in *ibid.* pp. 580–82.

cratic constitution inspired by the metropolitan model. What we have to ask ourselves is how far the African parties to these negotiations were ideologically committed to these constitutions? In Francophone and Anglophone Africa educated Africans soon learnt that the pen was mightier than the sword in dealing with their particular colonial masters and turned the democratic ideals and institutions of their masters against them and asked why they espoused democracy at home and denied it abroad. The Senegalese politician Lamine Gueye in his autobiography recalls the irony of the 'Liberté, Egalité et Fraternité' emblazoned on the offices of a colonial administration which practised none of these three virtues as far as their African subjects were concerned.[44] An educated chief like Tshekedi Khama in the then Bechuanaland Protectorate skilfully manipulated British press, parliament and public opinion to block measures of the local administration to which he was opposed. But if we examine his own life closely we find that while he was keen on his own rights, and went to great lengths to defend them, he was none too careful with respect to those of his own subjects.[45] David Williams has hypothesised that the emirs in Northern Nigeria finally agreed to back self-government and independence under the Sardauna of Sokoto because they believed he would be less insistent on the implementation of democracy than the British showed clear signs of being if they continued administering their country any longer.[46]

African leaders may have skilfully pressured the British and French to transfer their models and when finally they agreed to do so accepted them as a condition of gaining independence, just as Nkrumah had to accept a final election as a precondition of independence for Ghana.[47] But did this mean that they implicitly believed in them as anything other than as a means to an end? The answer is surely 'No'. Only thus can we explain the rapid dismantling of these constitutions in form or spirit by nearly all who were party to the independence agreements. A few days after Ghana's independence, Nkrumah gave a press conference in which he assured the world's press that 'We shall help [other African states] by our example of successfully working a parliamentary democracy'.[48] But within a few days more he had moved into Christiansborg Castle, the seat of the colonial governors, arranged for his own portrait to appear on currency and postage stamps, and started on the road to the acquisition of unchecked personal power. The commitment to liberal democracy thereafter tended to be the exclusive concern of the opposition, but how shallow this was was may be illustrated by the example of Siaka Stevens of Sierra Leone. His All People's Congress (APC) had

44. Lamine Gueye *Itinéraire africaine* (Paris 1966), p. 79.
45. See Michael Crowder 'Tshekedi Khama: Statesman' in R. F. Morton and Jeff Ramsay eds. *Botswana: Making of a Nation* (Gaborone, Longman) (forthcoming).
46. David Williams: Personal Communication.
47. Ofosu-Appiah *Danquah* pp. 130–1.
48. *West Africa* 16 March 1957.

campaigned against the ruling Sierra Leone People's Party (SLPP) in part on the basis that it was abusing democracy.   Having won the election despite heavy rigging by the Government, and finally acceding to power several coups later, Stevens set about creating the one party state that the SLPP had not quite dared to.   It is clear that for all but a few leaders— Seretse Khama of Botswana and Dauda Jawara of The Gambia being the notable exceptions—the commitment to liberal democracy was a transitory one.   Nor of course were the military who succeeded them so committed, coming from a very different tradition of dealing with people.

Was it not a staggering piece of arrogant paternalism that the European powers should prescribe for their African dependencies a model that had had such a chequered career on their own continent and criticise them for failing to work it?.   African leaders were for the most part aware of the many attacks on democracy experienced by Europe during the years that they had been under its tutelage.   They had seen how weak democracies could be in the face of a determined fascist leader like Mussolini.   Not all were convinced by their masters' condemnations of Hitler.   It is not for nothing that a fair number of African boys were named Adolf in the early forties.[49]   But democracy remained, in the eyes of the Western press, the panacea for Africa.   Thus there was general rejoicing at Nigeria's return to civilian rule in 1979 and general hostility to the military coup that brought it to an end in December 1983, even though there was rejoicing by the general population at the demise of a corrupt and increasingly oppressive regime.   A former Labour Minister in the British Foreign Office concerned with Africa, Ted Rowlands, was reported by *West Africa* as appearing to be calling for economic sanctions against Nigeria for 'abandoning democracy'.[50]   While the *Daily Express* referring to the new military ruler, General Buhari, wondered whether the Queen 'will take this despot's hand'.[51]

What African leaders surely appreciated more perceptively than those who wished liberal democratic constitutions on them was that liberal democracy had only worked in those countries of Europe where there was relative lack of inequality, a deep-rooted sense of national identity, and a consensus as to the ideal model for the government of the state.   Where, as in Zimbabwe, such conditions did not obtain, and where there were two major ethnic groups vying for power, the operation of the liberal democratic constitution became very close in character to the operation of democracy in Northern Ireland.   There was certainly genuine belief on the part of those African leaders who advocated the one-party state, however much later they were to pervert it to their own ends, that it would be less divisive than the

49. I have come across one Nigerian named Hitler, a Motswana named Mussolini, and been told of two sons of a Togolese called respectively Bismarck and Goebbels.
50. *West Africa* 16 January 1984.
51. Cited in *ibid*.

two-party model of the British or the multi-party model of the French.[52] Nor were African leaders particularly committed to the equitable distribution of resources that their election manifestoes promised and their talk of African socialism may have suggested. Since the means to independence was to be through the ballot box, they had necessarily to persuade the electorate by offering to implement programmes that would benefit them. With independence won, the behaviour of African politicians has differed little from that of the majority of office-seekers in promoting personal advancement and profit, with some pork barrelling for their homeboys. Africans were much more hard-nosed, realistic and even cynical about what independence portended. Rosy dreams were left to the departing colonial masters and the metropolitan press. Indeed as *West Africa* remarked almost petulantly at Ghana's independence celebrations 'the Accra crowds were much less demonstrative than expected'.[53] Its then editor, David Williams, tells the story of Sir Milton Margai who was overseeing the arrangements for the independence service in the Freetown Cathedral. When the Bishop suggested he might like to give a second thought to the choice of one hymn which contained what he felt was the inappropriate second verse: 'Though the darkness deepens, Lord with me abide'. 'Exactly' replied Sir Milton.[54] David Williams also tells of how journalists at Nigeria's independence had to file their stories three hours before the ceremonial lowering of the Union Jack in order to have their stories on the British breakfast table. All wrote of the dancing in the streets that followed the raising of the Nigerian flag. In fact when David Williams and a fellow-journalist toured the streets after the midnight ceremonial they met only desultory groups wending their way home. His colleague shouted out of the car: 'Dance, Dammit, you're meant to be dancing'.[55] To be fair, however, to the British, it must be remembered that the democratic dream was more enthusiastically supported in the corridors of Whitehall than in the offices of the District Officers who, as Sylvia Leith-Ross has shown in her memoirs of Nigeria, were much more apprehensive of its application to the societies among which they worked.[56]

I would like to conclude with the more positive assessment of the last quarter century of African history that I believe will be accorded by historians of the future. I need not record the failures of Africa—these can be read about daily in the papers.

52. Julius Nyerere immediately comes to mind. Another example is Mamadou Dia, the former Prime Minister of Senegal.
53. *West Africa* 16 March 1957. 'Ghana takes it calmly'. Two and a half years later *West Africa* used a similar headline 'Lagos takes it calmly' for its report on the independence celebrations of Nigeria.
54. David Williams: Personal Communication.
55. *ibid*.
56. Sylvia Leith-Ross *Stepping Stones: Memoirs of Colonial Nigeria, 1907–1960* (London, Peter Owen), 1983, in particular Section V covering the years 1951-55.

C: AFRICAN ACHIEVEMENT

I am convinced that historians of the future will find much more to the credit of Africa than current press punditry and academic despondency at present will admit.   And I think that their judgement will be made in the context of the colonial record.

Here it is instructive to listen to Julius Nyerere's recent justification *pro vita sua* made just after he relinquished the Presidency of Tanzania.[57]   It is instructive not least because Tanzania is usually cited as one of Africa's worst basket-cases in economic terms.   In 1961, he recalled, on the eve of independence and after nearly seventy years of colonial rule only 486,000 children were in primary school.   Today there are over three and a half million, in his own words 'a tremendous achievement unmatched anywhere else in Africa'.   In 1961 80% of the adult population was illiterate. Today, according to the Tanzanian Government, 85% can read and write. In 1961 only 11% of the population had access to clean water—today, Nyerere claims, nearly 50% have access to clean water within 450 yards of their homes.   The availability of health services, particularly in the rural areas has improved out of all recognition.   The ratio of doctors to population has been reduced from 1:830,000 to 1:26,000.   The mortality rate of infants has nearly halved while life expectancy for adults has risen from 35 to 51.

Of course all this was achieved at a tremendous cost to the economy with the accumulation of massive international debts.   We know that in many African countries these debts have been amassed not through genuine attempts at betterment of the lives of the people but by large scale squandering of resources and corruption.   Two points have to be made about the debts of African countries.   In many cases they were built up in a genuine attempt to make up for the sad development record of the colonial governments.   We should also remind ourselves that some of the spectacular failures in African development were part of development plans concocted largely in the metropole to buttress the colonial state, for instance the notorious Tanganyika groundnut scheme and the Gambia poultry project. Moreover, in the post-colonial era, many African development plans and projects were the outcome of advice by foreign experts.[58]

The financial strains experienced by the post-independence governments have also been due to a sometimes over-zealous concern to improve the inadequate communications systems left by the colonial powers and to build the foundations of an industrial infrastructure that would make them less dependent on supplies from the First World.   Much more directly responsible for these economic problems are facts such as these: in 1979, as Nyerere

57.   Interview with William E. Smith 'A Reporter at Large'.
58.   See the admirable critique of the role of foreign experts in African development in Paul Richards *Indigenous Agricultural Revolution* (London, Hutchinson University Library for Africa), 1985.

put it, Tanzania was paying nine times as much for its oil though using less than before the oil crisis began. To buy a seven ton truck in 1981 his country had to produce four times as much cotton, three times as many cashew nuts, ten times as much tobacco, and three times as much coffee as five years earlier.[59]

As Nyerere complained at the Cancun North–South summit in 1981:
Our balance of payment difficulties are enormous and getting greater. This is not because we are trying to live as though we were rich. It is because our already low income is constantly being reduced because of our participation in international trade... We find ourselves always selling cheap and buying dear... we are asking for a chance to earn our living in the international system.[60]

I believe that historians will also see these problems in this perspective, and I believe that, in the context of the colonial legacy and the economic vicissitudes of independence (whether self-inflicted or brought about by the caprices of the world market), they will marvel that by and large the post-colonial state in Africa has remained intact, often despite the machinations of erstwhile colonial powers or the conflicting interests of East and West as in the cases of Biafra, Chad and Angola. They will marvel that the map of Africa has remained largely the same as it was at independence and that there have been so few wars between the post-colonial states thought they were left with so many of the problems that in Europe have been the cause of war: ill-defined frontiers, split ethnic groups and so forth. In the thirty years period 1914–1944, as we know, Europe was ravaged by two major wars, as a result of which the boundaries of Europe were twice redrawn. In the thirty year period following the independence of Sudan in 1956, there has been marginal readjustment of the African map, and surprisingly little interstate hostility and when it has broken out it has usually been quickly resolved. Many potentially explosive situations have been defused by the little-known but often highly effective Conciliation Committee of the Organisation of African Unity.

Against the internal violence of Chad and Uganda we must set the large number of African countries where such violence has been minimal, and remember that even the three year long Biafran civil war in Nigeria came to an end without recrimination and in a spirit of reconciliation on the part of the victors that was without precedent in Europe or the Americas. We must also recall that when for instance South Africans use the examples of Uganda or Chad to argue against the transfer of power to their own African majority, the surprising thing is that the most secure group in Africa since independence has in fact been the whites themselves. We must further remind ourselves that some of the most extreme forms of violence

59. Julius Nyerere in interview with William E. Smith 'A Reporter at Large'.
60. Ibid.

perpetrated in post-colonial Africa have been by the whites of Rhodesia and
South Africa.

If it seems that I have presented this case as though it were that of a
defence lawyer, this has been deliberate.   Africa has in a very real sense
been on trial for the desperate situation in which she has found herself
twenty-odd years after independence.   The blame for this situation has
almost universally been placed upon African leaders.   I have tried to show
that that blame properly should be divided between these leaders and their
colonial predecessors.   I have also tried to show that the criteria by which
Africa is being judged are Eurocentric ones.   Finally I have suggested that
historians of the future will set against the many failures of African leaders
since independence their very real achievements which the Western press so
often ignores.   I rest my case.

Acknowledgments

Wright, Derek. "Fanon and Africa: A Retrospect." *Journal of Modern African Studies* 24 (1986): 679–89. Reprinted with the permission of Cambridge University Press. Courtesy of Yale University Sterling Memorial Library.

Flint, John. "Planned Decolonization and Its Failure in British Africa." *African Affairs* 82 (1983): 389–411. Reprinted with the permission of African Affairs, The Royal African Society. Courtesy of Yale University Sterling Memorial Library.

Lonsdale, John M. "Mau Maus of the Mind: Making Mau Mau and Remaking Kenya." *Journal of African History* 31 (1990): 393–421. Reprinted with the permission of Heldref Publications. Courtesy of Yale University Sterling Memorial Library.

Adamolekun, 'Ladipo. "The Road to Independence in French Tropical Africa." *Tarikh* 2 (1969): 72–85. Reprinted with the permission of the author. Courtesy of Yale University Sterling Memorial Library.

Gardinier, David E. "The Path to Independence in French Africa: Recent Historiography." *Africana Journal* 15 (1990): 15–38. Reprinted with the permission of Holmes & Meier Publishers, Inc. Courtesy of Yale University Sterling Memorial Library.

Suret-Canale, J. "Strike Movements as Part of the Anticolonial Struggle in French West Africa." *Tarikh* 5 (1977): 44–56. Courtesy of Yale University Sterling Memorial Library.

Johnson, R. W. "Sekou Touré and the Guinean Revolution." *African Affairs* 69 (1970): 350–65. Reprinted with the permission of African Affairs, The Royal African Society. Courtesy of Yale University Sterling Memorial Library.

Fuglestad, Finn. "Djibo Bakary, the French, and the Referendum of 1958 in Niger." *Journal of African History* 14 (1973): 313–30. Reprinted with the permission of Cambridge University Press. Courtesy of Yale University Sterling Memorial Library.

Geiger, Susan. "Women in Nationalist Struggle: TANU Activists in Dar Es Salaam." *International Journal of African Historical Studies* 20 (1987): 1–26. Reprinted with the permission of the African Studies Center. Courtesy of Yale University Sterling Memorial Library.

Van Donge, Jan Kees. "An Episode from the Independence Struggle in Zambia: A Case Study from Mwase Lundazi." *African Affairs* 84 (1985): 265–77. Reprinted with the permission of African Affairs, The Royal African Society. Courtesy of Yale University Sterling Memorial Library.

Tamuno, Tekena N. "Separatist Agitations in Nigeria Since 1914." *Journal of Modern African Studies* 8 (1970): 563–84. Reprinted with the permission of Cambridge University Press. Courtesy of Yale University Sterling Memorial Library.

Amaazee, Victor Bong. "The 'Igbo Scare' in the British Cameroons, c. 1945–61." *Journal of African History* 31 (1990): 281–93. Reprinted with the permission of Cambridge University Press. Courtesy of Yale University Sterling Memorial Library.

Allman, Jean Marie. "The Youngmen and the Porcupine: Class, Nationalism and Asante's Struggle for Self-determination, 1954–57." *Journal of African History* 31 (1990): 263–79. Reprinted with the permission of Cambridge University Press. Courtesy of Yale University Sterling Memorial Library.

Hancock, I. R. "Patriotism and Neo-Traditionalism in Buganda: The Kabaka Yekka ('The King Alone') Movement, 1961–1962." *Journal of African History* 11 (1970): 419–34. Reprinted with the permission of Cambridge University Press. Courtesy of Yale University Sterling Memorial Library.

Mohan, Jitendra. "Ghana, The Congo, and the United Nations." *Journal of Modern African Studies* 7 (1969): 369–406. Reprinted with the permission of Cambridge University Press. Courtesy of Yale University Sterling Memorial Library.

Rood, Leslie L. "Nationalisation and Indigenisation in Africa." *Journal of Modern African Studies* 14 (1976): 427–47. Reprinted with the permission of Cambridge University Press. Courtesy of Yale University Sterling Memorial Library.

July, Robert W. "Toward Cultural Independence in Africa: Some Illustrations from Nigeria and Ghana." *African Studies Review* 26

(1983): 119–31. Reprinted with the permission of the African Studies Association. Courtesy of Yale University Sterling Memorial Library.

Crowder, Michael. "Whose Dream Was It Anyway? Twenty-Five Years of African Independence." *African Affairs* 86 (1987): 7–24. Reprinted with the permission of African Affairs, The Royal African Society. Courtesy of Yale University Sterling Memorial Library.